BESTSELLING
BOOK SERIES

Series 7 Exam For Dummies

Cheat Sheet

Memorizing Important Figures and Formulas

You can't bring your notes (or this Cheat Sheet!) into the exam center, so be sure to squirrel the following info away in your brain and write it on the scrap paper provided *after* the test begins.

Adjust for stock splits (Chapter 6)

$$\frac{\text{Shares} \times \text{1st number}}{\text{2nd number}}$$

$$\frac{\text{Stock price} \times \text{2nd number}}{\text{1st number}}$$

Calculate the current yield of a stock or bond (Chapter 7)

$$\text{Current yield (CY)} = \frac{\text{annual interest}}{\text{market price}}$$

Calculate the conversion ratio of a convertible preferred stock or convertible bond (Chapter 7)

$$\text{Conversion ratio} = \frac{\text{par value}}{\text{conversion price}}$$

Options chart (Chapter 12)

Money Out	Money In
Investor spends money	Investor receives money

Long margin account formula (Chapter 9)

Long market value (LMV) − debit record (DR) = equity (EQ)

Short margin account formula (Chapter 9)

Short market value (SMV) + equity (EQ) = credit record (CR)

Balance sheet formula (Chapter 13)

Assets = liabilities + stockholder's equity

Calculate working capital (Chapter 13)

Working capital = current assets − current liabilities

Determine the outstanding shares (Chapter 6)

Outstanding shares = issued shares − treasury stock

Rights formula (Chapter 6)

$$\text{Value of a right}_{\text{cum rights}} = \frac{\text{market price (M)} - \text{subscription price (S)}}{\text{number of rights needed to purchase one share (N)} + 1}$$

Ex-rights formula (Chapter 6)

$$\text{Value of a right}_{\text{ex-rights}} = \frac{\text{market price (M)} - \text{subscription price (S)}}{\text{number of rights needed to purchase one share (N)}}$$

Calculate the taxable equivalent yield of a municipal bond (Chapter 8)

$$\text{Taxable equivalent yield (TEY)} = \frac{\text{municipal yield}}{100\% - \text{investor's tax bracket}}$$

Calculating the buying or shorting power (Chapter 9)

$$\text{Buying or shorting power} = \frac{\text{Special memorandum account (SMA)}}{\text{Regulation T}}$$

Calculate the sales charge % of a mutual fund (Chapter 10)

$$\text{Sales charge \%} = \frac{\text{ask} - \text{bid}}{\text{ask}} = \frac{\text{public offering price (POP)} - \text{net asset value (NAV)}}{\text{POP}}$$

Calculate the public offering price of a mutual fund (Chapter 10)

$$\text{Public offering price (POP)} = \frac{\text{net asset value (NAV)}}{100\% - \text{sales charge \%}}$$

Calculate the time value of an option (Chapter 12)

Premium (P) = intrinsic value (I) + time value (T)

Bond seesaw (Chapter 7)

Bond price	NY CY YTM YTC	Bond at par

Price/earnings ratio formula (Chapter 13)

$$\text{Price/earnings (P/E) ratio} = \frac{\text{market price}}{\text{earnings per share (EPS)}}$$

For Dummies: Bestselling Book Series for Beginners

Series 7 Exam For Dummies®

Cheat Sheet

Tackling Series 7 Questions

- Read the question carefully.
- Underline or highlight key words to avoid tricky detractors (except, unless, not).
- Identify the facts you need to answer the question and ignore the information you don't need.
- Use scrap paper to write down formulas and key points from the question, perform calculations, and draw diagrams.
- When you're unsure of the correct answer, eliminate as many wrong answers as possible.
- Work with the facts presented in the question and don't make the question more difficult than it is.
- If you don't know the answer, don't obsess. Take your best guess and mark it for review to return to later. As you go through the exam, another question may trigger your memory. If you still aren't sure of the answer when you return, remember these tips:
  - Select a more precise answer more often than a less precise answer.
  - Select a longer answer over a shorter answer.
  - When answering multiple choice questions, if you see two opposing answer choices, one must be right.
  - *Cannot be determined* is almost never the correct answer on the Series 7 exam.
  - In complex (two-tiered) questions, an answer choice of *none of the above* is almost always wrong; you can usually eliminate it.
- Keep track of time.

Tracking Your Timing

You have 1 minute and 22.8 seconds per question to complete 130 questions in each of the two sessions. Use the following schedule to track your progress:

Time Elapsed	Be Up to Question
30 minutes	22
1 hour	44
1½ hours	66
2 hours	88
2½ hours	110
3 hours	130

A Checklist for the Day Before

- ❑ Review your notes until noon.
- ❑ Get away from the books: Go out to dinner (skip the spicy foods and alcohol) or go to a movie — do whatever you want to rest your mind.
- ❑ Gather the items to bring with you to the exam site:
  - ❑ Your ID
  - ❑ Exam site directions
  - ❑ Layered clothing
  - ❑ Earplugs (if allowed)
  - ❑ A clock or watch
  - ❑ A snack/lunch
  - ❑ Your cellphone for emergencies (leave it in the car)
  - ❑ Study material and notes (leave them in the car)
- ❑ Set two alarm clocks. Leave enough time to get to the exam site an hour and a half early — one hour for more review and one half-hour for checking in.
- ❑ Get to bed early.

Establishing a Strong Study Routine

- Get into a consistent study routine on a daily basis; never separate yourself from your textbooks for more than one day.
- Stay focused. If you get stuck on a multipart question, break down the question into segments; if you run into trouble with a math question, draw diagrams.
- Take short, ten-minute breaks throughout the day to give your brain a chance to process information.
- Reinforce your knowledge every day by reviewing old information while learning new material.
- Make yourself some flash cards to use as study aids.
- Record your notes onto a tape recorder and play them back at night while you're falling asleep.
- Take several practice exams before you tackle the real deal. You should consistently score 80 to 85 percent on the sample tests to ensure that you're ready.

*The Series 7 is rated PG (Proctor Guarded). Proctors have been genetically altered to have eyes in the backs of their heads, and they'll catch you if you peek at this Cheat Sheet during the exam. Learn it and then burn it.

For Dummies: Bestselling Book Series for Beginners

Series 7
Exam

FOR

DUMMIES®

Series 7 Exam

FOR DUMMIES®

by Steven M. Rice

BICENTENNIAL
1807
WILEY
2007
BICENTENNIAL

Wiley Publishing, Inc.

Series 7 Exam For Dummies®

Published by
Wiley Publishing, Inc.
111 River St.
Hoboken, NJ 07030-5774
www.wiley.com

WILEY

About the Author

After earning a high score on the Series 7 exam in the mid '90s, **Steven M. Rice** began his career as a stockbroker for a broker dealership with offices in Nassau County, Long Island, and New York City. In addition to his duties as a registered representative, he also gained invaluable experience about securities registration rules and regulations when he worked in the firm's compliance office. But only after Steve began tutoring others in the firm to help them pass the Series 7 did he find his true calling as an instructor. Shortly thereafter, Steve became a founding partner and educator in Empire Stockbroker Training Institute (www.empirestockbroker.com), which has grown into one of the largest and most successful securities training schools in the country.

In addition to writing *Series 7 Exam For Dummies*, Steve developed and designed the Empire Stockbroker Training Institute online (*Series 7*, *Series 6*, *Series 63*, *Series 66*, and more) exams. Steve has also co-authored a complete library of securities training manuals for classroom use and for home study, including the *Series 4*, *Series 6*, *Series 7*, *Series 11*, *Series 24*, *Series 63*, *Series 65*, and *Series 66*. Steve's popular and highly acclaimed classes, online courses, and training manuals have helped tens of thousands of people achieve their goals and begin their lucrative new careers in the securities industry.

Steve lives on Long Island, NY, with his wife, Melissa Kollen-Rice, a real estate attorney, author of the book *Buying Real Estate Foreclosures,* and owner/instructor of LI Real Estate Training School (www.liret.com).

Dedication

I dedicate this book to my beautiful wife, Melissa. Melissa is the love of my life, my inspiration, and my best friend.

Author's Acknowledgments

A fantastic team over at Wiley Publishing made this book possible. I'd like to start by thanking my acquisitions editor, Michael Lewis, for seeing something in me that told him that I was the right man for the job. I believe that he may be one of the few people in this world who sleeps as little as my wife and I. Michael's rapid responses to my e-mails during the days, evenings, and weekends were quite comforting as I was beginning this journey.

Many thanks also go to my senior project editor, Alissa Schwipps, for her weekly, friendly little e-mails that helped keep me on track when I was wearing thin. Alissa's guidance and critiques were truly invaluable in the writing of this book. Alissa bought a new house during this project, and I'm sure she had quite a bit going on, making her new house a home, but she was always there when I needed her and is a professional all the way.

I would also like to thank my copy editor, Danielle Voirol, for making me a better writer. Danielle's suggestions on how to make the book more *Dummies* style ultimately made this book more fun to read for all of you.

Next, I'd like to thank the entire composition team and the technical editor, Nedra Mitchell. Although I didn't get a chance to communicate with any of them directly, this book wouldn't be possible without every one of them. Viewing the final product, I can tell you one thing: They are the best.

During this project, I wasn't able to put in my normal 60-hour week at my school. I'd like to thank my partner, Rueben Martinez, my office manager (and sister) Sharlene Wegner, and the rest of the staff at Empire Stockbroker Training Institute for picking up the slack so perfectly while I was out.

This book would have been much more difficult to write without my dad, Tom Rice. He has always been my role model, inspiring me as to how I want to live the rest of my life. I have the best dad a person could ask for, and I'm extremely blessed to have him, his wife Maggie, and my other sister Sharlet in my corner.

Finally, I want to thank my wife, Melissa. There's no way I could have finished this book if not for her. As a lawyer and real estate school owner, she's the busiest person I know. As busy as she is, she always makes me her top priority. Melissa was with me every day, every step of the way. She not only read every page of this book several times but also pre-edited and made great suggestions. Her undying love and support helped me through the toughest times. I am eternally grateful, and I love her forever.

Publisher's Acknowledgments

We're proud of this book; please send us your comments through our Dummies online registration form located at www.dummies.com/register/.

Some of the people who helped bring this book to market include the following:

Acquisitions, Editorial, and Media Development

Senior Project Editor: Alissa Schwipps

Acquisitions Editor: Michael Lewis

Copy Editor: Danielle Voirol

Technical Editor: Nedra E. Mitchell, CFP

Senior Editorial Manager: Jennifer Ehrlich

Media Project Supervisor: Laura Moss-Hollister

Media Development Specialist: Angela Denny

Media Development Manager: Laura VanWinkle

Editorial Assistants: Erin Calligan, Leeann Harney, Joe Niesen

Cartoons: Rich Tennant (www.the5thwave.com)

Composition Services

Project Coordinator: Lynsey Osborn

Layout and Graphics: Carrie A. Foster, Brooke Graczyk, Denny Hager, Joyce Haughey, Stephanie D. Jumper, Melanee Prendergast

Anniversary Logo Design: Richard Pacifico

Proofreaders: Arielle Mennelle, Christy Pingleton

Indexer: Valerie Haynes Perry

Publishing and Editorial for Consumer Dummies

Diane Graves Steele, Vice President and Publisher, Consumer Dummies

Joyce Pepple, Acquisitions Director, Consumer Dummies

Kristin A. Cocks, Product Development Director, Consumer Dummies

Michael Spring, Vice President and Publisher, Travel

Kelly Regan, Editorial Director, Travel

Publishing for Technology Dummies

Andy Cummings, Vice President and Publisher, Dummies Technology/General User

Composition Services

Gerry Fahey, Vice President of Production Services

Debbie Stailey, Director of Composition Services

Contents at a Glance

Table of Contents

Introduction

So you want to be a stockbroker? The good news is that a career in the securities field can be extremely lucrative and rewarding. The not-so-good news is that anyone who plans to become a stockbroker and sell securities in any of the 50 states must first pass the Series 7 exam, a monster of a test. And to accomplish this, you have to commit time and effort.

I passed the Series 7 exam the first time with a very high score, but it required weeks of study and sacrifice. Those who aren't totally prepared on exam day are in for an unpleasant wake-up call. I always get a few students in every class who've enrolled after they already failed the exam the first (or second) time they took it. Most of them initially expected the same easy ride that they'd experienced in high school or college. Not only were they wrong, but they also had to pay hundreds of dollars to re-register for the exam and wait another 30 days (a mandatory NASD rule) before they could retake the exam.

Back to the good news again. You're obviously interested in doing well, so you probably won't be one of those people. This book can help you pass the Series 7 and achieve your goal.

About This Book

This book is not a comprehensive content review. That's what textbooks are for. Rather, *Series 7 Exam For Dummies* is designed to be a supplement, a handy guide as you figure out how to think not only like a financial advisor but also like the test designers do (and no, I don't mean to tap into your potential as an evil mastermind).

I cover the topics that always appear on the test, offer formulas, provide definitions, and go over the foundational information you need to know. I also include lots of tips and memory tricks. But the real benefit from this book is finding out how to study and think through problems as well as you possibly can. That's why I help you choose a study program, explain how to handle specific question types, warn you about common mistakes, connect concepts, and show you how to pull questions apart and get to the bottom of what's being asked. You then get to apply this knowledge in two full-length practice tests — one in the book and one on the CD — so you get a taste of the Series 7 experience.

This is a reference book, and most sections are self-contained. In other words, you should be able to read a section and understand it without looking over the text that comes before it. When some background information would help, I give cross-references to related topics. Therefore, you can pretty much jump in and out whenever you find topics you like (and when you find those you don't). And like all good tour guides, I also point you to some other sites of interest — topics you should explore further on your own.

Conventions Used in This Book

I use the following conventions throughout the text to make things consistent and easy to understand:

- All Web addresses appear in `monofont`.

- New terms appear in *italics* and are closely followed by easy-to-understand definitions. Italics may also indicate emphasis.

I've scattered sample questions throughout this book so you can test your understanding of new info and get a feel for Series 7 questions. And of course, for those sections that don't include questions, remember that the practice tests that come with this book deal with all kinds of subjects.

I also use the language and lingo of the NASD. That means you see official names (like the Federal Reserve Board), nicknames (the Fed), and acronyms galore (like the FRB). That way, during the test, understanding the POPs, YTMs, TEYs, NAVs, EPSs, ADRs, LMVs, DRs, EQs, CPIs, GDPs, DPPs, ROPs, ODDs, OAAs, IDRs, GNMAs, FHLMCs, OBOs, CBOEs, PACs, TACs, and so on shouldn't be too much of a hassle.

What You're Not to Read

You don't have to read the Index straight through or dally over the Library of Congress number and other publisher information, but most of the information here is important — the basic, need-to-know ideas. You can skim through the topics you know well and spend more time on those you don't, but I do suggest looking everything over.

If you're short on time (as you probably are) and aren't ready for a break just yet, you can skip the sidebars, those little gray boxes that contain interesting but nonessential information.

Foolish Assumptions

While writing this book, I made a few assumptions about you and why you picked up this book. For starters, I assume that you're looking for a no-nonsense study guide to supplement your textbook or prep course — one that provides a ton of example questions and some sample exams. Look no further! Whether you're preparing to take the test for the first time, retaking the test after a less-than-stellar performance, or looking for a refresher before you recertify, this is the book for you!

How This Book Is Organized

This book is organized into six parts and 22 chapters. Each part explains the test itself or covers a major area of study on the Series 7 exam. A glance at the Table of Contents can give you the specifics, but here's a quick overview of what's in each part.

Part I: Gearing Up for the Series 7 Exam

In this part, Chapter 1 gives you an overview of the Series 7 exam format and the registration process for taking the exam. Chapter 2 introduces you to exam prep courses and the types of study materials available. It also helps you develop and stick to a study plan. Chapter 3 runs down the kinds of questions on the Series 7 exam and explains how to handle them, and Chapter 4 tells you what to expect on exam day.

Part II: Mastering Basic Security Investments

This part covers the securities (stocks and bonds) that form the foundation of an investor's portfolio. Chapter 5 covers the security registration process. Chapter 6 introduces you to stocks (common and preferred). Chapters 7 and 8 acquaint you with bonds (corporate, U.S., and municipal).

Part III: Delving Deeper: Security Investments with a Twist

Part III covers additional strategies for buying and selling securities. Chapter 9 describes the process by which investors borrow money to purchase securities by opening margin accounts. Chapter 10 covers the role of investment companies in helping investors diversify their portfolios. Chapter 11 reviews direct participation programs (DPPs), more commonly known as limited partnerships; it mentions their formation, function, structure, tax advantages, and tax disadvantages. Chapter 12 introduces options, another type of investment vehicle that savvy investors use.

Part IV: Playing Nicely: Serving Your Customers and Following the Rules

This part covers the stockbroker's role in scrutinizing a customer's account, monitoring market conditions that can affect the account, and making appropriate recommendations that meet each customer's individual investment goals.

Chapter 13 helps you identify market conditions that can affect a customer's investment objectives. Chapter 14 covers how new securities are brought to the market and how existing securities are traded on the market. Chapter 15 goes into taxes; it distinguishes between long term and short term capital gains and losses for income tax purposes, explains the effect of retirement plans on an individual's income taxes, and gives retirement plan contribution limits. Chapter 16 looks at rules and regulations; it reviews the stockbroker's responsibilities for opening, closing, transferring, and handling a customer's account.

Part V: Putting Your Knowledge to Good Use: A Practice Exam

Jackpot! In this part you can find two practice exams (Chapters 17 and 19) with 125 questions each — enough questions to simulate both 3-hour parts of the actual Series 7 (without those pesky experimental questions that don't count toward your score). To make the tests really useful, you also get the correct answers and explanations (Chapters 18 and 20). Completing and evaluating practice tests is one of the best ways to prepare for the Series 7 and to gauge your readiness for the real deal.

Part VI: The Part of Tens

This part is standard in all *For Dummies* books, and this book is no exception. In Chapter 21, I reveal ten Series 7 exam traps to avoid, and in Chapter 22, I give you ten ways to make money as a stockbroker.

Appendix

The Appendix tells you the computer system requirements, what you can find on the CD-ROM, and how to use the disc that comes with this book.

The CD-ROM

This book comes complete with a CD-ROM that includes an additional full-length practice exam different from the exam in the book. In order to familiarize yourself with the real-life exam experience, the questions are formatted to simulate the Series 7 test questions. The questions cover all topics tested on the Series 7 exam along with answers and explanations for each question.

Icons Used in This Book

To make this book easier to read and use, I include some icons to help you find and fathom key ideas and information.

This icon highlights example Series 7 test questions (which I follow with helpful answer explanations).

This icon is attached to shortcuts and insider advice for studying and passing the Series 7 exam.

This icon points to information that's especially important to remember in order to do well on the test.

This icon warns you away from actions that can harm your work and drop your score.

Where to Go from Here

Although you can read this book from start to finish, you can certainly work your way through in more creative ways. Where you start is up to you, though please, please don't start with the tests! Give yourself a good grounding in the content here, and then use the tests to evaluate your understanding and show you where to focus your studies. After you brush up on those topics, try out the practice tests on the CD-ROM.

You can flip to the topics you think you understand fairly well to boost your confidence or skip directly to whatever's giving you trouble — let the Index and the Table of Contents be your guides. If you have a good understanding of how to take the Series 7 exam, from how it's structured to how to tackle questions, then you can go directly to the chapters in Parts II or III, which address types of securities. If you're feeling shaky on the legal aspects, try the NASD rules and regulations in Part IV. Everyone, however, can probably benefit from Part I's test-taking basics and info on study plans. Wherever you go, feel free to take detours to your textbooks, flash cards, NASD Web sites, and any other resources for more information. Just remember to come back so you don't miss anything here!

Part I

Gearing Up for the Series 7 Exam

The 5th Wave   By Rich Tennant

" 'Stop limit orders,' 'debit put spreads'...
I prefer the days when my investment
options were printed on a card that told
me when to 'double down,' 'split,' 'stand,'
and 'take a hit.' "

In this part . . .

Are you looking for a job that can lead to wealth and success? Do you find satisfaction in helping people? Are you comfortable with mathematical calculations? If so, a career as a stockbroker is likely to be very rewarding for you.

By now, I'm sure you're aware of the hurdle that stands between you and your riches: the Series 7 exam. So in this part, I review the computerized exam format and the procedures for registering to take the exam, and I uncover the topics tested on the Series 7. I help you select the right study course and materials to prepare yourself for exam day, and I explain how to organize your study time efficiently and effectively — even when your time is limited. I also give you test-taking tips to maximize your chances of selecting the correct answer choices. Finally, I let you know what to expect on test day (because the only surprises that day should involve the triumphant return of your social life).

Chapter 1

So You Want to Sell Securities: Introducing the Series 7 Exam

. . . .

In This Chapter

▶ Introducing the Series 7

▶ Taking a look at companion tests

▶ Getting a sponsor and registering to take the exam

▶ Uncovering topics tested on the Series 7

▶ Understanding the computerized exam format

. . . .

Congratulations on your interest in becoming a stockbroker! But before you can lose yourself in the energy of the office, the eager voices of your clients, and the warm glow of success, you have to face the Series 7. In this chapter, I give you an overview of the Series 7 exam, including its purpose, structure, format, scoring, and some helpful tips to guide you through the registration procedure.

What Is the Series 7 Exam, Anyway?

The Series 7 exam qualifies you to hold the title General Securities Registered Representative (stockbroker), to sell many different types of securities, and to hopefully make stacks of money for your clients (and a bit for yourself). Series 7–licensed individuals are qualified to solicit, purchase, and/or sell securities products, including

  ✔ Corporate stocks and bonds

  ✔ Municipal bonds

  ✔ U.S. government bonds

  ✔ Options

  ✔ Direct participation programs (limited partnerships)

  ✔ Investment-company securities

  ✔ Variable contracts

The exam's purpose is to protect the investing public by ensuring that the registered reps who sell securities have mastered the skills and general knowledge that competent practicing stockbrokers need to have.

The Series 7 itself is a computer-based exam given at Prometric and Pearson VUE (Virtual University Enterprises) test centers throughout the United States. The 250-question exam, administered by the National Association of Securities Dealers (NASD), is six long, arduous hours in duration. A score of 70 percent or better can get candidates a passing grade and put big smiles on their faces.

The sections later in this chapter explain the setup of the Series 7 and give a rundown of how to register for the exam. If you have other questions, contact the NASD Call Center (Main NASD Telephone Number) at 301-590-6500 or visit www.nasd.com/RegistrationQualifications/BrokerGuidanceResponsibility.

Profiling the Series 7 Exam-Taker

The Series 7 exam is for people who want to

- Enter the securities industry
- Become registered representatives
- Work for a securities broker-dealer

Although some less-prestigious exams (for example, the Series 6 and 62) can qualify you to sell some securities, most broker-dealers want their rising stars (that's you) to have the Series 7 license. That way, you can work with almost the whole kit and caboodle — corporate stocks and bonds, municipal and U.S. government bonds, options, direct participation programs, investment companies, variable contracts, and so on.

People who have a long and sordid history of embezzlement, forgery, and fraud are generally disqualified and weeded out and precluded from taking the exam. Candidates must disclose any prior criminal records, and the NASD reviews each application on a case-by-case basis.

One's Not Enough: Tackling the Series 63 or Series 66

You don't have to pass any prerequisite exams before you can take the Series 7; however, you do need to pass the Series 63 or Series 66 to be able to work in the securities industry because these exams and the Series 7 are co-requisites in most states. You can take them in any order (in conjunction with the Series 7), but most people start studying for the Series 63 or 66 and register to take it right after passing the Series 7.

Note: Even if you live in a state that doesn't require either of these licenses, you still need to obtain one if you want to sell securities to someone who lives in a state that does require it. Just figure that your firm will require you to obtain the 63 or 66 to sell securities — your firm should tell you which one to take. The following sections explain what the two state-licensing exams cover.

Series 63: Uniform Securities Agent State Law Exam

The Series 63 is a 65-question test that the North American Securities Administrator Association (NASAA) developed, and it's designed to qualify candidates as securities agents. The Series 63 exam covers state securities regulation rules as well as rules prohibiting unethical and dishonest business practices (not that you'd do anything like that). The Series 63 is the most common test taken along with the Series 7, although the Series 66 is becoming more popular.

Series 66: Uniform Combined State Law Exam

The Series 66 is a 100-question NASAA exam that combines the Series 63 and the Series 65 (Uniform Investment Adviser). The Series 66 is designed to qualify candidates as both securities agents and investment adviser representatives (IARs). The Series 65 portion of the Series 66 allows you to collect a fee for just giving investment advice. This license is relatively new, and it'll most likely be required if you work for one of the bigger broker-dealers. More and more firms are requiring the Series 66 because it gives their registered reps an additional service to provide for their clients.

Securing Sponsorship and Signing Up

All candidates (that's you) must have a sponsoring broker in order to register for the Series 7 exam. After passing the exam, your license will be in your own name; however, you have to be working for a firm in order for your license to be active. Generally, a firm hires you and then acts as your sponsor.

The following sections explain the basic exam requirements and help you navigate your way through the exam registration process.

Filling out an application to enroll

For you to obtain admission to the Series 7, your sponsoring firm has to file an application form (called a *U-4*) and pay the required processing fees with the Central Registration Depository (CRD). The U-4 is an annoying little form with about a gazillion pages that requires you to remember where you were ten years ago. You're also required to submit your fingerprints, and you have to complete this step through an approved facility. Your firm will likely recommend the place they use — often the local police precinct. (Be advised that your sponsoring firm will probably frown upon your fingerprints if they're attached to your mug shot.)

If you want to see a preview of the U-4 registration form that you're responsible for filling out and that your firm has to submit, visit the NASD Web site (www.nasd.com) and search for U-4.

It's a date! Scheduling your exam

After your firm files the application with the Central Registration Depository and receives your enrollment notification, you can schedule an appointment to take the exam by contacting the Prometric or Pearson VUE Testing Center. Locate the test center nearest you by calling either the Prometric center (800-578-6273) or the Pearson VUE center (866-396-6273) during business hours. Or you can visit www.pearsonvue.com/nasd or www.prometric.com/nasd to schedule online.

Your Series 7 exam enrollment is valid for 120 days — you have to take the exam within this time frame. When scheduling your exam appointment, be ready to provide the exam administrators with

- ✔ Your name and Social Security number
- ✔ The name of your firm
- ✔ A telephone contact to reach you and your employer
- ✔ The name of the securities exam you're registering to take
- ✔ Your desired test date

Getting an appointment usually takes about two weeks, depending on the time of year (you may wait longer in the summer than around Christmas time). Prometric and Pearson VUE will confirm your appointment on the phone or via e-mail.

I suggest putting pressure on yourself and scheduling the exam a little sooner than you think you may be ready to take it; you can always move the test date back. You know yourself best, but I think most students study better when they have a target test date.

You have a choice of locations to take the exam. If you're a travelin' man (or woman), you may want to schedule your exam at a location far away (maybe even in a different state) to get the test date that you want.

After you have your test date set, you may find that you're ready sooner or will be ready later than your scheduled appointment. The exam center administrators are usually pretty accommodating about changing appointments and/or locations as long as you call before noon at least two business days before your test date.

You can get an extension from the 120-day enrollment only if you call within ten days of your enrollment expiration and if no earlier test dates are available.

Planning ahead for special accommodations

If you require special accommodations when taking your Series 7 exam, you can't schedule your exam online. You have to contact the NASD Special Conditions Team at 800-999-6647. Read on for info on what the test administrators can do if you have a disability or if English isn't your first language.

Asking about test center luxuries

Series 7 test centers are required to comply with NASD site guidelines; however, some of the older centers may not have the amenities that the newer ones do (such as lockers and earplugs). To protect yourself from a whole variety of unpleasant, unexpected site surprises on exam day, the NASD Web site (www.nasd.com) offers general information, including *Test Center Security*
Guidelines (including candidate ID requirements, personal items allowed, and provided aids), *Test Center Rules of Conduct,* and so on. For more site-specific questions, like whether a cafeteria, vending machines, or lockers are on site, ask the center's administrator when you schedule your test date.

Depending on your testing center, the NASD may have to authorize you to bring medical devices and supplies — such as insulin pumps, eye drops, and inhalers — into the testing room. If you need authorization, call NASD Field Support Services (FSS) at 800-999-6647 after scheduling the exam. For a list of personal items that may need approval, visit www.nasd.com/RegistrationQualifications/BrokerGuidanceResponsibility/Qualifications/NASDW_015104.

Americans with Disabilities Act (ADA) candidates

If you're disabled or learning impaired, the NASD provides testing modifications and aids in compliance with the provisions of the Americans with Disabilities Act (ADA). To qualify for ADA provisions, your disabilities have to permanently limit a major life activity, such as learning, speech, hearing, or vision.

To apply for special accommodations, you need to submit documentation from your physician or licensed health care professional to the NASD, along with a letter from your sponsoring firm requesting the special arrangements. Additionally, you have to submit the NASD Special Accommodations Eligibility Questionnaire and Special Accommodations Verification Request Form for all special arrangement requests (you can find links to the forms at www.nasd.com/RegistrationQualifications/BrokerGuidanceResponsibility/Qualifications/NASDW_010831).

You may request the accommodations you want approved; possible aids include

- Extra time
- A written exam (pencil and paper)
- A reader, writer, or recorder
- A sign language interpreter
- A large-print exam booklet
- Wheelchair-accessible locations

The NASD reserves the right to make all final decisions about accommodations on a case-by-case basis.

English as a second language (ESL) candidates

If English is your second language, you can request additional time to take the exam when you schedule your Series 7 test date. If the NASD approves, you receive an extra 30 minutes to complete each part (one hour total) of the Series 7 exam.

To qualify for this extra time, you have to provide the test center administrator with a letter from your firm, written in English on company letterhead, signed by your supervisor or manager, with your name and Social Security number. The letter should indicate that English is your second language. The supervisor's original signature has to be on the letter; a photocopy without the original signature won't be accepted.

Just in case: Cancelling as an option

If something comes up or if you feel you're just not ready, you can cancel your appointment to take the Series 7 exam without penalty if you do so before noon at least two business days before the exam date. If a holiday falls within the two-day cancellation period, you have to cancel an additional business day earlier. For example, if you're scheduled to take the exam Wednesday, January 17, you have to cancel before noon on the previous Monday, January 15. If Monday is a holiday, however, you have to cancel before noon on Friday, January 12.

If you're cancelling after the proscribed deadline, if you don't show up to take the exam, or if you show up too late to take the exam, NASD will charge your firm a cancellation fee equal to the Series 7 exam fee paid by your firm. Don't try the old "I forgot" excuse, because not only is it ineffective, but I'm somewhat sure that it's illegal in all 50 states, Canada, and the U.S. territories.

Taking a Peek at the Tested Topics

As a practical exam, the Series 7 requires you to master vocabulary, handle customer accounts, understand the rules and regulations that govern the securities industry, and yes, work with some math formulas. For ease of use (and because humans have a limited life span), this book focuses on the most commonly tested topics on the Series 7 exam. Here's an overview of what to expect:

- ✔ The underwriting process (how new securities come to market) (Chapter 5)
- ✔ Common and preferred stock (Chapter 6)
- ✔ Corporate bonds and U.S. government securities (Chapter 7)
- ✔ Securities issued by local governments (municipal bonds) (Chapter 8)
- ✔ Margin accounts (using money borrowed from broker-dealers to purchase securities) (Chapter 9)
- ✔ Investment companies (including mutual and closed-end funds) (Chapter 10)
- ✔ Direct participation programs (limited partnerships) (Chapter 11)
- ✔ Options (Chapter 12)
- ✔ Analyzing the benefits and risks associated with investments; making appropriate recommendations to customers (Chapter 13)
- ✔ Following how new securities are brought to the market and how existing securities are traded in the market (Chapter 14)
- ✔ Risk considerations and income-tax implications that stock market investors face (Chapter 15)
- ✔ Rules and regulations governing the purchase and sale of securities and the registered representative's responsibility for maintaining accurate recordkeeping (Chapter 16)

The NASD released a listing of the distribution of questions on the Series 7 exam. See Table 1-1 for the number of questions devoted to each activity that a registered rep performs.

Table 1-1	Distribution of Series 7 Exam Questions	
Activity Performed by a Registered Rep	*Number of Questions*	*Percent of Exam*
Prospecting for and qualifying customers	9	4%
Evaluating customer needs and objectives	4	2%
Providing customers with investment information and making suitable recommendations	123	49%
Handling customer accounts and account records	27	11%
Understanding and explaining the securities markets' organization and participants to customers	53	21%

Activity Performed by a Registered Rep	Number of Questions	Percent of Exam
Processing customer orders and transactions	13	5%
Monitoring economic and financial events; performing customer portfolio analysis and making suitable recommendations	21	8%
Total	**250**	**100%**

Each of these activities falls under multiple areas of study. For example, to correctly answer questions that address the topic of handling customer accounts, you have to know enough about different types of stocks, bonds, and so on to be able to guide your customers, including which investments are more beneficial to retirees and which work better for investors who are just entering the workforce.

Although Table 1-1 shows the outline of the exam, I (and most other study material providers) break the chapters down by similar content to keep you from having to jump back and forth through your study material.

Understanding the Exam Format and Other Exam Details

To make sure you don't walk into the testing center, take one look at the computer screen, go into shock, and start drooling on the keyboard, I use the next few sections to cover some of the things that you should expect from the Series 7 exam.

Reviewing the exam basics

The Series 7 exam is a computerized, closed book (no book), six-hour exam. The exam is graded on 250 multiple-choice questions, and it's divided into two three-hour sessions. You take a mandatory 30–60 minute break between sessions.

You can take bathroom breaks at any time, but the clock continues to tick away, so you may want to reconsider drinking a mega-jumbo iced latte in the morning before you arrive at the exam center.

For information on the types of questions to expect, see Chapter 3. Flip to Chapter 4 for an overview of how your exam day may progress.

Practicing on ten additional trial questions

To ensure that new questions to be introduced in future exams meet acceptable standards prior to inclusion, you answer ten additional, unidentified questions that don't count toward your score. In other words, you get 260 questions to answer (130 in each half), but only 250 are scored.

Note: If you see a question on the Series 7 that doesn't seem even remotely similar to anything that you've studied (or even heard about), it may very likely be an experimental question.

Mastering the computerized format and features

Although you don't need any previous computer experience to do well on the exam, your first encounter with a computerized exam shouldn't be on the date of the Series 7. Being familiar with the way the questions and answer choices will appear on the screen is essential. Figure 1-1 and the CD-ROM that comes with this book can help you prepare for exam day.

A friendly exam center employee will give you an introductory lesson to familiarize you with how to operate the computer before the exam session begins. Although the computer randomly selects the specific questions from each category, the operating system tracks the difficulty of each question and controls the selection criteria to ensure that your exam isn't ridiculously easier or harder than anyone else's.

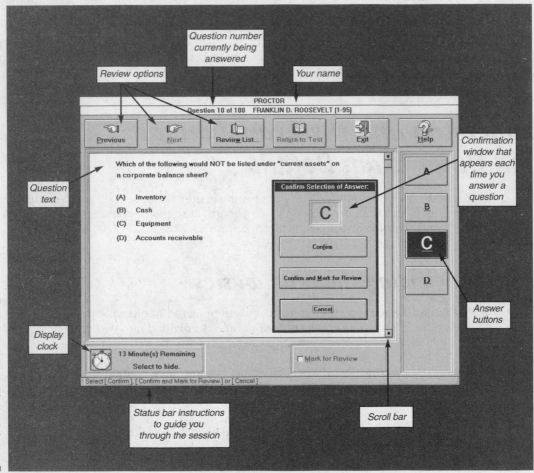

Figure 1-1:
The
PROCTOR
computer
system lets
you select
answers
and mark
them for
review.

2006 National Association of Securities Dealers, Inc. Reprinted with permission from NASD.

The following list describes some important computer exam features:

- ✔ Scroll bars for moving the questions on the screen
- ✔ A clock to help you track how much time you have left during each part (if the clock is driving you batty, you can hide it with a click of the mouse)
- ✔ A confirmation box that requires you to approve your answer choice before the computer proceeds to the next question

✔ An indication of which question you're currently on

✔ A choice of answering the questions by

- Typing in the letter for the correct answer on the keyboard

- Using the mouse to point and click on the correct answer

- At some test centers, using a computer with a touch screen that lets you select the answer by pressing lightly against the monitor with your fingertip

✔ The capability of changing your answers or marking questions that you're unsure of for later review, which allows you to go back and answer them at any time during that particular part

You can mark answers for review or change responses only for the part of the test you're currently taking. In other words, after you begin the second part, you can't go back and change answers from the first part.

Although you can review and change all your answers at the end of each half, don't. Your brain is going to feel like it went through a blender by the time you get there. Review only your *marked* questions and change the answers only if you're 100 percent sure that you made a mistake. As an instructor, I know that people change a right answer to a wrong one five times more often than a wrong one to a right one.

Instant gratification: Receiving and evaluating your score

Remember having to wait weeks for a standardized test score, hovering somewhere between eagerness and dread? Those days are gone. At the end of the Series 7, the system calculates your score and displays a grade result on the computer screen. Although the wait for your grade to pop up may feel like an eternity, it really takes only 30–45 seconds to see your grade. When you sign out, the test center administer will tackle you (well, approach you) and give

---

A little testing info from the NASD

The NASD Web site (www.nasd.com) is certainly worth checking out. It contains all the nitty-gritty details about the Series 7 and related exams. Use this Web site for the following:

✔ **NASD Current Uniform Registration Forms for Electronic Filing In WEB CRD:** This page includes the U-4 Series 7 registration forms and a link to the Uniform Forms Reference Guide, with contact numbers and other explanatory information for filers.

✔ **NASD Test Center Rules of Conduct:** Just in case you're unable to distinguish the Series 7 test center from that third period algebra class you had back in high school, the NASD gives you the rules and regulations for taking the Series 7 (do not hide a list of equations under the brim of your baseball cap, do not roam the halls during your restroom break, and do not pass notes, no matter how bored you are).

✔ **NASD Registration and Exam Requirements:** This section gives a comprehensive list of the categories of securities representatives and the exam requirements.

✔ **NASD Appointments and Enrollment:** Here you find NASD tips for scheduling appointments to take the Series 7 exam, info about obtaining extensions, and the exam cancellation policy.

✔ **NASD Registration Exam Fee Schedule:** Check out this page to see the fees for registering for the Series 7.

you a printed exam report with your grade and the diagnostic score results with your performance in the specific topics tested on your exam.

Each question on the Series 7 exam is worth 0.4 point, and candidates need a score of 70 or better to achieve a passing grade. This translates to 175 questions out of 250 that you have to answer correctly. The scores are rounded down, so a grade of 69.6 is scored as 69 on the Series 7. When I took the exam, one of the other students from my class got a 69.6 (which was rounded down to a 69), and he had the NASD review his exam to try and get him the extra point. Needless to say, the NASD ruled against him and he had to take the exam again.

You passed! Now what?

After you pass the Series 7, Series 63, and/or Series 66 exam, the NASD will send your firm confirmation that you passed. At that point, you can buy and sell securities for your customers in accordance with your firm's customary procedures.

To continue working as a registered rep, you'll need to fulfill the NASD's continuing education requirements. Within 120 days after your second anniversary as a registered rep, and every three years thereafter, you have to take a computer-based exam at either the Pearson VUE or Prometric exam center.

So you need a do-over: Retaking the exam

Sorry to end this chapter on a negative note, but the Series 7 is a difficult exam, and certainly a lot of people need a do-over.

If you fail the Series 7, your firm has to request a new test date and pay for you to retake the test. Your sponsors can send in one page of the U-4 requesting a new exam, or they can apply online through the Central Registration Depository (CRD) system. You should reapply immediately, though you have to schedule the new test date for at least 30 days after the day you failed (that's 30 days of prime studying time!). If you fail the exam three times, you're required to wait six months before you can retake the exam.

Use the time between exams to understand what went wrong and fix it. Here are some of the reasons people fail the Series 7 exam and some of the steps you can take to be successful:

✔ **Lack of preparation:** You have to follow, and stick to, a well-constructed plan of study. You have your diagnostic printout after you take the exam, and you can use that to focus on the areas of study where you fell short.

  Prep courses can help you identify and focus on the most commonly tested topics and provide valuable tips for mastering difficult math problems. Also consider tutoring sessions tailored to accommodate your busy schedule and pinpoint the areas of study where you need the most help.

✔ **Nerves won out:** Some people are just very nervous test-takers, and they need to go through the process to get comfortable in unfamiliar situations. Next time around, they know what to expect and pass with flying colors.

  The people who are the most nervous about taking the exam tend to be the ones who haven't prepared properly. Make sure that you're passing practice exams on a consistent basis with grades in at least the high 70s before you attempt to take the real exam.

✔ **Insufficient practice exams:** You need to take enough practice exams before you take the real test. I think getting used to the question formats and figuring out how to work through them is as important as learning the material to begin with.

Check out Chapter 2 for info on setting up a study schedule and making the most of your practice exams.

Chapter 2

Preparing for the Series 7 Exam

· ·

In This Chapter

▶ Investing in a prep course and choosing your own study materials

▶ Finding time to study and using study strategies

▶ Staying focused and building test-taking skills

▶ Evaluating your readiness

· ·

When you're preparing for the Series 7 exam, a good cup of java and an all-nighter just aren't gonna cut it. Neither are the frantic two-week study sessions that used to work miracles on final exams. The Series 7 is a mini-marathon of the test world, and as with all endurance events, you need to train for it both mentally and physically.

In this chapter, I discuss your options for studying to take the Series 7 exam. If you plan to enroll in a Series 7 exam prep course, I cover what to look for when selecting the course. I also help you organize your study time efficiently and effectively — even when your preparation time is limited.

Courses and Training Materials: Determining the Best Way to Study

When deciding which study materials to use, your first mission is to identify your learning style. Regardless of whether you understand and remember best by reading, writing, listening, or a combination of these methods, you have to select the training mode that best suits your needs.

If you're likely to benefit from a structured environment, you may be better off in a classroom setting. A prep course can also give you emotional guidance and support from your instructors and others in your class who are forging through this stressful ordeal with you. On the other hand, if you're the type of person who can initiate and follow a committed study schedule on your own every day, you may be able to pass the Series 7 exam without a prep course, and you can save the money you would've spent for classes. The following sections help you evaluate these options in more detail.

Back to school: Attending a prep course

People who learn best by reading, writing, and listening to an instructor benefit from attending prep courses. Unfortunately, not all Series 7 exam prep courses and training materials are created equally. Unlike high school or college courses, the content of Series 7 prep courses and the qualifications of the instructors who teach them aren't regulated by the state Department of Education, the SEC, the NASD, or any other government agency. Do some research to locate the Series 7 training course that works best for you.

The following sections explain some things to consider and questions to ask before enrolling. Take a look at the info you gather, and trust your gut. You should be able to get a good idea of whether training is the primary function of the company offering the prep course or whether the prep course exists to help the broker-dealer earn extra revenue to supplement his failing stockbroker business.

Training school background

To find information about the program, browse the training school's Web site or contact the school offices. Find out how many years the training school has been in business, and check with the Better Business Bureau or the Department of Consumer Affairs to see whether anyone has filed any complaints. I'd look for a school that has stayed in business at least five years. This staying power is generally a sign that the school is doing referral business from students who took the course and passed the Series 7.

Try to get recommendations from others who took the course. Word of mouth is an essential source of referrals for most businesses, and stockbroker training schools are no different. The stockbroker firm you're affiliated with (or will be affiliated with) should be able to recommend training schools.

Courses offered through a local high school's continuing-ed program can be equally as effective as those offered through an accredited university or a company that focuses solely on test prep, so long as the right instructors are teaching it. Read on.

Qualifications of the course instructor (s)

The instructor's qualifications and teaching style are even more important than the history of the company running the course (see the preceding section). An instructor should be not only knowledgeable but also energetic and entertaining enough to keep you awake during the not-so-exciting (all right, *boring*) parts.

When looking for a course, find out whether the teacher has taken — and passed — the Series 7 exam. If so, the instructor probably knows the kinds of questions that'll be asked and can help students focus on the relevant exam material. The instructor likely also developed good test taking skills and can share them with students.

Whether the instructor is a part-timer or full-timer may or may not be important. For example, a full-time instructor who teaches 30 classes a year probably has a better grasp on the material than a part-time instructor who teaches four classes a year. By the same token, an instructor who also owns the school where the course is being offered probably has greater interest in the success of the students than someone who's paid to teach the class by the hour. Use your best judgment.

Before you register, ask whether you can monitor a class for an hour or so with the instructor who'd be training you. If the company says no, I suggest finding another course because that course provider may have something to hide. Also, make sure the classroom is comfortable, clean, and conducive to learning.

Texts, course content, and extra help

To really benefit from a course, you need good resources — which come not only from the actual training materials but also from the people in the classroom. These elements affect how the class shapes up and what you actually learn:

- ✔ **Training material:** Will you have a textbook to study from or just some handouts? The instructor should provide you with textbooks that include sample exams, and a prep course should be loaded with in-class questions for you to work on. The course should also provide you with chapter exams that you can work on at night before the next session (yes, homework is a good thing). Remember, the more questions you see and answer, the better.

- ✔ **In-class practice tests:** You want a prep course that includes test sessions where the instructor grades your exams, identifies incorrect answers, and reviews the correct answers.

- ✔ **Instructor availability:** Ask whether the course instructors will be available to answer your questions after the course is over — not only at the end of the day but also during the weeks after you've completed the course and are preparing for the Series 7.

The practical details

The perfect course can't do you any good if you never show up for class. Here are some issues to consider about the course offering:

- ✔ **Days and times:** Make sure the class fits your schedule. If getting there on time is too stressful or you can't attend often enough to justify the expense, you won't benefit from registering to take the course.

- ✔ **Class size:** If more than 30 to 35 people are in the class, the instructor may not be able to give you the individual attention you need.

- ✔ **Cost:** Obviously, cost is a major concern, but it definitely shouldn't be your only consideration. Choosing a course because it's the least expensive one you can find may be a costly mistake if the course doesn't properly prepare you and you end up wasting your time and spending more money to retake the exam. You can expect to pay anywhere from $350 to $800 for a standard Series 7 prep course, including training course materials (textbooks and final exams).

Quite a few people don't pass the first time around, so find out whether the school charges a fee for retaking the prep course if you don't pass the Series 7 exam or even if you feel that you're not quite ready.

Selecting prep material to study on your own

If you're the type of person who can follow a committed study schedule on your own every day, you may be able to pass the Series 7 exam without a prep course. Many different types of study aids are available to help you prepare.

No matter what your learning style is, I'm a firm believer in textbooks as a primary training aid. Use the online courses, CDs, and flash cards as supplements to textbooks, because just by virtue of its portability and ease of use (you don't have to turn it on, plug it in, or have access to the Internet, and it can never, ever run out of batteries), the textbook is simply the most efficient and effective choice.

My personal favorites are the Empire Stockbroker Training Institute's *Series 7 Coursebook* and its companion, *Series 7 Final Exams* (www.empirestockbroker.com). The textbook focuses on the relevant exam topics, is easy to read and understand, and includes plenty of practice questions and detailed explanations. Securities Training Corporation (www.stcusa.com) and Kaplan Financial (www.kaplanfinancial.com) also publish quality Series 7 books. A lot of the better Series 7 course textbooks are available online.

In addition to *Series 7 Exam For Dummies* and a textbook, also consider investing in one or more of the following popular study aids:

- **Online courses:** For people who want to take a course but lack the time or a vehicle for commuting, instructor-led virtual classrooms may be an option. Students interact through online chats, e-mail, message boards, and/or phone conferences, and classes may be scheduled at specific times. Before purchasing an online course, you should see whether you can monitor one for an hour or so to see if it meets your needs.

  Note: Some so-called "online courses" may consist solely of a packet of study materials without any outside instruction. Make sure the course you sign up for has the features you want.

- **Online testing:** I'm all for online testing. Certainly, the more exams you take, the better. If the practice exam simulates the real test, it's even more valuable. With this study aid, you have access 24 hours a day, 7 days a week, and can pace yourself to take the exams at your leisure. Select a program with a couple thousand questions or more, along with answers and explanations.

- **CD-ROMs:** For the student who prefers interactive learning materials, CD-ROMs may offer everything from practice exams and tutorials to customizable study calendars. Computer programs vary, so shop around.

- **Audio CDs:** You may be able to find testing and audio-course CDs for the Series 7. This form of training can be beneficial as a review for people who already have a decent understanding of the course material. You can listen to taped material while on the go or in your home.

  Personally, I think recording your own notes — especially on topics you're having problems with — would be a better use of your time. Putting the info in your own words, saying ideas out loud, and listening to the recordings can really help reinforce the concepts.

- **Flash cards:** For those who already have a grasp on the subject matter, flash cards are good because you can tuck 'em in your pocket and look at 'em anytime you want. Commercial cards may be confusing and long-winded. You're better off making cards that focus on the areas that are most problematic for you.

Managing Your Study Time Wisely

Unless you're a direct descendent of Albert Einstein, you probably need to allow yourself as much time as possible to prepare for the Series 7 exam.

Get your affairs in order. Go to the dentist and get that sore tooth filled, pay your bills, get your flu shot, get your annual checkup, visit your friends and relatives, finish any critical home improvement projects. Basically, clear the decks as best you can so you can concentrate on your studies. The following sections can help you establish a study plan.

Blocking out some time to study

You have to use your time efficiently, and to accomplish this, you need to grab every spare moment and channel it into study time. If you're attending a Series 7 prep course, your instructors should help you (and your classmates) set up a study schedule for before, during, and after you complete the course.

If you're in charge of carving out your study time, then plan your study regime as if it were a full time, 40-hour-per-week job and leave yourself approximately 200–250 hours in a four- to six-week period to study. If you don't have a job (other than studying), I suggest that you put in at least five or six hours a day. (For advice on how to study well, please look at "Exploring Study Strategies"; the following section discusses setting up an actual schedule.)

Especially for those of you who continue to work at your full-time job, now may be the time to have a heart-to-heart with your boss to negotiate some extra study time. After all, you need to work this out only for the next six weeks. Can you take vacation time? Will your boss allow you flex time (where you agree to work two hours later each day for four days and have the fifth day off)? Can you arrange a quiet place at work to study during breaks and lunch time?

 Set aside a consistent time to study on a daily basis. If possible, schedule your study time around your internal clock. For example, if you're the type who needs a brass band to wake you up and get your mind functioning first thing in the morning but you're wide awake and ready to go at midnight, you may be better off with a study schedule that begins later in the day and lasts into the night. By contrast, if you're leaping out of bed like a jack-in-the-box at the crack of dawn but are dead on your feet by 10 p.m., a morning study schedule would be more favorable.

 You never know when extra time to study will present itself, so carry your textbooks or some flash cards with you whenever you leave home. You can read or drill yourself whenever you find some spare time — on the train, waiting in line, and yes, even during your trips to the restroom.

It's a plan: Getting into a study routine

Establishing and sticking to a study routine is essential. Many people find the Series 7 exam to be difficult because they have to absorb so much material in a relatively short time span, and most of the information on the test is easy to forget because it's not info you use every day. Therefore, you have to reinforce your knowledge on a daily basis by constantly reviewing and revisiting the old information while learning new material. You'll continue to follow this routine over and over and over again.

Setting up shop: Finding an ideal place to study

When you're first learning new material, set yourself up in a place where you have as few distractions as possible — the local library, a separate room, even the bathtub. One of my students used to retreat to his car in the driveway after dinner while his wife put their young kids to bed.

The exam room, with its small cubicles, places you in proximity with other people who are taking the exam at the same time. If clicks of the mouse, taps on the keyboard, the scratch of pencil on paper, and the frustrated sighs of less-prepared test-takers are likely to distract you, you may want to use earplugs, which are available at most exam centers. If, however, you don't want to use earplugs, you can prepare for the worst by subjecting yourself to a somewhat noisy study environment somewhere along the line. (When I was taking my exam before earplugs were permitted, construction crews were working in the next room. Luckily, I'd studied in noisy settings, or the sound of screw guns and workmen talking would've driven me to distraction!) Go to a coffee shop (or any populated establishment) during lunch hour, or turn on a fan or a radio to familiarize yourself with background noise while you're taking your practice exams.

Regardless of whether you have limited time, organizing yourself to cover all the topics you'll be tested on is crucial. If you're taking a prep course or home study course, a huge benefit is that during the course, your time will be allotted to learn and review all the subject matter.

If you're trying to study on your own, get yourself a course textbook and divide the pages by the number of days you have available for studying. Be sure to allow yourself an extra week or two for practice exams. Review each chapter and complete each chapter exam until you have a firm grasp on a majority of the information. Take notes, highlight, and review the material you're having problems with until you feel comfortable with the concepts. Initially, you'll spend a majority of your time on new material; after that, you'll spend your time reviewing and taking chapter quizzes.

During the last one to two weeks leading up to the exam, take as many practice exams as possible. Remember to review each exam thoroughly before moving onto the next exam. For more helpful tips, check out the section called "Exploring Study Strategies" later in this chapter.

Give it a rest: Taking short breaks

If you find yourself reading the same words over and over and wondering what the heck you just read, it's probably time to take a break. Taking short, 5–10-minute breaks can help you process and absorb information without confusing new ideas with the old.

When you reach your saturation point and really start zoning out, you can practice a bit of productive procrastination — walk the dog, shower, do some sit-ups and/or push-ups, grab a meal or a snack, or do anything else that lets you move around or take care of the little things that have to get done. Also, a little human contact can go a long way, provided you have the discipline to hit the books again.

Sometimes, taking a break from one study method can be as good as taking a break from studying altogether. Use multiple types of study material (textbooks, class notes, flash cards, and so on). If at any point during your study time you get sick of looking at a textbook, you can review your notes, flip through or create some flash cards, or take some online practice exams.

Staying focused from day to day

Passing the Series 7 exam is a rite of passage. It's your ticket to wealth, fame, and fortune (or at least a decent job). If you put the time and effort into studying for the Series 7, you'll be rewarded. If not, you'll have to go through this nightmare over and over again until you reach your objective. In the meantime, make yourself a resolution: Until you pass the Series 7, you will limit your social life, and most of your waking hours will revolve around one purpose — studying for the exam. Repeat after me: "This is my life for now."

During the time you're studying for the exam, an emergency that takes you away from your studies may arise, or you may just need to take a mental health day off on a weekend. If so, be sure that you never separate yourself from your textbooks for more than one day and that you jump right back into the Series 7 fire the next day.

Under no circumstances (except in the case of a family emergency) should you stop studying for more than one day within a two-week period. I've had students (who were doing quite well) come back to take another prep class because their test days were too far off and they'd put the books down for a while. The next thing they knew, they forgot half of what they learned. Fortunately, the information comes back faster the second time around.

To keep focused on your studies while not permanently forgetting about otherwise important life activities, prepare a file folder labeled "To-do's after I pass the Series 7." If anything comes up during the time you're studying, instead of interrupting your study time or stressing about things that need to be done, write down the major chore, task, or event on a piece of paper, place it in your to-do's file, and put it out of your mind.

Devoting time to practice tests

Certainly, while you're first going over the new material, you spend most of your time learning the information and taking chapter quizzes. When you feel like you have a good handle on the material, you should start taking full practice exams to see where you stand. (This book includes questions throughout the chapters and two 125-question practice exams with answers and explanations. I also include a CD-ROM with 250 questions, answers, and explanations.) The last one or two weeks before the exam should be almost entirely devoted to taking practice exams and reviewing them.

After you move into the practice test phase, use your textbooks only as reference tools for looking up information you don't understand. Always completely review a practice exam before you move on to the next one. And don't listen to the people who say you have to take three or four practice exams a day; you're better off taking one exam per day and spending twice as long reviewing it as you spent taking it. This method (at least in theory) ensures that you know the subject matter and that you won't make the same mistakes twice.

Practice exams can help you gauge whether you're ready for the real Series 7. See "Knowing When You're Ready," at the end of the chapter, for details.

If you run out of exams to take, purchase more or see whether someone else in your firm has a different book with tests you can borrow. Even though some companies make tests that are somewhat ridiculous, they're still better than taking the same exams over and over again.

Avoiding study groups

Unless your study group includes your instructor, I'd avoid a study group like the plague. The problem with study groups is that everyone wants to study the information that he or she is having problems with. If everyone is having a problem with the same thing, who can help you? I strongly feel that your time is better spent studying on your own.

If you really feel you'd benefit from studying with someone else, try to arrange a tutoring session with a Series 7 instructor.

Staying in shape

Ignoring the importance of physical and mental fitness when you prepare to take the Series 7 exam is a big mistake. The exam itself (and the prep time you put into your study schedule) is physically demanding and mentally exhausting. You have to be alert and able to concentrate on difficult questions for two three-hour sessions. In the weeks leading up to the test, any exercise you can do to keep yourself physically fit — including cardiovascular exercise such as jogging or bike riding — can help out. A workout also gives you a great reason to take a study break.

Exploring Study Strategies

The more ways you work with a piece of information, the better you'll be able to recall it. Here are some study strategies to supplement your routine of reading your textbook and taking practice exams:

- **Aim to understand concepts and relationships, not just formulas and definitions.** Having a good grasp of how ideas are related can provide a safety net for when rote memory fails; you may be able to make educated guesses, recreate formulas, or come up with something to jog your memory. When you see an equation, try to figure out where the numbers come from and what the formula really tells you.

- **Create an outline of your notes or write flash cards.** Using your own words, try to put the more difficult areas of study into an outline or on flash cards. The whole process of condensing large mountains of information into your own abbreviated outline helps you process and absorb difficult concepts.

- **Mark up your textbook.** You don't have to return your textbook to the library, so use the margins to rephrase ideas, draw diagrams, repeat formulas or equations, and highlight unfamiliar words.

- **Tape yourself reading your notes and then play back the tape at night while you're falling sleep or when you're driving.** Although the play-it-at-night technique has been known to give some people nightmares, this temporary condition usually clears up after the exam. I've also heard some people proclaim the nighttime playback is "as soothing as Sominex." (If it prevents you from falling asleep, turn off the tape and opt for getting some rest.)

  Note: While you're sleeping, the brain may process ideas you learned during your waking hours; however, you generally have to be paying attention to remember something new. The main benefit comes from making the initial recording and letting study material be the last thing you hear before you fall asleep.

- **Use sticky notes to flag difficult topics or concepts.** As you study, put a sticky note on a section or page in the book where you need more work. After you have your book(s) filled with stickies, just study those difficult areas (where the stickies are); when you feel you have a good grasp on the information, remove the note from the book. As you learn more and more, whittle down the number of pages with stickies until you've removed them all from the textbook.

Developing Solid Test-Taking Skills

To be successful, you have to master the concepts that form the basis of the questions and, equally importantly, you need to develop your test-taking skills. The best way to develop test-taking skills is to take practice tests, such as the ones in this book and on the accompanying CD-ROM.

Read the question carefully

Don't be fooled. Exam creators love to trip you up by making you jump ahead and answer the question (incorrectly) before you read the entire problem. You know what I mean — where one of the last words in the call (specific inquiry) of the question is worded in the negative, like "all of the following are true except," or "which of the following is the least likely to," and so on. When reviewing the answers to a practice test, these questions cause some students to groan or slap themselves in the head when they realize their mistake. Don't worry — this common reaction usually goes away after you start getting better at taking exams.

Look for phrases that lead to the topic tested

Try to identify the specific category that the question is testing you on. If you study for the number of hours that I recommend to you (see "Blocking out some time to study"), you've most likely covered the material at some point and should be able to identify the topic that the question applies to. After you know the topic, your brain can retrieve the information you need from its mental file cabinet, making it easier for you to focus on the applicable rule, equation, or concept, and you can answer the question correctly.

Work with what you have

If possible, work with the facts in the question and *only* the facts in the question. Too often, students add their own interpretation to the question and turn a straightforward problem into a mess. Use the facts that are given, dump the garbage information that isn't necessary to answer the question, and don't make the question more difficult or assume that there's more to the question than what appears.

Adding information into a question seems to be a very common practice for students (for example, they ask, "Yeah, but what if he were married?"). My standard answer is, "Did it say that in the question?" and the response is *no*. Don't make your life more difficult by adding your own feelings into the question; answer the question that was given to you.

Don't obsess; mark for review

If you experience brain freeze while taking the exam, don't panic or waste valuable time on one question. Eliminate any answer(s) that you know must be wrong (if any), take your best guess, and *mark the question for review* so you can easily return to it later. The question may even resolve itself. For example, another question may trigger your memory as you continue to take the exam, and the correct answer may become clear.

Keep track of time

Time yourself so you're always aware of how much time you have left to complete your exam. One way to do so is to figure out which question you need to be up to at the end of each half-hour; use that as a benchmark to keep track of your progress. In each of your two sessions, you have three hours to complete the exam. You have to answer 130 questions in each session (5 don't count toward your score). This gives you 1.38 minutes (or 1 minute and 22.8 seconds) to answer each question.

Translating these numbers to half-hour benchmarks gets you the following results:

Time	Number of Questions Completed
30 minutes	22
1 hour	44
1.5 hours	66
2 hours	88
2.5 hours	110
3 hours	130

Memorize these benchmarks, write them on your scrap paper (or dry erase board) as soon as the exam administrators allow you to begin, and keep referring to your watch or the clock on the computer screen to track your progress in relation to the benchmark. If you find yourself falling behind, pick up your pace. If you're really falling behind, mark the lengthier, more difficult questions for review and spend your time answering the easier questions. Why waste two minutes on one long question for 0.4 of a point when you could've answered two shorter questions in that time and earned twice as many points?

Most students don't have a problem finishing the Series 7 exam on time. If you easily and consistently finish 125-question Series 7 practice exams in less than 3 hours, you should be okay on the real Series 7.

The clock on the computer screen is a tool that can help you keep track of your time. If you find yourself obsessing over the clock to the point that you can't concentrate on the question in front of you, hide it by clicking on the lower left-hand corner of the computer screen.

Master the process of elimination

The Series 7 exam is a standardized exam. This format makes it similar to other practical exams of this type: The best way to find the correct answer may be to eliminate, one at a time, the incorrect answers. I help you develop this crucial skill as you tackle the topic-specific questions throughout the book.

Maintain your concentration

To maintain your concentration, read the *stem* of the question (the last question before the answer choices) first to keep yourself focused on what the question is asking. Next, read through the entire problem (including the stem) to get a grip on the facts you have to consider to select the correct answer. You can then anticipate the correct answer and read all answer choices to see whether your anticipated answer is there. If you don't see your answer and none of the other choices seem to fit, reread the stem to see whether you missed an important fact. Check out Chapter 3 for more detailed test-taking tips.

You can also take care to keep yourself physically alert. The last hour or so of each session will probably be the most difficult. I recommend that you eat a small protein bar to help you keep your levels of energy and concentration high prior to starting your test. Forget the high sugar/high-carb foods; leave them for after the exam. These foods boost your sugar level temporarily, but when the level drops, your energy and concentration levels will sink like a lead balloon.

Speaking of low energy levels, to keep yourself alert if you feel yourself fading, get up and get a drink of water, splash some water on your face, stretch, dig your fingernails into your palms of your hands, do whatever you have to do to keep yourself focused on the exam so you don't make sloppy mistakes.

Think carefully before changing your answers

In general, if you've selected an answer and you can't really explain why, maybe it was just a *gut* answer. You're five times more likely to change to a wrong answer than to the right one, so change answers only if

- You didn't read the question correctly the first time and missed a major point that changes the answer choice (for example, you didn't see the word *except* at the end of the question).
- You're absolutely sure you made a mistake.

Use the scrap paper wisely

In the testing room, you receive six pieces of letter-sized scrap paper (or a dry erase board), all of which will be collected — so restrain yourself from writing any obscenities about the exam or its creators. Here are some more productive ways to use this valuable resource:

- **Mark for review.** You have to answer each question before you can go to the next, so if you're not sure of the correct answer, eliminate the wrong answers, take your best guess, and mark the question for review later. On your scrap paper, write down the numbers of any questions you want to check before the end of the session.

- **Eliminate wrong answers.** You can't write on the computer screen, so for each question, you may find it easier to write *A*, *B*, *C*, and *D* on your scrap paper (in a column) as they appear on the screen and eliminate answers directly on your paper.

- **Do a brain dump.** After your exam begins and before your brain gets cluttered with the Series 7 exam questions, use your scrap paper to jot down the formulas you memorized or topic matters that were giving you problems so that you can refresh your memory during the exam. Your scrap paper will be collected at the end of the first session, so repeat the brain dump process after you begin the exam in the afternoon session.

When doing a brain dump, write only the things that you're really having problems with. You know — the ones that you needed to study the morning of the test. Don't worry about cataloguing things you already know and feel comfortable with, because it's a waste of your time (and paper). Those items should come to the surface of your brain as soon as you need them.

- **Time yourself.** If you have a problem with timing, you can pace yourself to avoid running out of time by using the clock on the computer. Another option is to write down your half-hour benchmarks (listed in the "Keep track of time" section earlier) on your scrap paper to make sure you stay on track.

If you find yourself spending more time watching the clock than working on the questions, feel free to hide it (the "Keep track of time" section earlier explains how). The clock is supposed to be a useful tool, not a hindrance.

- **Perform calculations and draw diagrams.** Use the scrap paper to work out math problems, to create seesaws, or to make any other diagrams that help you rack up your points.

Knowing When You're Ready

Your goal is to consistently score 80 to 85 percent on the sample tests that you take to ensure that you're ready for the real exam.

To determine your readiness, consider your scores on the practice exams the *first time* you take them. In other words, don't convince yourself that you're ready if you're getting 85 percents on exams that you've already taken three times. If you take a practice exam more than once, you may just be remembering the answers. I'm not against taking the same exams more than once, but don't use exams you've taken before to gauge how prepared you are.

My company and some other companies sell an exam as a final benchmark to test a student's readiness to take the Series 7 exam. We call ours The Annihilator — a 250-question exam designed to be four-to-six points harder than the real exam. Students who pass with a 70 or better are most likely ready to take the Series 7.

Chapter 3

Examining Question Types and How to Master Them

. . . .

In This Chapter

▶ Exploring the composition of Series 7 exam questions

▶ Analyzing the purpose and intent of the question

▶ Identifying the correct answer

▶ Mastering the process of elimination

. . . .

Yes, I know, I know: "Why can't they just ask regular questions?" This problem has perplexed Series 7 test takers throughout the ages (all right, maybe not, but it *does* bug me). The test designers have riddled the old pick-the-best-answer questions with all kinds of pitfalls. The people in charge want you to choose combinations of correct answers and pick out exceptions; they expect you to pull numbers from balance sheets and apply complex formulas; and, as if you didn't have enough to worry about, they even give you extraneous information to try to trip you up. Sheesh!

In this chapter, I introduce you to the types of questions to expect on the Series 7 exam, how to analyze the facts in the questions, and how to identify what the examiners are *really* testing you on. I also show you how to use the process of elimination to find the right answer, and if all else fails, how to logically guess the best answer.

Familiarizing Yourself with Question Formats

The Series 7 exam is a beast of a test that poses questions in many different ways. You have to deal with multi-tiered Roman numeral nightmares, open- and closed-ended sentences, and killers like *except* and *not*. In this section, I show you how the examiners phrase the questions and the ways they can trip you up if you aren't careful.

Working with the straight shooters: The more straightforward type

Straightforward question types include a group of sentences with the facts followed by a question or incomplete sentence; you then get four answer choices, one of which correctly answers the question or completes the idea.

Closed-stem questions

You can find more closed-stem questions than any other question type on the Series 7 exam, so you better get a handle on answering these babies for sure. Thankfully, closed-stem questions are fairly run-of-the-mill. They begin with one or more sentences of information and end with a question (and appropriately enough, a question mark). The question mark is what makes closed-stem questions different from open-stem questions, which I discuss in the next section. Your answer choices lettered A through D may be complete or incomplete sentences. Here's a basic closed-stem question:

Mr. Bearishnikoff is a conservative investor. Which of the following investments would you recommend to him?

(A) Put options

(B) Long-term income adjustment bonds

(C) Common stock of an aggressive growth company

(D) Treasury notes

The answer is D. The first sentence tells you that Mr. Bearishnikoff is a conservative investor. This detail is all the information you need to answer the question correctly, because you know that conservative investors aren't looking to take a lot of investment risks and that Treasury notes (T-notes) are considered the safest of all securities — they're backed by the fact that the government can always print more money to pay off the securities that it issues.

Of course, sometimes the phrasing of the answer choices can help you immediately cut down on the answer choices. For instance, Mr. Bearishnikoff would probably balk at investing in an *aggressive growth* company, which certainly doesn't sound stable or safe. Check out the section titled "Picking up clues when you're virtually clueless: The process of elimination" for details on raising your odds of answering questions correctly.

By the way, the *you* in the question refers to you on your good days, when you're considerate and rational and have had sufficient amounts of sleep. Your client probably wouldn't appreciate any rogue-elephant investing, even if you think Mr. Bearishnikoff should be more daring because of whatever life situation you've pictured for him. The question also assumes normal market conditions, so don't recommend a different investment because you think the government is going to collapse and T-notes are going to take a dive. Just accept the conditions the problem presents to you.

Be careful to focus only on the information you need to answer the question. The Series 7 exam creators have an annoying tendency to include extra details in the question (such as the maturity date, coupon rate, investor's age, and so on) that you may or may not need. See "Focusing on key information," later in this chapter, for some tips on zeroing in on the necessary info.

Open-stem questions

An open-stem question poses the problem as an incomplete sentence, and your mission, should you choose to accept it, is to complete the sentence with the correct answer. The following example shows how you can skillfully finish other people's thoughts:

The initial maturity on a standard option is

(A) three months

(B) six months

(C) nine months

(D) one year

The answer is C. Options (see Chapter 12) give the purchaser the right to buy or sell securities at a fixed price. Options are considered derivatives (securities that derive their value from another security) because they're linked to an underlying security. Standard options have an initial maturity of nine months. On the other hand, Long-term Equity AnticiPation Securities (LEAPS) may have initial maturities of one, two, or three years. In a case like this, the question asks about a standard option; therefore, you don't assume that it's a LEAP.

The preceding example is quite easy. Anyone who's been studying for the Series 7 exam should know the answer. However, what makes the Series 7 so difficult is that the exam is loaded with so many date-oriented details. Not only do you have to memorize the initial maturities of all the different securities, but unfortunately (and believe me, I feel your pain), you also have to remember a truckload of time frames (like accounts are frozen for 90 days, new securities can't be purchased on margin for 30 days, an options account agreement must be returned within 15 days after the account is approved, and so on).

Date-oriented details are excellent material to include in your flash cards. See Chapter 2 for more study suggestions.

Encountering quirky questions with qualifiers

To answer questions with qualifiers, you have to find the best answer to the question; if not for the qualifier (*most, least, best, except,* or *not*), most of the answers would be correct.

Working with extremes: Most, least, best

Recognizing the qualifier in the question stem and carefully reading every single answer choice are very important. Check out this example:

Which of the following companies would be MOST affected by interest rate fluctuations?

(A) SKNK Perfume Corp.

(B) Bulb Utility Co.

(C) Crapco Vitamin Supplements, Inc.

(D) LQD Water Bottling Co.

The answer is B. Although all companies may be somewhat affected by interest rate fluctuations, the question uses the word *most.* If interest rates increase, companies have to issue bonds with higher coupon (interest) rates. This higher rate, in turn, greatly affects the companies' bottom lines. Therefore, you're looking for a company that issues a lot of bonds. Utility companies are most affected by interest rate fluctuations because they're highly leveraged (issue a lot of bonds).

Making exceptions: Except or not

With an *except* or *not* question, you're looking for the answer that's *the exception* to the rule stated in the stem of the question. In other words, the correct answer is always the *false* answer. The question can be open (as it is in the next example) or closed.

Right off the bat, look for an *except* or *not* in the stem of every question on the Series 7. Many students who really know their material accidentally pick the wrong answer on a few questions because they carelessly miss the *except* or *not.*

Take a look at an exception problem:

A stockholder owns 800 shares of WHY common stock. WHY stockholders were given cumulative voting rights. If there are three vacancies on the board of directors, stockholders can cast any of the following votes EXCEPT

(A) 800 for one candidate

(B) 800 for each candidate

(C) 2,400 for one candidate

(D) 900 for each candidate

The answer is D. Cumulative voting rights give smaller stockholders (not heightwise, but in the number of shares owned) an easier chance to gain representation on the board of directors because a stockholder may combine his or her total voting rights and vote the cumulative total in any way he or she wants. Here, the stockholder has a total of 2,400 votes to cast (800 shares × 3 vacancies = 2,400 votes).

In this example, you may be tempted to select answers A, B, or C, any of which would be correct if you were asked for the number of votes this stockholder *could* cast. For example, the stockholder can use the 800 shares to vote for only one candidate, and the investor doesn't have to use all 2,400 votes (choice A). Answer B is another possible voting arrangement because nobody said the stockholder has to use all the votes for one candidate. Choice C is another option because the stockholder has a total of 2,400 votes to cast. In this question, however, you're looking for the number of votes the stockholder *can't* cast because the word *except* in the question stem requires you to find a false answer. Therefore, D is the correct answer because 900 votes for each candidate (900 × 3) would require the stockholder to cast a total of 2,700 votes.

If you're one of the unlucky people who get an "all of the following are false except" question, you have to find the *true* answer. Don't forget, two negatives in a sentence make a positive statement. You may want to try rephrasing the question so you know whether you're looking for a true or false answer.

Roman hell: Complex multiple choice

Yes, the Series 7 exam creators even sneak complex (two-tiered) Roman numeral questions in on you. They can pose the question by asking you to put something in order, or they can ask you to find the best combination in a series of answer choices. To make things even more enjoyable, sometimes they even add *except* and *not* to the question (see the preceding section).

Imposing order: Ranking questions

To answer a ranking question, you have to choose the answer that places the information in the correct order — for example, first to last, last to first, highest to lowest, lowest to highest, and so on. Check out the following example:

In which order, from first to last, are the following actions taken when opening a new options account?

   I. Send the customer an ODD.

  II. Have the ROP approve the account.

 III. Execute the transaction.

 IV. Have the customer send in an OAA.

(A) I, II, III, IV

(B) II, I, IV, III

(C) III, I, II, IV

(D) I, III, II, IV

The answer is A. Wasn't it nice of me to arrange all the answers in order for you? Because option transactions are so risky, the customer has to receive an options risk disclosure document (ODD) prior to opening the account. Roman numeral I has to come first, so you can immediately eliminate answer choices B and C, giving you a 50 percent chance of answering correctly. After the client receives the ODD, the registered options principal (ROP) needs to approve the account before any transactions can be executed; II has to come before III, so you can finish the problem here — the answer is A. Last but not least, the customer signs and returns an options account agreement (OAA) within 15 days after the account is approved by the ROP.

Taking two at a time

The Roman numeral format also appears on the Series 7 with questions that offer two answer choices as the correct response. In these types of questions, you choose the responses that best answer the question:

Which TWO of the following are the minimum requirements for an investor to be considered accredited?

   I. An individual with a net worth of $500,000

   II. An individual with a net worth of $1,000,000

   III. An individual who earns $200,000 per year

   IV. An individual who earns $300,000 per year

   (A) I and III

   (B) I and IV

   (C) II and III

   (D) II and IV

The answer is C. Roman numerals I and II both deal with net worth; III and IV deal with earnings. Therefore, you're dealing with two questions in one: To be accredited, what are

   ✔ An individual's minimum net worth?

   ✔ An individual's minimum income?

To be considered an accredited (sophisticated) investor, the minimum requirement is a net worth of $1,000,000 and/or a yearly income of $200,000. If the word *minimum* were not used in the question, answer IV would also be correct.

A little mystery: Dealing with an unknown number of correct statements

In the preceding section, the question states that only two responses can be correct. The following question may have one, three, or four correct answers. You can recognize this type of question simply by glancing at your answer choices. To make the problem more difficult (don't hate me, now), I add an *except* because I'm feeling really good about you, and I just know you're up to it:

All of the following are considered violations EXCEPT

   I. rehypothecation

   II. commingling

   III. odd lot transactions

   IV. forward pricing

   (A) I only

   (B) II only

   (C) I, III, and IV only

   (D) I, II, III, and IV

The answer is C. The only violation out of the choices listed is commingling. *Commingling* occurs when a broker-dealer combines a customer's account with that of the broker-dealer's or combines a customer's fully paid securities with margined securities. (Chapter 16 can fill you in on rules and regulations.)

You're looking for the choices that are *not* violations, so you want to identify the actions that are allowed. If you eliminate commingling, Roman numeral II, your choices are A (I only) or C (I, III, and IV only). You know that I is correct because it's in both answer choices, so you need to evaluate only III and IV. (You have to check only one of these because you know that if III is correct, IV must be as well; if III is false, so is IV.) Odd lot transactions (III) are ones for fewer than 100 shares (a round lot) and are okay. Forward pricing (IV) is what mutual funds do with orders placed by investors, allowing them to purchase or sell at the next price (usually at the end of the day), which is also okay. Answer C is correct because it's the only one that lists all three correct choices (I, III, and IV).

Looking at exhibits: Series 7 diagram questions

The Series 7 exam also gives some exhibit questions, which may include newspaper clippings, option prices, bond prices, trading patterns, a specialist's book, income statements, balance sheets, and so on. Out of the exhibit questions you get, some of them just require you to find the correct information; others require a little calculating. I wouldn't be too concerned about them if I were you because most of them are quite easy.

Take a look at the following problem:

GHI Corporation Balance Sheet at 12-31-XX
(In Thousands)

Assets		Liabilities	
Cash and cash equivalents	$8,000	Accounts payable	$1,000
Receivables (net)	$1,000	Wages payable	$800
Inventory	+$3,000	Taxes payable	$700
Total current assets	**$12,000**	Interest payable	+ $500
		Total current liabilities	$3,000
Notes receivable due after one year	$1,000	Long-term debt 8%	+$4,000
		Total liabilities	**$7,000**
Property, plant, and equipment (net)	$4,000		
Goodwill	+$1,000	**Stockholder's Equity**	
Total long-term assets	**$6,000**	Preferred stock $100 par 9%	$2,000
		Common stock $1 par	$2,000
		Paid-in capital	$4,000
Total assets	**$18,000**	Retained earnings	+$3,000
		Total stockholder's equity	**$11,000**
		Total liabilities and stockholder's equity	**$18,000**

What is the working capital of GHI Corp.?

(A) $7,000

(B) $7,000,000

(C) $9,000

(D) $9,000,000

The answer is D. This example accurately portrays the difficulty level of most of the exhibit questions on the Series 7 exam. After you remember the formula for working capital (see Chapter 13), you simply have to find the information you need — the current assets and current liabilities — on the balance sheet so you can answer the question:

Working capital = current assets – current liabilities

= $12,000,000 – $3,000,000

= $9,000,000

You may wonder why the answer is in millions instead of thousands. If you notice, the top of the balance sheet says "in thousands," which tells you that you have to multiply the numbers in the balance sheet by 1,000.

Be careful when you answer exhibit questions that you don't miss labels like "in thousands" in headings or scales on a graph that would change your answer. Almost nothing is worse than missing a question that you know how to figure out because you carelessly overlooked something right in front of you.

The following question has you locate information on call options:

Option			Calls		Puts	
CDE	Strike Price	Expiration	Vol	Last	Vol	Last
68.50	65	Aug	10	3.75	90	0.10
68.50	65	Sep	40	4.50	120	0.80
68.50	65	Nov	20	6.75	4	1.80
68.50	65	Feb	21	7.00	—	—
68.50	70	Aug	140	0.40	5	2.00
68.50	70	Sep	155	1.70	1	3.00
68.50	70	Nov	28	3.00	30	4.35
68.50	75	Feb	40	2.60	—	—
68.50	80	Nov	70	0.65	—	—

What is the time value of a CDE Nov 65 call?

(A) 4.00

(B) 3.25

(C) 3.00

(D) 2.40

The answer is B. This question involves options (see Chapter 12 for calculations and more information). The first step is to find the premium for the CDE Nov 65 call in the exhibit. To accomplish this, line up the 65 strike price with the Nov expiration month; you find it in the third row of data. Follow that row over to the fifth column to get the premium for the Nov 65 call. In this case, it's 6.75. Next, use the following formula P = I + T, where P = premium, I = intrinsic value (the in-the-money amount), and T = time value (how long an investor has to use the option).

First, enter the premium into the equation. Next, you have to determine the intrinsic value (how much the option is in-the-money). Call options go in-the-money when the price of the stock is above the strike price. The stock price is 68.50 (left column) and the strike price is 65, so the option is 3.50 in-the-money (68.50 – 65 = 3.50). After placing those two numbers (6.75 and 3.50) in the equation, you see that the time value has to be 3.25:

$$P = I + T$$
$$6.75 = 3.50 + T$$
$$T = 3.25$$

Shredding the Questions: Tips and Tricks

In Chapter 2, I give you general exam proficiency tips. In this section, I show you how to improve your analysis of topic-specific Series 7 questions. I also provide you with more sample exam questions to further demonstrate the art of choosing the correct answers.

Focusing on key information

The Series 7 exam questions can be particularly difficult if you rush through the exam and miss details that change the meaning of the question.

When you first start taking practice exams, read through the question to determine what's being asked; then go back to the beginning of the problem to identify the key facts and underline and/or highlight them in your textbooks. Marking the questions may seem time-consuming when you first begin to study, but if you get into the habit of picking out key words in each question, zoning in on the important information should be second nature by the time you take the test. Of course, you can't underline items on the computer screen at the testing center (the test center administrators may get upset if you write on the computer screen). So instead, if you find yourself getting distracted by useless information, use the scrap paper to write down the information you do need.

This example zeroes in on the essential information:

A 55-year-old investor purchases a <u>6 percent</u> DEF convertible mortgage bond at 90 with 10 years until maturity. If the bond is currently trading at <u>97</u>, <u>what is the current yield</u>?

(A) 5.72%

(B) 6.00%

(C) 6.19%

(D) 6.67%

The answer is C. When determining the current yield of a bond, all you need is the market price of the bond and the coupon (interest) rate (see Chapter 7). The fact that the investor is 55 years old or that the bond is a convertible mortgage bond that was purchased at $900 (90 percent of $1,000 par) with 10 years until maturity means nothing to the question. Underline or highlight what you do need (6 percent, 97, current yield) so you don't get distracted.

To determine the current yield, divide the annual interest by the market price. The annual interest is $60 (6 percent of $1,000 par) and the market price is $970 (97 percent of $1,000 par):

$$\text{Current yield} = \frac{\text{annual interest}}{\text{market price}} = \frac{\$60}{\$970} = 6.19\%$$

To avoid confusion when faced with a math problem, read the stem of the question to determine what's being asked; before you consider the rest of the question, jot down the formula you need to calculate your answer.

Answer me this: Picking the correct answer

The Series 7 exam is a practical, multiple-choice exam. The correct answer has to be one of the choices. This setup means you don't have to *provide* the correct answer; you just have to *recognize* it when you see it.

Picking up clues when you're virtually clueless: The process of elimination

When you don't straight-out know an answer, your approach can definitely make the difference between passing and failing the exam. Your best strategy may be eliminating the wrong answers. In theory, you should be able to eliminate, one by one, three incorrect answers for each question.

Even if you can't eliminate three incorrect answers, you'll most certainly be able to eliminate one or two answers that are definitely wrong. Don't try to guess the right answer until you've axed as many wrong answers as you can. Obviously, if you can get the choices down to two potential answers, you have a 50-50 chance of answering correctly.

For an answer choice to be correct, every aspect has to be correct, and the selection has to specifically answer the question that's asked. As a rule of thumb on the Series 7 exam, a more-precise answer is correct more often than a less-precise answer, and a longer answer usually (but not always) prevails over a short answer.

If a response is potentially correct, write *T* for *true* next to the answer in your practice exam, and if a response is wrong, eliminate it by writing *F* for *false* next to the answer. If you do this step correctly, you should end up with three Fs and one T, and the T is the correct answer. Or if the question is looking for a false answer, you should end up with three Ts and one F. On the actual test, you can write A through D on your scrap paper and mark the answer choices appropriately.

Always look to eliminate any wrong answers that you can. Pay attention to the wording, and get rid of choices that simply sound wrong or make statements that are too broad or absolute. If you're still undecided, use your scrap paper to write down the question number and the answer choices that remain. Take your best guess and mark the answer for review. When you review, look at your scrap paper to help you zone in on your potential answers. Change your answer only if you're sure you made a mistake.

Getting down with numbers: Eliminating some math

The process of elimination can get you out of some messy calculations. When dealing with math, look at the answer choices before you begin working out the problem. You may be able to get the answer without doing any calculations at all. For instance, if you have a forward stock split, you know that the number of shares has to increase and that the price of the stock has to decrease (see Chapter 6). If three of the answers fail to meet these conditions, you have your answer right off the bat.

Stop opposing me: Dealing with opposite answers

When answering multiple choice questions, if you see two opposing answer choices, only one can be right. Traditionally, in practical exams like the Series 7, when you see two answer choices that are completely opposite from each other, the exam creators are trying to test your knowledge of the correct rule, procedure, or law, so one of those opposing choices will most likely be the correct answer. Take a look at the example:

Which of the following is TRUE of UGMA accounts?

(A) There can be only one minor and one custodian per account.

(B) There can be more than one minor and one custodian per account.

(C) Securities can only be purchased on margin.

(D) They must be set up for children who have reached the age of majority.

The answer is A. If you look at the answers, you notice that answers A and B oppose each other. If you have two opposing answers, in almost all cases, one of them has to be right. Therefore, you can ignore answers C and D, which gives you a 50 percent chance of getting the answer right. Uniform Gifts to Minors Act (UGMA) accounts are set up for minors who are too young to have their own accounts. Each account is limited to one minor and one custodian. (See Chapter 16 for details on custodial accounts.)

Facing Roman numerals: Not as hard as you think

Complex (two-tiered) multiple-choice questions, with both Roman numerals and letters, can be really frustrating because they usually signal the test taker (you) that you need more than one correct answer. Well, today's your lucky day, because I show you a shortcut that can help you blow these questions right out of the water.

Traditionally, the first tier of these types of questions gives you several answer choices preceded by Roman numerals; the second tier (preceded by letters) provides you with choices about which Roman numeral answers are correct. Fifteen different combinations of I, II, III, and IV are possible (16 if you count "none of the above," which is almost never correct), but each problem can list only four of them in the answer choices. Because of the limited answer choices, you may not have to evaluate every statement — certain combinations of Roman numerals may be logically impossible.

Read the question carefully, and then mark *T* for *true* or *F* for *false* next to the Roman numerals to indicate whether they're correct answers to the question. If the Roman numeral is correct, circle that number on the choices that follow the letters in the second tier. If the Roman numeral is false, all the letter answers that include that numeral must also be false, and you can cross them out. If you're really lucky, three of the Roman numerals can be eliminated right away, leaving you with one answer choice.

Look over a Roman numeral question:

Which of the following is TRUE of the NASD 5% policy?

    I. It covers commissions charged to customers when executing trades on an agency basis.

    II. It covers markups on stock sold to customers from inventory.

    III. It covers markdowns on stock purchased from customers for inventory.

    IV. Riskless and simultaneous are covered.

(A) I and IV only

(B) IV only

(C) II and III only

(D) I, II, III, and IV

The answer is D. The NASD 5% policy applies to non-exempt securities sold to or purchased from customers. This situation is one where you should look at the Roman numerals and pick out whatever answers you know answer the question. For example, if you know Roman numeral I is right (which it is), put a T (for true) next to it. Next, look at answer choices A, B, C, and D, and eliminate answers B and C, because neither one includes Roman numeral I. Because both answers that remain, A and D, include Roman numerals I and IV, you don't even have to bother reading Roman numeral IV — it's in both remaining answers, so you know it has to be true. Write T next to Roman numeral IV. If you know that either Roman numeral II or III is correct (which they both are), the answer has to be D because it's the only one that lists all the correct choices.

Don't make the same mistake twice

When studying for the Series 7 exam, the practice exams can help you pinpoint your weaker areas of knowledge. The questions you answer incorrectly can be your best learning tools if you thoroughly review the explanations for each wrong answer. You may be tempted to jump from one practice exam to the next without taking adequate time to review your wrong answers. Don't do it! If you put the effort into finding out why your choices were wrong when you're practicing, you're less likely to repeat the same mistake on the Series 7 exam, when it really counts.

Chapter 4

Surviving Test Day

- -

- -

*Y*ou've done your homework, taken practice exams, and completed your prep course, and now the day of reckoning is upon you. You're ready to exchange the gazillion hours of study and hard work for your Series 7 license. The last hurdle awaits you at the test center.

In this chapter, I give you a snapshot of the Series 7 exam experience so you know the procedure before, during, and after you take the exam and can hit the ground running.

Composing Yourself the Day Before

On the day before the exam, review the information that you're still having problems with until noon; then call it a day. Get away from the books, go out to dinner (maybe skip the spicy foods and alcohol), go to a movie. Rest your mind. If you've put the required time and effort into studying up to now, you'll benefit more from a good night's rest than anything you can learn in the final hours the night before your exam. Taking the evening off can help prevent brain fatigue and make zoning into exam mode easier tomorrow, when it counts the most.

Before you go to sleep, gather the items you need to take with you to the exam. If you prepare yourself the night before, you'll be more relaxed on exam day. Here are some activities to complete the night before the exam to finalize your preparations for the big day:

✔ Make sure you have the proper government-issued ID bearing your name, signature, and a recent photo. The name on your ID must identically match the name on the Web CRD registration form. Expired ID won't be accepted. Official (primary) identification can be in the form of a valid passport, a driver's license, or a military ID card.

If the military ID doesn't have a signature, you need to bring a secondary form of ID with a signature. Secondary ID can be a valid credit card, a bank automatic-teller machine (ATM) card, a library card, a U.S. Social Security card, an employee ID/work badge, or a school ID.

✔ Pack earplugs (if allowed — ask when you schedule your exam).

✔ Put your lunch and/or a snack with the rest of the stuff.

✔ Bring study materials — including the topics and/or math formulas you're having trouble with — for a final review before you enter the test center.

Doing test runs in the final weeks

Getting too little sleep (you'll be a nervous wreck) or too much sleep (you'll be in a stupor) the night before the exam can be a disaster. For the week before the exam (if possible), follow the routine you'll be following on the day of your exam. Set your alarm at the same time you'll wake up on exam day, take your practice exams for two three-hour intervals at the same time as you'll be taking the real exam, and so on.

Also, the day of the exam is not the time to find out that a big construction project is underway on the exact route you're taking to get to the test center, the traffic is backed up for miles, and you'll be at least an hour late. The last thing you need to worry about on exam day is getting to the test center late and having to reschedule your exam.

To help avoid this disaster, do a test run sometime before the test date. Travel the route you'll take at the same time (and, if possible, on the same day of the week) as your exam date to get a preview of what you can expect. You may even be able to check your local newspaper for details on upcoming construction or repairs that may affect roadways and public transportation. Having an alternate route established in advance is also a good idea in case your route of choice isn't the best option on exam day.

✔ Have your watch ready to make sure you're on time, that you don't take too long between the first and second halves of the exam, and that you complete both sessions before your time is up.

✔ Lay out your clothes (dress in layers in case the test center is like either your refrigerator or your oven).

✔ Review the directions to the exam site. Make sure you have a charged cell phone and the test center number in case you get lost.

Additionally, you have to bring at least one finger with you, preferably yours, so that the exam administrators can take a fingerprint (though you probably have that packed already).

You can't bring study material, textbooks, briefcases, purses, electronic devices, cell phones, notes of any kind, or your really smart friend with you into the testing room. Calculators, pencils, and scrap paper will be provided for you at the exam center, and the exam administrators will collect the calculators, pencils, and all scrap paper (used and unused) at the end of each session.

Making the Most of the Morning

Now the big day is here. Certainly, you don't have to dress up for the pictures the Series 7 administrator takes, but you should at least do what you need to do to feel awake and alive and good about yourself (do some push-ups, take a shower, shave, whatever).

Be sure to eat at least a light breakfast. You may feel like you're too nervous to eat, but if you're hungry when you take the exam, you won't be able to concentrate. And if you overeat, you'll be wasting valuable energy (and blood flow!) digesting the meal — energy your brain needs to sustain you. To avoid an energy crash, I suggest a protein bar, fruit, and/or veggies rather than sugar or carbs.

Grab everything you packed up the night before (see the preceding section) and head out the door.

Leave your home in time to arrive at the test center at least 30 minutes before your scheduled exam so you have time to check in. I recommend that you arrive at the test center 1½ hours before the exam — 1 hour to review the topics and/or math formulas that you're having problems with and a half-hour to check in.

Arriving on the Scene

The Series 7 exams are administered by Thompson Prometric and Pearson VUE, and you can contact either company for additional information. In this section, I cover the steps to take upon your arrival at the exam center.

In Chapter 1, I discuss the availability of special accommodations if you're disabled or learning impaired or if English is your second language. If you require special accommodations, contact the NASD Special Conditions Team at (800) 999-6647 for information about registration and for instructions about arriving at the exam center.

Taking advantage of one last chance to cram

The information you review just before the exam will be on the surface of your mind. When you arrive at the exam center (or even during your commute if you take public transportation), do some last-minute cramming. Review the topics and/or math formulas you're having trouble with. The formulas on the Cheat Sheet in this book may be helpful.

Each Series 7 exam center is set up differently; you may find areas in the building where you can study, or you may have to study outside in your car, on a bench, or at a nearby coffee shop. When you're ready to enter the exam center (a half hour before the exam) you can leave your books in your vehicle, or some locations have a locker you can use for storing personal property while you're taking the exam.

Signing in

To enter the Series 7 exam center, you have to provide the administrators with valid ID. (See "Composing Yourself the Day Before" for what's considered to be valid.) When inside the test center, you have to sign in and get photographed and fingerprinted. In addition, before you begin the exam, you have to read a form called the Rules of Conduct and agree to the terms. A preview of the Rules of Conduct is available on the NASD Web site (www.nasd.com/ RegistrationQualifications/BrokerGuidanceResponsibility/Qualifications/ NASDW_016189).

Getting seated

Basically, the only things you may bring into the testing room are your own sweet self and possibly a set of earplugs. You can store all other personal property in a locker at the exam center. (All new testing sites are supposed to have lockers, but some older sites may have been grandfathered without them. You can ask when you make your appointment.) For a list of the (mostly) medical items you can bring into the exam room, including which ones need inspection or pre-authorization, visit www.nasd.com/RegistrationQualifications/ BrokerGuidanceResponsibility/Qualifications/NASDW_015104.

Some exam centers have vending machines with snacks and drinks, but you can't even bring chewing gum into the exam room. I don't know why — maybe because of the noise, or maybe so the exam staff doesn't have to scrape gum wads off computer screens.

The exam administrators escort you to the exam room. In the testing room, you receive six 8½-x-11-inch pieces of scrap paper (or a dry erase board), a pencil, and a basic calculator. You'll have to return the paper, pencil, and calculator to the exam center administrators at the end of the session (yes, even the unused scrap paper). You can't bring anything else into the cubicle where you'll take the exam.

Taking the Exam

Take a deep breath, crack your knuckles, and get ready to make things count — this Series 7 exam is the genuine article. The exam is six long hours in duration, and you're graded on a total of 250 questions. The test designers have even prepared a bonus for you: To ensure that new questions to be introduced in future exams meet acceptable standards, you also answer 10 additional, unidentified questions that don't count toward your score. Lucky you! This means that you answer 260 questions, but only 250 really count.

You get three hours to answer 130 questions in the first half of the exam and three hours to answer 130 questions in the second half. In between the two sessions, you have a much-needed 30- to 60-minute break.

Most test centers offer the inspirational creature comforts of the office: You take your Series 7 in a cubicle (approximately 4 feet wide) with a computer and a small desk area. You may leave your cubicle for restroom breaks at any time, if necessary. The clock continues to run, however, so try to limit your intake of fluids before each session.

Tackling the first half

Just before you begin your first session, a member of the test center staff will walk you through the steps of how to use the computerized system. Don't worry — you don't need any previous computer experience to understand the way the computer operates (it's that easy). If you do have any tech problems during the test, you can use the help button or summon the exam administrators. A picture of how a question appears on the computer screen is in Chapter 1.

As the test begins, you're ready to put all those test-taking skills to use (check out Chapter 2 for a rundown of what those skills are). So write down everything you think you're likely to forget, right off the bat. Keep track of time. Mark questions for review. Concentrate on the facts in question, and look for key words that can give you clues. Use your amazing powers of elimination to identify wrong answer choices. Work your magic with specific question types (see Chapter 3). You've done your homework, so be confident.

You can't return to the first-session questions after finishing the session and signing out of your computer, so before the first session ends, double check the answers you marked for review. Don't change any answers unless you're certain your answer was wrong.

If you're one of those speed demons (and I hope you're not) who finishes each half of the test in an hour and are tempted to review all your answers, don't do it. Go over only the questions you marked for review. If you try to review all the questions, not only will you drive yourself bonkers, but you'll also do more harm than good by second-guessing your right answers.

Staying relaxed, focused, and conscious

Here are some ways to keep stress at bay and make sure you're giving the test the attention it deserves:

- ✔ If you feel tense, take a few slow, deep breaths and give yourself a mini-massage.

- ✔ If you find yourself growing tired, stretch, sit up straight, or go to the restroom just for a chance to walk around.

- ✔ Give your eyes a rest from the computer screen by looking away from the computer every so often.

- ✔ If you're having trouble focusing, write down significant details from the question. If you're stuck on a multipart question, break down the question into segments. Try drawing diagrams. If you're still having trouble, choose a tentative answer and mark the question for review.

- ✔ Don't lose track of your mission here — now is not the time to let up. Visualize success and hang in there!

After completing the first session, you get to leave your cubicle and take a short break.

Taking a break: At long last lunch

After the first session, you get a minimum of 30 minutes and a maximum of 60 minutes for a lunch break before you begin the second session. You may have an upset stomach by this point, but you'll definitely benefit from eating something — first, to keep up your energy level and second, to keep yourself from being distracted by the sounds your empty stomach would otherwise serenade you with during the second half of the exam.

Many test centers have vending machines on site; others have a full cafeteria. Select protein bars, water, fruit, and other food that'll increase your stamina and provide you with longer lasting energy. Remember, you can also bring your own food and keep it in your locker to eat after the first half.

After sitting at the computer for three hours, it may be a good idea to force yourself to walk around a bit, stand up, and fraternize with fellow test-takers and work off some nervous energy (or at least try to wake yourself up).

The test center Rules of Conduct say that during the break (and after the exam is completed), candidates may not discuss the exam with others, even those who are taking a different exam. Enjoy other topics of conversation.

Heading down the home stretch: Completing the second half

You follow the same procedure for taking the second half of the exam that you did in the first half. You get on the computer and answer another 130 questions in three hours.

You may find your endurance tested during the last hour or so. If your energy level and concentration starts slipping and time allows, you may want to take a bathroom break and splash some water on your face to wake yourself up. If nothing else, the walk should at least get your blood flowing.

After you complete the second half of the exam, look over the questions you marked for review. As with the first half, change answers only if you're absolutely, 100 percent sure you made a mistake. Everyone is on his or her own time schedule, so as soon as you're done with your review, you're ready for the moment of truth.

Getting the Results: Drum Roll Please . . .

You've completed many hours of studying. You've deprived yourself of weekend parties and long afternoons of leisure. Your social life has been almost nonexistent, and if you're the type who becomes unpleasant when in a stressful state of being, you may have alienated the people who used to hang out with you.

After surviving six hours of mental abuse from taking the Series 7 exam, you're ready to push the button that reveals your score and can change your life.

The time may seem much longer, but in reality, you have to wait approximately 30 seconds before your score is revealed. Your grade and the word *passed* or *failed* appear on the computer screen. If your grade is 70 or better, you passed the exam. (Please remember that you're now a professional and refrain from doing a victory dance in the middle of the test center.) If your score is less than 70, you didn't pass the exam. Don't call your friends and tell them you've decided to become an astronaut or firefighter instead. You can retake the test, so you may still have a future on Wall Street. See Chapter 1 for what to do next.

After you receive your exam score, you can leave your cubicle. Bring your scrap paper, pencil, and calculator with you, and turn them over to the exam center staff.

Regardless of whether you passed or failed the exam, you receive a printout of your grade and the breakdown of your performance on the Series 7 exam topics. Employers receive a copy of the results in the mail, or if tied into the NASD computer system, they can get results online.

Part II
Mastering Basic Security Investments

The 5th Wave — By Rich Tennant

I took a modified Series 7 exam. Now, I'm certified as an investment advisor, representative, a securities agent, and a grief counselor.

In this part . . .

For the Series 7 exam (and to be a successful stock-broker) you have to develop the skills to help customers distinguish the securities that meet their needs from those that don't. To accomplish this, you need to be able to analyze customers' individual investment profiles, identify the securities that are available on the marketplace, and help the customers select the securities that can meet their financial objectives.

In this part, I introduce the basic securities — stocks and bonds, including municipal securities — that form the foundation of an investor's portfolio. These chapters review the registration procedure that securities go through before they can be sold to the public and reveal which securities are exempt from registration. Finally, they help you distinguish common stock from preferred stock, corporate bonds from U.S. bonds, and municipal bonds from general obligation bonds.

Chapter 5

Underwriting Securities

• •

• •

All issuers of securities need a starting point, just as all securities need a birth date (just not the kind that's celebrated with funny looking hats and a cake). Most securities go through a registration procedure before the public can buy them. The Series 7 exam tests your ability to recognize the players and institutions involved in the registration process.

In this chapter, I cover topics related to bringing new issues to market. You find out about key players, types of security offerings, kinds of securities that don't need to be registered, and other details about the underwriting process. (Check out the "For Further Review" section at the end of this chapter for a list of related topics you should be well-versed on before taking the test.) This chapter also includes a few practice questions to help you measure how well you understand the topic.

Bringing New Issues to the Market

A lot of things need to happen before securities hit the market. Not only do the securities have to be registered, but the issuer has to find a company (like your firm) to sell the securities to the public. The Series 7 exam tests your expertise in answering questions about this process.

Starting out: What the issuer does

For an entity to become a corporation, the founders must file a document called a *corporate charter* (bylaws) in the home state of its business. Included in the corporate charter are the names of the founders, the type of business, the place of business, the amount of shares that can be issued, and so on. If a corporation wants to sell securities to the public, it has to register with states and the Securities and Exchange Commission (SEC). Read on for info on how the registration process works.

The securities acts

Registration helps ensure that securities issued to the public adhere to certain regulations (though anti-fraud rules also apply to exempt securities). The following acts are designed to protect investors from unscrupulous issuers, firms, and salespeople (see Chapter 16 for details on other rules and regulations).

The Securities Act of 1933: This act — also called the Truth in Securities Act, the Paper Act, the Full Disclosure Act, and the New Issues Act — regulates new issues of corporate securities. An issuer of corporate securities must provide full and fair disclosure about itself and the offering. Included in this act are rules to prevent fraud and deception.

The Securities Exchange Act of 1934: The Act of 1934, which established the SEC, was enacted to protect investors by regulating the over-the-counter (OTC) market and exchanges (such as the NYSE). (Chapter 14 can tell you more about markets.) In addition, the Act of 1934 regulates

- The extension of credit in margin accounts (see Chapter 9)
- Transactions by insiders
- Customer accounts
- Trading activities

The Trust Indenture Act of 1939: This act prohibits bond issues valued at over $5,000,000 from being offered to investors without an indenture. The trust *indenture* is a written agreement that protects investors by disclosing the particulars of the issue (coupon rate, maturity date, any collateral backing the bond, and so on). As part of the Trust Indenture Act of 1939, all companies must hire a trustee who's responsible for protecting the rights of bondholders.

Registering securities with the SEC

When a company wants to go public (sell stock to public investors), it has to file a prospectus and a registration statement with the SEC (see "Getting the skinny on the issue and issuer: The prospectus" later in the chapter).

The *registration statement* includes

- The issuer's name and a description of its business
- The names and addresses of all of the company's officers and directors
- What the proceeds of the sale will be used for
- The company's capitalization

Blue skies: Registering with the states

All *blue sky laws,* or state laws that apply to security offerings and sales, say that in order to sell a security to a customer, the broker-dealer (brokerage firm), the registered representative, and the security must be registered in the customer's state. The issuer is responsible for registering the security not only with the SEC but also in each state in which the securities are to be sold.

Here are the methods of state security registration:

- **Notification (registration by filing):** Notification is the simplest form of registration for established companies. Companies who have previously sold securities in a state can renew their previous application.
- **Coordination:** This method involves registering with the SEC and states at the same time. The SEC helps companies meet the blue sky laws by notifying all states in which the securities are to be sold.
- **Qualification:** Companies use this registration method for securities that are exempt from registration with the SEC but require registration with the state.

Role call: Introducing the team players

The following list explains who's involved in the securities registration and selling process. Registered reps can work for any of these firms:

- **Investment banking firm:** An investment banking firm is an institution (a broker-dealer) that's in the business of helping issuers raise money. You can think of investment bankers as the brains of the operation, because they help the issuer decide what securities to issue, how much to issue, the selling price, and so on. Not only do investment bankers advise issuers, but they usually underwrite the issue and may also become the managing underwriter in the offering of new securities.

- **Underwriter:** The underwriter is a broker-dealer that helps the issuer bring new securities to the public. Underwriters purchase the securities from the issuer and sell them to the public for a nice profit (yippee!).

- **Syndicate:** When an issue is too large for one firm to handle, the syndicate manager (managing underwriter) forms a syndicate to help sell the securities and relieve some of the financial burden on the managing underwriter. Each syndicate member is responsible for selling a portion of the securities to the public (see the upcoming section titled "Agreeing to sell your share: Western versus Eastern accounts" for details).

- **Managing (lead) underwriter:** The managing underwriter (syndicate manager) is the head cheese who's responsible for putting together a syndicate and dealing directly with the issuer. The managing underwriter receives financial compensation (buckets-o-bucks) for each and every share sold.

- **Selling group:** In the event that the syndicate members feel that they need more help selling the securities, they can recruit selling group members. These members are brokerage firms that aren't part of the syndicate. Selling group members help distribute shares to the public but don't make a financial commitment (do not purchase shares from the issuer) and therefore receive less money per share when selling shares to the public.

Who gets what: Distributing the profits

When larger issues come to market, the underwriter (lead underwriter) often has to form a syndicate to help sell the securities. When selling the securities to the public, each entity (lead underwriter, syndicate members, selling group, and so on — see the preceding section) receives a different portion of the selling profits. I list the terms in order from the highest dollar amount to the lowest:

- **The spread:** The spread is the difference between the amount the syndicate pays the issuer when purchasing new shares or bonds and the public offering price for each share or bond sold. For example, if the issuer sells shares to the syndicate for $8.00 per share and the syndicate turns around and sells them to the public for $9.00 per share, the spread is $1.00 (or $9.00 − $8.00). Naturally, you get the following formula:

  Spread = public offering price − price paid to the issuer

  So the spread is just the initial profit from selling the security; you still have to divvy it up among the salespeople. The syndicate splits the spread into the manager's fee and the takedown, so you get the following equation:

  Spread = syndicate manager's fee + takedown

✔ **Takedown:** The takedown is the profit that each syndicate member makes when selling shares or bonds to the public. Remember that the syndicate members are the ones taking the financial risk and therefore deserve the lion's share of the sales proceeds. You can use the spread formula (spread = manager's fee + takedown) to calculate this value. For example, if the spread is $1.00 and the manager's fee is $0.15, the takedown is $0.85 ($1.00 – $0.15).

- **Concession:** The concession is the profit that the selling group makes when selling shares or bonds to the public. Selling group members don't step up to the plate financially and therefore don't receive as much of the sales proceeds as syndicate members do. The concession is paid out of the takedown. The profit made by syndicate members on shares or bonds sold by the selling group is called the *additional takedown*.

    Takedown = additional takedown + concession

- **Reallowance:** The portion of the takedown that's available for firms that aren't part of the syndicate or selling group is the *reallowance*. For example, assume ABC Corporation is in the process of issuing new shares. One of your customers calls you up to let you know that she's interested in purchasing shares of ABC Corporation from you, but you're not one of the official distributors of the stock. No sweat. You'd contact the syndicate manager, who'd give you a discount off the public offering price (POP). That discount is the reallowance.

✔ **Syndicate manager's fee:** This part of the spread is the profit the syndicate manager makes on shares or bonds sold by anyone. This fee is usually the smallest of all of the listed fees.

The following question tests your knowledge of distribution of profits:

Nogo Auto Corp., which specializes in fuel-efficient cars, is in the process of selling new shares of their company to the public. Nogo contacts Thor Broker-Dealer Corp. to underwrite the securities. Thor realizes that the issue is too big to underwrite by itself, so it forms a syndicate. Nogo will receive $15.00 per share for each share issued and the public offering price will be $16.20. If the manager's fee is $0.25 per share and the concession is $0.40 per share, what is the additional takedown?

(A) $0.55

(B) $0.80

(C) $0.95

(D) $1.20

The answer is A. This question is a little tricky because you have to determine the takedown (the profit syndicate members make) before you can figure out the additional takedown. The additional takedown is the profit syndicate members make on shares sold by the selling group. The spread of $1.20 ($16.20 selling price – $15.00 to Nogo) is made up of the manager's fee of $0.25 and the takedown of $0.95 ($1.20 spread – $0.25 manager's fee). If the syndicate members sell the shares by themselves, they receive the takedown of $0.95 per share. However, if the selling group sells the shares, the selling group would receive the concession of $0.40 per share. The concession is paid out of the takedown, and thus, the additional takedown is $0.55 per share ($0.95 – $0.40).

Agreeing to sell your share: Western versus Eastern accounts

The *syndicate agreement,* also called the *agreement among underwriters,* is the contract among syndicate members. This agreement includes the fee structure (who gets what — see the preceding section). In addition to the bucks that each member of the syndicate gets when selling shares or bonds, the syndicate agreement lays out each syndicate member's amount of commitment (how many shares or bonds each party will sell); the syndicate manager can set up underwritings on a Western or Eastern account basis:

- ✓ **Western (divided) account:** In this securities underwriting, the syndicate agreement states that each syndicate member is responsible only for the shares or bonds originally allocated to it. If a syndicate member commits to selling 500,000 shares and sells them all, the syndicate member doesn't have to sell any more.

  To distinguish an Eastern account from a Western account, remember the phrase *wild, wild West,* because back in the day, each man (or *syndicate member* in this case) was for himself.

- ✓ **Eastern (undivided) account:** In this securities underwriting, the syndicate agreement states that each syndicate member is responsible not only for the shares or bonds originally allocated to it but also for a portion of the shares or bonds left unsold by other (apparently less aggressive) members. If a syndicate member was originally responsible for 10 percent of the new issue, it would be responsible for 10 percent of the shares or bonds left unsold by other members.

The following question tests your knowledge of Eastern and Western accounts:

A syndicate is underwriting $5,000,000 worth of municipal general obligation bonds. There are 10 syndicate members each with an equal participation. Firm A, which is part of the syndicate, sells its entire allotment. However, $1,000,000 worth of bonds remain unsold by other members of the syndicate. If the syndicate agreement was set up on an Eastern account basis, what is Firm A's responsibility regarding the unsold bonds?

(A) No responsibility

(B) $100,000 worth of bonds

(C) $200,000 worth of bonds

(D) $1,000,000 worth of bonds

The answer is B. Your key to this question is that the underwriting was done on an Eastern account basis. On an Eastern account basis, the underwriters (because they're so nice) have to help the slackers sell the shares of unsold bonds. Firm A sold all its bonds, so it has to help sell the remaining bonds that the other syndicate members didn't sell. Firm A's responsibility is in proportion to its original responsibility. Because it was responsible for 10 percent of the original issue (10 syndicate members with equal participation), it's responsible for selling 10 percent of the unsold bonds:

10% × $1,000,000 of unsold bonds = $100,000 worth of bonds

If the underwriting had been on a Western account basis, the answer would've been A.

Registering the securities

Unless the securities are exempt from registration (see "Exempt Securities" later in the chapter), the issuer has to go through a registration process with the Securities and Exchange Commission (SEC). The Series 7 tests you on the following items that relate to securities registration.

Cooling-off period

After the issuer files a registration statement with the SEC, a 20-day cooling-off period begins. During the 20-day (and often longer) cooling-off period, the good old SEC reviews the registration statement. At the end of the cooling-off period, the issue will (hopefully) be cleared for sale to the public.

During the cooling-off period, the underwriter (or underwriters) can obtain indications of interest from investors who may want to purchase the issue. Registered reps (like you in the not-too-distant future) scramble to get indications of interest from prospective purchasers of the securities.

Indications of interest aren't binding on customers or underwriters. A customer always has the prerogative to change his or her mind, and underwriters may not have enough shares available to meet everyone's needs.

A *tombstone ad* — a newspaper ad that's shaped like a, well, tombstone (it's rectangular with black borders) — is simply an announcement (but not an offer) of a new security for sale. It's the only advertisement allowed during the cooling-off period. These ads contain just a simple statement of facts about the new issue (for example, the issuer, type of security, amount of shares or bonds available, underwriter's name, and so on). Tombstone ads are optional.

Also during the cooling-off period, the underwriters and selling group members use the preliminary prospectus to obtain indications of interest from prospective customers. The preliminary prospectus must be made available to all customers who are interested in the new issue during the cooling-off period. I talk more about what that prospectus has to include in the "Getting the skinny on the issue and issuer: The prospectus" section a little later in this chapter.

Due diligence meeting

Toward the end of the cooling-off period, the underwriter holds a due diligence meeting. During this meeting, the underwriter provides information about the issue and what the issuer will use the proceeds of sale for. The meeting is designed to provide the information to syndicate members, selling groups, brokers, analysts, institutions, and so on.

The last time syndicate members can back out of an underwriting agreement is toward the end of the cooling-off period (around the time of the due diligence meeting). You can assume that if syndicate members are backing out, it's most likely due to negative market conditions.

Getting the skinny on the issue and issuer: The prospectus

The issuer prepares a preliminary prospectus (sometimes with the help of the underwriter) that's sent in with the registration statement. The preliminary prospectus must be available for potential purchasers when the issue is in registration (in the cooling-off period) with the SEC. The preliminary prospectus is abbreviated, but it contains all essential facts about the issuer and issue except for the final offering price (public offering price, or POP) and the *effective date* (the date that the issue will first be sold).

A preliminary prospectus is sometimes called a *red herring,* not because it smells fishy (or is totally misleading and irrelevant) but because it has a statement in red lettering on the cover stating that it's not the final prospectus and that some items may change before the final version.

The *final prospectus,* which is prepared toward the end of the cooling-off period, is a legal document that the issuer prepares; it contains material information about the issuer and new issue of securities. The final prospectus has to be available to all potential purchasers of the issue. It includes

- The final offering price
- The underwriter's spread (profit the underwriters make per share)
- The delivery date (when the securities will be available)

Counting the securities along the way

When a company issues securities and they're traded in the market, someone has to be responsible to keep track of the owners of the securities, and someone has to make sure that no more securities are in the market than there are supposed to be. These jobs are assigned to the registrar and transfer agent.

The *registrar* is an independent entity that works along with a company's transfer agent and maintains a record of stock and bond owners. The main function of a registrar is to make sure that the outstanding shares don't exceed the amount of stock the issuer authorizes under its corporate charter (bylaws — rules the company lives by).

The *transfer agent* maintains records of a corporation's stock and bond owners (much like a registrar) but also mails and cancels stock certificates as necessary.

An easy way to keep these folks straight is to remember that a registrar is responsible for counting things and a transfer agent is responsible for transferring or sending things.

Getting Up to Speed on the Types of Securities Offerings

Table 5-1 deals with different types of offerings that you (as a mega-broker) should be familiar with. The offerings that follow usually require the services of an underwriter or underwriting syndicate to sell the securities to the public.

Table 5-1	Types of Securities Offerings	
Type	*Description*	*Who Profits*
Initial public offering (IPO)	The first time an issuer sells stock to the public to raise capital; issuers usually hold back some stock for future primary offerings.	The bulk of the moolah raised goes to the issuer, and the rest goes to the underwriters.

(continued)

Table 5-1 *(continued)*

Type	Description	Who Profits
Primary offering	An offering of new securities from an issuer that has previously issued securities; a company can have an initial public offering and several primary offerings if it wants.	The proceeds of sale go the issuer and underwriters.
Secondary offering	A sale of a large block of outstanding (stockholder-owned) securities or previously outstanding securities (*treasury stock,* or stock the issuer has repurchased); typically, one or more major stockholders of a corporation are the ones who make the secondary offerings; new investors are essentially buying used, so the number of shares outstanding doesn't change.	The sales proceeds don't go to the issuer (except with treasury stock); it goes to the big shots selling the securities.
Split (combined) offering	A combination of a primary and secondary offering, with both new and outstanding securities.	A portion of the sales proceeds goes to the issuer, and a portion goes to the selling stockholders.

For IPOs, a final prospectus needs to be available to all purchasers of the IPO for 90 days after the *effective date* (the first day the security starts trading).

With primary, secondary, or combined offerings, a final prospectus has to be available to all purchasers of the primary offering for 25 days after the effective date for all issuers whose securities are already listed on an exchange or NASDAQ. If an issuer has already issued securities but not on an exchange or NASDAQ, the final prospectus has to be available for 40 days after the effective date.

The following question tests your knowledge on the types of offerings, whether new or outstanding:

DEF Corp. is offering 2,000,000 shares of its common stock to the public; 1,500,000 shares are authorized but previously unissued, and insiders of the company are selling the other 500,000 shares. Which of the following are TRUE about this offering?

   I. The EPS of DEF will increase.

  II. The EPS of DEF will decrease.

 III. The number of outstanding shares will increase by 500,000.

 IV. The number of outstanding shares will increase by 1,500,000.

 (A) I and III

 (B) I and IV

 (C) II and III

 (D) II and IV

The answer is D. This offering is a combined, or split, offering. The 1,500,000 shares that were previously unissued is a primary offering, and the 500,000 shares held by insiders is a secondary offering. Answering this question correctly requires a little bit of deduction on your part. You first have to note that unissued shares aren't considered part of the outstanding shares (because for stockholders, owning the shares before they're even offered would be a pretty impressive feat!). Because 1,500,000 shares were previously unissued (kept by the company for future use), the number of outstanding shares increases by that amount. When considering whether the earnings per share (EPS) increases or decreases, look at what happened. You can assume that the company earned the same amount of money. Now that same amount of money has to be divided among 1,500,000 more shares. Therefore, you deduce that the EPS would decrease, not increase.

Reviewing Exemptions

Certain securities are exempt from registration because of the type of security or the type of transaction. You may find the securities that are exempt because of who's issuing them a bit easier to recognize. You'll probably have to spend a little more time on the securities that are exempt from registration because of the type of transaction.

Exempt securities

Certain securities are exempt from the registration requirements under the Securities Act of 1933. Either these securities come from issuers that have a high level of creditworthiness, or another government regulatory agency has some sort of jurisdiction over the issuer of the securities. These securities include

- ✔ Securities issued by the U.S. government or federal agencies
- ✔ Municipal bonds (local government bonds)
- ✔ Securities issued by banks, savings institutions, and credit unions
- ✔ Public utility stocks or bonds
- ✔ Securities issued by religious, educational, or nonprofit organizations
- ✔ Notes, bills of exchange, bankers' acceptances, and commercial paper with an initial maturity of 270 days or less
- ✔ Insurance policies and fixed annuities

Fixed annuities are exempt from SEC registration because the issuing insurance company guarantees the payout. However, variable annuities require registration because the payout varies depending on the performance of the securities held in the separate account. For more info on annuities and other packaged securities, see Chapter 10.

Exempt transactions

Some securities that corporations offer may be exempt from the full registration requirements of the Securities Act of 1933 due to the nature of the sale. The following list shows you these exemptions:

✔ **Intrastate offerings (Rule 147):** An intrastate offering is, naturally, an offering of securities within one state. For such an offering to be exempt from SEC registration, the company must be incorporated in the state in which it's selling securities, 80 percent of its business has to be within the state, and it may sell securities only to residents of the state. The securities still require registration at the state level.

Don't confuse *intra*state offerings (securities sold in one state) with *inter*state offerings (securities sold in many states). *Inter*state offerings do need SEC registration. To help you remember, think of an interstate roadway, which continues from one state to the next.

✔ **Regulation A (Reg A) offerings:** An offering of securities worth $5,000,000 or less within a 12-month period is Regulation A. Although this company may seem large to you, it's relatively small in market terms. Regulation A offerings are exempt from the full registration requirements but you still have to file a simplified registration.

✔ **Regulation D (Reg D) offerings:** Also known as a private placement, a Regulation D offering is an offering to no more than 35 unaccredited investors per year. Companies who issue securities through private placement are allowed to raise an unlimited amount of money but are limited on the number of unaccredited investors. Sales of Reg D securities are subject to the sales limitations as set forth under Rule 144.

An *accredited investor* is one with a net worth of $1,000,000 or more or an investor who's had a yearly income of at least $200,000 (for an individual investor) or $300,000 (for joint income with spouse) for the previous two years and is expected to earn at least that much in the current year.

✔ **Rule 144:** This rule covers the sale of restricted, unregistered, and control securities. According to Rule 144, sellers of these securities must wait at least one year prior to selling the securities to the public. Additionally, the most an investor can sell at one time is 1 percent of the outstanding shares or the average weekly trading volume for the previous four weeks, whichever is greater.

The following example tests your ability to answer restricted-stock questions:

John Bullini purchased shares of restricted stock and wants to sell under Rule 144. John has fully paid for the shares and has held them for over one year. There are 1,500,000 shares outstanding. Form 144 is filed on Monday, May 28, and the weekly trading volume for the restricted stock is as follows:

Week Ending	Trading Volume
May 25	16,000 shares
May 18	15,000 shares
May 11	17,000 shares
May 4	15,000 shares
April 27	18,000 shares

What is the maximum number of shares John can sell with this filing?

(A) 15,000

(B) 15,750

(C) 16,200

(D) 16,250

The answer is B. The test writers often try to trick you on the Series 7 exam by giving you at least an extra week more than you need to answer the question. Because John has held his restricted stock for over a year, he can sell 1 percent of the outstanding shares or the averaged weekly trading volume for the previous four weeks, whichever is greater:

$$1\% \times 1,500,000 \text{ shares outstanding} = 15,000 \text{ shares}$$

$$\frac{16,000 + 15,000 + 17,000 + 15,000}{4 \text{ weeks}} = \frac{63,000}{4 \text{ weeks}} = 15,750 \text{ shares}$$

In this case, the previous four weeks are the top four in the list, but be careful; the examiners could've used the bottom four just as easily if they'd wanted a different look for the table. Figure out 1 percent of the outstanding shares by multiplying the outstanding shares by 1 percent (easy, right?). In this case, you come up with an answer of 15,000 shares. That's one possible answer. The other possible answer is the average weekly trading volume for the previous four weeks. Add the trading volume for the previous four weeks (the top four in the chart) and divide by 4 to get an answer of 15,750 shares. Because you're looking for the greater, the answer is B.

Even securities exempt from registration are subject to anti-fraud rules. All securities are subject to anti-fraud provisions of the Securities Act of 1933, which requires issuers to provide accurate information regarding any securities offered to the public.

For Further Review

To be properly prepared for the Series 7, you need to know the information in this chapter and have a good handle on the following terms and ideas related to underwriting securities:

- Negotiated versus competitive underwritings
- Firm commitment, all or none, mini-max, and best efforts underwritings
- Shelf offering Rule 415
- Deficiency letter
- Stabilizing price
- Penalty bid
- Pegging
- Market-out clause
- Rule 144A
- Rule 145
- Rule 2790
- Qualified institutional buyer (QIB)

Chapter 6

Corporate Ownership: Equity Securities

Equity securities — such as common and preferred stock — represent ownership interest in the issuing company. All publicly held corporations issue equity securities to investors. Investors love these securities because they've historically outperformed most other investments, so an average (or above-average in your case) stockbroker sells more of these types of securities than any other kind.

The Series 7 exam tests you on your ability to recognize the types of equity securities and on some other basic information. Although you may find that the Series 7 doesn't test you heavily on the info here, this chapter forms a strong foundation for many other chapters in the book. I think that you'll find it difficult (if not impossible) to understand what an option or mutual fund is if you don't know what a stock is. Needless to say, even though this chapter is small, don't ignore it or it may come back to bite you.

In this chapter, I cover the Series 7 exam topics that are the most tested and most difficult to understand relating to company ownership. (Check out the "For Further Review" section at the end of this chapter for a list of related topics not covered in this chapter that you should know before you take the test.) This chapter also gives you plenty of examples to familiarize you with the types of equities securities questions on the Series 7 exam.

Beginning with the Basics: Common Stock

Corporations issue common stock (as well as other securities) to raise business capital. As an equity security, common stock represents ownership of the issuing corporation. If a corporation issues 1,000,000 shares of stock, each share represents one-millionth ownership of the issuing corporation. Read on for the ins and outs of common stock.

Understanding a stockholder's voting rights

One of the most basic rights that common stockholders receive is voting rights. Every so often, a corporation may have investors vote to change members on the board of directors. Although investors may be able to vote on other issues (like stock splits — see "Splitting common stock" later in this chapter), the Series 7 focuses on voting to change board members.

Because having all stockholders actually attend the annual corporate meeting to vote would be difficult, stockholders usually vote by *proxy*, or absentee ballot.

Statutory (regular) voting

Statutory or regular voting is the most common type of voting that corporations offer to their shareholders. This type of voting is quite straightforward. Investors receive one vote for every share that they own multiplied by the number of positions to be filled on the board of directors (or issues to be decided). However, investors have to *split the votes evenly* for each item on the ballot.

For example, if an investor owns 500 shares and there are four positions to be filled on the board of directors, the investor has a total of 2,000 votes (500 shares × 4 candidates), which the investor must split evenly among all open positions (500 each). The investor votes yes or no for each candidate.

Cumulative voting

Cumulative voting is a little different from statutory voting (see the preceding section). Although the investor still gets the same number of overall votes as if the corporation had offered statutory voting, the stockholder can vote the shares in any way he or she sees fit. Cumulative voting gives smaller shareholders (in terms of shares) an easier chance to gain representation on the board of directors.

For example, if an investor owns 1,000 shares and three positions on the board of directors are open, the investor would have a total of 3,000 votes (1,000 shares × 3 candidates), which the investor can vote for any candidate(s) in any way he or she sees fit.

Cumulative voting doesn't give an investor more voting power, just more voting flexibility. The only way to get more voting power is to buy more shares.

The following question tests your ability to answer a cumulative voting question:

Bella Bearishnikoff owns 800 shares of CBA common stock. It is time for CBA to have its annual shareholders' meeting, and there are four candidates for the board of directors. CBA offers its shareholders cumulative voting. Which of the following are acceptable votes from Bella?

    I. 800 votes for each of the four candidates

    II. 2,000 votes for one candidate and 400 votes for each of the other candidates

    III. 3,200 votes for one candidate

    IV. 3,200 votes for each of the candidates

  (A) I only

  (B) II and III

  (C) I, II, and III

  (D) I, III, and IV

The answer is C. Ms. Bearishnikoff has a total of 3,200 votes (800 shares × 4 candidates). Because CBA offers cumulative voting, she can vote the 3,200 votes in any way she likes. Roman numerals I, II, and III are all correct because none of those choices require more than 3,200 votes. However, IV would require 12,800 votes. As a side note, if the question had asked about statutory voting, the answer would've been A.

Categorizing shares corporations can sell

All publicly held corporations have a certain quantity of shares that they can sell based on their corporate charter. These shares are broken down into a few categories depending on whether the issuer or investors hold the shares:

✔ **Authorized shares:** Authorized shares are the number of shares of stock that a corporation can issue. The issuer's *corporate charter* (bylaws, a document filed with the state that identifies the names of the founders of the corporation, its objectives, and so on) states the number of authorized shares. Although a corporation may be authorized to issue a certain number of shares, the issuer usually holds back a large percentage of the authorized stock (which it can sell later through a primary offering — see Chapter 5 for details on offerings).

✔ **Issued shares:** Issued shares are the portion of authorized shares that the issuer has sold to the public to raise money.

✔ **Outstanding shares:** Outstanding shares are the number of shares that are in investors' hands. This quantity may or may not be the same number as the issued shares. At times, an issuer may decide to repurchase its stock to either help increase the demand (and the price) of the stock trading in the market or to avoid a *hostile takeover* (when another company is trying to gain control of the issuer). Stock that the issuer repurchases is called *treasury stock*.

The standard formula for outstanding shares follows:

Outstanding shares = issued shares – treasury stock

The following question tests your understanding of outstanding shares:

ZZZ Bedding Corp. is authorized to issue 2,000,000 shares of common stock. However, ZZZ issued only 800,000 shares to the public. One year later, ZZZ repurchased 150,000 shares to increase the demand on the outstanding shares. How many shares does ZZZ have outstanding?

(A) 650,000

(B) 800,000

(C) 1,200,000

(D) 1,850,000

The answer is A. You probably didn't have too much difficulty with this one. All the question is asking is how many shares are still outstanding in the market. Check out the following equation:

Outstanding = issued – treasury

= 800,000 – 150,000

= 650,000

Because ZZZ issued only 800,000 shares of the 2,000,000 that it's authorized to issue, the most ZZZ ever had in the market was 800,000. However, a year after issuing those shares, ZZZ repurchased 150,000 shares, giving the company treasury stock. Therefore, the amount of outstanding shares is 650,000.

Considering the par value of common stock

Par value for common stock is not as important to investors as it is for bondholders and preferred stockholders (see the later "Considering the characteristics of preferred stock" section). *Par value* for common stock is more or less a bookkeeping value for the issuer. Although issuers may set the par value at $1 (or $5, $10, or whatever), the selling price is usually much more. A stock's par value has no relation to the market price of the stock.

The amount over par value that an issuer receives for selling stock is called *paid-in capital, paid-in surplus,* or *capital surplus.*

The stated par value is printed on the stock certificate; it changes if the issuer splits its stock (see the next section). You should be aware that an issuer can also issue *no par value stock* (stock issued without a stated par value); a lack of par value doesn't affect investors.

Splitting common stock

You may ask yourself, "Why would a company split its stock?" The obvious answer is that the company wants to make the market price of the security more attractive. The normal unit of trading is 100 shares of stock (a *round lot*) and if the price of a security gets too high, the number of investors who can purchase it becomes limited. You can imagine that if a company like Microsoft were to never split its stock (which it's already done nine times), a round lot would cost investors (at the time of this writing) about $750,000. Know a lot of investors who could afford that?

Companies may alternatively use a reverse split, consolidating shares so they can raise the price of the stock and perhaps boost investor confidence. The next couple sections take you through splits so you know them forward and backward.

Stockholders can vote on stock splits (please see "Understanding a stockholder's voting rights" earlier in the chapter for info on types of voting). Be aware that after a stock split, investors may have more or fewer votes, but they still hold the same percentage of votes. When a company splits its stock, the number of authorized shares needs to be changed on the *corporate charter* (see the earlier section "Categorizing shares corporations can sell").

Forward splits

During a *forward stock split,* the number of shares increases and the price decreases without affecting the total market value of outstanding shares. After a company forward splits its stock, investors receive additional shares, but the market price (and par value) per share drops. A forward split can be a 2-for-1, 3-for-1, 3-for-2, and so on.

Use the following calculation to figure out an investor's position after an A-for-B split:

$$\text{Shares after split} = \text{shares} \times \frac{A}{B}$$

$$\text{Price after split} = \text{stock price} \times \frac{B}{A}$$

The following question tests your ability to answer a stock split question:

Bob Billingham owns 1,200 shares of DEF common stock at a current market price of $90 per share. If DEF splits its stock 3-for-1, what would Bob's position be after the split?

(A) 400 shares at $270 per share

(B) 400 shares at $90 per share

(C) 3,600 shares at $33.33 per share

(D) 3,600 shares at $30 per share

The answer is D. A forward stock split, like a 3-for-1, increases the number of shares and decreases the price of the stock, so you can immediately cross off choices A and B. Now check your work:

$$1,200 \text{ shares} \times \frac{3}{1} = 3,600 \text{ shares}$$

$$\$90 \times \frac{1}{3} = \$30$$

A good way to double check your work is to make sure that the overall value of the investment doesn't change after the split. Using the example, Bob had $108,000 worth of DEF (1,200 shares × $90) before the split, and after the split he has $108,000 worth of DEF (3,600 shares × $30).

Reverse splits

A reverse split has the opposite effect on a security than a forward split does; with a reverse split, the market price of the security increases and the number of shares decreases. As with forward stock splits, the overall market value of the securities doesn't change. A company may reverse split its stock if the market price gets too low and potential investors may think there's a problem with the company.

In the event of a reverse split, investors usually have to send in their old shares to the transfer agent to receive the new shares. If a company were executing a 1-for-3 reverse split, investors would receive one new share for every three sent in.

You can use the same formula to determine an investor's position after a reverse split that you use for forward splits.

The following question tests your ability to answer a reverse stock split question:

Betty Billings owns 3,600 shares of GHI common stock at a current market price of $2 per share. If GHI reverse splits its stock 1-for-5, what would Betty's position be after the split?

(A) 600 shares at $10 per share

(B) 720 shares at $10 per share

(C) 18,000 shares at $0.40 per share

(D) 18,000 shares at $10 per share

The answer is B. With a reverse split, the number of shares has to decrease and the price has to increase, so you can immediately eliminate choices C and D. Check your work:

$$3,600 \text{ shares} \times \frac{1}{5} = 720 \text{ shares}$$

$$\$2 \times \frac{5}{1} = \$10$$

Sharing corporate profits through dividends

Occasionally (if the board of directors is in a good mood), a corporation may decide to issue a dividend to investors. The Series 7 exam expects you to know the forms of dividends an investor can receive and how the dividends affect both the market price of the stock and an investor's position. Although the investor can receive dividends in cash, stock, or *property forms* (stock of a subsidiary company or sample products made by the issuer), I focus on cash and stock dividends because those scenarios are more likely.

Investors can't vote on dividends; instead, the board of directors decides dividend payouts. You can imagine that if this decision were left in the investor's hands, they'd vote for dividends weekly! For more info on voting, see "Understanding a stockholder's voting rights," earlier in this chapter.

Cash dividends

Cash dividends are a way for a corporation to share its profits with shareholders. When an investor receives cash dividends, it's a taxable event. Corporations aren't required to pay dividends; however, dividends provide a good incentive for investors to hold onto stock that isn't experiencing much growth. Although cash dividends are nice, the market price of the stock falls on the *ex-dividend date* (the first day the stock trades without a dividend) to reflect the dividend paid:

Stock price – dividend = price on ex-dividend date

Try your hand at answering a cash dividend question:

ABC stock is trading for $49.50 on the day prior to the ex-dividend date. If ABC previously announced a $0.75 dividend, what will be the next day's opening price?

(A) $48.25

(B) $48.75

(C) $49.50

(D) $50.25

The answer is B. Check your work:

$49.50 – $0.75 = $48.75

The math's as simple as that. Because stocks are now trading in pennies instead of eighths, calculating the price on the ex-dividend date is a snap.

Stock dividends

Stock dividends are just like forward stock splits in that the investor receives more shares of stock (see "Spitting common stock"), only the corporation gives a percentage dividend (5 percent, 10 percent, and so on) instead of splitting the stock 2-for-1, 3-for-1, or whatever. Unlike cash dividends, stock dividends aren't taxable to the stockholder because the investor's overall value of investment doesn't change.

The primary reason for a company to give investors a stock dividend is to make the market price more attractive to investors (if the market price gets too high, it limits the number of investors who can purchase the stock), thus adding liquidity to the stock.

The following question tests your expertise in answering stock dividend questions:

Terry Trader owns 400 shares of OXX common stock at $33 per share. OXX previously declared a 10 percent stock dividend. Assuming no change in the market price of OXX prior to the dividend, what is Terry's position after the dividend?

(A) 400 shares at $30

(B) 440 shares at $33

(C) 400 shares at $36.30

(D) 440 shares at $30

The answer is D. In this case, you can find the answer without doing any math. Because the number of shares increases, the price of the stock has to decrease. Therefore, the only answer that works is D. I can't guarantee that you'll get a question where you don't have to do the math, but don't rule it out; scan the answer choices before pulling out your calculator.

Anyway, here's how the numbers work. You have to remember that the investor's overall value of investment doesn't change. Terry gets a 10 percent stock dividend, so she receives 10 percent more shares. Now Terry has 440 shares of OXX (400 shares + 40 shares [10 percent of 400]). Next, you need to determine her overall value of investment:

400 shares × $33 = $13,200

Because the overall value of investment doesn't change, Terry needs to have $13,200 worth of OXX after the dividend:

$$\frac{\$13,200}{440 \text{ shares}} = \$30 \text{ per share}$$

Terry's position after the split is 440 shares at $30 per share.

Getting Preferential Treatment: Preferred Stock

Equity securities represent shares of ownership in a company, and debt securities, well, represent debt (see Chapters 7 and 8 for info on debt securities). Although preferred stock has some characteristics of both equity and debt securities, preferred stock is an equity security because it represents ownership of the issuing corporation the same way that common stock does.

Considering characteristics of preferred stock

One advantage of purchasing preferred stock over common stock is that preferred shareholders receive money back (if there's any left) before common stockholders do if the issuer declares bankruptcy. However, the main difference between preferred stock and common stock has to do with dividends. Issuers of common stock pay a cash dividend only if the company's in a position to share corporate profits. By contrast, issuers of preferred stock are required to pay consistent cash dividends. Preferred stock generally has a par value of $100 per share and tends to trade in the market somewhere close to that par value.

Some of the drawbacks of investing in preferred stock over common stock are the lack of voting rights, the higher cost per share (usually), and limited growth. You can assume for Series 7 exam purposes that preferred stockholders don't receive voting rights unless they fail to receive their expected dividends (a few other exceptions exist, but they're nothing you need to worry about now). Also, because the price of preferred stock remains relatively stable, preferred stockholders may miss out on potential gains that common stockholders may realize.

If the issuer can't make a payment because earnings are low, then in most cases, owners of preferred stock are still owed the missing dividend payment(s). The dividend (sharing of profits) that preferred stockholders receive is based on par value. Thus, although par value may be nothing more than a bookkeeping value when you're dealing with common stock, par value is definitely important to preferred stockholders.

To calculate the annual dividend, multiply the percentage of the dividend by the par value. For instance, if a customer owns a preferred stock that pays an 8 percent dividend and the par value is $100, you set up the following equation:

8% preferred stock × $100 par = $8 per year in dividends

If the issuer were to pay this dividend quarterly (once every three months), an investor would receive $2 every three months.

When working on a dividend question on preferred stock, you need to look for the par value in the problem. It's normally $100, but it could be $25, $50, and so on.

Getting familiar with types of preferred stock

You need to be aware of several types of preferred stock for the Series 7. This section gives you a brief explanation of the types and some of their characteristics. Some preferred stock may be a combination of the different types, as in cumulative convertible preferred stock. Here are the distinctions between noncumulative and cumulative preferred stock:

- **Noncumulative (straight) preferred:** This type of preferred stock is rare. The main feature of preferred stock is that investors receive a consistent cash dividend. In the event that the issuer doesn't pay the dividend, the company usually still owes it to investors. This isn't the case for noncumulative preferred stock. If the preferred stock is noncumulative and the issuer fails to pay a dividend, the issuer doesn't owe it to investors. An investor may choose noncumulative preferred stock over common stock because the company is still supposed to pay a consistent cash dividend.

- **Cumulative preferred:** Cumulative preferred stock is more common. If an investor owns cumulative preferred stock and doesn't receive an expected dividend, the issuer still owes that dividend. If the issuer declares a common dividend, the issuer first has to make up all delinquent payments to cumulative preferred stockholders.

The following question tests your understanding of cumulative preferred stock:

An investor owns ABC 8 percent cumulative preferred stock ($100 par). In the first year, ABC paid $6 in dividends. In the second year, it paid $4 in dividends. If a common dividend is declared the following year, how much must the preferred shareholders receive?

(A) $6

(B) $8

(C) $12

(D) $14

The answer is D. Because ABC is cumulative preferred stock, issuers have to catch up preferred stockholders on all outstanding dividends before common shareholders receive a dividend. In this example, the investor is supposed to receive $8 per year in dividends (8% × $100 par). In the first year, the issuer shorted the investor $2; in the second year, $4. The investor hasn't yet received payment for the following year, so he or she is owed $8. Add up these debts:

($8 – $6) + ($8 – $4) + $8 = $2 + $4 + $8 = $14

All preferred stock has to be either cumulative or noncumulative. Both types may have other features, including the ability to turn into other kinds of stock, offerings of extra dividends, and other VIP treatment; other variations may increase the investors' risks. I run through some of these traits in the list that follows:

- **Convertible preferred:** Convertible preferred stock allows investors to trade their preferred stock for common stock of the same company at any time. Because the issuers are providing investors with another way to make money, investors usually receive a lower dividend payment than with regular preferred stock.

  The *conversion price* is the dollar price at which a convertible preferred stock par value can be exchanged into a share of common stock. When the convertible preferred stock is first issued, the conversion price is specified and is based on par value. The *conversion ratio* tells you the number of shares of common stock that an investor receives for converting one share of preferred stock.

  You can use the following conversion ratio formula for convertible preferred stock and also for convertible bonds (see Chapter 7 for info on debt securities).

  $$\text{Conversion ratio} = \frac{\text{par value}}{\text{conversion price}}$$

  The conversion ratio helps you determine a *parity price* where the convertible preferred stock and common stock would be trading equally. For example, say you have a convertible preferred stock that's exchangeable for four shares of common stock. If the convertible preferred stock is trading at $100 and the common stock is trading at $25, they're on parity because four shares of stock at $25 equal $100. However, if there's a disparity in the exchange values, converting may be profitable. If the convertible preferred stock is trading at $100 and the common stock is trading at $28, the common stock is trading above parity; converting makes sense because investors are exchanging $100 worth of securities for $112 worth of securities ($28 × 4).

- **Callable preferred:** Callable preferred stock allows the issuer to buy back the preferred stock at any time at a price on the certificate. This stock is a little riskier for investors because they don't have control over how long they can hold the stock, so corporations usually pay a higher dividend than on regular preferred stock.

- **Participating preferred:** Although rarely issued, participating preferred stock allows the investors to receive common dividends in addition to the usual preferred dividends.

- **Prior (senior) preferred:** Preferred stockholders receive compensation before common stockholders in the event of corporate bankruptcy. In this case, senior preferred stockholders receive compensation even before other preferred stockholders. Because of the extra safety factor, senior preferred stock pays a slightly lower dividend than other preferred stock from the same issuer.

- **Adjustable (floating rate) preferred:** Holders of adjustable preferred stock receive a dividend that's reset every six months to match movements in the prevailing interest rates. Because the dividend adjusts to changing interest rates, the stock price remains more stable.

The following example gives you an idea of how to determine the conversion ratio:

If ABC preferred stock ($100 par) is convertible into common stock for $25, what is the conversion ratio?

(A) 1 share

(B) 4 shares

(C) 25 shares

(D) 100 shares

The answer is B. This equation is about as simple as the math gets on the Series 7 exam. Because the $100 par value preferred stock is convertible into common stock for $25, it's convertible into four shares:

$$\text{Conversion ratio} = \frac{\text{par value}}{\text{conversion price}} = \frac{\$100}{\$25} = 4 \text{ shares}$$

If you'd like to have more fun (and I use that term loosely) with convertible securities, please visit the convertible bond section in Chapter 7.

Securities with a Twist

Some securities fall outside the boundaries of the more normal common and preferred stock, but I still include them in this equities chapter because they involve ownership in a company or the opportunity to get it. This section gives you an overview of those special securities.

Opening national borders: ADRs

American Depositary Receipts (ADRs) are receipts for foreign securities traded in the U.S. ADRs are negotiable certificates (they can be sold or transferred to another party) that represent a specific number of shares (usually one to ten) of a foreign stock. ADR investors may or may not have voting privileges. U.S. banks issue them, therefore investors receive dividends in U.S. dollars. The stock certificates are held in a foreign branch of a U.S. bank (the custodian bank) and, to exchange their ADRs for the actual shares, investors return the ADRs to the bank that's holding the shares. In addition to the risks associated with stock ownership in general, ADR owners are also subject to currency risk (the risk that the value of the security declines because the value of the currency of the issuing corporation falls in relation to the U.S. dollar). For information on how the strength of the dollar affects the relative prices of goods in the international market, flip to Chapter 13.

Rights: The right to buy new shares at a discount

Corporations offer rights (subscription or preemptive rights) to their common stockholders. To maintain their proportionate ownership of the corporation, *rights* allow existing stockholders to purchase new shares of the corporation at a discount directly from the issuer, before the shares are offered to the public. Stockholders receive one right for each share owned. The rights are short-term (usually 30 to 45 days). The rights are marketable and may be sold by the stockholders to other investors. If existing stockholders don't purchase all the shares, the issuer offers any unsold shares to a standby underwriter. A *standby underwriter* is a broker-dealer that purchases any stock that wasn't sold in the rights offering and then resells the shares to other investors.

For the Series 7, you can assume that common stockholders automatically receive rights.

Because rights allow investors to purchase the shares at a discount, rights have a theoretical value. The board of directors determines that value when they decide how many rights investors need to purchase a share, as well as the discounted price offered to investors. To determine the value of a right, you can use one of two basic formulas: the cum rights formula or the ex-rights formula. Look closely at the question to determine which one you need. The following sections explore each.

Using the cum rights formula

You may have to find the value of a right while shares are still trading with rights attached. To find out how much of a discount each right provides, you can simply take the difference between the market price and the subscription price, divide that by the number of rights, and come up with a nice, round number. But not so fast! On the *ex-date* (the first day the stock trades without rights), the market price will drop by the value of the right. Before the ex-date, you can find the value of a right by using the cum (Latin for *with*) rights formula:

$$\text{Value of a right}_{\text{cum rights}} = \frac{M \text{ (market price)} - S \text{ (subscription price)}}{N \text{ (number of rights needed to purchase one share)} + 1}$$

The +1 in the denominator accounts for the later drop in the market price. Try out the following rights question:

DEF Corp. is issuing new shares through a rights offering. If a new share costs $16 plus four rights and the stock trades at $20, what is the theoretical value of a right prior to the ex-date?

(A) $0.20

(B) $0.80

(C) $1.00

(D) $1.20

The answer is B. The stock is trading with (cum) rights (the words *prior to the ex-date* in the problem should tip you off), so you need to use the cum rights formula to figure out the value of a right:

$$\frac{M - S}{N + 1} = \frac{\$20 - \$16}{4 + 1} = \frac{4}{5} = \$0.80$$

The theoretical value of a right is $0.80.

Using the ex-rights formula

When you calculate the value of a right on the *ex-date* (the first day the stock trades without rights), the market price has already fallen by the value of the right. You simply have to use the new market price and the subscription price to figure out the discount per right. If the stock is trading ex-rights, use the following formula to figure out the value of a right:

$$\text{Value of a right}_{\text{ex-rights}} = \frac{M \text{ (market price)} - S \text{ (subscription price)}}{N \text{ (number of rights needed to purchase one share)}}$$

The cum rights and ex-rights formulas are the same except for the +1 in the denominator. Because *ex* means *without,* remember that the *ex* formula is *without* the +1.

Warrants: The right to buy stock at a fixed price

Warrants are certificates that entitle the holder to buy a specific amount of stock at a fixed price; they're usually issued along with a new bond or stock offering. Warrant holders have no voting rights and receive no dividends. Bundled bonds and warrants or bundled stock and warrants are called *units.* They are long term and sometimes perpetual (without an expiration-date). Warrants are *sweeteners* because they're something that the issuer throws into the new offering to make the deal more appealing; however, warrants can also be sold separately on the market. When warrants are originally issued, the warrant's exercise price is set well above the underlying stock's market price.

For example, suppose QRS warrants give investors the right to buy QRS common stock at $20 per share when QRS common stock is trading at $12. Certainly, exercising their warrants to purchase QRS stock at $20 wouldn't make sense for investors when they can buy QRS stock in the market at $12. However, if QRS rises above $20 per share, holders of warrants can exercise their warrants and purchase the stock from the issuer at $20.

For Further Review

To be properly prepared to take the Series 7 exam, you need to know the information in this chapter and have a good handle on the following terms and ideas related to equity securities:

- ✔ Registrar and transfer agents
- ✔ Stockholders' rights
- ✔ Proxies
- ✔ Non-voting stock
- ✔ Limited liability
- ✔ Sinking-fund provisions for preferred stock
- ✔ Preferred stock preference upon corporate dissolution
- ✔ Residual claim on assets

Chapter 7

Debt Securities: Corporate and U.S. Government Loans

*I*nstead of giving up a portion of their company (via stock certificates), corporations can borrow money from investors by selling bonds. Local governments (through municipal bonds) and the U.S. government also issue bonds. For Series 7 exam purposes, most bonds are considered safer than stocks.

Bondholders aren't owners of a company like stockholders are; they're creditors. Bondholders lend money to an institution for a fixed period of time and receive interest for doing so. This arrangement allows the institution to borrow money on its terms (with its chosen maturity date, scheduled interest payments, interest rate, and so on), which it wouldn't have been able to do had it borrowed from a lending institution.

The Series 7 exam tests you on your ability to understand the different types of bonds issued, terminology, and yes, some math. This chapter has you covered in topics relating to corporate and U.S. government debt securities. Check out the "For Further Review" section at the end of this chapter for a list of related topics, and pay attention to the example questions along the way.

Bond Terms, Types, and Traits

Before you delve deeper into bonds, make sure you have a good handle on the basics. Understanding the bond basics is a building block that can make all the rest of the bond stuff easier. In this section, I first do a review of the basic bond terminology and then move on to some bond characteristics.

Remembering bond terminology

The Series 7 exam designers expect you to know general bond terminology. (And I give it to you here — that's why I get paid the big bucks!) In this section, I help you reinforce the information you may have already learned from a prep course or study material (or are in the process of learning). This stuff is basic, but the Series 7 exam does test it:

✔ **Maturity date:** All issued bonds have a stated maturity date (for example, 20 years, 30 years, and so on). The maturity date is the year bondholders get paid back for the loans they made. At maturity, bondholders receive par value (see the next bullet).

✔ **Par value:** Par value is the face value of the bond. Although par value isn't significant to common stockholders (who use it solely for bookkeeping purposes), it's important to bondholders. For Series 7 exam purposes, you can assume that the par value for each bond is $1,000 unless otherwise stated in the question.

Bond prices are quoted as a percentage of par value, often without the percent sign. A bond trading at 100 is trading at 100 percent of $1,000 par. Regardless of whether investors purchase a bond for $850 (85), $1,000 (100), or $1,050 (105), they'll receive par value at the maturity date of the bond, usually with interest payments along the way. Corporate bonds are usually quoted in increments of ⅛% (⅛% = 0.00125 or $1.25), so a corporate bond quoted at 99⅜ (99.375%) would be trading at $993.75.

✔ **Coupon rate:** Of course, investors aren't lending money to issuers for nothing; investors receive interest for providing loans to the issuer. The coupon rate on the bond tells the investors how much annual interest they'll receive.

The coupon rate is expressed as a percentage of par value. For example, a bond with a coupon rate of 6 percent would pay annual interest of $60 (6% × $1,000 par value). You can assume that bonds pay interest semiannually unless otherwise stated. So in this example, the investor would receive $30 every six months.

Bondholders receive *interest* (payment for the use of the money loaned), and stockholders receive *dividends* (a sharing of profits).

✔ **The bond indenture:** The *indenture* (also known as *deed of trust*) is the legal agreement between the issuer and the investor. It's printed on or attached to the bond certificate. All indentures contain basic terms:

- The maturity date
- The par value
- The coupon rate (interest rate) and interest payment dates
- Any collateral securing the bond (see "Comparing secured and unsecured bonds" later in this chapter)
- Any callable or convertible features (check out "Contrasting callable and put bonds" and "Popping the top on convertible bonds" later in this chapter)

The bond indenture also includes the name of a trustee. A *trustee* is an organization that administers a bond issue for an institution. It ensures that the bond issuer meets all the terms and conditions associated with the borrowing. Essentially, the trustee tries to make sure that the issuer does the right thing.

The following question tests your knowledge of bond interest:

Jane Q. Investor purchased 100 AA rated bonds issued by COW Corp. Jane purchased the bonds at 105 percent of par value, and they are currently trading in the market at 104. If the coupon rate is 7½ percent, how much annual interest does Jane receive?

(A) $37.50

(B) $75.00

(C) $3,750.00

(D) $7,500.00

The answer is D. This is a nice, easy question after you wade through the information that you don't need. You need only the number of bonds and the coupon rate to figure out the answer. Don't let yourself get distracted by the rating, purchase price, or market price. That information is there to confuse you.

Jane purchased 100 bonds at $1,000 par (remember you can assume $1,000 par) with a coupon rate of 7½ percent, so do the math:

100 bonds × $1,000 par × 7½% = $7,500.00

Answer C would've been correct if the question had asked for the semiannual interest.

Identifying types of bond certificates

To make your life even more interesting, bond certificates can be delivered in different forms. Even though some types of bonds are no longer being issued, you'll still be tested on them when taking the Series 7 exam. Take a look:

- **Bearer bonds:** Bearer bonds are also known as *coupon bonds* because they have bearer coupons attached. This type of bond is not registered in a particular person's name. Instead, the holder submits coupons (representing interest payments) to the issuer once every six months to receive the stated interest amount. Because of the inherent risk of bearer bonds (like cash, they can be lost or stolen), they're no longer issued. Why, you ask, do you have to study them if they're no longer issued? Many of them haven't yet matured and are still trading in the market.

- **Partially registered bonds:** Partially registered bonds are also called *registered coupon bonds* or *registered as to principal only*. This is a bond in which the principal (par value) — but not interest — is registered in the investor's name. Therefore, the bearer coupon payments can go to anyone, but only the person named on the bond can claim the principal payment at maturity. As with bearer bonds, this type of bond is no longer issued, but it's still traded in the market.

- **Fully registered bonds:** Fully registered bonds are currently the most common form of bond certificates. This type of bond is registered in an investor's name and does not have any bearer coupons attached. An investor doesn't have to submit coupons to receive the semiannual interest payments; the investor receives the interest automatically.

- **Book entry certificates:** Book entry certificates, or book entry securities, are recorded in electronic records called *book entries;* thus, the investor doesn't receive certificates or coupons. The U.S. government usually issues its securities in book entry form. Although a majority of the bonds trading in the market are bearer, fully registered, or partially registered, book entry certificates are becoming more popular.

On the Series 7 exam, all bearer and partially registered bonds that are in default should be delivered *with* any unpaid coupons attached.

Now try your hand at a question about bond certificates:

Which of the following types of bond certificates require the investor to turn in coupons in order to receive interest payments?

   I. Book entry bonds

  II. Fully registered bonds

 III. Bearer bonds

 IV. Partially registered bonds

(A) I and III

(B) III and IV

(C) I, II, and IV

(D) I, III, and IV

The answer is B. Here you see an example of a complex multiple-choice question. If you remember that book entry bonds don't require the investor to mail in anything, you know Roman numeral I is wrong; therefore, you can immediately cross off answers A, C, and D. Both bearer bonds and partially registered bonds require the investor to turn in coupons to the issuer in order to receive interest payments. Book entry bondholders and fully registered bondholders receive interest from the issuer automatically without turning anything in.

Following bond issue and maturity schedules

Not only can bond certificates be in different forms, but they can also be scheduled with different types of maturities. Maturity schedules depend on the issuer's needs. The following list presents an explanation of the types of bond issues and maturity schedules:

- **Term bonds:** Term bonds are all issued at the same time and have the same maturity date. For example, if a company issues $20,000,000 worth of term bonds, they may all mature in 20 years. Because of the large payment that's due at maturity, most corporations issuing this type of bond have a sinking fund. Most corporations issue term bonds because they lock in a coupon rate for a long period of time.

    A corporation creates a *sinking fund* when it sets aside money over time in order to retire its debt. Investors like to see that a sinking fund is in place because it lowers the likelihood of *default* (the risk that the issuer can't pay interest or par value back at maturity).

- **Series bonds:** These bonds are issued in successive years but have only one maturity date. Issuers of series bonds pay interest only on the bonds that they've issued so far. Construction companies that are building developments in several phases would issue this type of bond.

- **Serial bonds:** In this type of bond issue, a portion of the outstanding bonds mature at regular intervals (for example, 10 percent of the entire issue matures yearly). These are usually issued by corporations and municipalities to fund projects that provide regular income streams. Most municipal (local government) bonds are issued with serial maturity.

    A serial bond that has more bonds maturing on the final maturity date is called a *balloon issue.*

The Series 7 exam focuses mainly on term and serial bonds. A typical Series 7 exam question may ask, "Which of the following types of bonds is most likely to have a sinking fund?"

Comparing secured and unsecured bonds

The assets of the issuer may or may not back bonds. You should assume for test purposes that bonds backed by *collateral* (assets that the issuer owns) are considered safer for the investor. *Secured bonds,* or bonds backed by collateral, involve a pledge from the issuer that a specific asset (for instance, property) will be sold to pay off the outstanding debt in the event of default. Obviously, with all else being equal, secured bonds normally have a lower yield than unsecured bonds.

The Series 7 tests several types of secured bonds:

- **Mortgage bonds:** These bonds are backed by property that the issuer owns. In the event of default or bankruptcy, the issuer would have to liquidate the property to pay off the outstanding bonds.

- **Equipment trusts:** This type of bond is mainly issued by transportation companies and is backed by equipment they own (for instance, airplanes or trucks). If the company defaults on its bonds, it sells the assets backing the bonds to satisfy the debt.

- **Collateral trusts:** These bonds are backed by financial assets (stocks and bonds) that the issuer owns. A *trustee* (a financial institution the issuer hires) holds the assets and sells them to pay off the bonds in the event of default.

- **Guaranteed bonds:** Guaranteed bonds are backed by a firm other than the original issuer, usually a parent company. If the issuer defaults, the parent company pays off the bonds.

Unsecured bonds are the opposite of secured bonds: These bonds are not backed by any assets whatsoever, only by the good faith and credit of the issuer. If a reputable company that's been around for a long time issues the bonds, the bonds aren't considered too risky. If they're issued by a relatively new company or one with a bad credit rating, hold onto your seat! Again, for Series 7 exam purposes, assume that unsecured bonds are riskier than secured bonds. Here's the lineup of unsecured bonds:

- **Debentures:** These bonds are backed only by the issuer's good word and written agreement (the indenture) stating that the issuer will pay the investor interest when due (usually semiannually) and par value at maturity.

- **Income bonds:** These bonds are the riskiest of all. The issuer promises to pay par value back at maturity and will make interest payments only if earnings are high enough. Companies in the process of reorganization usually issue these bonds at a deep discount (for example, the bonds sell for $500 and mature at par, or $1,000). For test purposes (and real world purposes), you shouldn't recommend these bonds to investors who can't afford to take a lot of risk.

Because secured bonds are considered safer than unsecured bonds, secured bonds normally have lower coupon rates. You can assume that for the Series 7, the more risk an investor takes, the more reward he or she will receive. Remember the saying "more risk equals more reward." More reward may be in the form of a higher coupon rate or a lower purchase price. Either one, or both, would lead to a higher yield for the investor.

Check out the following question for an example of how the Series 7 may test your knowledge of the types of bonds:

Jon Bearishnikoff is a 62-year-old investor who has 50 percent of his portfolio invested in common stock of up-and-coming companies. The other 50 percent of his portfolio is invested in a variety of stocks of more secure companies. Jon would like to start investing in bonds. Jon is concerned about the safety of his investment. Which of the following bonds would you LEAST likely recommend?

(A) Collateral trust bonds

(B) Mortgage bonds

(C) Equipment trust bonds

(D) Income bonds

The answer is D. This problem includes a lot of garbage information that you don't need to answer the question. One of your jobs (should you decide to accept it) is to dance your way through the question and cherry-pick the information that you do need. The last sentence is usually the most important one when answering a question. Jon is looking for safety; therefore, you'd least likely recommend income bonds because they're usually issued by companies in the process of reorganizing. As a side note, if you become Jon's broker, he shouldn't have 100 percent of his investments in stock. At Jon's age, he should have at least 60 percent of his portfolio in bonds.

Making Basic Bond Price and Yield Calculations

The Series 7 exam tests your knowledge of bond prices, bond yields, and how to calculate them. In this section, I review the relationship between bond prices and bond yields. I also show you how accrued interest can affect how much customers have to pay for the bond.

There's an inverse relationship between outstanding bond prices and yields. You can assume for Series 7 exam purposes that if interest rates decrease, outstanding bond prices increase and vice versa. Say, for example, that a company issued bonds with a 7 percent coupon rate for $1,000. After the bonds are on the market, interest rates decrease. The company can now issue bonds with a 6 percent coupon rate. Investors with the 7 percent bonds are in a very good position right now and can demand a premium for their bonds. Before I show you how the "seesaw" works, make sure you understand the different yields.

Finding bond yields

The following sections review the types of bond yields and how the Series 7 exam tests this topic.

Nominal yield (coupon rate)

The *nominal yield* (NY) is the easiest yield to understand because it's the coupon rate on the face of the bonds. For Series 7 exam purposes, you can assume that the coupon rate will remain fixed for the life of a bond. If you have a 7 percent bond, the bond will pay $70 per year interest (7% × $1,000 par value). When a problem states that a security is a 7 percent (or 6 percent or whatever) bond, it's giving the nominal yield.

Current yield

The *current yield* (CY) is the annual rate of return on a security. The CY of a bond changes when the market price changes; you can determine the CY by dividing the annual interest by the market price:

$$\text{Current yield (CY)} = \frac{\text{annual interest}}{\text{market price}}$$

The following question involves bond yields:

Monique Moneybags purchased one XYZ convertible mortgage bond at 105. Two years later, the bond is trading at 98. If the coupon rate of the bond is 6%, what is the current yield of the bond?

(A) 5.7%

(B) 6.0%

(C) 6.1%

(D) Cannot be determined

The answer is C. Yes, I'm giving you a question with a lot of unnecessary information. All I can tell you is that unfortunately, you'll have to get used to it. The Series 7 exam is notorious for inserting useless (and sometimes misleading) information into the question to daze and confuse you. In this case, you need only the annual interest and the market price to calculate the answer. Use the following formula to get your answer:

$$CY = \frac{\text{annual interest}}{\text{market price}} = \frac{\$60}{\$980} = 6.1\%$$

The annual interest is $60 (6% coupon rate × $1,000 par value), and the current market price is $980 (98% of $1,000 par). The facts that the bond is convertible (bondholders can trade it for common stock — see "Popping the top on convertible bonds" later in this chapter) or a mortgage bond (backed by the issuer's property) and that it was purchased at 105 ($1,050) are irrelevant.

"Cannot be determined" is almost never the correct answer on the Series 7 exam.

Yield to maturity (basis)

The *yield to maturity* (YTM) is the yield an investor can expect if holding the bond until maturity. The YTM takes into account not only the market price but also par value, the coupon rate, and the amount of time until maturity. When someone yells to you, "Hey, what's that bond yielding?" (all right, maybe I run in a different circle of friends), he or she is asking for the YTM. The formula for YTM is as follows:

$$YTM = \frac{\text{annual interest} + \text{annual accretion } or - \text{annual amortization}}{(\text{market price} + \text{par value}) / 2}$$

$$\text{Annual accretion} = \frac{\text{par value} - \text{market price}}{\text{years until maturity}}$$

$$\text{Annual amortization} = \frac{\text{market price} - \text{par value}}{\text{years until maturity}}$$

This formula can be difficult to remember. If you have it down, kudos (whatever that means) to you. It's tested (although somewhat rarely) on the Series 7 exam, and you may be one of the unlucky blokes who need this formula. For more on accretion and amortization, please visit Chapter 15.

Yield to call

The *yield to call* (YTC) is the amount that the investor receives if the bond is called prior to maturity. The calculations are similar to those for the YTM (see the preceding section), but you'd substitute the call price for the par value. The chances of needing it on the Series 7 exam are even more remote than needing the YTM calculations.

Using seesaw calculations for price and yields

In this section, I show you how to use a "seesaw" to help you better visualize the relationship between bond prices and yields. I know this method is a little goofy, but I'll do *almost* anything to help you pass the Series 7 exam.

Higher numbers make the seesaw rise, and lower numbers make it fall. Looking at the following diagram, you can see that if a bond is at par, the seesaw remains level. If the prices decrease, the yields increase, and if the prices increase, the yields decrease. The center support (△) represents the nominal yield (coupon rate) of the bond because it remains constant no matter what happens to the prices or other yields. (*Note:* In the seesaw, NY stands for *nominal yield,* CY is *current yield,* YTM is *yield to maturity,* and YTC is *yield to call.*)

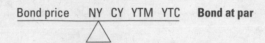

Check out the following problem and its explanation, which show you how to put the seesaw in motion:

Jonathan Bullinski purchased an 8 percent ABC bond yielding 9 percent. He purchased the bond at

(A) a discount

(B) par

(C) a premium

(D) a price that cannot be determined

The answer is A. The question states that the nominal yield is 8 percent and the bond is yielding 9 percent. The 9 percent is the yield to maturity:

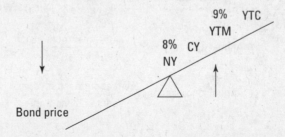

Because the YTM is greater than the NY, the right side of the seesaw goes up and the left side of the seesaw goes down. This means that the investor paid a price that was at a discount (below par). You can also determine that the current yield (CY) would have to be in between 8 and 9 percent and the yield to call (YTC) would have to be greater than 9 percent.

If the YTM were lower than the NY, the seesaw would tip the opposite way, and the price would've been at a premium rather than at a discount.

Calculating accrued interest

When investors purchase bonds in the market, they may have to pay an additional cost besides the market price (and, of course, your commission). The additional cost is called accrued interest. *Accrued interest,* which is due when bonds are purchased between coupon dates, is the portion of the interest still due to the seller. As you may remember, bonds pay interest once every six months. If an investor holds onto a bond for five months out of a six-month period, he or she is entitled to ⅚ of that next interest payment; that's accrued interest.

When taking the Series 7 exam, you need to be able to calculate the number of days of accrued interest that the buyer owes the seller. Although you can calculate the accrued interest with a few different methods, I'm here to make your life easier by showing you one of the simplest ways.

Accrued interest on corporate and municipal bonds is calculated on a 360-day year and assumes 30-day months. Accrued interest on U.S. government bonds is calculated using the actual days per year and actual days per month.

The following sample question tests your ability to figure out this prorated amount:

Skippy Skippington III purchased a 6 percent corporate bond on Friday, October 21. The coupon dates are January 1 and July 1. How many days of accrued interest does Skippy owe?

(A) 115

(B) 117

(C) 120

(D) 122

The answer is A. You have to begin your calculations from the settlement date (the date that the issuer records the new owner's name). Corporate and municipal bonds settle in three business days. You're thrown a slight curveball in this question because you have to contend with a weekend.

Accrued interest is calculated from the previous coupon date up to, but not including, the settlement date.

Now you're probably asking yourself, "What the heck does that mean?" I can show you a nice, easy way to calculate the answer. Using the preceding example, assume that the settlement date is October 26. You would write it as 10/26 (tenth month and 26th day). The previous coupon date would be 7/1 (July 1). You can now set up a subtraction problem:

$$
\begin{array}{r}
10 / 26 \\
- \ 7 / \ 1 \\
\hline
3 / 25
\end{array}
$$
3 / 25   (3 months × 30-day months) + 25 days = 115 days of accrued interest

First subtract the seventh month (July) from the tenth month (October). You end up with three months. Because corporate and municipal bonds calculate accrued interest using 30-day months, you have to multiply three months by 30 days to get an answer of 90 days. Subtract the previous coupon date (1) from the settlement date (26) to get an answer of 25 days. Add the 90 days and 25 days together, and you get 115 days as your answer.

Read carefully. To try to trip you up, the Series 7 exam writers may include the settlement date in the question. If this is the case, you don't need to add days to the trade date.

You can use the same formula to calculate accrued interest on U.S. government securities (for basic information, see "Exploring U.S. Government Securities" later in the chapter). However, U.S. government securities settle in one business day, not three. Additionally, U.S. government securities are calculated using actual days per month. The following example shows you how to calculate interest for a U.S. government securities question:

Skippy Skippington IV purchased a 5 percent T-bond on Monday, November 18. The coupon dates are January 1 and July 1. How many days of accrued interest does Skippy owe?

(A) 135

(B) 138

(C) 141

(D) 142

The answer is C. Please note the following calculations:

$$
\begin{array}{ll}
11/19 & \text{The T-bond settled in one business day} \\
-\ 7/\ 1 & \text{The previous coupon date} \\
\hline
4/18 & \text{(4 months} \times \text{30-day months) + 18 days = 138 days} \\
& \qquad\qquad\qquad\qquad +\ \underline{3\ \text{days}}\ \text{for July, Aug., and Oct.} \\
& \qquad\qquad\qquad\qquad 141\ \text{days of accrued interest}
\end{array}
$$

To get the settlement date, you have to add only one business day. Because the trade date is Monday, November 18, the settlement date is Tuesday, November 19 (11/19). Next, subtract the previous coupon date of July 1 (7/1), and you get an answer of 4 months/18 days. If you multiply the months by 30 as I do in the preceding example and add the days, you end up with 138 days. At this point, you add one day for each of the months that have 31 days. Your answer is 141 days.

Your 31-day months are January, March, May, July, August, October, and December. All the rest of the months have 30 days, except for February, which has 28. For February, you'd subtract two days. I know that you're thinking: "What about leap year?" I haven't heard of anyone getting a leap-year question yet, but if you are that unlucky person, you'd subtract only one day for February.

Determining the Best Investment: Comparing Bonds

As you grind your way through Series 7 exam questions, you may be asked to determine the best investment for a particular investor. You need to carefully look at the question for clues to help you choose the correct answer (for instance, is the investor looking for safety? Is the investor close to retirement?). Consider several factors, including credit rating, callable and put features, and convertible features.

Considering bond credit ratings

The institutions that rate bonds are most interested in the likelihood of *default* (the likelihood the interest and principal won't be paid when due). For the Series 7 exam, you can assume that the higher the credit rating, the safer the bond and, therefore, the lower the yield.

The two main bond credit rating companies are Moody's and Standard & Poor's. Standard & Poor's ratings of BB and lower and Moody's ratings of Ba and lower are considered *junk bonds* or *high yield bonds,* which have a high likelihood of default, as Table 7-1 explains. (Another credit rating service, called Fitch, uses the same rating symbols as Standard & Poor's.) ***Note:*** Different sources may show some slight variations in how S&P and Moody's ratings compare; however, the relationships here are the most common.

Table 7-1	Bond Credit Ratings (by Quality)	
S&P (Standard & Poor's)	*Quality*	*Moody's*
AAA	Highest quality	Aaa
AA	High quality	Aa
A	Upper medium	A
DDD	Lower medium	Baa
BB	Speculative (junk)	Ba
B	Speculative (junk): Interest or principal payments missed	B
C	Speculative (junk): No interest being paid	Caa
D	In default	D

As if these categories weren't enough, Standard & Poor's can break down each category even further by adding a + or a – after the letter category. The + would be the high end of the category, and – would be the lower end of the category. If you see no + or –, the bond is in the middle of the category. Moody's can further break down a category by adding a 1, 2, or 3. The 1 is the highest, 2 is the middle, and 3 is the lowest.

The rating company with the capital letters (S&P) uses all capital letters (AAA, AA, and so on). Additionally, S&P has an &, which is like a plus sign (+) between the two letters. Noting this can help you remember that S&P uses pluses and minuses within the categories.

Here's a typical bond-ratings question:

Place the following Standard & Poor's bond ratings in order from highest to lowest.

    I. A+

   II. AA

  III. A–

  IV. BBB+

(A) I, II, III, IV

(B) I, III, II, IV

(C) IV, I, II, III

(D) II, I, III, IV

The correct answer is D. When answering this type of question, always look at the letters first. The only time pluses or minuses come into play is when two answers have the same letters, as in choices I and III. The highest choice is AA, followed by A+ because it's higher than A–, which is even higher than BBB+.

Contrasting callable and put bonds

As you may know, bonds can be issued in callable and put form. Your mission for the Series 7 exam is to know which is better for investors and when bonds are likely to be called or put.

✔ **Callable bonds:** A *callable bond* is a bond that the issuer has the right to buy back from investors at the price stated on the indenture (deed of trust). Callable bonds are riskier for the investors because investors can't control how long they can hold onto the bonds. Because callable bonds are riskier for the investor, they're usually issued with a higher coupon rate (more risk = more reward).

Most callable bonds are issued with call protection. *Call protection* is the amount of time (usually several years) that an issuer has to wait before calling its bonds. Some callable bonds also have a *call premium,* which is an amount over par value that an issuer has to pay if calling its bonds in the early years.

✔ **Put bonds:** Put bonds are better for investors. *Put bonds* allow the investor to "put" the bonds back (redeem them) to the issuer at any time at the price stated on the indenture. Because the investors have the control, put bonds are (of course) rarely issued. Because these bonds provide more flexibility to investors (who have an interest in the bond and stock prices), put bonds usually have a lower coupon rate.

Remember, there's a direct correlation between interest rates and when bonds are called or put. Issuers call bonds when interest rates decrease; investors put bonds when interest rates increase. Check out the following question to see how this works:

Issuers would call their bonds when interest rates

(A) increase

(B) decrease

(C) stay the same

(D) are fluctuating

The correct answer is B. Being adaptable when taking the Series 7 exam can certainly help your cause. In this question, you have to look from the issuer's point of view, not the investor's. An issuer would call bonds when interest rates decrease because he or she could then redeem the bonds with the higher coupon payments and issue bonds with lower coupon payments to save money. Conversely, investors would put their bonds back to the issuer when interest rates increase so they could invest their money at a higher interest rate.

You can assume for Series 7 exam purposes that if interest rates increase, bond yields increase.

Popping the top on convertible bonds

Bonds that are convertible into common stock are called *convertible bonds*. Convertible bonds are attractive to investors because investors have an interest in the bond price as well as the price of the underlying stock. The Series 7 exam tests your expertise on whether converting a bond makes sense for an investor. This determination requires you to calculate the parity price of the bond or stock.

Parity occurs when a convertible bond and its underlying stock (the stock it's convertible into) are trading equally (that is, when a bond trading for $1,100 is convertible into $1,100 worth of stock).

When answering Series 7 exam questions relating to convertible bonds, you always need to get the *conversion ratio* (the number of shares that the bond is convertible into). Here's the formula for the conversion ratio:

$$\text{Conversion ratio} = \frac{\text{par value}}{\text{conversion price}}$$

You can then use the conversion ratio to calculate the parity price:

Parity price of the bond = market price of the stock × conversion ratio

Use the formula to answer the next example question:

Jane Q. Investor purchased a 6 percent DIM convertible bond. Her DIM bond is currently trading at 106, and the underlying stock is trading at 26. If the conversion price is 25, which of the following are TRUE?

I. The stock is trading above parity.

II. The stock is trading below parity.

III. Converting the bond would be profitable.

IV. Converting the bond would not be profitable.

(A) I and III

(B) I and IV

(C) II and III

(D) II and IV

The answer is D. You can cross out two answers right away. If the stock is trading above parity, converting will always be profitable. And if the stock is trading below parity, converting wouldn't be profitable. Therefore, you can eliminate answers B and C right away. You've just increased your odds of getting the question correct from 25 to 50 percent. To increase your odds from 50 to 100 percent, please follow these equations:

$$\text{Conversion ratio} = \frac{\text{par value}}{\text{conversion price}} = \frac{\$1,000}{\$25} = 40 \text{ shares}$$

parity price of the bond = market price of the stock × conversion ratio
= $26 × 40 shares = $1,040

Currently, the bond is trading for $1,060 (106 × $1,000 par) and is convertible into stock valued at $1,040 (the parity price of the bond). Because the value of the bond is greater than the converted value of the stock, the stock is trading below parity and converting wouldn't be profitable.

Here's another problem that involves parity price:

Victoria purchased a Spanko, Inc., convertible bond at 115 with a conversion ratio of 25. If the common stock for Spanko, Inc., is currently $48 per share, when should Victoria convert her bond?

(A) Right away

(B) When the common stock falls below $46 per share

(C) When the common stock increases to $50 per share

(D) Never, because bonds are safer investments than stocks

The answer is A. Always assume for test purposes that if the stock is trading above parity, the investor should convert. You don't need to figure out the conversion ratio because it was already given in the question. Here's how to solve:

Parity price of the bond = market price of the stock × conversion ratio

= $48 × 25 shares = $1,200

The bond is currently trading at $1,150 (115 × $1,000 par) and is convertible into $1,200 worth of stock. It certainly makes sense for the investor to convert at this point. Although you can try to make a point for answer C, it's not correct. On the Series 7 exam, if the stock is above parity, convert the bond. Convertible bonds and the underlying stock always seek parity. Even though $50 per share would be better than $48, the bond would also increase in price, and the conversion may not end up being as profitable.

Sometimes companies force a conversion (*forced* conversion) by calling bonds at a price that's less than parity. In this situation, converting is more advantageous for investors.

Exploring U.S. Government Securities

On the Series 7 exam, you need to know the basic types of U.S. government securities, their initial maturities, and certain characteristics.

As you may already know, the U.S. government also issues bonds. U.S. government bonds are considered the safest of all securities. Yes, you did read that correctly: the *safest of all securities*. I feel it's worth repeating. How can U.S. government securities be so safe when we're running such a large deficit? Guess what — I don't know, and you don't need to know, either. I can only assume that the U.S. government can always print more currency to make payments on their securities if needed.

Note: With government bonds, you use some of the same types of calculations as you use for corporate bonds. The methods for determining accrued interest, for instance, are very similar. For more information, see "Calculating accrued interest," earlier in this chapter.

Understanding the types and characteristics of U.S. government securities

Table 7-2 gives you an overview of different types of U.S. government securities and their specifics. You should remember all the information in the following chart so you can ace U.S. government securities questions on the Series 7 exam.

Table 7-2	U.S. Government Securities and Time until Maturity	
Security	**Initial Maturity**	**Characteristics**
T-bills (Treasury bills)	4, 13, and 26 weeks	Issued at a discount and mature at par
T-notes (Treasury notes)	2, 3, 5, and 10 years	Pay interest every 6 months
T-bonds (Treasury bonds)	10 to 30 years	Pay interest every 6 months
T-STRIPS (Separate Trading of Registered Interest and Principal of Securities)	6 months to 30 years	Issued at a discount and mature at par
TIPS* (Treasury Inflation-Protected Securities)	5, 10, and 20 years	Pay interest every 6 months; par value and interest payments adjust according to inflation or deflation

* TIPS are tied to the Consumer Price Index (CPI), which measures inflation. The par value changes according to inflation. If inflation is high (prices of goods and services are increasing), the par value increases. If we're in a period of deflation (prices on goods and services are decreasing), the par value decreases. Because investors are getting a percentage of par value as their interest payments, the interest payments vary along with the par value.

For the Series 7, remember that the interest received on U.S. government securities is exempt from state and local taxes. The interest received on municipal bonds is exempt from federal taxes (although I get into that a little more in the next chapter). Chapter 15 gives you the scoop on taxes.

The following question concerns various types of bonds and U.S. government securities:

One of your new customers calls to tell you that his wife just had a baby. He would like to start saving for the child's higher education. He has $30,000 to invest and seems genuinely concerned about the safety of his investment. Which of the following securities would you MOST likely recommend to help him meet his goals?

(A) AA-rated corporate bonds with 18 years until maturity

(B) T-STRIPS with 18 years until maturity

(C) T-bonds with 18 years until maturity

(D) High-yielding corporate bonds

The answer is B. The question gives you a couple clues. The investor is concerned about safety, so answer D is definitely out. High-yielding corporate bonds are low-rated bonds and are a speculative (risky) investment. Out of the other three choices, B makes the most sense. If this customer invests $30,000 in the AA rated corporate bonds or the T-bonds, he'll receive

$30,000 at maturity, along with interest payments along the way. However, interest entails risk. T-STRIPS, on the other hand, don't pay interest, so investors can purchase them at a discount. Because the bonds mature in 18 years, perhaps this investor can purchase the T-STRIPS for around $400 each. He could buy 75 bonds with $1,000 par value which would probably be worth $75,000 in 18 years.

When you see a question on the Series 7 exam about the best investment when planning for a future event (for instance, college), the answer will most likely be either zero-coupon bonds or T-STRIPS.

In the tranches: Delving into packaged mortgages (CMOs)

Just when you thought you were going to get out of debt securities relatively unscathed, you have collateralized mortgage obligations (CMOs) thrown at you. *CMOs* are annoying little (or big) debt securities backed by pools of mortgages (GNMA/Ginnie Mae, FNMA/Fannie Mae, FHLMC/Freddie Mac). What makes matters worse is that you probably won't sell one in your entire career. However, CMOs are on the Series 7 exam, and you need to know the basics in order to answer these questions correctly.

CMOs don't have a set maturity date and are subject to things called *extension risk* and *prepayment risk*. Take a look at these terms:

- **Average life:** The average amount of time until a mortgage is refinanced or paid off; for example, a 30-year mortgage may have an average life of 17 years

- **Prepayment risk:** The risk that a *tranche* (slice or portion of the loan) will be called sooner than expected due to decreasing interest rates; more people refinance when interest rates are low

- **Extension risk:** The risk that a tranche will be called later than expected due to a less-than-normal amount of refinancing; extension occurs when interest rates are high

CMOs are also broken down into tranches (slices) of varying maturity dates. The basic type of CMO has tranches that are paid in a specific sequence. All tranches receive regular interest payments, but only the tranche with the shortest maturity receives principal payments. After the shortest tranche is retired, the second-shortest receives principal payments until that tranche is retired, and then the principal is paid to the next tranche. This type of structure is known as a *plain vanilla* offering. The following list describes other types of CMO tranches (although I discuss several types of tranches, the most important ones on the Series 7 exam are the PAC, TAC, companion, and Z-tranches):

- **Planned amortization class (PAC) tranches:** This is the most common type of CMO because it has the most certain prepayment date. The prepayment and extension risk can be somewhat negated by a companion tranche, which assumes a greater degree of the risk. Because of the relative safety of PAC tranches, they usually have the lowest yields.

- **Targeted amortization class (TAC) tranches:** This is the second-safest CMO. TAC tranche-holders have somewhat less-certain principal payments and are more subject to prepayment and extension risk. TAC tranches have yields that are low but not as low as those of PAC tranches.

- **Companion tranches (support bonds):** Companion tranches are included in every CMO that has PAC or TAC tranches. Companion tranches absorb prepayment risk associated with CMOs. The average life of a companion tranche varies greatly depending on interest rate fluctuations. Because there's more risk associated with companion tranches, they have higher yields.

- **Z-tranches (accrual bonds):** Z-tranches are usually the last tranche (they have longest maturity) in a series of PAC or companion tranches. Z-tranches don't receive interest or principal until all the other tranches in the series have been retired. The market value of Z-tranches can fluctuate widely. Z-tranches are somewhat similar to a zero-coupon bond (which is bought at a discount and does not receive interest along the way).

- **Principal-only (PO) tranches:** Principal-only tranches are purchased at a price deeply discounted below face value. Investors receive face value through regularly scheduled mortgage payments and prepayments. The market value of a PO increases if interest rates drop and prepayments increase.

- **Interest-only (IO) tranches:** Any CMOs with principal-only tranches will also have interest-only tranches. IOs are sold at a deep discount below their expected value based on the principal amount used to calculate the amount of interest due. Contrary to PO tranches, the market value of an IO increases if interest rates increase and prepayments decrease.

- **Floating rate tranches:** These tranches appear with CMOs in which the interest rates are tied to an interest rate index (for instance, London Interbank Offered Rate/LIBOR). Investors can use these investments to hedge interest rate risk on other investments.

The following question tests your understanding of tranches:

Companion tranches support

    I. PO tranches

    II. PAC tranches

    III. TAC tranches

    IV. IO tranches

(A) I only

(B) II only

(C) II and III only

(D) II, III, and IV

The answer is C. Companion tranches absorb the prepayment risk associated with CMOs. All PAC and TAC tranches are supported by a companion tranche.

I know that this information is a lot to take in and may be a little confusing. Remembering the basics can help you get most of the questions correct: PAC tranches are the safest; TAC tranches are the second safest; companion tranches support PAC and TAC tranches; and Z-tranches have the longest maturity.

Playing It Safe: Short-Term Loans or Money Market Instruments

Every Series 7 exam includes a few questions on money market instruments. *Money market instruments* are relatively safe short-term loans that can be issued by corporations, banks, the U.S. government, and municipalities. Most have maturities of 1 year or less, and they're usually issued at a discount and mature at par value. The following list reviews some basic characteristics of money market instruments to help you earn an easy point or two on the Series 7 exam:

- **Repurchase agreements:** Repurchase agreements (Repos) are a contract between a buyer and a seller. The seller of the securities (usually T-bills) agrees to buy them back at a previously determined price and time. Repos are short-term loans.

- **Federal Funds:** Federal Funds are loans between banks to help meet reserve requirements. Federal Funds are usually overnight loans for which the rates are changing constantly depending on supply and demand.

  Reserve requirements are the percentage of deposits that member banks must hold each night. Banks that aren't able to meet their reserve requirements may borrow from other banks at the Fed Funds rate. For more info on the Fed Funds rate and other tools that the Federal Reserve Board uses to influence money supply, see Chapter 13.

- **Corporate commercial paper:** Commercial paper is unsecured corporate debt. Commercial paper is issued at a discount and matures at par value. Commercial paper is issued with an initial maturity of 270 days or less and is exempt from SEC registration.

- **Negotiable certificates of deposit:** A negotiable certificate of deposit is sometimes called a Jumbo CD because it's a CD with a large denomination, usually $1,000,000 or more. Jumbo CDs are low-risk investments and can be sold to other investors.

- **Eurodollars:** Eurodollars are American dollars held by a foreign bank outside the U.S. This situation is usually the result of payments made to overseas companies. Eurodollars are not to be confused with Eurodollar bonds (dollar-denominated bonds issued and held overseas).

- **Bankers' acceptances:** A bankers' acceptance (BA) is a *time-draft* (short-term credit investment) created by a company whose payment is guaranteed by a bank. Companies use BAs for the importing and exporting of goods.

- **T-bills:** The U.S. government issues T-bills at a discount, and they have initial maturities of 4, 13, or 26 weeks. U.S. government securities are considered the safest of all securities.

Here's what a question on money market instruments may look like:

SNK Surfboard Company wants to import boogie boards from an Italian manufacturer in Sicily. SNK would use which of the following money market instruments to finance the importing of the boogie boards?

(A) T-bills

(B) Collateral trust bonds

(C) Repurchase agreements

(D) Banker's acceptances

The answer is D. You can eliminate answer B right away because collateral trust bonds aren't money market instruments; they're secured long-term bonds. Bankers' acceptances are like a post-dated check that's used specifically for importing and exporting goods. Word association can help you here. If you see *importing, exporting,* or *time draft,* your answer is probably bankers' acceptance (BA).

For Further Review

I want you to be as prepared as possible to take the Series 7 exam, so I've compiled a list of items relating to this chapter that the Series 7 exam may test you on. Please look at the items one at a time and make sure you have a good handle on each of them:

- EE Bonds (U.S. Savings Bonds), HH bonds, and I bonds
- U.S. Government Agency Securities — Federal Farm Credit Consolidated Systemwide Bank, Federal Home Loan Bank, and Student Loan Marketing Association (Sallie Mae)
- Mortgage-backed securities — GNMAs (Ginnie Maes), FNMAs (Fannie Maes), and FHLMCs (Freddie Macs)
- Arbitrage
- Forced conversion
- Bond retirement (by redemption, refunding, or conversion)
- Good delivery for bonds
- Long coupons
- Comparative safety of different debt securities
- Sinking funds
- Trust Indenture Act of 1939
- Call protection and call premium
- Zero-coupon bonds
- Trustees
- Anti-dilution covenants
- Bonds trading flat

Chapter 8

Municipal Bonds: Local Government Securities

- -

In This Chapter

▶ Understanding municipal bond basics

▶ Comparing general obligation bonds to revenue bonds

▶ Reviewing other types of municipal bonds

▶ Recognizing sources of municipal bond information

▶ Reviewing additional topics tested

- -

*M*unicipal bonds are securities that state governments, local governments, or U.S. territories issue. The municipality uses the money it borrows from investors to fund and support projects such as roads, sewer systems, hospitals, and so on.

Even though you're most likely going to spend a majority of your time selling equity securities (stocks), for some unknown reason, the Series 7 tests heavily on municipal securities. As a matter of fact, municipal bonds are one of the most heavily tested areas on the entire exam. If you've flipped ahead, you may have noticed that this chapter isn't one of the biggest in the book. Why is that? Well, I cover a lot of the bond basics such as par value, maturity, types of maturities (term, serial, and balloon), the seesaw, and so on in Chapter 7. Also, you can find some of the underwriting information in Chapter 5.

In this chapter, I cover the Series 7 exam topics that are the most tested and most difficult to understand relating to municipal bonds. This chapter and the real exam focus mainly on the differences between GO (general obligation) bonds and revenue bonds. (Check out the "For Further Review" section for a list of related topics that you should have a firm grasp on before you take the test.) This chapter also gives you plenty of example questions for practice.

General Obligation Bonds: Backing Bonds with Taxes

Most Series 7 municipal test questions are on general obligation (GO) bonds. The following sections help you prepare.

General characteristics of GOs

When you're preparing to take the Series 7 exam, you need to recognize and remember a few items that are specific to GO bonds:

- ✓ **They fund non-revenue producing facilities.** GO bonds are not self-supporting because municipalities issue them to build or support projects that don't bring in enough (or any) money to help pay off the bonds. GOs fund schools, libraries, police departments, fire stations, and so on.
- ✓ **They're backed by the full faith and credit (taxing power) of the municipality.** The taxes of the people living in the municipality back general obligation bonds.
- ✓ **They require voter approval.** Because the generous taxes of the people living in the municipality back the bonds, those same people have the right to vote on the project.

The following question tests your knowledge of GO bonds:

Which of the following projects are MORE likely to be financed by general obligation bonds than revenue bonds?

    I. New municipal hospital

    II. Public sports arena

    III. New junior high school

    IV. New library

    (A) I and II only

    (B) III and IV only

    (C) I and III only

    (D) I, III, and IV only

The answer is B. Remember that GO bonds are issued to fund non-revenue producing projects. A new municipal hospital and a public sports arena will produce income that can back revenue bonds. However, a new junior high school and a new library need the support of taxes to pay off the bonds and, therefore, are more likely to be financed by GO bonds.

Analyzing GO bonds

The Series 7 exam tests your ability to analyze different types of securities and help a customer make a decision that best suits his or her needs. You should be able to analyze a GO bond like you'd analyze other investments; however, because they're backed by taxes rather than sales of goods and services (like most corporations are), GO bonds have different components to look at when analyzing the safety of the issue.

Dealing with debt

One factor that influences the safety of a GO bond is the municipality's ability to deal with debt. First, make sure you consider the issuer's name; you can look at previous issues that the municipality had and find out whether it was able to pay off the debt in a timely manner.

In addition to the municipality's name (and credit history), you want to look at current debt. *Net overall debt* includes the debt that the municipality owes directly plus the portion of the overlapping debt that the municipality is responsible for:

- **Net direct debt:** The debt that the municipality obtained on its own. Net direct debt comes from both GO bonds and short-term municipal notes (see the later section "Don't Forget Municipal Notes!"). Revenue bonds are not included in the net direct debt because they're self-supporting (see "Dealing with Revenue Bonds: Raising Money for Utilities").

- **Overlapping debt:** Overlapping debt occurs when several authorities in a geographic area have the ability to tax the same residents. Take, for example, my wife's and my home-away-from-home, Las Vegas. Not only does Las Vegas have its own debt, but because it's part of Clark County, the Las Vegas residents are also responsible for part of Clark County's debt. In addition, because Las Vegas is in Nevada, the residents of Las Vegas are responsible for a portion of Nevada's debt.

To determine the debt *per capita* (per person), take the debt (overall, direct, or overlapping) and divide it by the number of people in the municipality. Obviously, for an investor, the lower this number is, the better.

Bringing in taxes, fees, and fines

Taxes are one of life's little certainties, and they're the driving force behind paying investors for their GO bonds. Property taxes (which local municipalities, not states, collect), sales taxes, traffic fines, and licensing fees put money in the municipal coffers and eventually in investors' hands. Here are some factors that affect the safety of a GO bond:

- **Property values:** *Ad valorem* (property) taxes are the largest source of backing for GO bonds. Even though people living in a municipality would like their property values to be low (at least for tax purposes), people investing in municipal bonds would like the property values to be high. The higher the assessed value, the more taxes collected and the easier it'll be for the municipality to pay off its debt.

When you're dealing with Series 7 questions that ask you to calculate the ad valorem taxes for an individual, always go with the assessed value, not the market value. Ad valorem taxes are based on mills, or thousandths of a dollar (1 mill = $0.001). To help you remember that a mill equals 0.001, remember that *mills* has two *l*s, so you need to have two zeros after the decimal point.

- **Population:** Obviously, the more people who live in a municipality and pay taxes to back the bond issue, the better. Also, the population trend is important. Investors would like to see more people moving into a municipality than moving out.

- **Tax base:** The tax base is comprised of the number of people living in the municipality, the assessed property values, and how much the average person makes. Larger tax bases are ideal.

- **Sales per capita:** Because sales taxes also support GO bonds, the amount of sales per capita (the amount of goods the average person buys) is also important.

- **Traffic fines and licensing fees:** You know that $100 speeding ticket that you got last month? The money that you paid in fines helped pay off some of the municipality's debt. I hope that makes you feel better.

Municipal GO bonds are backed by the huge taxing power of a municipality, so GO bonds usually have higher ratings and lower yields than revenue bonds. Because investors aren't taking as much risk, they don't get as much reward (lower yields).

Try your hand at a question involving property taxes, an issue that affects the safety of GO bonds:

An individual has a house with a market value of $350,000 and an assessed value of $300,000. What is the ad valorem tax if the tax rate is 16 mills?

(A) $480

(B) $560

(C) $4,800

(D) $5,600

The answer is C. First make sure that you start with the assessed value; multiply it by the tax rate and then by 0.001 to get the answer:

$$\$300,000 \times 16 \times 0.001 = \$4,800$$

To keep yourself from making a careless mistake, multiply the three numbers separately; the tax rate may be single or double digits. Multiplying by 0.001 means moving a decimal point three places to the left, so 16 mills is $0.016, not $0.0016. In this case, if you'd multiplied $300,000 by 0.0016 (or 1.6 mills), you would've gotten a wrong answer, choice A.

Dealing with Revenue Bonds: Raising Money for Utilities

Unlike the tax-backed GO bonds (see the preceding sections), *revenue bonds* are issued to fund municipal facilities that'll generate enough income to support the bonds. These bonds raise money for certain utilities, toll roads, airports, hospitals, student loans, and so on.

A municipality can also issue *industrial development revenue bonds* (IDRs) to finance the construction of a facility for a corporation that moves into that municipality. Remember that even though a municipality issues IDRs, they're actually backed by lease payments made by a corporation. Because the corporation is backing the bonds, the credit rating of the bonds is derived from the credit rating of the corporation.

Because IDRs are backed by a corporation rather than a municipality, IDRs are generally considered the riskiest municipal bonds. Additionally, because these bonds are issued for the benefit of a corporation and not the municipality, the interest income may not be federally tax free to investors subject to the alternative minimum tax (AMT).

General characteristics of revenue bonds

Before taking the Series 7 exam, you need to recognize and remember a couple items that are specific to revenue bonds:

- ✔ **They don't need voter approval.** Because revenue bonds fund a revenue-producing facility and therefore aren't backed by taxes, they don't require voter approval. The revenues that the facility generates should be sufficient to pay off the debt.

- ✔ **They require a feasibility study.** Prior to issuing revenue bonds, the municipality hires consultants to prepare a feasibility study. The study basically answers the question *does this make sense?* The study includes estimates of revenues that the facility could generate, along with any economic, operating, or engineering aspects of the project that would be of interest to the municipality.

Analyzing revenue bonds

As with any investment, you should check out the specifics of the security. For instance, when gauging the safety of a revenue bond, you want to look at *call features* (whether the issuer has the right to force investors to redeem their bonds early). You can assume that if a bond is callable, it has a higher yield than a non-callable bond because the investor is taking more risk (the investor doesn't know how long he or she can hold onto the bond).

For Series 7 exam purposes, and if you ever sell one or more revenue bonds, you also need to be familiar with the revenue-bond-specific items in this section. For instance, municipal revenue bonds involve covenants, wonderful little promises that protect investors by holding the issuer legally accountable. Table 8-1 shows some of the promises that municipalities make on the municipal bond indenture.

Table 8-1	Revenue Bond Covenants
Type of Covenant	*Promises That the Municipality Will*
Rate covenant	Charge sufficient fees to people using the facility to be able to pay expenses and the debt service (principal and interest on the bonds)
Maintenance covenant	Adequately take care of the facility and any equipment so the facility continues to earn revenue
Insurance covenant	Adequately insure the facility

If you see the word *covenant* on the Series 7 exam, immediately think of revenue bonds.

Obviously, municipalities don't want to default on their loans. That's why issuers use the *additional bonds test,* which says that if the municipality is going to issue more bonds backed by the same project, it must prove that the revenues will be sufficient to cover all the bonds. The indenture on the initial bonds may be open-ended or closed-ended. If it's open-ended, additional bonds will have equal claims to the assets. If it's closed-ended, any other bonds issued are subordinate (lower rank) to the original issue.

A *catastrophe clause* states that if a facility is destroyed due to a catastrophic event such as a flood, hurricane, tornado, and so on, the municipality will use the insurance that it purchased to call the bonds and pay back bondholders.

The *flow of funds* relates only to revenue bonds. The flow of funds tells you what a municipality does with the money collected from the revenue-producing facility that's backing the bonds. Typically, the flow of funds is as follows:

1. **Operation and maintenance:** This item is normally the first that the municipality pays from revenues it receives. If the municipality doesn't adequately maintain the facility and pay its employees, it'll cease to run.

2. **Debt service:** Usually the next item paid after the operation and maintenance is the *debt service* (principal and interest on the bonds).

3. **Debt service reserve:** After paying the first two items, the municipality puts aside money into the debt service reserve to pay one year's debt service.

4. **Reserve maintenance fund:** This fund helps supplement the general maintenance fund.

5. **Renewal and replacement fund:** This fund is for exactly what you'd expect — renewal projects (updating and modernizing) and replacement of equipment.

6. **Surplus fund:** Municipalities can use this fund for several purposes, such as redeeming bonds, paying for improvements, and so on.

Revenues are normally dispersed as I describe in the preceding list. This system is called a *net revenue pledge* because the *net revenues* (revenues after paying operation and maintenance expenses) are used to pay the debt service. However, if the municipality pays the debt service before paying the operation and maintenance, it is called a *gross revenue pledge*.

The *debt service coverage ratio* is an indication of the ability of a municipal issuer to meet the debt service (principal and interest) payments on its bonds. The higher the debt service coverage ratio, the more likely the issuer is to be able to meet interest and principal payments on time.

The following question tests your debt service coverage ratio knowledge. Use the following formula to answer:

$$\text{Debt service coverage ratio} = \frac{\text{net or gross revenues}}{\text{principal} + \text{interest}}$$

A municipality generates \$10,000,000 in revenues from a facility. It must pay off \$6,000,000 in operating and maintenance expenses, \$1,500,000 in principal, and \$500,000 in interest. Under a net revenue pledge, what is the debt service coverage ratio?

  (A) 1 to 1

  (B) 1.5 to 1

  (C) 2 to 1

  (D) 4 to 1

The answer is C. Because the question states that the municipality is using a net revenue pledge, you have to calculate the net revenues. First, using the earlier equation, figure the net revenues by subtracting the operation and maintenance (\$6,000,000) from the gross revenues (\$10,000,000), which gives you \$4,000,000. Next, take the \$4,000,000 and divide it by the combined principal and interest. The principal is \$1,500,000 and the interest is \$500,000, which gives you a total of \$2,000,000. After dividing the \$4,000,000 by \$2,000,000, you come up with an answer of 2 to 1, which means that the municipality brought in two times the amount of money needed to pay the debt service (principal and interest). A debt service ratio of 2 to 1 is considered adequate for a municipality to pay off its debt.

Here's how your equation should look:

$$\text{Debt service coverage ratio} = \frac{\text{net revenues}}{\text{principal} + \text{interest}}$$

$$= \frac{\$10,000,000 - \$6,000,000}{\$1,500,000 + \$500,000} = \frac{\$4,000,000}{\$2,000,000} = 2 \text{ to } 1$$

If the question doesn't specifically ask for gross revenues or net revenues, you can assume net because that's the more common way that a municipality pays off its debt.

Examining Other Types of Municipal Bonds on the Test

Along with standard revenue and GO bonds (see the earlier sections on these topics), you're required to know the specifics of the following bonds:

- ✔ **Special tax bonds:** These bonds are secured by one or more taxes other than ad valorem (property) taxes. These bonds may be backed by sales taxes on fuel, tobacco, alcohol, and so on.

- ✔ **Special assessment (special district) bonds:** These bonds are issued to fund the construction of sidewalks, streets, sewers, and so on. Special assessment bonds are backed by taxes only on the properties that benefit from the improvements. In other words, if people who live a few blocks away from you get all new sidewalks, they'll be taxed for it, not you.

- ✔ **Double-barreled bonds:** These bonds are basically a combination of revenue and GO bonds. Municipalities issue these bonds to fund revenue-producing facilities (toll bridges, water and sewer facilities, and so on), but if the revenues taken in aren't enough to pay off the debt, tax revenues make up the deficiency.

- ✔ **Public housing authority bonds (PHAs):** These bonds are also called new housing authority (NHA) bonds and are issued by local housing authorities to build and improve low-income housing. These bonds are backed by U.S. government subsidies, and if the issuer can't pay off the debt, the U.S. government makes up any shortfalls.

Because PHAs are backed by the issuer and the U.S. government, they're considered the safest municipal bonds and would get a Standard & Poor's credit rating of AAA.

- ✔ **Moral obligation bonds:** These bonds are issued by a municipality but backed by a pledge from the state government to pay off the debt if the municipality can't. These bonds have the additional backing of the state and are considered safe. Moral obligation bonds need legislative approval to be issued.

Because they're called moral obligation bonds, the state has a *moral* responsibility, but not a legal obligation, to help pay off the debt if the municipality can't.

The following question tests your ability to answer questions about the safety of municipal bonds:

Rank the following municipal bonds in order from safest to riskiest.

  I. Revenue bonds

 II. Moral obligation bonds

III. Public housing authority bonds

IV. Industrial development revenue bonds

(A) I, II, III, IV

(B) III, II, I, IV

(C) II, III, IV, I

(D) II, IV, III, I

The answer is B. If you remember that public housing authority bonds are considered the safest of the municipal bonds because they're backed by U.S. government subsidies, this question's easy, because only one answer choice starts with III. Anyway, public housing authority bonds have a AAA credit rating; moral obligation bonds, which are also considered very safe because the state government has a moral obligation to help pay off the debt if needed, follow. Next come revenue bonds, which are backed by a revenue-producing facility. You should also remember that industrial development revenue bonds (IDRs) are considered the riskiest municipal bonds because although they're technically municipal bonds, they're backed only by lease payments made by a corporation.

Don't Forget Municipal Notes!

When municipalities need short-term (interim) financing, municipal notes come into play. These notes bring money into the municipality until other revenues are received. Municipal notes typically have maturities of one year or less (typically three to five months). Know the different types of municipal notes for the Series 7 exam:

- **Tax anticipation notes (TANs):** These notes provide financing for current operations in anticipation of future taxes that the municipality will collect.

- **Revenue anticipation notes (RANs):** These bonds provide financing for current operations in anticipation of future revenues that the municipality will collect.

- **Tax and revenue anticipation notes (TRANs):** These notes are a combination of TANs and RANs.

- **Bond anticipation notes (BANs):** These bonds provide interim financing for the municipality while it's waiting for long-term bonds to be issued.

- **Construction loan notes (CLNs):** These notes provide interim financing for the construction of multifamily apartment buildings.

- **Project notes (PNs):** These bonds provide interim financing for the building of subsidized housing for low-income families.

AON (all or none) is an order qualifier (fill an entire order at a specific price or not at all) or type of underwriting; it is not a municipal note, no matter how much it looks like one.

Municipal notes are not rated the same as municipal or corporate bonds (AAA, AA, A, and so on). Municipal notes have ratings as follows (from best to worst):

- **Moody's:** MIG 1, MIG 2, MIG 3, MIG 4

- **Standard & Poor's:** SP-1, SP-2, SP-3

- **Fitch:** F-1, F-2, F-3

The following question tests your knowledge of municipal notes:

Suffolk County, NY, would like to even out its cash flow. Which of the following municipal notes would Suffolk County MOST likely issue?

(A) RANs

(B) BANs

(C) CLNs

(D) TANs

The answer is D. You have to use a little common sense to answer this one. Because the question doesn't state that the municipality is constructing housing or issuing long-term bonds, you should cross out answers B and C. Likewise, you can't assume that the municipality will be collecting revenues from some project, so answer A is out. However, municipalities collect property taxes at regular intervals, so D is the best choice.

Understanding the Taxes on Municipal Bonds

Municipal bonds typically have the lowest yields of all bonds. You may think that because U.S. government securities (T-bills, T-notes, T-bonds, and so on) are the safest of all securities, that they should have the lowest yields. Not so, because municipal bonds have a tax advantage that U.S. government bonds don't have: The interest received on municipal bonds is federally tax free.

Comparing municipal and corporate bonds equally

The *taxable equivalent yield* (TEY) tells you what the interest rate of a municipal bond would be if it weren't federally tax free. You need the following formula to compare municipal bonds and corporate bonds equally:

$$\text{Taxable equivalent yield} = \frac{\text{municipal yield}}{100\% - \text{investor's tax bracket}}$$

Because the investor's tax bracket comes into play with municipal bonds, municipal bonds are better suited for investors in higher tax brackets.

The following question tests your ability to answer a TEY question:

Mrs. Stevenson is an investor who is in the 30 percent tax bracket. Which of the following securities would provide Mrs. Stevenson with the BEST after-tax yield?

(A) 5 percent GO bond

(B) 6 percent T-bond

(C) 7 percent equipment trust bond

(D) 7 percent mortgage bond

The answer is A. If you're looking at this question straight up without considering any tax advantages, the answer would be either C or D. However, you have to remember that the investor has to pay federal taxes on the interest received from the T-bond, equipment trust bond, and mortgage bond but doesn't have to pay federal taxes on the interest received from the GO municipal bond. So you need to set up the TEY equation to be able to compare all of the bonds equally:

$$\text{TEY} = \frac{\text{municipal yield}}{100\% - \text{investor's tax bracket}} = \frac{5\%}{100\% - 30\%} = \frac{5\%}{70\%} = 7.14\%$$

Looking into the Series 7 examiners' heads, you have to ask yourself, "Why would they be asking me this question?" Well, because they want to make sure that you know that the interest received on municipal bonds is federally tax free. Therefore, if you somehow forget the formula, you're still likely to be right if you pick municipal bond as the answer when you get a question like the preceding one.

Note: Although this situation is less likely, the Series 7 may ask you to determine the *municipal equivalent yield* (MEY), which is yield on a taxable bond after paying taxes. Once you have that yield, you can compare it to a municipal bond to help determine the best investment for one of your customers. The formula for the municipal equivalent yield is

MEY = municipal yield × (100% – investor's tax bracket)

Scot free! Taking a look at triple tax-free municipal bonds

Bonds that U.S. territories (and federal districts) issue are triple tax-free (the interest is not taxed on the federal, state, or local level). These places include

- Puerto Rico
- Guam
- U.S. Virgin Islands
- American Samoa
- Washington, D.C.

Additionally, in most cases (there are a few exceptions), if you buy a municipal bond issued within your own state, the interest will be triple tax-free.

Unless you see the U.S. territories or Washington, D.C., in a municipal bond question, don't assume that the bonds are triple tax-free. Even if the question states that the investor buys a municipal bond issued within his or her own state, don't assume that it's triple tax-free unless the question specifically states that it is.

The tax advantage of municipal bonds applies only to interest received. If investors sell municipal bonds for more than they paid for them, the investors have to pay taxes on the capital gains.

Following Municipal Bond Rules

Yes, unfortunately, the Series 7 tests you on rules relating to municipal bonds. Rules are a part of life and a part of the Series 7 exam. This section covers just a few rules that are specific to municipal securities, but if you're itching for more regulations, don't worry — you can see plenty more rules in my favorite (and I use that term loosely) chapter: Chapter 16.

The 90-day apprenticeship period

The 90-day apprenticeship period rule says that new registered representatives can't engage in any municipal securities business with the public for their first 90 days in the industry. During this time, a registered rep may deal only with securities professionals such as dealers, and they may not receive commissions during this time.

The 90-day apprenticeship period applies only to municipal bonds. Fortunately, you can still receive commissions from selling other types of securities.

Confirmations

All confirmations of trades must be sent or given to customers at or before the completion of the transaction (settlement date). Municipal securities settle *regular way* in three business days after the trade date. The following items are included on the confirmation:

- The broker-dealer's name, address, and phone number
- The capacity of the trade (whether the firm acted as a broker or dealer)
- The dollar amount of the commission (if the firm's acting as a broker)
- The customer's name
- Any bond particulars, such as the issuer's name, interest rate, maturity, call features (if any), and so on
- The trade date, time of execution, and the settlement date
- Committee on Uniform Securities Identification Procedures (CUSIP) identification number (if there is one)
- Bond yield and dollar price
- Any accrued interest
- The registration form (registered as to principal only, book entry, or fully registered)
- Whether the bonds have been called or pre-refunded
- Any unusual facts about the security

Advertising and record keeping

A brokerage firm has to keep all advertising for a minimum of three years, and these ads must be easily accessible (not in a bus storage locker) for at least two years.

The Municipal Securities Rulemaking Board (MSRB) requires a principal (manager) to approve all advertising material of the firm prior to its first use. The principal must ensure that the advertising is accurate and true.

 Advertising includes any material designed for use in the public media. Advertising includes offering circulars, market and form letters, summaries of official statements, and so on. However, preliminary and final official statements are not considered advertising because they're prepared by the issuer and therefore do not require approval from a principal.

Gifts

According to MSRB rules, municipal securities dealers can't give gifts to customers valued at more than $100 per year. (The board kind of has this thing against bribery.) Business expenses are exempt from the rule.

 If you get a question on the Series 7 exam relating to what qualifies as a gift, remember that business expenses are exempt. Business expenses can be airline tickets (for the customer to meet with you, not for the customer to vacation in the Bahamas), hotel expenses (for the customer's lodging while he or she is meeting with you), business meals, and so on.

Commissions

Although no particular guideline states what percentage broker-dealers can charge (as with the NASD 5% policy — see Chapter 16), all commissions, markups, and markdowns must be fair and reasonable, and policies can't discriminate among customers. The items that firms should consider follow:

✔ The market value of the securities at the time of the trade.

✔ The total dollar amount of the transaction. Although you're going to charge more money for a larger transaction, the percentage charged is usually lower.

✔ The difficulty of the trade. If you had to jump through hoops to make sure the trade was completed, you're entitled to charge more.

✔ The fact that you and the firm that you work for are entitled to make a profit (which is, of course, the reason you got involved in the business to begin with).

You can't take race, ethnicity, religion, gender, sexual orientation, disability, age, funny accents, or how much you like the client into account.

Gathering Municipal Bond Info

As with other investments, you need to be able to locate information if you're going to sell municipal securities to investors. You may find that information about municipal bonds is not as readily available as it is for most other securities. Some municipal bonds are relatively *thin* issues (not many are sold or traded) or may be of interest only to investors in a particular geographic location. This section reviews some of the information that you have to know to ace the Series 7 exam.

The Bond Buyer

The Bond Buyer, which is published Monday through Friday every week, is a newspaper about municipal issues. It includes information about new municipal bonds. Included in *The Bond Buyer* are the following statistics and information:

✔ **The visible supply:** The total dollar amount of municipal bonds expected to reach the market within the next 30 days

✔ **The placement ratio:** The percentage of new issues this week as compared to new issues offered for sale the previous week

✔ **Official notice of sale:** Municipalities looking to accept underwriting bids for new issues of municipal bonds publish the official notice of sale in *The Bond Buyer;* the official notice of sale includes

• When and where bids can be submitted

• The total amount of the sale

• Amount of the good-faith deposit

• The type of bond being offered (GO or revenue)

• Methods for calculating cost (net interest cost or true interest cost)

• The taxes backing the issue

Because GO bonds are backed by taxes paid by people living in the municipality, issuers are more likely to take bids by underwriters for GO bonds than for revenue bonds. The winning bid has the lowest net interest cost to the issuer (the lowest interest rate and/or the highest purchase price).

The Bond Buyer also offers some pretty nifty municipal bond indexes. Here they are now:

✔ ***The Bond Buyer's* Index:** Also called the 20-bond index, this index measures the average yield of 20 municipal bonds with 20 years to maturity; all these bonds have a rating of A or better.

To help you remember that *The Bond Buyer's* Index has 20 bonds with 20 years to maturity, remember that two *B*s equals two *20*s.

✔ **The eleven-bond index:** This index should be a nice, easy one for you to remember because it's the average yield of 11 bonds (of course) from the 20-bond index with a rating of AA or better.

✔ **The revenue bond index:** Also called the RevDex, this index is the average yield of 25 revenue bonds with 30 years to maturity rated A or better.

✔ **The municipal bond index:** Also called the 40-bond index, this index is the average dollar price of 40 highly traded GO and revenue bonds with an average maturity of 20 years with a rating of A or better.

Munifacts

Munifacts is a wire service provided by subscription to *The Bond Buyer;* it provides general information about proposed municipal securities, municipal securities prices, and general information relevant to the municipal bond market. Munifacts is of particular interest to municipal bond traders because it provides information about not only new municipal bonds but also municipal bonds in the secondary market.

The bond resolution (indenture)

A *bond resolution* (indenture) provides investors with contract terms including the coupon rate, years until maturity, collateral backing the bond (if any), and so on. Although not required by law, almost every municipal bond comes with a bond indenture, which is printed on the face of most municipal bond certificates. It makes the bonds more marketable because the indenture serves as a contract between the municipality and a trustee that was appointed to protect the investors' rights. Included in the indenture are the flow of funds (see "Dealing with Revenue Bonds: Raising Money for Utilities," earlier in this chapter) and any assets that may be backing the issue.

Legal opinion

Printed on the face of municipal bond certificates, the legal opinion is prepared and signed by a *municipal bond counsel* (attorney). The purpose of the legal opinion is to verify that the issue is legally binding on the issuer and conforms to tax laws. Additionally, the legal opinion may also state that interest received from the bonds is tax exempt.

The broker's broker

Yes, a *broker's broker* is exactly what you would expect: a broker for brokers. Broker's brokers specialize in trading municipal bonds with institutional customers (banks and municipal brokers) and not with public customers. Broker's brokers help municipal dealers sell unsold portions of a municipal bond issue. Additionally, broker's brokers maintain the anonymity of their clients.

By definition, a broker has no inventory and does not make a market in securities.

If a bond is stamped *ex-legal,* it does not contain a legal opinion.

Here are the two types of legal opinions:

✔ **Qualified legal opinion:** The bond counsel has some reservations about the issue.

✔ **Unqualified legal opinion:** The bond counsel is issuing a legal opinion without reservations.

Normally, you'd think of *qualified* as a good thing and *unqualified* as a bad thing. For legal opinions, think the opposite!

Official statement

Municipal bonds don't have a prospectus; instead, municipalities provide an official statement. The *official statement* is the document that the issuer prepares; it states what the funds will be used for, provides information about the municipality, and details how the funds will be repaid. The official statement also includes

✔ The offering terms

✔ The underwriting spread (see Chapter 5)

✔ A description of the bonds

✔ A description of the issuer

✔ The offering price

✔ The feasibility statement

✔ The legal opinion

For Further Review

I'd love for you to be as prepared as possible to take the Series 7 exam, so I've compiled a list of Series 7 exam information related to this chapter that may show up on the test. Please take a look at the items one at a time and make sure you know each of them well.

✔ Underwriting municipal bonds (see Chapter 5)

✔ Competitive underwritings versus negotiated underwritings

✔ Allocation of orders priority

- Underwriters and conflicts of interest
- Control relationships
- Reoffering yields
- Blue List
- When-issued
- Good delivery
- Alternative minimum tax (AMT)
- Municipal bond insurance
- Ratings for municipal bonds
- Additional Municipal Securities Rulemaking Board (MSRB) Rules
- The *G* Rules, specifically G-6, G-7, G-10, G-11, G-12, G-13, G-15, G-16, G-17, G-18, G-19, G-20, G-21, G-22, G-23, G-24, G-25, G-27, G-28, G-29, G-30, G-31, G-32, G-33, G-37, and G-39
- Enforcers of MSRB rules
- Reciprocal agreement
- Forms of ownership (bearer, registered as to principal only, fully registered, and book entry) (see Chapter 7)
- Zero-coupon municipal securities
- Municipal bond quotes (basis price, dollar price) (see Chapter 7)
- Original issue discount (OID)
- Factors affecting the marketability of municipal bonds (rating, maturity, call features, coupon rate, block size, liquidity, dollar price, and so on)
- Diversification of municipal bonds
- Call or put features (see Chapter 7)
- Escrowed to maturity
- Accrued interest (see Chapter 7)
- Capital gains or losses
- Purchasing municipal securities on margin
- Tax-exempt commercial paper
- Basis points

Part III

Delving Deeper: Security Investments with a Twist

The 5th Wave   By Rich Tennant

"The first thing we should do is get you two into a good mutual fund. Let me get out the 'Magic 8-Ball' and we'll run some options."

In this part . . .

Besides stocks and bonds, you have to be familiar with other security investment categories, first to pass the Series 7 exam and then to be more successful in your career as a stockbroker. In this part, I introduce the process by which investors open margin accounts to borrow money for purchasing securities. I also discuss the role of investment companies in helping investors diversify their portfolios. Next, I explain limited partnerships — their formation, function, structure, tax advantages, and tax disadvantages. Last but not least, I introduce you to options, an investment vehicle that allows investors to buy and sell securities at a fixed price; and just as importantly, I provide you with simple charts that help you master difficult options math calculations for the Series 7 exam.

Chapter 9

Borrowing Money and Securities: The Long and Short of Margin Accounts

· ·

· ·

*T*his chapter describes the process by which investors borrow money from a broker-dealer to purchase securities or borrow the securities themselves. The good news for you as a registered rep is that this process allows you to sell more securities than a customer may normally purchase, thus leading to more money in your pocket (a greater commission). However, margin accounts are not without an additional degree of risk (which a lot of people found out back in 1929). Margin accounts are great if the securities held in the account are going in the right direction but horrible if they aren't.

In this chapter, I cover the Series 7 exam topics relating to short and long margin accounts and show you how to put those math skills to use. I also suggest related topics to study in the "For Further Review" section at the end of this chapter. And of course, I give you plenty of practice questions.

Practice a lot of these questions because this stuff is tricky. The biggest mistake students make is mixing up the equations for long and short accounts. By doing the equations over and over again, you can avoid this pitfall. Additionally, the more questions that you practice now, the easier the calculations will be for you to recall when you're taking the real exam.

Introducing Long and Short Margin Accounts

In margin accounts, investors either borrow some money to buy securities or borrow the securities themselves. As a result, margin accounts come in two varieties: long and short.

As you may remember, *long* means *to buy*. With a *long margin account,* the customer buys securities by coming up with a certain percentage of the purchase price of the securities and borrowing the balance from the broker-dealer. These optimistic investors are hoping for a bull market, because they want to sell the securities sometime later for a profit.

With a *short margin account,* an investor is borrowing securities to immediately sell in the market. The process sounds a bit backwards, but the investor is selling things he or she doesn't actually own yet. Hopefully, for this bearish customer, the price of the security will decrease so the investor can purchase the shares in the market at a lower price and then return them to the lender.

When a customer buys securities, he or she can purchase the securities in a cash or margin account, but when a customer sells short securities, the transaction must be executed in a margin account.

Playing by the Federal Reserve Board's Rules

The Securities Exchange Act of 1934 gives the Federal Reserve Board (FRB) the authority to regulate the extension of credit to customers in the securities industry. In addition to Regulation T (see the following section), the FRB decides which securities can be purchased on margin. All exchange-listed stocks and bonds, NASDAQ stocks, and non-NASDAQ over-the-counter issues approved by the FRB can be purchased on margin. (Chapter 13 can tell you more about the FRB and its role in influencing money supply.)

Regulation T

Regulation T is the Federal Reserve Board rule that covers the credit broker-dealers may extend to customers who are purchasing securities. Currently for margin accounts both long and short, Regulation T (Reg T) requires customers to deposit at least 50 percent of the current market value of the securities purchased on margin, and the balance is borrowed from the broker-dealer.

Regulation T is currently set at 50 percent; however, firms not willing to take as much risk may increase the house margin requirement to 55 percent, 60 percent, 65 percent, and so on. When you're taking the Series 7 exam, you should assume 50 percent unless the question states a different percentage.

Regulation T applies not only to margin accounts but also to cash accounts (see Chapter 16). When customers are purchasing securities in cash accounts, they have a certain number of business days to pay for the trade (one, three, or five). This delay is an extension of credit; therefore, it falls under Regulation T.

Reg T also identifies which securities can be purchased on margin and which ones can't. Securities that may be purchased on margin include

- Exchange-listed securities
- NASDAQ stocks
- Non-NASDAQ over-the-counter (OTC) securities approved by the Federal Reserve Board

Margin call

A *margin call* (also know as a *Fed call, federal call,* or *Reg T call*) is the broker-dealer's demand for a customer to deposit money in a margin account when purchasing or shorting (selling short) securities. If a customer is buying securities on margin, a customer may also deposit fully paid securities to meet the margin call.

For both long and short margin accounts, the margin call is the dollar amount of securities purchased (or shorted) multiplied by Regulation T (50 percent). So, for example, if an investor purchases $50,000 worth of securities on margin, the margin call would be $25,000. Here's how you figure that:

Margin call = the current market value of the securities × Reg T

= $50,000 × 50% = $25,000

Opening a Margin Account: The Initial Requirements

The initial margin requirements for short and long accounts apply to the *first* transaction in a margin account only. After the account is established, the investor can purchase or short securities just by depositing Regulation T of the current market value of the securities purchased or shorted.

For an initial purchase in a margin account, customers must deposit a minimum of equity in their margin accounts. Currently, Regulation T calls for a minimum deposit of 50 percent of the current market value of the securities purchased or sold short. However, the National Association of Securities Dealers (NASD) and the New York Stock Exchange (NYSE) call for a minimum deposit of $2,000 or ask customers to pay for the securities in full.

 Pay attention to the wording of the question. Phrases like "opens a margin account," "in an initial transaction in a margin account," and so on indicate that the question is asking for the initial margin requirement rather than a margin call (see the preceding section for info on margin calls).

Starting long accounts

To open a long margin account, the customer is required to deposit Regulation T or $2,000, whichever is greater. The exception to this rule occurs when a customer is purchasing less than $2,000 worth of securities on margin. In this case, the customer pays for the transaction in full. It certainly wouldn't make sense for a customer to purchase $1,000 of securities on margin and pay $2,000 when he or she could pay $1,000 if it were purchased in a cash account. Even if the customer pays in full, the account is still considered a margin account because the customer can make future purchases on margin as soon as he or she has over $2,000 in equity.

Table 9-1 shows you how Regulation T and the NASD/NYSE requirements affect how much customers have to deposit when opening long margin accounts.

Table 9-1	Deposit Requirements for Long Margin Accounts		
Dollar Amount of Purchase	*Regulation T Requirement*	*NASD/NYSE Requirement*	*Customer Must Deposit*
$6,000	$3,000	$2,000	$3,000
$3,000	$1,500	$2,000	$2,000
$1,000	$500	$1,000	$1,000

In short, here's how much an investor has to deposit:

Purchase Price	Amount Owed
Initial purchase < $2,000	Pay in full
$2,000 ≤ initial purchase ≤ $4,000	$2,000
Initial purchase > $4,000	Reg T (50% of market value)

Opening short accounts

The minimum deposit for short accounts is fairly easy to remember. The $2,000 minimum required by the NASD and NYSE applies to short margin accounts. Because of the additional risk investors take when selling short securities, the $2,000 minimum always applies, even if the customer is selling short only $300 worth of securities. In this case, the customer must deposit 50 percent of the current market value of securities or $2,000, whichever is greater. Here's the breakdown:

Purchase Price	Amount Owed
Initial purchase ≤ $4,000	$2,000
Initial purchase > $4,000	Reg T (50% of market value)

Calculating Debit and Equity in Long Margin Accounts

The Series 7 asks you to calculate the numbers in a long margin account, which isn't too difficult if you take it one step at a time. The basic long margin account formula is as follows:

$$LMV - DR = EQ$$

In other words, *long market value minus debit balance equals equity.* The following sections describe the variables of this equation.

Long market value . . .

The *long market value* (LMV) is the current market value of the securities purchased in a margin account. The LMV does not remain fixed; it changes as the market value of the securities changes. Certainly, if an investor is long (owns) the securities, he or she would want the LMV to increase.

When a customer purchases securities on margin, the margin call (the amount the customer has to come up with) is based on the LMV of the securities. With Regulation T set at 50 percent, an investor would have to deposit 50 percent of the value of the securities purchased on margin.

. . . *Minus debit balance* . . .

DR is the *debit balance* (also called the *debit record* or *debit register*); it's the amount of money that a customer owes a brokerage firm after purchasing securities on margin. The debit balance remains the same unless the customer pays back a portion of the amount borrowed by either selling securities in the account or by adding money to the account through dividends or payments.

Note: Although you aren't as likely to see a question about it on the Series 7 exam, the debit balance may be increased by interest charges imposed by the broker-dealer.

So, for example, if an investor purchases $20,000 worth of securities on margin, the debit balance would be $10,000. First you have to determine the margin call:

Margin call = LMV × Reg T

= $20,000 × 50% = $10,000

Then use the margin call and the following formula to determine the debit balance:

DR = LMV – margin call

= $20,000 – $10,000 = $10,000

. . . *Equals equity*

The *equity* (EQ) is the investor's portion of the account. When an investor initially opens a margin account, the equity is equal to the margin call. However, the equity changes as the market value of the securities in the account increases or decreases. When an investor has more equity than the Regulation T requirement, he or she has excess equity, and if an investor has less equity than the Regulation T requirement, his or her account would be restricted (see the later "Checking out restricted accounts" section).

Note: When an investor has excess equity, he or she develops SMA (see "Let the Good Times Roll: Handling Excess Equity," later in the chapter). Remember that the SMA is built into the equity, not an addition to it. When a customer uses or removes SMA, the equity decreases and the debit balance increases.

Putting it all together

The following question tests your ability to determine the debit balance in a long margin account:

Mr. Downey buys 1,000 shares of DEF common stock at $40 in a margin account. After Mr. Downey meets the margin call, what is the debit balance?

(A) $16,000

(B) $20,000

(C) $24,000

(D) $30,000

The answer is B. I know what you're thinking: "This is too easy." If the Series 7 gods are smiling down on you, you may actually get a question this straightforward. However, even if you don't, you still need a starting point, and this is a good one. First, set up the equation:

$$LMV - DR = EQ$$

Mr. Downey purchased $40,000 worth of stock (1,000 shares × $40 per share), so you need to enter $40,000 under the LMV (long market value). Next, figure out how much he needs to pay. Multiply the $40,000 × 50 percent (Regulation T), and you know that Mr. Downey has to come up with $20,000, which goes under the EQ (the investor's portion of the account). If the LMV is $40,000 and the EQ is $20,000, the DR (debit balance) has to be $20,000:

$$\$40,000 - DR = \$20,000$$
$$DR = \$20,000$$

Making Short Work of Calculations in Short Margin Accounts

On the Series 7 exam, you may be asked to calculate the numbers in a short margin account. You have to start by setting up the formula correctly. The basic short margin account formula is as follows:

$$SMV + EQ = CR$$

In other words, *short market value plus equity equals the credit balance.* The following sections describe the variables of this equation.

When a customer purchases securities, he or she has the choice of whether to pay in full or purchase on margin. When a customer is selling short securities (selling borrowed securities), there is no option: The transactions must be executed in a margin account.

Short market value . . .

The *short market value* (SMV) is the current market value of the securities sold short in a margin account. Just as the LMV in a long account varies (see the earlier "Long market value . . ." section), so does the SMV. The SMV changes as the market value of the securities changes. If an investor is short the securities (sold borrowed securities), he or she would want the SMV to decrease so the customer could repurchase the securities at a lower price.

When a customer sells short securities on margin, the margin call (the amount the customer has to come up with) is based on the SMV of the securities. With Regulation T set at 50 percent, an investor would have to deposit 50 percent of the value of the securities purchased on margin.

. . . Plus equity . . .

The *equity* (EQ) is the investor's part of the account. When an investor initially opens a short margin account, the equity is equal to $2,000 or Reg T (50 percent of the market value of the security), whichever is greater.

In a short margin account, the equity increases when the SMV of the securities decreases; when the SMV of the securities increases, the equity decreases.

When an investor has more equity than the Regulation T requirement, he or she has excess equity and develops SMA (see the upcoming section titled "Let the Good Times Roll: Handling Excess Equity"); if an investor has less equity than the Reg T requirement, the account is restricted (see "Checking out restricted accounts," later in this chapter).

. . . Equals the credit balance

There's no debit balance (DR) in a short margin account because investors aren't borrowing money; they're borrowing securities. Instead, short margin accounts have a *credit balance* (also called a *credit record, credit register,* or *CR* for short). The credit balance is initially made up of the amount of money the investor received for selling the stock short (the *short market value*) and the amount that the investor had to deposit into the margin account to pay for the trade (the *equity*). The credit balance remains fixed unless the investor removes excess equity, more securities are shorted, or the investor covers some of his or her short positions.

For example, if in an initial transaction in a margin account, an investor sells short $50,000 worth of securities, the credit balance is $75,000. First you determine the margin call:

> Margin call = SMV × Reg T (50%)
>
> = $50,000 × 50% = $25,000

Then use the margin call and the following formula to determine the credit balance:

> CR = SMV + margin call
>
> = $50,000 + $25,000 = $75,000

Putting the equation together

The following question tests your ability to determine the credit balance in a short margin account:

In an existing short margin account, Melissa Rice sold short 1,000 shares of HIJ common stock at $30. Prior to this transaction, the short market value of securities in the account was $52,000 and the equity was $25,000. What is Melissa's credit balance after the transaction?

(A) $15,000

(B) $45,000

(C) $77,000

(D) $122,000

The answer is D. This question is a little more difficult because the transaction happened in an existing margin account. Prior to this transaction, Melissa had a short market value (SMV) of $52,000 and an equity of $25,000, which means that the CR was $77,000:

> SMV + EQ = CR
>
> $52,000 + $25,000 = CR
>
> CR = $77,000

Because you know the existing CR, you only need to determine what happened to it as a result of the new transaction. Melissa shorted another $30,000 worth of stock (1,000 shares × $30 per share), so you need to enter $30,000 under the SMV (short market value). Next, figure out how much she needs to pay. Multiply the $30,000 × 50 percent (Regulation T), and you know that Melissa has to come up with $15,000, which goes under the EQ (the investor's portion of the account). If the SMV increases by $30,000 and the EQ increases by $15,000, the CR (credit balance) has to increase by $45,000:

$$SMV + EQ = CR$$
$$\$30,000 + \$15,000 = CR$$
$$CR = \$45,000$$

Because the initial credit balance was $77,000 and it increased by $45,000, the credit balance after the transaction is $122,000.

Let the Good Times Roll: Handling Excess Equity

Special memorandum account (SMA) is a line of credit that a customer can borrow from his or her margin account or use to purchase more securities on margin. If all is right in the universe and the market goes in the right direction, the customer actually has more equity in the margin account than needed, which generates SMA. If a customer removes the SMA, he or she is borrowing money from the margin account; therefore

- ✔ The equity is reduced for both long and short margin accounts
- ✔ The debit balance (the amount owed to the brokerage firm) is increased for long margin accounts
- ✔ The credit balance is decreased for short margin accounts

After SMA is generated in a long or short account, it doesn't go away until a customer uses it, even if the account becomes restricted (see "Checking out restricted accounts," later in this chapter, for info on restriction). You can think of SMA as establishing credit; after you establish credit (like on a credit card), it remains there until you use it.

SMA for long margin accounts

When an investor purchases on margin, that customer has a leveraged position, so he or she has an interest in a larger amount of securities than he or she would've had if he or she had paid in full. When a customer has a long margin account, excess equity is created when the value of the securities in the account increases and the equity in the account increases above the margin requirement.

The following question tests your ability to answer a question on excess equity:

Mrs. Glorious purchased 1,000 shares of DUD Corp. on margin at $50 per share. If DUD is currently trading at $70 per share, what is Mrs. Glorious' excess equity?

(A) $5,000

(B) $7,500

(C) $10,000

(D) $20,000

The answer is C. This question throws you a little curveball because you have to set up a new equation when the market price changes. You first need to find the debit balance. Mrs. Glorious purchased $50,000 worth of securities (1,000 shares at $50 per share), so enter $50,000 under the LMV (long market value). Then Mrs. Glorious had to deposit the Regulation T (50%) amount of the purchase, so enter $25,000 (50% × $50,000) under the EQ (the investor's portion of the account). This means she borrowed $25,000 (the DR) from the broker-dealer:

$$LMV - DR = EQ$$
$$\$50,000 - DR = \$25,000$$
$$DR = \$25,000$$

Now the curveball: Next, the LMV changes to $70,000 ($70 × 1,000 shares). Because the DR (the amount borrowed from the broker-dealer) doesn't change, you bring the $25,000 to your new equation. You find that the EQ has increased to $45,000:

$$LMV - DR = EQ$$
$$\$70,000 - \$25,000 = EQ$$
$$\$45,000 = EQ$$

Now multiply the LMV by Regulation T to get the margin requirement, the amount that Mrs. Glorious should have in EQ to be at 50 percent. Take the $35,000 ($70,000 × 50%) and compare it to the EQ. Because Mrs. Glorious has $45,000 in equity, she has $10,000 in excess equity ($10,000 more than she needs):

$$Margin\ requirement = Reg\ T \times LMV$$
$$= 50\% \times \$70,000 = \$35,000$$

$$SMA = EQ - margin\ requirement$$
$$= \$45,000 - \$35,000 = \$10,000$$

The *R* in *DR* should help you remember that the debit balance *remains* the same as the market price changes.

SMA for short margin accounts

Unlike in a long account, an investor with a short margin account earns excess equity when the price of the securities in the margin account decreases. SMA is a credit line that investors can withdraw as cash or use to help purchase or sell short more securities on margin.

Excess equity is the amount of equity that a customer has in a margin account that's above the Regulation T requirement.

The following question tests your knowledge on determining excess equity for a short account:

Mrs. Rice sold short 1,000 shares of HIJ Corp. on margin at $60 per share. If HIJ is currently trading at $50 per share, what is Mrs. Rice's excess equity?

(A) $5,000

(B) $7,500

(C) $10,000

(D) $15,000

The answer is D. This question has a twist because you have to use a new equation when the market price changes. Start by setting up the equation to find the credit balance. Mrs. Rice sold short $60,000 worth of securities (1,000 shares at $60 per share), so enter $60,000 under the SMV (short market value). Then Mrs. Rice had to deposit the Regulation T (50%) amount of the purchase, so enter $30,000 (50% × $60,000) under the EQ (the investor's portion of the account). The credit balance (CR) has to be $90,000:

SMV + EQ = CR

$60,000 + $30,000 = CR

$90,000 = CR

Next, the SMV changes to $50,000 ($50 × 1,000 shares), so you need to calculate the investor's current equity. Put that value under the SMV. In a short account, the CR remains the same as the market price changes, so you need to bring the $90,000 straight down from the previous equation. This means that the EQ has increased to $40,000 (the difference between $50,000 and $90,000):

SMV + EQ = CR

$50,000 + EQ = $90,000

EQ = $40,000

Now multiply the SMV by Regulation T to get the amount that Mrs. Rice should have in equity to be at 50 percent. Compare the margin requirement of $25,000 ($50,000 × 50%) to the current equity. Because Mrs. Rice has $40,000 in equity, she has $15,000 in excess equity ($15,000 more than she needs):

Margin requirement = Reg T × SMV

= 50% × $50,000 = $25,000

SMA = EQ – margin requirement

= $40,000 – $25,000 = $15,000

The *R* in *CR* should help you remember that the credit balance *remains* the same as the market price changes.

Playing it SMA/RT: Using buying and shorting power for good

Buying power (for long accounts) and *shorting power* (for short accounts) are the dollar amount of securities a customer can purchase on margin using his or her excess equity (SMA). You calculate both by dividing the SMA by Reg T:

$$\text{Buying or shorting power} = \frac{\text{SMA}}{\text{Reg T}}$$

To help you calculate the buying or shorting power in a margin account, remember the phrase *People who are SMA/RT use their buying (or shorting) power.* This phrase can help you remember that to determine the buying or shorting power, you need to divide the SMA by Regulation T. As long as Regulation T is at 50 percent, you probably don't need this tip because the power will always be double the SMA ($1,000 SMA could purchase $2,000 worth of securities on margin). However, if Regulation T (or house requirements) is anything other than 50 percent, this formula becomes very important.

Try your hand at the following question:

Mr. Smith has a long margin account with a market value of $20,000, a debit balance of $5,000, an equity of $15,000, and an SMA of $3,000. If Regulation T is set at 60 percent, what is the buying power?

(A) $3,000

(B) $5,000

(C) $6,000

(D) No buying power

The answer is B. Because the question is nice enough to supply you with the SMA, you didn't have to figure it on your own. The buying power of a margin account is how much in securities an investor can buy (or sell short) without depositing additional funds. All you need to do is divide the SMA by Regulation T:

$$\text{Buying power} = \frac{\text{SMA}}{\text{Reg T}} = \frac{\$3,000}{60\%} = \$5,000$$

Looking at Limits When the Market Goes the Wrong Way

Often, securities don't go in the direction customers hope for. When this happens in a margin account, investors lose money at an accelerated rate. If the equity in a margin account drops below the Regulation T (or house) requirement, the account becomes restricted. However, if the equity in a long margin account drops below 25 percent (30 percent for a short account), the situation becomes much more serious. Read on for info on restricted accounts and minimum maintenance.

Checking out restricted accounts

In previous sections, everything has been coming up roses, but what if the market price of the securities held in a long margin account decreases instead of increasing? What if the securities in a short margin account show wild success? If this happens, the account becomes restricted. *Restricted accounts* show up when the equity in the account is below the margin requirement. However, a restricted account doesn't mean that investors can't buy (or short) securities in the margin account; investors may still buy or short securities in the margin account by coming up with the margin requirement of the new purchase.

Restricted long margin accounts

A restricted account is calculated the same way as the excess equity (see the earlier section "Let the Good Times Roll: Handling Excess Equity"), only the investor has less than 50 percent of the long market value (LMV) in equity instead of more than 50 percent. Check out the following example:

Macy Bullhorn purchased 500 shares of LMN common stock on margin when LMN was trading at $30 per share. If LMN is currently trading at $25 per share, by how much is Macy's margin account restricted?

(A) $1,250

(B) $2,500

(C) $5,000

(D) $6,250

The answer is A. You may notice the similarities between figuring out excess equity and determining whether an account is restricted. If an account is restricted, the account contains less equity than needed to be at 50 percent of the LMV. First figure out Macy's debit balance. Macy purchased $15,000 worth of securities (500 shares at $30 per share), so enter $15,000 under the LMV (long market value). Then Macy had to deposit the Reg T (50 percent) amount of the purchase, so enter $7,500 (50% × $15,000) under the EQ (the investor's portion of the account). She borrowed $7,500 (the DR) from the broker-dealer:

$$LMV - DR = EQ$$
$$\$15,000 - DR = \$7,500$$
$$DR = \$7,500$$

Next, find the investor's current equity. The LMV changed to $12,500 ($25 × 500 shares), so enter that under the LMV. Because the DR (the amount borrowed from the broker-dealer) doesn't change, you bring the $7,500 straight down from the preceding equation. You find that the EQ has decreased to $5,000 ($12,500 – $7,500):

$$LMV - DR = EQ$$
$$\$12,500 - \$7,500 = EQ$$
$$\$5,000 = EQ$$

Now multiply the LMV by Reg T to get the margin requirement, the amount Macy should have in equity to be at 50 percent. Take the $6,250 ($12,500 × 50%) and compare it to the current equity. Because Macy has only $5,000 in equity, her account is restricted by $1,250:

$$\text{Margin requirement} = Reg\ T \times LMV$$
$$= 50\% \times \$12,500 = \$6,250$$

$$\text{Restriction} = \text{margin requirement} - EQ$$
$$= \$6,250 - \$5,000 = \$1,250$$

You can calculate the excess equity (SMA) or determine whether an account is restricted in pretty much the same way. If the investor has more equity than needed, it's SMA; if the investor has less than needed, the account is restricted.

Restricted short margin accounts

If the market price of the securities held in a short margin account were to increase instead of decreasing, things wouldn't be so great. If this happens, the account becomes restricted. You can figure out whether the account is restricted the same way you figure out the excess equity, only the investor has less than 50 percent of the SMV in equity instead of more than 50 percent.

The following question tests your knowledge of restricted short accounts:

Mr. Willing sold short 400 shares of RST common stock on margin at $40 per share. If RST is currently trading at $44 per share, how much is the account restricted?

(A) $2,400

(B) $6,400

(C) $8,800

(D) $16,000

The answer is A. First figure out the credit balance. Mr. Willing sold short $16,000 worth of securities (400 shares at $40 per share), so enter $16,000 under the SMV (short market value). Then Mr. Willing had to deposit the Reg (50 percent) amount of the purchase, so enter $8,000 (50% × $16,000) under the EQ (the investor's portion of the account). This means that the credit balance (CR) has to be $24,000:

$$SMV + EQ = CR$$
$$\$16,000 + \$8,000 = CR$$
$$\$24,000 = CR$$

Next, find Mr. Willing's current equity. The SMV changes to $17,600 ($44 × 400 shares), so you need to put that under the SMV in a new equation. In a short account, the CR remains the same as the market price changes, so you need to bring the $24,000 straight from the preceding equation. You can see that the EQ has decreased to $6,100 (the difference between $17,600 and $24,000):

$$SMV + EQ = CR$$
$$\$17,600 + EQ = \$24,000$$
$$EQ = \$6,400$$

Now multiply the SMV by Regulation T to get the amount Mr. Willing should have in equity to be at 50 percent. Take the $8,800 ($17,600 × 50%) and compare it to the EQ. Because Mr. Willing has only $6,400 in equity, his account is restricted by $2,400 ($2,400 less than the Reg T requirement).

$$Margin\ requirement = Reg\ T \times SMV$$
$$= 50\% \times \$17,600 = \$8,800$$

$$Restriction = margin\ requirement - EQ$$
$$= \$8,800 - \$6,400 = \$2,400$$

Keeping up with minimum maintenance

A margin account can be left restricted, but if a margin account falls below minimum maintenance, the situation is much more serious. Customers have to deal with a *maintenance call* (or *maintenance margin call* or *Fed call*), which requires investors to deposit money into the margin account immediately.

Minimum maintenance on a long

Minimum maintenance on a long ma
I'm sure that you'll be happy to knov
accounts (see the preceding section

Mark Smithers III purchased 1,000 s
was trading at $55 per share. If UVV
maintenance call?

(A) $1,250

(B) $7,500

(C) $8,750

(D) $10,000

The answer is A. You may notice that the equation looks almost exactly the same as the previous two examples except for the last step. An account may be left restricted, but if it falls below minimum maintenance, the customer must come up with enough money (or fully paid securities) to bring the account above minimum maintenance right away.

First find use the market value at the time of purchase to determine the debit balance. Mark purchased $55,000 worth of securities (1,000 shares at $55 per share), so enter $55,000 under the LMV (long market value). Then Mark had to deposit the Reg T (50%) amount of the purchase, so enter $27,500 (50% × $55,000) under the EQ (the customer's portion of the account). You find that he borrowed $27,500 (the DR) from the broker-dealer:

$$LMV - DR = EQ$$
$$\$55,000 - DR = \$27,500$$
$$DR = \$27,500$$

Then find Mark's current equity. The LMV changed to $35,000 ($35 × 1,000 shares), so you need to put that value under the LMV. Because the DR (the amount borrowed from the broker-dealer) doesn't change, you bring the $27,500 straight down. Therefore, the EQ has decreased to $7,500:

$$LMV - DR = EQ$$
$$\$35,000 - \$27,500 = EQ$$
$$\$7,500 = EQ$$

Now multiply the LMV by the 25 percent minimum maintenance requirement to get the amount Mark should have in equity to be at minimum maintenance. Take the $8,750 ($35,000 × 25%) and compare it to the current equity. Because Mike has only $7,500 in equity, he'll receive a maintenance call of $1,250:

$$Maintenance\ EQ = minimum\ maintenance\ \% \times LMV$$
$$= 25\% \times \$35,000 = \$8,750$$

$$Maintenance\ call = maintenance\ EQ - EQ$$
$$= \$8,750 - \$7,500 = \$1,250$$

Minimum maintenance on a short account

As with long margin accounts, short margin accounts can be left restricted, but if a margin account falls below minimum maintenance, the customer gets hit with a maintenance call. Minimum maintenance on a short margin account is 30 percent of the current market value. The rest of the calculations are similar to figuring out the SMA or how much the account is restricted (see "Checking out restricted accounts," earlier in this chapter) until you get to the last step.

Minimum maintenance for a long account is 25 percent of the current market value, and minimum maintenance on a short account is 30 percent of the current market value.

The following question tests your knowledge in determining the maintenance call for short accounts:

Mrs. Martinez sold short 1,000 shares of XYZ common stock on margin at $50 per share. If XYZ is currently trading at $60 per share, what is the maintenance call?

(A) $0

(B) $2,000

(C) $3,000

(D) $8,000

The answer is C. First find Mrs. Martinez's credit balance. Mrs. Martinez sold short $50,000 worth of securities (1,000 shares at $50 per share), so enter $50,000 under the SMV (short market value). Then Mrs. Martinez had to deposit the Reg T (50 percent) amount of the purchase, so enter $25,000 (50% × $50,000) under the EQ (the investor's portion of the account). The credit balance (CR) has to be $75,000:

$$SMV + EQ = CR$$
$$\$50,000 + \$25,000 = CR$$
$$\$75,000 = CR$$

Next, find Mrs. Martinez's current equity. The SMV changed to $60,000 ($60 × 1,000 shares), so you need to put that value under the SMV. In a short account, the CR remains the same as the market price changes, so the CR is $75,000. Therefore, the equity has decreased to $15,000:

$$SMV + EQ = CR$$
$$\$60,000 + EQ = \$75,000$$
$$EQ = \$15,000$$

Now multiply the SMV by 30 percent to get the amount Mrs. Martinez should have in equity to be at minimum maintenance. Take the $18,000 ($60,000 × 30%) and compare it to the equity. Because Mrs. Martinez has only $15,000 in equity, she'll receive a maintenance call of $3,000:

$$Maintenance\ EQ = minimum\ maintenance\ \% \times SMV$$
$$= 30\% \times \$60,000 = \$18,000$$

$$Maintenance\ call = maintenance\ EQ - EQ$$
$$= \$18,000 - \$15,000 = \$3,000$$

For Further Review

I want you to be as prepared as possible to answer any possible margin question that can come your way on the Series 7 exam. Although I cover the main topics related to margin accounts and hopefully have given you some more confidence when answering margin math questions, you also need to have a good understanding of the items that follow to be truly prepared to ace the margin questions on the exam:

- Margin requirement for U.S. government securities and municipal bonds
- Waiting period for buying new securities on margin
- Credit agreement
- Loan consent form
- Which securities can be purchased on margin and which ones can't
- Effect of dividends or cash deposits on a margin account
- Effect of interest charges on long margin accounts
- Calculating combined long and short margin accounts
- Loan value
- Hypothecation and rehypothecation
- Buying and selling simultaneously
- Where the money goes when securities are sold
- Dollar value of securities that must be deposited or liquidated to meet a margin/maintenance call
- Margin requirement when selling short low-priced securities
- LEAPS (long-term options) purchased on margin

Chapter 10

Delivering Diversification with Packaged Securities

Diversification is key when you're helping customers set up a portfolio of securities, and it's fairly easy when your customer has a good deal of money to invest. But what if an investor has limited resources? Certainly, such investors can't afford to buy several different securities, and you don't want to limit your customer to only one (heaven forbid it should go belly up). Packaged securities to the rescue! These securities, such as investment companies, REITs, and annuities, offer variety within one security by investing a customer's money in a diversified pool of securities . . . for a fee, of course. A bit of profit-driven teamwork can ensure your customers' investments are much safer than, say, the blackjack tables in Vegas.

In this chapter, I cover topics relating to investment companies, REITs, and annuities. Mutual funds and closed investment funds are only the beginning. I also discuss face-amount certificate companies, trusts like UITs and REITs, and annuities. The "For Further Review" section at the end of this chapter can help you round out your studies, and the practice questions in this chapter may put you in that question-answering mood.

Diversifying through Management Investment Companies

The Investment Company Act of 1940 divides investment companies into three main types: management investment companies, face-amount certificate companies, and unit investment trusts. This section focuses on management investment companies, which the Series 7 tests more than the other types. I cover the other types in the aptly named "Considering Other Investment Company Options" section later on.

Management companies, which are by far the most familiar type of investment company, are actively managed by a portfolio manager, who receives a fee for making investment decisions for a fund.

Comparing open- and closed-end funds

Management companies have to be either open-end or closed-end funds. Make sure you know the difference between the two.

Closed-end funds

Unlike open-end funds, closed-end funds have a fixed number of shares outstanding (hence the word *closed*). Closed-end funds act more like stock than open-end funds because they issue new shares to the public, and after that, the shares are bought and sold in the market. Because they trade on the market, they're often called *publicly traded funds*. Although the net asset value of closed-end and open-end funds are figured the same, the public offering price is determined a little differently:

- **Net asset value (NAV):** The net asset value or net asset value per share is the parity price where the fund should be trading. You determine it by dividing the value of the securities held by the fund by the number of shares outstanding. Only closed-end funds may trade below the NAV (at a discount).

- **Public offering price (POP):** For closed-end funds, the public offering price (the ask price) depends more on supply and demand than the NAV. Investors of closed-end funds pay the POP (current market price) plus a broker's commission.

Note: Although closed-end funds are not purchased from and redeemed with the issuer, they do offer a high degree of liquidity. After the initial offering, they can be purchased or sold either on an exchange or over-the-counter (OTC).

Open-end (mutual) funds

An open-end fund is more commonly known as a *mutual fund*. As with closed-end funds, mutual funds invest in many different securities to provide diversification for investors. The key difference is that mutual funds are constantly issuing and redeeming shares, which provides liquidity for investors. Because open-end fund shares are continuous offerings of new shares, a mutual fund prospectus must always be available. You need to understand the makings of the net asset value and the public offering price when taking the Series 7 exam:

- **Net asset value (NAV):** Fortunately, the net asset value or net asset value per share is determined the same way for both open and closed-end funds — by dividing the securities held by the fund by the number of shares outstanding; however, with open-end funds, the NAV is the bid price. When investors redeem shares of a mutual fund, they receive the NAV. Mutual funds can't ever trade below the NAV.

- **Public offering price (POP):** For mutual funds, the public offering price (the ask price) is the *NAV plus a sales charge.*

  If a mutual fund doesn't charge a sales charge, it's called a *no-load fund.*

Open and closed: Focusing on their differences

You can expect at least a few of the Series 7 questions relating to investment companies to test you on the differences between open-end and closed-end funds. Table 10-1 should help you zone in on the major distinctions.

Table 10-1	Comparing Open-End and Closed-End Funds	
Category	*Closed-End*	*Open-End*
Capitalization	One-time offering of securities (fixed number of shares outstanding)	Continuous offering of new shares (no fixed number of shares outstanding)
Pricing the fund	Investors purchase at the current market value (public offering price, or POP) plus a commission	Investors purchase at the net asset value (NAV) plus a sales charge
Issues	Common stock, preferred stock, and debt securities	Common stock only
Shares purchased	Shares can be purchased in full only	Shares can be purchased in full or fractions (up to three decimal places)
Purchased and sold	Initial public offerings go through underwriters; after that, investors purchase and sell shares either over-the-counter or on an exchange (no redemption)	Shares are sold and redeemed by the fund only

The key difference between open-end and closed-end funds is the method of capitalization. An open-end (mutual) fund is a continuous offering of new securities, and a closed-end fund is a one-time offering of new securities.

Keeping your customer's investment objectives in mind

Unlike investors in face-amount certificate companies and unit investment trusts (see "Considering Other Investment Company Options," still to come), investors of open-end and closed-end funds have many choices available. Investors may be looking for safety, growth, a combination, and so on. This section gives you a glimpse into those investment choices.

The single most important consideration for customers who invest in investment companies is the fund's investment objectives. This feature surpasses even the sales charge or management fees. As a registered rep, one of your primary jobs will be to help investors decide which type of fund would be best for them. The test-designers want to know you can handle that job. Comparing between like-type funds is secondary. So without further ado, here are the major types (although variables within each fund can make a fund riskier or safer, I've placed the list in the normal order from safest to riskiest):

✔ **Money market fund:** This fund (as you've probably guessed) invests in money market instruments (short-term debt securities). You need to know the specifics of this fund more than other ones. Here are the key points:

- They usually provide a check-writing feature (they give you a checkbook) as a way of redeeming shares.
- They are always no-load (there's no sales charge).
- They compute dividends daily and credit them monthly.
- There's no penalty for early redemption.

- **Income fund:** The primary objective of income funds is to provide current revenue (not growth) for investors. This type of fund invests most of its assets in a diversified portfolio of debt securities that pay interest and in preferred and common stock of companies that are known to pay consistent dividends in cash.

    Income funds are considered much safer (more conservative investments) than growth funds. You can assume for Series 7 exam (and real life) purposes that income funds are better investment choices for retirees and investors who are looking for a steady cash flow without much risk.

- **Balanced fund:** A balance fund is a combination of a growth fund and income fund. Balanced funds invest in common stocks, preferred stocks, long-term bonds, and short-term bonds, aiming to provide both income and capital appreciation while minimizing risk. These funds don't get hammered too badly when the market is bearish but usually underperform when the market is bullish.

- **Growth fund:** This fund is exactly what you'd expect it to be; growth funds invest most of their assets in a diversified portfolio of the common stock of relatively new companies, looking for big increases in the stock prices. Growth funds offer a higher potential for growth but usually at a higher risk for the investor. This type of fund is ideal for an investor who's looking for long-term capital appreciation potential.

    Because of the inherent risk of investing in growth funds, they're better for younger investors who can take the risk because they have more time to recover their losses.

- **Specialized (sector) fund:** A specialized or sector fund is a type of fund that invests primarily in the securities of a single industry or geographical area. A specialized fund may invest only in financial services, health care, automotive stocks, Japanese securities, and so on. Because specialized funds are limited in their investments, you can assume that they're a little riskier than the average fund.

- **Hedge fund:** This fund that uses leverage (purchasing on margin — see Chapter 9), options (Chapter 12), short sales, and other speculative investment strategies. Hedge funds usually perform better in a bearish market than the other funds do. This fund is considered the most speculative (riskiest) investment company.

The key thing is not to let the variety of funds distract you too much. So many different funds are out there that the choices could drive you crazy. I list the main types, but funds could invest by objective (as listed above) or composition, such as with foreign stock funds (which invest in foreign securities), tax-exempt funds (which invest in municipal bonds), U.S. government funds, and so on. The composition of the fund should help you match it with your customer's objectives. For instance, a customer looking for safety and income may invest in a U.S. government bond fund.

Dealing with discounts and methods of investing

Investors who have the extra funds available may be able to receive a reduced sales charge for large dollar purchases. Breakpoints and the letter of intent are available to investors of open-end funds only. Dollar cost averaging and fixed share averaging are most often used for open-end fund purchases but may apply to other investments as well.

Breakpoints

Funds have an investment adviser (portfolio manager) who gets paid a percentage of the value of the securities held in the fund. Therefore, one way to entice investors to spend more is to reduce the sales charge when they spend a certain minimum amount of money. That's where the breakpoint comes in.

Management investment companies divide purchase amounts into different tiers. Within a certain range, investors all pay the same sales charge percent. But when investors spend enough to put them in the next tier (when they hit the *breakpoint*), they get a reduced sales charge. Breakpoints have no set schedule, so they vary from fund to fund.

Here are a few key points for you to remember for the Series 7 exam:

✔ Breakpoints must be disclosed in the prospectus.

✔ Breakpoints are *not* available to partnerships or *investment clubs* (several people pooling money together to receive reduced sales charges)

✔ Breakpoints are generally available to individual investors, joint accounts with family members, and corporations.

Letters of intent

A *letter of intent* (LOI) signed by an investor allows him or her to receive a breakpoint (quantity discount) right away with the initial purchase, even if the investor didn't yet deposit enough money to get the breakpoint. This document states that as long as the investor deposits enough within a 13-month period, he or she will receive the discounted sales charge right away.

Here are a few specifics about the letter of intent that you need to know for the Series 7:

✔ The investor has *13 months* after the first deposit to live up to the terms of the letter of intent in order to maintain the reduced sales charge.

✔ The LOI may be *backdated for up to 90 days*, meaning that it may apply to a previous purchase. However, remember that if the LOI applies to a previous purchase, the 13-month period starts from the date of that transaction.

✔ While the investor is under the letter of intent, shares are held in escrow to pay for the difference in the sales charge. If the investor doesn't live up to the terms of the obligation, the fund sells the shares held in escrow.

Here's how a letter of intent may work. Suppose, for instance, that Mr. Smith purchased $2,000 worth of ABC Growth Fund two months ago and has another $7,000 to invest in the fund right now. Mr. Smith believes that he'll keep investing in ABC Growth Fund and would like to get a reduced sales charge for investments of $10,000 and up (see Table 10-2 for the breakpoints).

Table 10-2	Breakpoints for ABC Growth Fund
Purchase Amount	*Sales Charge*
$1–$9,999	7%
$10,000–$19,999	6%
$20,000–$39,999	4%
$40,000 and up	2%

Mr. Smith signs a letter of intent and would like it to apply to his previous purchase. Because his previous purchase was two months ago, Mr. Smith has only another 11 months to invest the remaining $8,000 into ABC Growth Fund. Mr. Smith will receive the 6 percent sales charge on his $7,000 investment right now, which would be reduced by the overage he paid on the previous investment of $2,000. In other words, he'll pay only $400 sales charge on the current investment ($420 for this transaction minus the $20 overpaid from the previous investment) when he invests the $7,000. As long as Mr. Smith deposits the additional $1,000 by the end of the letter of intent's time frame, he'll pay the 6 percent sales charge. However, if Mr. Smith doesn't live up to the terms of the agreement, ABC Growth fund will sell the shares held in escrow to pay for the difference in the sales charge.

Investors may redeem their shares at any time. Even if an investor is under the letter of intent, he or she may still redeem the shares. The letter of intent is binding on the fund only.

Dollar cost averaging

If an investor is employing the *dollar-cost-averaging* formula, he or she is investing the same dollar amount into the same investment periodically. Although dollar cost averaging is primarily used for mutual funds, people can use it for other investments as well. Dollar cost averaging benefits the investor when the price of the security is *fluctuating*. The investor ends up buying more shares when the price is low and fewer shares when the price is high by depositing the same amount of money each time he or she makes a purchase.

Dollar cost averaging results in an *average cost per share* that is *lower than the average price per share* if the price of the fund fluctuates.

The following question tests your understanding of dollar cost averaging:

Mrs. Johnson deposits $1,000 into DEF growth fund in four separate months. The purchase prices of the fund are as follows:

> **Month 1:** $40
>
> **Month 2:** $50
>
> **Month 3:** $50
>
> **Month 4:** $40

What is the average cost per share for Mrs. Johnson?

(A) $40.00

(B) $44.44

(C) $45.00

(D) $48.35

The answer is B. On the surface, this question may look very easy to you, but answer C is the average price per share, not the average cost. Remember that because Mrs. Johnson is investing the same amount of money each month, she's able to buy more shares when the price is low and less when the price is high. In the first and fourth months, when the price was $40 per share, she was able to buy 25 shares each time. In the second and third month, she was able to buy only 20 shares each time:

1st and 4th months: $\dfrac{\$1,000 \text{ invested}}{\$40 \text{ per share}} = 25$ shares per month

2nd and 3rd months: $\dfrac{\$1,000 \text{ invested}}{\$50 \text{ per share}} = 20$ shares per month

Over the four months, Mrs. Johnson invested a total of $4,000 and purchased a total of 90 shares (25 + 20 + 20 + 25). The average cost per share is $44.44:

$$\text{Average cost per share} = \frac{\text{total amount invested}}{\text{No. of shares purchased}} = \frac{\$4,000}{90 \text{ shares}} = \$44.44$$

Use your sense of logic and watch for ways to eliminate answer choices, and you may get away with doing very little math. Here, you can answer the question by finding the average price per share, which is *not* what the question is looking for. With dollar cost averaging, buying more when the price is low drives the average cost down; therefore, the average cost per share has to be between the minimum price per share ($40) and the average price per share ($45). The only number that fits the criteria is $44.44, or choice B.

You should be prepared to calculate the average cost per share, the average price per share ($45), or the amount saved per share ($0.56).

Fixed share averaging

Fixed share averaging is a nice, easy concept that doesn't require you to remember any more formulas. *Fixed share averaging* is just buying the same number of shares of a security (20 shares, 50 shares, 100 shares, and so on) every so often (monthly, quarterly, and so on). Investors don't get any savings with this type of plan like they do with dollar cost averaging, but it does force investors to be disciplined and consistent with their investing.

Figuring the sales charge and public offering price of open-end funds

Yes, every chapter seems to have more formulas, but these formulas are pretty straightforward and shouldn't cause you too many sleepless nights. You need to know two basic formulas to determine the sales charge and public offering price of open-end funds.

Sales charge percent

The sales charge is part of the public offering price (POP), or ask price, not something tacked on afterward like a sales tax. One of the tricks for calculating the sales charge for open-end funds is remembering that the POP equals 100 percent. Therefore, if the sales charge is 8 percent, the net asset value (NAV) is 92 percent of the POP. The formula for determining the sales charge percent is as follows:

$$\text{Sales charge \%} = \frac{\text{ask} - \text{bid}}{\text{ask}} = \frac{\text{POP} - \text{NAV}}{\text{POP}}$$

The following question tests your expertise in calculating the sales charge of a mutual fund:

ABC Aggressive Growth Fund has a net asset value of $9.20 and a public offering price of $10.00. What is the sales charge percent?

(A) 6.8 percent

(B) 7.5 percent

(C) 8 percent

(D) 8.7 percent

The answer is C. The first thing that you have to do is set up the equation. Start with the POP of $10.00 and subtract the NAV of $9.20 to get $0.80. Next, divide the $0.80 by the POP of $10.00 to get the sales charge of 8 percent:

$$\text{Sales charge \%} = \frac{\text{POP} - \text{NAV}}{\text{POP}} = \frac{\$10.00 - \$9.20}{\$10.00} = \frac{\$0.80}{\$10.00} = 8\%$$

To help you remember that the ask (offer) price of a fund is the same as the POP, remember to *ask* your *POP* about it.

Public offering price (POP)

When taking the Series 7 exam, you may be asked to figure out the public offering price of a mutual fund when you're given only the sales charge percent and the NAV.

Remember, the sales charge is already a part of the POP, so the sales charge is *not* equal to the sales charge percent times the NAV. Use the following formula to figure out how much an investor has to pay to buy shares of the fund when you know only the NAV and the sales charge percent:

$$\text{Public offering price} = \frac{\text{net asset value}}{100\% - \text{sales charge \%}}$$

The following question tests your ability to answer a POP question:

DEF Aggressive Growth Fund has an NAV of $9.12 and a POP of $9.91. If there is a 5 percent sales charge for investments of $30,000 and up, how many shares can an investor who is depositing $50,000 purchase?

(A) 5,045.409 shares

(B) 5,208.333 shares

(C) 5,219.207 shares

(D) 5,482.456 shares

The answer is B. Don't let the decimals throw you off; mutual funds can sell fractional shares. This investor isn't going to be paying the POP of $9.91 per share because he or she is receiving a breakpoint for a large dollar purchase (see "Breakpoints," earlier in this chapter). To figure out the POP for this investor, set up the formula:

$$\text{POP} = \frac{\text{NAV}}{100\% - \text{sales charge \%}} = \frac{\$9.12}{100\% - 5\%} = \frac{\$9.12}{95\%} = \$9.60 \text{ per share}$$

After working out the formula, you see that the investor is paying $9.60 per share instead of $9.91. Next, determine the number of shares the investor can purchase by dividing the amount of the investment by the cost per share:

$$\frac{\$50,000 \text{ invested}}{\$9.60 \text{ per share}} = 5,208.333 \text{ shares}$$

This investor is able to purchase 5,208.333 shares because of the breakpoint. Without the breakpoint, the investor would've been able to purchase only 5,045.409 shares.

Considering Other Investment Company Options

A couple other types of investment companies — face-amount certificate companies and unit investment trusts (UITs) — aren't as popular as they used to be. Unfortunately, even though you may never sell any, you do need to know them for the Series 7 exam. You probably won't see more than a question or two on these topics.

Face-amount certificate companies

A *face-amount certificate* is a type of investment company that's similar to a zero-coupon bond (see Chapter 7); investors make either a lump sum payment or periodic payments in return for a larger future payment. The issuer of a face-amount certificate guarantees payment of the face amount (a fixed sum) to the investor at a preset date. Very few face-amount certificate companies are around today.

Unit investment trusts (UITs)

A *unit investment trust* (UIT) is a registered investment company that purchases a fixed portfolio of income-producing securities (typically bonds) and holds them in trust, which means that a UIT acts as a holding company for its investors. Then the company issues redeemable shares (units) that represent investors' interest in the trust. Any capital gains, interest, and/or dividends are passed on to shareholders at regular intervals. Here are the two main types of these trusts:

- **Fixed investment trust:** These companies invest in a portfolio of debt securities, and the trust terminates when all the bonds in the portfolio mature.
- **Participating trust:** These companies invest in shares of mutual funds. The mutual funds that the trust holds don't change, but the securities held by the underlying mutual funds do.

Because the portfolio of securities is fixed, UITs don't employ investment advisers and therefore have no investment adviser fees. Nice break!

Reducing Real Estate Risk with REITs

A *real estate investment trust* (REIT) is a trust that invests in real-estate-related projects such as properties, mortgage loans, and construction loans. REITs pool the capital of many investors to manage property and/or purchase mortgage loans. As with other trusts, they issue shares to investors representing their interest in the trust. REITs may be listed on an exchange or can trade over-the-counter (OTC) (see Chapter 14 for more info on markets). They also provide real estate diversification and liquidity for investors.

Equity REITs take equity positions in real estate properties; the income is derived from rent collected or profits made when the properties are sold. *Mortgage REITs* purchase construction loans and mortgages. The trust receives the interest paid on the loans and in turn passes it on to the owners of the trust (the investors).

REITs can *avoid* being taxed like a corporation if

- At least 75 percent of the income comes from real-estate-related activities
- At least 75 percent of the REITs assets are in real estate, government securities, and/or cash
- At least 90 percent of the net income received is distributed to shareholders (who pay taxes on the income)

Don't get REITs confused with real estate limited partnerships (which I cover in Chapter 11). Limited partnerships pass through income and write-offs to investors; REITs just pass through income.

Don't kill yourself worrying too much about REITs (not that you would); you shouldn't get more than one or two questions on the Series 7 exam relating to REITs.

Adding Annuities to a Portfolio

Annuities are similar to mutual funds, except annuities are designed to provide supplemental retirement income for investors. Life insurance companies issue annuities, and these investments provide guaranteed payments for the life of the holder. The Series 7 tests you on the two basic types of annuities, fixed and variable. Because variable annuities are considered securities and fixed annuities are not (because of the guaranteed payout), most of the annuity questions will be on variable annuities.

Gather very specific information about your client before making recommendations. Annuities have been under the watchful eye of state insurance commissions and the SEC due to inappropriate recommendations from some brokers. Annuities typically aren't recommended for younger clients, for clients older than 75, or for a client's entire investment portfolio. For information on portfolio and securities analysis, see Chapter 13.

Looking at fixed annuities

The main thing for you to remember about *fixed annuities* is that they have fixed rates of return that the issuer guarantees. Investors pay money into fixed annuities, and the money is deposited into the insurance company's general account. After the investor starts receiving payments from the fixed annuity (usually monthly), the payments remain the same for the remainder of the investor's life. Because of the guaranteed payout, fixed annuities are *not* considered securities and therefore are exempt from SEC registration requirements.

Because the payouts associated with a fixed annuity remain the same, they're subject to *purchasing power risk* (the risk that the investment won't keep up with inflation). An investor who received payments of $1,000 per month in the 1970s may have been able to survive; however, that amount today may not even pay the grocery bill.

Checking out variable annuities

Insurance companies introduced variable annuities as a way to keep pace with (or hopefully exceed) inflation. In a fixed annuity, the insurance company bears the inflation risk; however, in a variable annuity, the investment risk is borne by the investor. Because the investors assume the investment risk, variable annuities are considered securities and must be registered with the SEC. All variable annuities have to be sold with a prospectus, and only individuals who hold appropriate securities and insurance licenses can sell them.

The money that investors deposit is held in a *separate account* (separate from the insurance company's other business) because the money is invested differently. The separate account is invested in securities such as common stock, bonds, mutual funds, and so on, with the hope that the investments will keep pace with or exceed the inflation rate.

The *assumed interest rate* (AIR) is a projection of the performance of the securities in the separate account over the life of the variable annuity contract. If the assumed interest rate is 4 percent and the performance of the securities in the separate account is equal to 4 percent, the investor will receive the payouts that he or she expects. However, if the securities outperform the AIR, the investor will receive higher payouts than expected. And unfortunately, if the securities held in the separate account underperform the AIR, the investor will get lower payouts than expected.

Putting money into (and receiving money from) annuities

Investors have choices when purchasing annuities and getting distributions. Depending on investors' needs, they may choose a lump sum payment or multiple payments. Also, investors have a choice of how they want to get their distributions at retirement.

Looking at the pay-in phase

Payments into both fixed and variable annuities are made from after-tax dollars, meaning that the investor can't write the payments off on his or her taxes. However, payments into both fixed and variable annuities grow on a tax-deferred basis (are not taxed until the money is withdrawn). If an investor has contributed $80,000 into a variable annuity that's now worth $120,000, the investor would be taxed only on the $40,000 difference because he or she already paid taxes on the contribution. If an annuitant dies during the pay-in phase, most annuity contracts require a death benefit to be paid to the annuitant's beneficiary.

Note: During the pay-in phase, an investor of a variable annuity purchases *accumulation units*. These units are similar to shares of a mutual fund.

Investors have a few payment options to select when purchasing fixed or variable annuities. Here's the rundown of options:

- ✔ **Single payment deferred annuity:** An investor purchases the annuity with a lump sum payment, and the payouts are delayed until some pre-determined date.

- ✔ **Periodic payment deferred annuity:** An investor makes periodic payments (usually monthly) into the annuity, and the payouts are delayed until some pre-determined date; this is the most common type of annuity.

- ✔ **Immediate annuity:** An investor purchases the annuity with a large sum, and the payouts begin within a couple months.

Getting the payout

Investors of both fixed and variable annuities have several payout options. These options may cover just the *annuitant* (investor) or the annuitant and a survivor. No matter what type of payout option the investor chooses, he or she will be taxed on the amount above the contribution. The earnings grow on a tax-deferred basis, and the investor is not taxed on the earnings until withdrawal at retirement.

Note: During the payout phase of a variable annuity, accumulation units are converted into a fixed number of *annuity units.* Investors receive a fixed number of annuity units periodically (usually monthly) with a variable value, depending on the performance of the securities in the separate account.

When an investor purchases an annuity, he or she has to decide which of the payout options works best for him or her:

- **Life annuity:** This type of payment option provides income for the life of the *annuitant* (the individual covered by the annuity); however, after the annuitant dies, the insurance company stops making payments. This type of annuity is riskiest for the investor because if the annuitant dies earlier than expected, the insurance company gets to keep the leftover annuity money. Because it's the riskiest type of annuity for the annuitant, it has the highest payouts of all the options.

- **Life annuity with period certain:** This payout option guarantees payment to the annuitant for a minimum number of years (10, 20, and so on). For example, if the annuitant were to purchase an annuity with a 20-year guarantee and die after 7 years, a named beneficiary would receive the payments for the remaining 13 years.

- **Joint life with last survivor annuity:** This option guarantees payments over the lives of two individuals. As you can imagine, this type of annuity is typically set up for a husband and wife. If the wife dies first, the husband receives payments until his death. If the husband dies first, his wife receives payments until her death. Because this type of annuity covers the lifespans of two individuals, it has the lowest payouts.

All annuities have a *mortality guarantee.* This guarantee means that the investor receives payments as long as he or she lives, even if it's beyond his or her life expectancy.

For Further Review

Although I cover the main topics related to these packaged securities and hopefully have given you a leg up on your competition, you also need to have a good understanding of the items in the following list:

- Functions of the board of directors
- The custodian bank
- Transfer agent
- The investment adviser and fees
- The underwriter's functions
- Trust indenture
- Advertising
- Tax treatment
- Shareholders' rights
- Automatic reinvestments
- Redemption fee
- Payout or withdrawal plans

- ✔ Conversion privileges
- ✔ Regulated investment companies
- ✔ Conduit theory
- ✔ Constant dollar plan
- ✔ Forward pricing
- ✔ Maximum sales charge percent
- ✔ Contractual plans
- ✔ Margin on mutual funds
- ✔ Diversified investment companies
- ✔ Tax treatment of REITs
- ✔ Separate accounts investment policy
- ✔ Surrender value of accumulation units

Chapter 11

Working with Direct Participation Programs

. . . .

In This Chapter

▶ Understanding the specifics of DPPs

▶ Distinguishing a limited partner from a general partner

▶ Looking at the different types of DPPs

▶ Reviewing additional topics tested

. . . .

Direct participation programs (DPPs) can raise money to invest in real estate, oil and gas, equipment leasing, and so on. More commonly known as limited partnerships, these businesses are somewhat similar to corporations (stockholder owned companies). However, limited partners have some specific tax advantages (and disadvantages) that stockholders don't have. According to tax laws, limited partnerships are not taxed directly; the income or losses are passed directly through to the investors.

DPPs were once known as tax shelters because of the tax benefits to investors; however, tax law changes have taken away a lot of these advantages. As a result, DPPs have somewhat fallen out of favor for investors (though not entirely for the test designers).

In this chapter, I explain the differences between limited and general partners as well as the types of partnerships, their particular risks, and potential rewards. The info here can help you examine those risks and rewards and determine suitability for investors. You can also check out the "For Further Review" section at the end of this chapter for a list of related topics on the Series 7. As always, I give you some practice questions to go along with the rest of the questions in this book.

Searching for Identity: What DPPs Are (and Are Not)

As stockholders are owners of a corporation, limited (and general) partners are owners of a *direct participation program (DPP)*. The key difference for people investing in DPPs is that they'll be required to tie up their investment dollars for a long period of time, though they'll receive tax advantages for doing so. Most DPPs are set up for real estate projects, oil and gas projects, or equipment leasing.

The IRS determines whether an enterprise is a corporation or a limited partnership. For a limited partnership to actually be considered (and taxed) like a limited partnership, it has to *avoid* at least two of the following corporate characteristics (usually the last ones):

✔ **Having a centralized management:** Corporations have management in one place. The challenges of having a limited partnership exist when it's being managed from several locations make this corporate trait quite difficult for a partnership to avoid.

✔ **Providing limited liability:** Corporate shareholders have limited liability; well, so do limited partners. Corporate shareholders are limited to the amount invested, and limited partners are limited to the amount invested plus a portion of any recourse loans taken out by the partnership (if any). Providing limited liability is pretty much unavoidable.

✔ **Having perpetual (never-ending) life:** Unlike corporations, which hope to last forever, limited partnerships are set up for a definite period of time. Limited partnerships are dissolved at a predetermined time — for example, when its goals are met or after a set number of years.

✔ **Having free transferability of partnership interest:** DPPs are difficult to get in and out of. Unlike with a stock purchase, where anyone can freely buy and sell shares, not only do limited partners have to pass your scrutiny (as a registered rep), but they also require approval of the general partner. DPP investors (limited partners) must show that they have enough money to invest initially, plus have liquidity in other investments in the event that the partnership needs a loan.

For Series 7 exam purposes, you should remember that the easiest corporate characteristics for a partnership to avoid are perpetual life (continuity of life) and having free transferability of shares; the most difficult to avoid are providing limited liability and having a centralized management.

The DPP Characters: General and Limited Partners

By law, limited partnerships require at least one limited partner and one general partner. Limited partners are the investors, and general partners are the managers. When you're looking at general and limited partners, you should focus on *who can and can't do what*.

General partners are responsible for the day-to-day decision making (overseeing operations, deciding when to buy or sell, choosing what to invest in, and so on) for the partnership. Limited partners (your investors) provide the bulk of the money for the partnership but, unlike general partners, can't make any of the partnership's investment decisions. Table 11-1 lays out the key things to remember about general and limited partners for the Series 7.

Table 11-1	Comparing General and Limited Partners	
Category	*General Partners*	*Limited Partners*
Decision making	Are legally bound to make decisions in the best interest of the partnership; make all the partnership's day-to-day decisions	Have voting rights but can't make decisions for the partnership
Tasks	Buy and sell property for the partnership; manage the partnership assets	Provide capital; vote; can keep general partners in check by reviewing books

Category	General Partners	Limited Partners
Liability and litigation	Have unlimited liability (can be sued and held personally liable for all partnership debts and losses)	Have limited liability (limited to the amount invested and a proportionate share of any recourse loans taken by the partnership)
		Can inspect *all* the partnership books; can sue the general partner or can sue to dissolve the partnership
Financial involvement	Maintain a financial interest in the partnership	Provide money contributed to the partnership, recourse debt of the partnership, and non-recourse debt for real estate DPPs
Financial rewards	Receive compensation for managing the partnership	Receive their proportion of profits and losses
Conflicts of interest	Can't borrow money from the partnership; can't compete against the partnership (for example, they can't manage two buildings for two different partnerships in close proximity to each other)	None; can invest in competing partnerships

Pushing through Partnership Paperwork

For the Series 7, you need to know about certain paperwork that's specific to limited partnerships. In the following sections, I discuss the three required documents necessary for a limited partnership to exist.

Partnership agreement

The *partnership agreement* is a document that includes the rights and responsibilities of the limited and general partners. Included in the agreement are the general partner's rights to

- Charge a management fee for making decisions for the partnership
- Enter the partnership into contracts
- Decide whether cash distributions will be made to the limited partners
- Accept or decline limited partners

Certificate of limited partnership

The *certificate of limited partnership* is the legal agreement between the general and limited partners filed in the home state of the partnership. The certificate of limited partnership includes basic information such as the name of the partnership and its primary place of business, the names and addresses of the limited and general partner(s), as well as:

> ✔ The objectives (goals) of the partnership and length of time it's expected to last
>
> ✔ The amount contributed by each partner, plus future expected investments
>
> ✔ How the profits are to be distributed
>
> ✔ The roles of the participants
>
> ✔ How the partnership can be dissolved
>
> ✔ Whether a limited partner can sell or assign his or her interest in the partnership

If any significant changes are made to the partnership, such as adding new limited partners, the certificate of limited partnership must be amended.

Subscription agreement

The *subscription agreement* is an application form that potential limited partners have to complete. The general partner uses this agreement to determine whether an investor is suitable to become a limited partner. The general partner has to sign the subscription agreement to officially accept an investor into the DPP.

One of your jobs as a registered rep is to review the agreement to ensure (to the best of your ability) that the information the investor provides is complete and accurate. Besides the investor's payment, the subscription agreement has to include items such as the investor's net worth and annual income, a statement explaining the risks of investing in the partnership, and a power of attorney that allows the general partner to make partnership investment decisions for the limited partner.

The following question tests your ability to answer questions about DPP paperwork:

All of the following statements are TRUE regarding the subscription agreement EXCEPT

(A) A general partner must sign the agreement to officially accept a limited partner.

(B) A registered rep must first examine the subscription agreement to make sure that the investor has provided accurate information.

(C) After the general partner has signed the subscription agreement, it gives the limited partner power of attorney to conduct business on behalf of the partnership.

(D) The subscription agreement is usually sent to the general partner with some form of payment.

The answer is C. The test designers want to know that you understand what this document is and that you have a grasp of who does what. The subscription agreement is a form that the potential limited partner fills out; then the registered rep reviews the document before sending it (with the investor's payment) to the general partner, who signs to accept the terms. Choice B shows where the registered rep (that's you!) comes in. Here, you assume that the "investor" is the potential limited partner, so choice B checks out.

Because this is an *except* question, the correct answer is C; the subscription agreement gives the *general partner,* not the limited partner, power of attorney to make decisions for the partnership. If you remember that limited partners don't really do much in the way of decision making (as I explain earlier in "The DPP Characters: General and Limited Partners"), you can spot the false answer right away.

Passive Income and Losses: Looking at Taxes on Partnerships

DPPs used to be called *tax shelters* because DPPs flow through (pass through) not only income but also losses to investors (corporations only flow through income). Prior to 1986, investors could write off these losses against income from other investments. Then the IRS stepped in because they felt that this write-off was too much of an advantage for investors (or the IRS wasn't making enough money) and decided to give DPPs their own tax category. Now, because investors are not actively involved in earning the income, taxes on DPPs are classified as *passive income* and *passive losses*. (See Chapter 15 for more info on taxes and types of income.)

The key thing to remember for Series 7 purposes is that investors can write off passive losses only against passive income from other DPP investments.

Checking Out Types of Partnerships

Certainly partnerships can be formed to run any sort of business that you can imagine, but the Series 7 exam focuses on the big three: real estate, equipment leasing, and oil and gas. You should be able to identify the risks and potential rewards for each of the following types of partnerships.

Because of the risks associated with some of the different types of DPPs, investors should have the ability to tie up their money for a long period of time and be able to recover from a loss of all of the money invested in case the partnership never becomes profitable.

Building on real estate partnership info

Real estate partnerships include programs that invest in raw land, new construction, existing properties, or government-assisted housing. You need to know the differences among the types of programs, along with their risks and potential rewards. Here are the types of real estate DPPs, from riskiest to safest:

✔ **Raw land:** This type of DPP invests in undeveloped land, looking for long-term capital appreciation; raw land DPPs don't build on or rent out the property. The partnership hopes the property purchased will appreciate in value so that the DPP can sell the property for more than the purchase price plus all expenses.

Raw land DPPs are looked at as the riskiest real estate DPP because the partnership doesn't have any cash flow (no rental or sales income), and the value of the land may not increase or may actually decrease.

✔ **New construction:** This type of DPP purchases property for the purpose of building. After completing the construction, the partnership goal is to sell the property and structure at a profit after all expenses. Building costs may be more than expected, and the partnership doesn't receive income until the property is sold, but the DPP can benefit from appreciation on both the land and the structure. Although this investment is speculative, it's not as risky as a raw land DPP.

✔ **Existing properties:** This type of DPP purchases existing properties, looking to generate a regular stream of rental income. Because the properties already exist, this DPP generates immediate cash flow. The risk with this type of DPP is that the maintenance or repair expenses will eat into the profit or that tenants won't renew their leases. The properties already exist and are producing income, so the risk for this type of DPP is relatively low.

✔ **Public housing (government-assisted housing programs):** This type of real estate DPP develops low-income and retirement housing. The focus of this type of DPP is to earn consistent income and receive tax credits. The U.S. government (through U.S. government subsidies), under Housing and Urban Development (HUD), makes up any deficient rent payments. Appreciation potential is low and maintenance costs can be high, but the DPP does benefit from a little government security. Public housing DPPs are backed by the U.S. government and therefore are considered the safest real estate DPP.

The following question tests your understanding of real estate DPPs:

Which of the following types of real estate DPPs has the fewest write-offs?

(A) Raw land

(B) New construction

(C) Existing properties

(D) Public housing

The answer is A. DPPs that invest in raw land are buying property and sitting on it with the hope it'll be worth more in the future. Because the DPP isn't spending money on improving the property and land can't be depreciated, raw land DPPs have the fewest write-offs.

Gearing up with equipment leasing

Although you may be tested on equipment leasing programs on the Series 7 exam, it's the least tested type of DPP. Equipment leasing programs purchase equipment (trucks, heavy machinery, computers, or you name it) and lease it out to other businesses. The objective is to obtain steady cash flow and depreciation write-offs. The two types of leasing arrangements you should be aware of are the operating lease and the full payout lease:

✔ **Operating lease:** This type of equipment leasing program purchases equipment and leases it out for a short period of time. The DPP doesn't receive the full value of the equipment during the first lease. This type of arrangement allows the DPP to lease out the equipment several times during the life of the machinery.

✔ **Full payout lease:** This type of equipment leasing program purchases the equipment and leases it out for a long period of time. The DPP receives enough income from the first lease to cover the cost of the equipment and any financing costs. Usually, the initial lease lasts for the useful life of the equipment.

The main thing to remember about equipment leasing is that the operating lease is riskier because the equipment becomes less valuable or outdated over time and, therefore, less rentable.

Strengthening your grasp on oil and gas

Oil and gas partnerships include programs that produce income, are speculative in nature, or are a combination of the two. You need to know how the types of programs differ, along with their risks and potential rewards. Oil and gas partnerships also have certain tax advantages that are unique:

- ✔ **Intangible drilling costs (IDCs):** IDCs are write-offs for drilling expenses. The word _intangible_ is your clue that you're not talking about actual equipment. These costs include wages for employees, fuel, repairs, hauling of equipment, insurance, and so on. IDCs are usually completely deductible in the tax year in which the intangible costs occurred. IDC deductions are only for the drilling and preparing of a well for the production of oil and gas. Therefore, when a well is producing, IDC write-offs are not allowed.

- ✔ **Tangible drilling costs (TDCs):** TDCs are write-offs on items purchased that have salvage value (items that can be resold). All oil and gas DPPs have TDCs, which includes costs for purchasing items such as storage tanks, well equipment, and so on. These costs are not immediately written off but are _depreciated_ (deducted) over seven years. Depreciation may be claimed on a straight-line (an equal amount each year) or an accelerated basis (writing off more in the early years and less in the later years).

IDCs are fully deductible in the current year; TDCs are depreciated (deductible) over several years.

- ✔ **Depletion:** Depletion is a tax deduction that allows partnerships that deal with natural resources (such as oil and gas) to deduct for the decreasing supply of the resource. Partnerships can claim depletion deductions only on the amount of natural resources sold (not extracted and put in storage for future sale).

Depletion deductions are only for DPPs that deal with natural resources. On the Series 7 exam, the only DPP you should have to worry about with depletion deductions is oil and gas.

When investing in oil, partnerships can pioneer new territory, drill near existing wells, buy producing wells, or try a combination of those methods. For Series 7 exam purposes, exploratory programs are the riskiest oil and gas DPPs because oil may never be found, and income programs are the safest oil and gas DPPs. To make your life easier (hopefully), I've composed a DPP comparison chart that should help you focus in on the main points of each type of oil and gas DPP. See Table 11-2.

Table 11-2	Advantages and Risks of Various Oil and Gas DPPs		
Type	**Objective**	**Advantages**	**Risks**
Exploratory (wildcatting)	Locate and drill for oil in unproven, undiscovered areas	Long-term capital appreciation potential; high returns for discovery of new oil or gas reserves	Riskiest oil and gas DPP because new oil reserves may never be found; high IDCs because the DPP isn't working with producing wells
Developmental	To drill near producing wells with the hope of finding new reserves	Long-term capital appreciation potential with less risk than exploratory programs	Although oil will likely be found, the property's expensive and the drilling costs may be higher than expected; the risk of dry holes (non-producing wells) is still somewhat high; medium level of IDCs
Income	To provide immediate income by purchasing producing wells	The partnership generates immediate cash flow; no IDCs	High initial costs. The least risky of the oil and gas DPPs. However, there is the risk that the well could dry up or gas prices could lower

(continued)

Table 11-2 *(continued)*

Type	Objective	Advantages	Risks
Combination	To provide income to help pay for the cost of finding new oil reserves	To be able to offset the costs of drilling new wells by using income generated by existing wells	This type of program has the risks and potential rewards of all of the programs combined

The following question concerns different DPP investments:

Mr. Smith has money invested in a limited partnership that's expecting to have a significant amount of income over the next one to two years. Which of the following programs would BEST help Mr. Smith shelter the MOST of that income?

(A) Oil and gas exploratory

(B) Raw land purchasing

(C) Equipment leasing

(D) Real estate existing property

The answer is A. Oil and gas exploratory programs spend a lot of money attempting to find and drill for oil. These programs have high IDCs (intangible drilling costs), which are fully tax-deductible when the drilling occurs. Therefore, the oil and gas exploratory programs have the largest write-offs in the early years, which could help Mr. Smith offset some or all of his passive income from the other limited partnership.

For Further Review

You should have a grasp of the items in this section for the Series 7. Look over these additional DPP-related topics and make sure you know them prior to taking the real deal:

- ✔ Functional allocation
- ✔ Private placement
- ✔ Public offering
- ✔ Syndicator
- ✔ Limited partner's cost basis
- ✔ Depreciation and depletion deductions
- ✔ Accelerated depreciation versus straight-line depreciation
- ✔ Crossover point
- ✔ Recourse debt and non-recourse debt
- ✔ Recapture
- ✔ Dissolution of a partnership
- ✔ Abusive shelter
- ✔ Blind pool

Chapter 12

Options: The Right to Buy or Sell at a Fixed Price

- -

In This Chapter

▶ Understanding the specifics of options

▶ Feeling comfortable with an options chart

▶ Calculating the maximum loss, maximum gain, and break-even points

▶ Dealing with unconventional options

▶ Reviewing additional topics tested

- -

Welcome to the wonderful world of options. I'm sure you've heard the stories about the difficulty of options. Put your mind at ease — I'm here to make your life easier. Maybe I'm a little warped, but options are my favorite part of the Series 7 exam! Options are one of the more heavily tested areas, and you can expect around 40 questions on the Series 7.

A lot of the questions are simple calculations, so in this chapter, I show you how to put numbers into an options chart to make even the more difficult calculations simple. I give you plenty of example questions so you can put those math skills to good use. I also give you a general tour of the options basics — calls and puts, in- and out-of-the-money, and so on — and introduce you to the unique LEAPS and capped options. The "For Further Review" section wraps things up and suggests what else to study.

Brushing Up on Option Basics

Options are just another investment vehicle that (hopefully) more-savvy investors can use. An owner of an *option* has the right, but not the obligation, to buy or sell an underlying security (stock, bond, and so on) at a fixed price; as derivatives, options draw their value from that underlying security. Investors may either *exercise* the option (buy or sell the security at the fixed price) or trade the option in the market.

All option strategies (whether simple or sophisticated), when broken down, are made up of simple call and/or put options. After going over how to read an option, I explain a basic call option and help you figure out how to work with that before moving on to a put option. After you've sufficiently mastered the basics, the rest (the more difficult strategies later in this chapter) should be easier.

Reading an option

To answer Series 7 questions relating to options, you have to be able to read an option. The following example shows you how an option may appear on the Series 7:

> Buy 1 XYZ Apr 60 call at 5

Here are the seven elements of the option order ticket and how they apply to the example:

1. **Whether the investor is buying or selling the option — buy**

   When an investor buys (*longs, holds, owns,* and so on) an option, he or she is in a position of power; that investor controls the option and decides whether and when to exercise the option. If an investor is selling (*shorting* or *writing*) an option, he or she is obligated to live up to the terms of the contract and must either purchase or sell the underlying stock if the holder exercises the option.

2. **The contract size — 1**

   You can assume that one option contract is for *100 shares* of the underlying stock. Although this idea isn't as heavily tested on the Series 7 exam, an investor may buy or sell multiple options (for example, five) if he or she is interested in having a position in more shares of stock. If an investor owns five option contracts, he or she is interested in 500 shares of stock (check out "Multiple option contracts" later in the chapter for more information on this topic).

3. **The name of the stock — XYZ**

   In this case, XYZ is the underlying stock that the investor has a right to purchase at a fixed price.

4. **The expiration month for the options — Apr**

   All options are owned for a fixed period of time. The initial expiration for most options is *9 months* from the issue date. Options expire at 11:59 p.m. EST (10:59 p.m. CST) on the Saturday following the third Friday of the expiration month. Remembering the EST (Eastern Standard Time) is generally easier than recalling the CST (Central Standard Time) because 11:59 p.m. EST is right before midnight.

   Don't confuse the option's expiration date with the third Saturday of the expiration month; if the expiration month starts on a Saturday, the option expires on the fourth Saturday.

5. **The strike (exercise) price of the option — 60**

   When the holder *exercises* the option, he or she uses the option contract to make the seller of the option buy or sell the underlying stock at the strike price. In this case, if the holder were to exercise the option, the holder of the option would be able to purchase 100 shares of XYZ at $60 per share.

6. **The type of option — call**

   An investor can buy or sell a call option or buy or sell a put option. Calls give investors the right to buy the underlying security at a set price; puts give the right to sell.

7. **The premium — 5**

   Of course, an option investor doesn't get to have the option for nothing. An investor buys the option at the premium. In this case, the premium is 5, so a purchaser would have to pay $500 (5 × 100 shares per option).

Looking at call options: The right to buy

A *call option* gives the holder (owner) the right to buy 100 shares of a security at a fixed price and the seller the obligation to sell the stock at the fixed price. Owners of call options are bullish (picture a bull charging forward) because the investors want the price of the stock to increase. If the price of the stock increases above the strike price, holders can either exercise the option (buy the stock at a good price) or sell the option for a profit. By contrast, sellers of call options are bearish (imagine a bear hibernating for the winter) because they want the price of the stock to decrease.

For example, assume that Ms. Smith buys 1 DEF October 40 call option. Ms. Smith bought the right to purchase 100 shares of DEF at 40. If the price of DEF increases to over $40 per share, this option could become very valuable to Ms. Smith, because she could purchase the stock at $40 per share and sell it at the market price or sell the option at a higher price.

If DEF never eclipses the 40 strike (exercise) price, then the option doesn't work out for poor Ms. Smith and she would not exercise the option. However, it does work out for the seller of the option, because the seller receives a premium for selling the option that he or she gets to keep.

Checking out put options: The right to sell

You can think of a put option as being the opposite of a call option (see the preceding section). The holder of a *put option* has the right to sell 100 shares of a security at a fixed price, and the writer (seller) of a put option has the obligation to buy the stock if exercised. Owners of put options are bearish because the investors want the price of the stock to decrease (so they can buy the stock at market price and immediately sell it at the higher strike price or sell their option at a higher premium). However, sellers of put options are bullish (they want the price of the stock to increase), because that would keep the option from going in-the-money and allow them to keep the premiums they received.

For example, assume that Mr. Jones buys 1 ABC October 60 put option. Mr. Jones is buying the right to sell 100 shares of ABC at 60. If the price of ABC decreases to less than $60 per share, this could become very valuable to Mr. Jones. If you were in Mr. Jones' shoes and ABC were to drop to $50 per share, you could purchase the stock in the market and exercise (use) the option to sell the stock at $60 per share, which would make you (the new Mr. Jones) very happy.

If ABC never drops below the 60 strike (exercise) price, then the option doesn't work out for Mr. Jones and he would not exercise the option. However, it does work out for the seller of the option, because the seller receives a premium for selling the option that he or she gets to keep.

Getting your money back: Options in-, at-, or out-of-the-money

To determine whether an option is in- or out-of-the-money, you have to figure out whether the investor would be able to get some of that money back if the option were exercised.

You can figure out how much an option is in-the-money or out-of-the-money by finding the difference between the market value and the strike price. Here's how you know where-in-the-money an option is:

- When an option is *in-the-money*, exercising the option lets investors sell a security for more than its current market value or purchase it for less — a pretty good deal.

  The *intrinsic value* of an option is the amount that the option is in-the-money; if an option is out-of-the-money or at-the-money, the intrinsic value is zero.

- When an option is *out-of-the-money*, exercising the option means investors can't get the best prices; they'd have to buy the security for more than its market value or sell it for less. Obviously, holders of options that are out-of-the-money don't exercise them.

- When the strike price is the same as the market price, the option is *at-the-money;* this is true whether the option is a call or a put.

Call options — the right to buy — go in-the-money when the price of the stock is above the strike price. Suppose, for instance, that an investor buys a DEF 60 call option and that DEF is trading at 62. In this case, the option would be in-the-money by two points (the option's intrinsic value). If that same investor were to buy that DEF 60 call option when DEF was trading at 55, the option would be out-of-the-money by five points (with an intrinsic value of zero).

A put option — the right to sell — goes in-the-money when the price of the stock drops below the strike price. For example, a TUV 80 call option is in-the-money when the price of TUV drops below 80. The reverse holds as well: If a put option is in-the-money when the price of the stock is below the strike price, it must be out-of-the-money when the price of the stock is above the strike price.

Don't take the cost of the option (the premium) into consideration when determining whether an option is in-the-money or out-of-the-money. Having an option that's in-the-money is not the same as making a profit. (See the next section for info on premiums.)

Use the phrases *call up* and *put down* to recall when an option goes in-the-money. *Call up* should help you remember that a *call* option is in-the-money when the market price is *up* above the strike price. *Put down* should help you remember that a *put* option is in-the-money when the market price is *down* below the strike price.

The following question tests your knowledge of options being in- or out-of-the-money:

Which TWO of the following options are in-the-money if ABC is trading at 62 and DEF is trading at 44?

   I. An ABC Oct 60 call option

  II. An ABC Oct 70 call option

 III. A DEF May 40 put option

 IV. A DEF May 50 put option

(A) I and III

(B) I and IV

(C) II and III

(D) II and IV

The answer is B. Start with the strike (exercise) prices. You're *calling up* or *putting down* from the strike prices, not from the market prices. Because call options go in-the-money when the market price is above the strike price, answer I is the only one that works for ABC. An ABC 60 call option would be in-the-money when the price of ABC is above 60. ABC is currently trading at 62, so that 60 call option is in-the-money. For the ABC 70 call option to be in-the-money, ABC would have to be trading higher than 70. Next, use *put down* for the DEF put options, because put options go in-the-money when the price of the stock goes below the strike price. Therefore, answer IV makes sense because DEF is trading at 44, and that's below the DEF 50 put strike price, not the 40 put strike price.

Paying the premium: The cost of an option

The *premium* of an option is the amount that the purchaser pays for the option. The premium may increase or decrease depending on whether an option goes in- or out-of-the-money, gets closer to expiration, and so on. The premium is made up of many different factors, including

- Whether the option is in-the-money (see the preceding section)
- The amount of time the investor has to use the option
- The volatility of the underlying security
- Investor sentiment (for example, whether buying calls on ABC stock the cool thing to do right now)

One of the questions you may run across on the Series 7 exam requires you to figure out the time value of an option premium. *Time value* has to do with how long you have until an option expires. There's no set standard for time value, such as every month until an option expires costs buyers an extra $100. However, what you can assume is that if two options have everything in common except for the expiration month, the one with the longer expiration will have a higher premium. Hopefully, the following equation can help keep you from getting a "pit" in your stomach:

$$P = I + T$$

In this formula, *P* is the premium or cost of the option, *I* is the intrinsic value of the option (the amount the option is in-the-money), and *T* is the time value of an option.

For example, here's how you find the time value for a BIF Oct 50 call option if the premium is 6 and BIF is trading at 52: Call options (the right to buy) go in-the-money when the price of the stock goes above the strike price (*call up* — see the preceding section). Because BIF is trading at 52 and the option is a 50 call option, it's two points in-the-money; therefore, the intrinsic value is two. Because the premium is six and the intrinsic value is two, the premium must include four as a time value:

$$P = I + T$$
$$6 = 2 + T$$
$$T = 4$$

The following question tests your knowledge of using P = I + T:

Use the following chart to answer the question.

Stock	Strike Price	Calls		Puts	
LMN		July	Oct	July	Oct
40.50	30	13	14.5	0.25	0.50
40.50	40	2.5	4.5	1.5	2.75
40.50	50	0.25	0.75	10.5	12

What is the time value of an LMN Oct 30 call?

(A) 2.5

(B) 4

(C) 6.25

(D) 9.5

The answer is B. I threw you a curveball by giving you a chart similar to what you may see on the Series 7 exam. I hope you're able to find the premium that you need to answer the question. Most of the exhibits you get on the Series 7 are simple, and solving the problem is just a matter of locating the information you need.

Using the chart, the first column shows the price of the stock trading in the market, the second column shows the strike prices for the options, and the rest of the chart shows the premiums for the calls and puts and the expiration months. Scan the chart under the October calls, which is in the fourth column; then look for the 30 strike price, which is in the first row of data. The column and row intersect at a premium of 14.5.

Now you need to find the intrinsic value (how much the option is in-the-money). Remember that call options go in-the-money when the price of the stock is above the strike price (call up). This is a 30 call option and the price of the stock is 40.50, which is 10.5 above the strike price. Plug in the numbers, and you find that the premium includes a time value of 4:

P (premium) = I (intrinsic value) + T (time value)

$$14.5 = 10.5 + T$$

$$T = 4$$

Incorporating Standard Option Math

I'm here to make your life easier. Prep courses use several different types of charts and formulas to figure out things such as gains or losses, break-even points, maximum gain or loss, and so on. I believe that the easiest way is to use the options chart that follows. It's a simple *Money Out, Money In* chart you can use to plug in numbers. What's great about this chart is that you don't even necessarily have to understand what the heck is going on to determine the answer to most options questions. As this chapter progresses, I show you how incredibly useful the options chart can be.

Money Out	Money In

If it looks basic, it is — and that's the idea. Any time an investor spends money, you place that value in the Money Out side of the options chart, and any time an investor receives money, you place the number in the Money In side of the chart.

Calls same: Buying or selling call options

The most basic options calculations involve buying or selling call or put options. Although using the options chart may not be totally necessary for the more basic calculations (such as the one that follows in the next section), working with the chart now can help you get used to the tool for when the Series 7 exam tests your sanity with more-complex calculations.

As you work with options charts, you may notice a pattern when determining maximum losses and gains. Table 12-1 gives you a quick reference concerning the maximum gain or maximum loss an investor faces when buying or selling call options. Notice that the buyer's loss is equal to the seller's gain (and vice versa).

Table 12-1	Maximum Gains and Losses for Call Options	
Buying or Selling	_Maximum Loss_	_Maximum Gain_
Buying a call	Premium	Unlimited
Selling a call	Unlimited	Premium

The key phrase to remember when working with call options is _calls same,_ which means that the premium and the strike price go on the same side of the options chart.

Buying call options

The following steps show you how to calculate the maximum loss and gain for holders of call options (the right to buy). I also show you how to find the break-even point. Here's the order ticket for the example calculations:

Buy 1 XYZ Oct 40 call at 5

1. Find the maximum loss.

The holder of an option doesn't have to exercise it, so the most he or she can lose is the premium. The premium is five, so this investor purchased the option for $500 ($5 \times 100$ shares per option); therefore, you enter that value in the Money Out side of the options chart (think "money out of the investor's pocket"). According to the chart, the maximum loss (the most this investor can lose) is $500.

Money Out	Money In
$500	

2. Determine the maximum gain.

To calculate the maximum gain, you have to exercise the option at the strike price. The strike price is 40, so you enter $4,000 (40 strike price × 100 shares per option) under its premium (which you added to the chart when calculating maximum loss); exercising the call means buying the stock, so that's Money Out. When exercising call options, always put the multiplied strike price under its premium because *calls same* (the premium and the strike price go on the same side of the options chart).

Money Out	Money In
$500	
$4,000	

Because you've already determined the maximum loss, look at the Money In portion of the options chart. The Money In is empty, so the maximum gain (the most money the investor can make) is unlimited.

When you see a question about the break-even point, the Series 7 examiners are asking, "At what point does this investor not have a gain or loss?" The simplest way to figure out this point for a call option is to use *call up* (remember that call options go in-the-money when the price of the stock goes above the strike price — see "Options in-, at-, or out-of-the-money"). When using *call up,* you add the strike price to the premium:

Strike + premium = 40 + 5 = 45

For this investor, the break-even point is 45. This number makes sense because he or she paid $5 for the option, so the option has to go $5 in-the-money for the investor to recoup the amount he or she paid. *Note:* The break-even point is always the same for the buyer and the seller.

Selling call options

Here, I show you how to find the maximum gain and loss, as well as the break-even point, for sellers of call options. Here's the order ticket for the example calculations:

Sell 1 ZYX Oct 60 call at 2

1. Determine the maximum gain.

The seller makes money only if the holder fails to exercise the option or exercises it when the option is in-the-money by less than the premium received. This investor sold the option for $200 (2 × 100 shares per option); therefore, you enter that amount in the Money In side of the options chart. According to the chart, the maximum gain (the most that this investor can make) is the $200 premium received. *Note:* The exercised strike price of $6,000 (60 × 100 shares) doesn't come into play when determining the maximum gain in this example because the holder of the option would exercise the option only if it were in-the-money.

Money Out	Money In
	$200

2. Find the maximum loss.

To calculate the maximum loss, you need to exercise the option at the strike price. The strike price is 60, so you enter $6,000 (60 strike price × 100 shares per option) under its premium. The $6,000 goes in the Money In side of the options chart because this investor had to sell the stock to the holder at the strike price (60 × 100 shares). When exercising call options, always enter the multiplied strike price under its premium because *calls same* (the premium and the strike price go on the same side of the options chart).

Money Out	Money In
	$200
	$6,000

You've already determined the maximum gain; now look at the Money Out portion of the options chart. The Money Out is empty, so the maximum loss (the most money the investor can lose) is unlimited.

When you see a question about the break-even point, the examiners are asking you, "At what point does this investor not have a gain or loss?" The simplest way to figure this out for a call option is to use *call up.* When using *call up,* you add the strike price to the premium:

Strike + premium = 60 + 2 = 62

For this investor, the break-even point is 62. This makes sense because he or she received $2 for the option, so the option has to go $2 in-the-money for this investor to lose the amount that he or she received for selling the option. Call options go in-the-money when the price of the stock goes above the strike price.

Puts switch: Buying or selling put options

Fortunately, when you're calculating the buying or selling of put options (the right to sell), you use the options chart in the same way but with a slight change (see the preceding section for info on call options). Instead of using *calls same* as you do with call options, you use *puts switch* — in other words, you place the premium and the strike price on opposite sides of the options chart.

Table 12-2 can give you a quick reference as to the maximum gain or maximum loss an investor faces when buying or selling put options.

Table 12-2	Maximum Gains and Losses for Put Options	
Buying or Selling	*Maximum Loss*	*Maximum Gain*
Buying a put	Premium	(Strike − premium) × 100 shares
Selling a put	(Strike − premium) × 100 shares	Premium

Buying put options

This section explains how to find the maximum loss, maximum gain, and the break-even point for buyers (holders) of put options. Here's the ticket order for the calculations:

Buy 1 TUV Oct 55 put at 6

1. **Find the maximum loss.**

   Exercising an option is, well, optional for the holder, so buyers of put options can't lose more than the premium. Because this investor purchased the option for $600 ($6 \times 100$ shares per option), you enter that value in the Money Out side of the options chart. The maximum loss (the most that this investor can lose) is the $600 premium paid.

Money Out	Money In
$600	

2. **Determine the maximum gain.**

   To find the maximum gain, you have to exercise the option at the strike price. The strike price is 55, so you enter $5,500 (55 strike price × 100 shares per option) on the opposite side of the options chart because *puts switch* (the premium and the strike price go on opposite sides of the options chart). Exercising the option means selling the underlying stock, so that $5,500 is Money In.

Money Out	Money In
$600	$5,500

   You've already determined the maximum loss; now look at the Money In portion of the options chart. Because you find $4,900 more Money In than Money Out ($5,500 – $600), the maximum gain is $4,900.

The break-even point is the security price where the investor doesn't have a gain or loss. The simplest way to figure this point out for a call option is to use *put down* (put options go in-the-money when the price of the stock goes below the strike price). When using *put down,* you subtract the premium from the strike price:

Strike – premium = 55 – 6 = 49

For this investor, the break-even point is 49. The investor paid $6 for the option, so the option has to go $6 in-the-money in order for this investor to recoup the amount that he or she paid. As with call options, the break-even point is always the same for the buyer and the seller.

Selling put options

The following steps show you how to calculate the maximum gain and loss for the seller of a put option. I also demonstrate calculations for the break-even point. Here's the ticket order for the example:

Sell 1 TUV Sep 30 put at 8

1. Determine the maximum gain.

The seller makes money only if the holder of the option fails to exercise it. This investor sold the option for $800 (8 × 100 shares per option); you put that number in the Money In side of the options chart. The maximum gain (the most this investor can make) is $800.

Money Out	Money In
	$800

2. Find the maximum loss.

To calculate the maximum loss, you have to exercise the option at the strike price. The strike price is 30, so you place $3,000 (30 strike price × 100 shares per option) on the opposite side of the options chart because *puts switch* (the premium and strike price go on opposite sides of the options chart).

Money Out	Money In
$3,000	$800

You've already determined the maximum gain; now look at the Money Out portion of the options chart and compare it to the Money In. The maximum potential loss for this investor is the $2,200 difference between the Money Out and Money In.

You calculate the break-even point for buying or selling puts the same way: You use *put down* (the strike price minus the premium) to figure out the break-even point:

Strike – premium = 30 – 8 = 22

For this investor, the break even-point is 22. Because this investor received $8 for the option, the option has to go $8 in-the-money for this investor to lose the amount he or she received for selling the option. Put options go in-the-money when the price of the stock goes below the strike price (put down).

Trading options: Opening and closing transactions

Although some investors hold onto their options long enough to actually exercise them, a lot of investors trade options the way that they'd trade other investments. On the Series 7, not only do you need to know the difference between opening and closing transactions, but you also have to be able to calculate the profit or loss for an investor trading options. This process is actually pretty easy when you break it down.

Putting things back where you found them: Doing opposite transactions

When distinguishing between opening and closing transactions, your key is to know whether this transaction is the first time or the second time the investor buys or sells an option: The first time is an *opening*, and the second time is a *closing*.

Here are your opening transactions:

- ✔ **Opening purchase:** An opening purchase occurs when an investor first buys a call or a put.

- ✔ **Opening sale:** An opening sale is when an investor first sells a call or a put.

If an investor already has an option position, the investor has to close that position by doing the opposite — through a closing transaction. If the investor originally purchased the option, he or she has to sell to close it. By contrast, if he or she originally sold the option, he or she has to purchase to close. Here are the two types of closing transactions:

- ✔ **Closing purchase:** A closing purchase occurs when an investor buys himself or herself out of a previous option position that he or she sold. For example, if an investor sold an XYZ Oct 40 call (opening sale), he or she would have to buy an XYZ Oct 40 call to close out the position. The second transaction is a closing purchase.

- ✔ **Closing sale:** A closing sale occurs when an investor sells himself or herself out of a previous option position that he or she purchased. For example, if an investor bought an ABC Sep 60 put (opening purchase), he or she would have to sell an ABC Sep 60 put to close out the position. The second transaction is a closing sale.

When determining opening or closing transactions, whether the transactions are both calls or both puts doesn't matter.

The following question tests your knowledge of opening and closing transactions:

Mr. Dimpledell previously bought 1 XYZ Oct 65 call at 8 when the market price of XYZ was 64. XYZ is currently trading at 69, and Mr. Dimpledell decides that now would be a good time to sell the option that he previously purchased. The second option order ticket would be marked

(A) opening sale

(B) opening purchase

(C) closing sale

(D) closing purchase

The answer is C. This is the second time that Mr. Dimpledell does something with the option that he owns; therefore, the move has to be a closing transaction, and you can immediately eliminate answers A and B. Mr. Dimpledell has to sell himself out of the position because he owned the option. The second order ticket would have to be marked *closing sale*.

Tricks of the options trade: Calculating gains and losses

In addition to knowing how to mark the order ticket, you also have to be able to figure out an investor's gain or loss when trading options. You shouldn't find this task too difficult after you master the options chart. The key thing to remember is that when an investor closes, he or she does the opposite of what he or she did before.

The following question tests your mastery of options trades:

Mrs. Cleveland purchased 100 shares of DPY stock at $50 per share. Two weeks later, Mrs. Cleveland sold 1 DPY Oct 55 call at 6. Mrs. Cleveland held that position for three months before selling the DPY stock at $52 per share and closing the DPY Oct 55 call at 4. What is Mrs. Cleveland's gain or loss on the transactions?

(A) $400 gain

(B) $400 loss

(C) $600 gain

(D) no gain or loss

The answer is A. This question introduces stock trades as well as options transactions, but that's no problem. The options chart works for questions involving actual stocks and options or just options.

When you approach the transactions one at a time, the problem-solving process is actually pretty straightforward. Mrs. Cleveland purchased 100 shares of DPY stock at $50 per share for a total of $5,000; therefore, you enter $5,000 in the Money Out side of the options chart. Next, she sold the DPY 55 call for a premium of 6, so you need to enter $600 (6 × 100 shares per option) on the Money In side of the chart because she received money for selling that option.

Three months later, Mrs. Cleveland sold the stock for $5,200 ($52 per share × 100 shares) and received money for selling the stock. Place the $5,200 in the Money In side of the options chart. When closing the option, the customer has to do the opposite of what she did before. Originally, Mrs. Cleveland sold the option, so to close, she has to buy the option (make a closing purchase). She purchased the option for $400 (4 × 100 shares per option), so enter $400 in the Money Out side of the options chart. All that's left for you to do is total up the two sides. Mrs. Cleveland has $5,800 in and $5,400 out for a gain of $400.

Money Out	Money In
$5,000	$600
$400	$5,200
$5,400	$5,800

Mastering Complex Option Calculations

You may not be happy to hear this, but some investors out there will make your life difficult. But, hey, don't be too upset, because working with these customers is how you're going to earn your six- or seven-figures-a-year salary (not including pennies). The Series 7 exam also tests your knowledge on more-complex option strategies. Of course, you can use an options chart to make your life much easier.

Long straddles and combinations

Straddles are option positions in which the investor buys a call and a put or sells a call and a put on the same underlying security with the same strike (exercise) price and same expiration month; if the securities are the same but the strike prices and/or expiration months are different, you have a *combination* instead. What's nice is that combinations and straddles are virtually the same and the calculations are performed the same way.

This section deals with long positions, which involve purchases. (See "Short straddles and combinations" for info on sales.)

Long straddle

A *long straddle* is buying a call and a put with the same underlying stock, same strike price, and same expiration month. Investors who are expecting *volatility* in the underlying security purchase long straddles. These investors aren't sure which direction the stock will go, so they're covering their bases. They own a call option in case the price of the stock increases, and they own a put option in case the price of the stock decreases. Here's an example of a long straddle:

> Buy 1 DEF Oct 40 call at 6
>
> Buy 1 DEF Oct 40 put at 3

In order to have a long straddle (or combination) you must have two buys.

Long combination

A *long combination* is buying a call and a put for the same underlying stock with a different strike price and/or expiration month. As with straddles (see the preceding "Long straddle" section), an investor of a long combination is looking for a security that's volatile. The investor isn't sure which direction the security is going, so he or she is buying a call in case the security increases in value and a put in case it decreases in value. Here's what a long combination may look like:

> Buy 1 LMN Oct 40 call at 6
>
> Buy 1 LMN Oct 30 put at 1

To distinguish a combination from a straddle, look at the expiration months and the strike (exercise) prices. If either is different, you're dealing with a combination.

The following example tests your skill at distinguishing a straddle from a combination:

An investor who owns 1 XYZ Oct 40 call option would like to establish a long combination. Which of the following option positions would fulfill his needs?

(A) Write 1 XYZ Jan 40 put

(B) Buy 1 XZY Oct 30 put

(C) Buy 1 XYZ Oct 40 put

(D) Buy 1 XYZ Jan 30 put

The answer is D. You can cross off answer A right away because a long combination requires two purchases; answer A is a sell (write), so it can't be right. You can cross off B, too, because although it looks ever so close, it involves a different security. Answer C would've been correct if the question had indicated that the investor was looking for a straddle. A *long combination*, however, is buying a call and buying a put for the same security with different expiration months and/or different strike prices. Therefore, the only answer that works is D.

Try another problem to practice using the options chart (see the earlier "Incorporating Standard Option Math" section for the basics on buying and exercising options):

An investor buys 1 ABC Mar 60 call at 6 and buys 1 ABC Mar 50 put at 3. ABC subsequently increases to 68. The investor exercises the call and immediately sells the stock in the market. After the put expires unexercised, what is the investor's gain or loss?

(A) $100 gain

(B) $100 loss

(C) $500 gain

(D) $500 loss

The answer is B. The investor bought the call for $600 (6 × 100 shares per option), so you have to enter $600 in the Money Out section of the options chart because that was money paid from the investor's pocket. After that, the investor purchased the put for $300 (3 × 100 shares per option), so you have to enter $300 in the Money Out section of the chart. The next sentence states that the stock increased to 68, but it doesn't tell you to do anything with that yet, so you don't.

Next, you have to exercise the call option at the call strike price (always exercise at the strike price) and place the $6,000 (60 strike price × 100 shares per option) under its premium, because *calls same* (the premium and strike price go on the same side of the options chart). This investor sold the stock in the market for $6,800 (68 × 100 shares per option), which is Money In the investor's pocket. Total up each side, and you see that this investor has a loss of $100.

Money Out	Money In
$600	
$300	
$6,000	$6,800
$6,900	$6,800

When you get an option question with several steps (like the preceding one), look for the action words to tell you what to do. Action words include

✔ Buys, holds, owns, longs

✔ Sells, writes, shorts

✔ Exercises

Every time you see an action word, think of it as a clue to remind you that you have to put something in the options chart.

Short straddles and combinations

Short positions involve selling a call and a put with the same underlying stock. In straddles, the calls and puts have the same strike price and expiration month; with combinations, one of these values may differ.

Short straddle

A *short straddle* is selling a call and a put with the same underlying stock, same strike price, and same expiration month. An investor who is short a straddle is looking for *stability*. These investors are looking for a stock that's not going to change too much in price. If the stock doesn't move in price, these investors will be able to keep the premiums they received for selling the options. A short straddle may look like this:

> Sell 1 GHI Oct 50 call at 9

> Sell 1 GHI Oct 50 put at 2

In order to have a short straddle (or combination), you must have two sells.

Short combination

A *short combination* involves selling a call and a put for the same underlying stock with a different strike price and/or expiration month. Similar to a short straddle, an investor who sells a combination is looking for a security with stability. The investor is hoping the securities don't go in-the-money so the options are not exercised and he or she gets to keep the premiums received. A short combination may look like this:

> Sell 1 QRS Dec 60 call at 4

> Sell 1 QRS Mar 55 put at 3

Fortunately, for both straddles and combinations, you can calculate the maximum gain and maximum loss by just placing the premiums in the options chart. No exercising is necessary. For instance, suppose an investor has the following ticket orders:

> Sell 1 TUV Jul 45 call at 6

> Sell 1 TUV Jul 40 put at 3

Here's how you find the maximum potential loss and gain:

1. **Find the investor's maximum potential gain.**

   This problem involves a combination because the strike prices are different. However, if it were a straddle, you'd figure out the answer the same way. Place the premiums in the options chart. The investor sold the call for $600 (6 × 100 shares per option) and the put for $300 (3 × 100 shares per option). The transactions are both *sells,* so they have to go in the Money In side of the options chart. Add the numbers, and you can see that the maximum that this investor can gain (if the options never go in-the-money) is the $900 ($600 + $300) in premiums that he or she received.

Money Out	Money In
	$600
	$300
	$900

2. **Determine the investor's maximum potential loss.**

   With straddles and combinations, the premiums help you determine both the maximum potential gain and the maximum potential loss. After entering the premiums in the options chart, you may notice that the Money Out side of the chart is empty, so the investor's maximum potential loss is unlimited.

Straddles and combinations are a combination of calls and puts; therefore, you can find two break-even points (one on the way up and one on the way down). You must first add the two premiums together, because the investor either paid money twice (bought the call and bought the put) or received money twice (sold the call and sold the put). In this case, after you add the two premiums together, the total is 9 (6 + 3). Next, you use *call up* and add the combined premiums to the call strike price to get one break-even point. To get the other break-even point, use *put down* and subtract the combined premiums from the put strike price. This investor's break-even points are 31 and 54:

Combined premium: 6 + 3 = 9

Call up: Call strike + combined premium = 45 + 9 = 54

Put down: Put strike – combined premium = 40 – 9 = 31

You always have two break-even points for straddles and combinations. Make sure you *call up* (add the combined premiums to the call strike price) and *put down* (subtract the combined premiums from the put strike price) to get the break-even points.

Spreads

Investors create a *spread* position by buying an option and selling an option on the same underlying security. The maximum gain or loss with a spread position is limited. Investors create spread positions to either limit their potential loss or to reduce the premium paid.

Call spread

An investor creates a *call spread* position when buying a call and selling a call on the same underlying security. Additionally, the strike prices and/or expiration months have to be different. Here's what a call spread may look like:

Buy 1 JKL Aug 50 call at 9

Sell 1 JKL Aug 60 call at 2

The following section shows you how to find the maximum gain, minimum gain, and break-even points for spreads.

Put spread

An investor creates a *put spread* position when buying a put and selling a put on the same underlying stock with different expiration month and/or strike prices. Here's an example of a put spread position:

Buy 1 MNO Sep 30 put at 1

Sell 1 MNO Sep 40 put at 8

The options chart can make figuring out the particulars, such as the maximum gain, maximum loss, and break-even points easier. Here's how you find these numbers, using the preceding put spread numbers:

1. **Determine the maximum gain.**

   Begin by entering the premiums in the options chart. This investor bought the 30 put option for $100 (1 × 100 shares per option), so that $100 is Money Out of his or her pocket. Then this investor sold the 40 put for a premium of $800 (8 × 100 shares per option), which you enter in the Money In side of the chart because he or she received money for selling that option.

Money Out	Money In
$100	$800

You end up with more Money In than Money Out; therefore, the investor's maximum potential gain is $700 ($800 in minus $100 out).

To help you recognize a spread, notice that when you put the two premiums in the options chart, they are *spread apart* (one on either side).

2. **Find the maximum loss.**

You already calculated the maximum gain, so next you need to exercise both options to get the maximum loss. When exercising put options, enter the strike prices (multiplied by 100 shares) on the opposite side of the chart from its premium because *puts switch* (go on the opposite side of the chart from its premium). First, exercise the 30 put and enter $3,000 (30 × 100 shares per option) in the Money In side of the chart, which is opposite from the $100 premium. Next, exercise the 40 put and enter $4,000 (40 × 100 shares per option) in the Money Out side of the options chart, which is opposite its $800 premium. Total up the two sides, and you see that the maximum potential loss is $300 ($4,100 out minus $3,800 in).

Money Out	Money In
$100	$800
$4,000	$3,000
$4,100	$3,800

Placing just the premiums in the options chart can give you the maximum potential gain or maximum potential loss but not both. To find the other answer, you must exercise both options.

To find the break-even point, begin by finding the difference between the two premiums because you had one buy and one sell:

Adjusted premium = 8 − 1 = 7

This is a put spread; therefore, you have to subtract the 7 from the higher strike price. The higher strike price is 40, so the break-even point is 33:

Break-even point (put spread) = higher strike price − adjusted premium = 40 − 7 = 33

For call spreads, you have to *add* the adjusted premium (after you've subtracted the smaller premium from the larger one) to the lower strike price. For put spreads, you *subtract* the adjusted premium from the higher strike price.

The following question tests your ability to determine the break-even point on spreads:

Miguel Hammer purchased 1 Apr 40 call at 9 and shorted 1 Apr 50 call at 3. What is Miguel's break-even point?

(A) 43

(B) 46

(C) 49

(D) 53

The answer is B. You should first focus on the buy and the sell. If the investor is buying one option and selling another, you should be able to recognize it as a spread. Therefore, you have to find the difference between the two premiums:

Adjusted premium = 9 – 3 = 6

Next, because it's a call spread, you have to add the adjusted premium (after subtracting the smaller from the larger) to the call strike (exercise) price to get the break-even point:

Break-even point (call spread) = 40 + 6 = 46

The following question tests your ability to answer a spread story question:

Mrs. Peabody purchased 1 DEF Mar 60 put at 5 and wrote 1 DEF Mar 65 put at 9 when DEF was trading at 68. Six months later, with DEF trading at 61, Mrs. Peabody's DEF Mar 65 put was exercised. Mrs. Peabody held the shares of DEF for another two months before selling them in the market for $62 per share. Mrs. Peabody's Mar 60 put expired without ever going in-the-money. What is Mrs. Peabody's gain or loss?

(A) $100 loss

(B) $100 gain

(C) $700 loss

(D) $700 gain

The answer is B. I like to call such problems *story* questions because they take you on a journey, and this one is a tricky one. If you got this right, you're a master of spreads.

Begin by placing transactions in the correct side of the options chart. Because Mrs. Peabody purchased the DEF Mar 60 put at 5, you have to enter $500 (5 × 100 shares per option) on the Money Out side of the options chart because she spent that much to purchase the option. After that, she sold a DEF Mar 65 put for 9 and received $900 (9 × 100 shares per option) Money In for selling that option. The fact that DEF was trading at 61 when the option was exercised means nothing in this question, so feel free to ignore it.

Next, you have to exercise the 65 put that Mrs. Peabody sold. Because *puts switch,* you enter the strike price (multiplied by 100 shares) in the opposite side of the options chart from its premium. After you place the $6,500 in the Money Out section of the options chart, you have to sell the stock that Mrs. Peabody purchased when her option was exercised. She sold the stock in the market for $6,200 ($62 market price × 100 shares) and received cash for that transaction, so enter $6,200 in the Money In section of the chart. Total up the two sides, and you can see that good old Mrs. Peabody has a gain of $100.

Money Out	Money In
$500	$900
$6,500	$6,200
$7,000	$7,100

Just like other option story questions (with several things happening), enter only items in the options chart when you see action words. Remember, every time you see an action word such as *purchased, wrote, exercised, sold,* and so on, you know that you have to enter something in the options chart.

Got it covered: Stock/option contracts

When an investor purchases or sells option contracts on securities he or she owns, that investor has chosen an excellent way to protect against loss or to bring additional funds into his or her account. The most common form is when an investor sells covered call options.

If an investor is selling a call option against a security that he or she owns, the investor is considered to be *covered*. He or she is covered because if the option is exercised, the investor has the stock to deliver.

Take the following position as an example:

> Buy 100 shares of QRS at $47 per share
>
> Sell 1 QRS Dec 55 call at 4

1. **Find this investor's maximum potential loss.**

   Place the purchases and sales in the options chart. This investor purchased 100 shares of QRS stock at $47 per share for a total of $4,700. That's money spent, so enter $4,700 in the Money Out side of the options chart. Next, this investor sold 1 QRS Dec 55 call for a total premium of $400 (4 × 100 shares per option) and received money for selling that option, so you enter $400 in the Money In section of the options chart.

Money Out	Money In
$4,700	$400

   This investor has more Money Out than Money In, so the investor's maximum potential loss is $4,300 ($4,700 minus $400).

2. **Determine the investor's maximum potential gain.**

   Placing the two transactions (in this case the stock purchase and the option sale) in the options chart helps you calculate the maximum gain or maximum loss. You've already calculated the maximum loss, so to find the maximum gain, you need to exercise the option. You always exercise at the strike price, which in this case is 55. Take the $5,500 (55 × 100 shares per option) and place it under its premium because *calls same,* which means that the exercised strike price and the premium go on the same side of the chart. Total the two sides and you find that there's $1,200 more Money In than Money Out, so that's the investor's maximum potential gain.

Money Out	Money In
$4,700	$400
	$5,500
$4,700	$5,900

When the investor is covered, finding the break-even point is nice and easy for stock and options. Although you can use the options chart, you really don't need to in this case. First, look at how much the investor paid for the stock, and then look at how much more he or she paid for the option or received for the option. Find the difference, and you have your break-even point:

> $47 stock price – $4 option premium = $43 break-even point

Because this investor paid $47 per share for the stock and received back $4 per share for selling the option, this investor would need to receive another $43 per share to break even.

Here's how to find the break-even point for stock and options:

- ✔ If the investor purchased twice (bought the stock and the option), add the stock price and the premium.

- ✔ If the investor sold twice (sold short the stock and sold an option), add the stock price and the premium.

- ✔ If the investor had one buy and one sell (for example, bought the stock and sold the option or sold short the stock and bought the option), you subtract the premium from the stock price.

The following example tests your knowledge on stock and option problems:

Mr. Bullwork sold short 100 shares of DIM common stock at $25 per share and bought 1 DIM Aug 30 call at 3 to hedge his position. What is Mr. Bullwork's maximum potential loss from this strategy?

(A) $300

(B) $800

(C) $2,200

(D) $2,700

The answer is B. As always, you need to enter the initial purchase and sale into the options chart and see what you have. Your friend and client, Mr. Bullwork, sold short 100 shares of DIM common stock at $25 per share for a total of $2,500. Because Mr. Bullwork received the $2,500 for selling short, you have to put $2,500 in the Money In side of the options chart. Next, Mr. Bullwork purchased a DIM Aug 30 call to hedge (protect) his position in case the stock started increasing in value. You have to enter the $300 (3 × 100 shares per option) in the Money Out side of the options chart, because he paid money to purchase the option. Stop and take a look and see whether that calculation answered the question.

Money Out	Money In
$300	$2,500

You see more Money In at this point than Money Out, so you have a maximum gain, not a maximum loss; therefore, you have to exercise the option to get the answer you need. Make sure you exercise the option at the strike price. The strike price is 30, so enter $3,000 under its premium because *calls same* (the premium and multiplied strike price go on the same side of the chart). Total up the two sides, and you see that the maximum potential loss for Mr. Bullwork is $800 ($3,300 − $2,500):

Money Out	Money In
$300	$2,500
$3,000	
3,300	$2,500

Off the charts: Multiple option contracts

Now before you start freaking out, working with multiple option contracts is not that much more difficult than working with single contracts. This change is just simply a matter of an investor's buying two, three, four, or more of the same option contract at one time. I guide you through the steps in this section.

When you work with multiple option contracts, approach the problem as though you were dealing with only one contract. You can easily do so by taking the multiple (the number of contracts) and placing it to the side of the options chart so you don't forget. Calculate the maximum potential loss or gain for a single contract, and then multiply that answer by the number of contracts.

The following sample calculations use this ticket order:

> Buy 6 ABC Oct 40 calls at 7
>
> Sell 6 ABC Oct 55 calls at 2

1. **Find the investor's maximum potential loss.**

   Take the number of contracts (in this case it's six) and place it to the side of the options chart. Now this problem is as simple as the other options I mention in the earlier sections. In this case, you can look at the problem as though the investor is buying a call for $700 (7 × 100 shares per option), which is Money Out of the investor's pocket. Next, the investor sold (wrote) the ABC Oct 55 call for $200 (2 × 100 shares per option). Because this transaction is a sale, you enter it in the Money In side of the options chart. The investor has $700 out and $200 in; therefore, the maximum loss per option is $500. Now, you can look at the multiple. Take the maximum loss and multiply it by six (six options on each side), and you end up with a maximum loss of $3,000 for this investor.

×6	Money Out	Money In
	$700	$200

   Maximum loss = $500 per option × 6 = $3,000

   Note: Some option strategies include having a different number of options on each side. However, you're unlikely to be tested on these strategies on the Series 7. These strategies are covered more in the Series 4 exam (Registered Option's Principal).

2. **Determine the investor's maximum potential gain.**

   When dealing with spreads, the premiums give you the maximum gain or the maximum loss but not both. Because you've already so expertly determined the investor's maximum potential loss, you need to exercise both options to get the maximum potential gain. Approach the question as if you were dealing with only one option on each side. Multiply the strike price of 40 by 100 shares per option to get $4,000. Enter $4,000 under its premium of $700, because *calls same* (the premium and the strike price go on the same side of the chart). After that, you can exercise the 55 call to get $5,500 (55 strike price × 100 shares per option). Enter $5,500 under its premium of $200 because *calls same*. Total up the two sides, and you have $1,000 more Money In than Money Out ($5,700 – $4,700). That value is the maximum gain for one option on each side. Because this investor has six options on each side, multiply the $1,000 by six to get $6,000 for this investor's maximum potential gain.

(×6) Money Out	Money In
$700	$200
$4,000	$5,500
$4,700	$5,700

Maximum gain = $1,000 per option × 6 = $6,000

What's nice about finding the break-even point is that it works out the same whether the investor has 1, 10, 30, or more options on either side of the market. In this case, the investor bought one option and sold the other, so you need to find the difference between the two premiums. After subtracting the two premiums, you end up with an answer of 5:

Adjusted premium = 7 − 2 = 5

This is a call spread (buy a call and sell a call — see the earlier section on spreads), so you need to add the adjusted premium (5) to the lower strike price (40) to get the break-even point. In this case, the break-even point is 45:

Break-even point (call spread) = 40 + 5 = 45

Follow the same strategy for all option transactions (spreads, straddles, combinations, and so on) when dealing with multiple options: Always take the contract size and move it to the outside of the options chart when calculating the maximum gain or loss. Then multiply the gain or loss by the number of contracts.

You have to worry (and I use that term loosely) about not only multiple option contracts but also multiple options and multiples of 100 shares of stock purchases or sales. This process is a piece of cake if you follow the rules that I give you. Check out the example, which uses the following position:

Buy 400 shares of ABC common stock at $36

Buy 4 ABC Oct 30 puts at 4

1. **Determine the investor's maximum potential gain.**

   This investor purchased 400 shares of stock and four options, which gives you a multiple of four. Take the multiple and move it to the outside of the options chart. You can then look at the problem as though the investor has only 100 shares of stock and 1 option, because you'll deal with the contract size later. First, enter the $3,600 that the investor paid for the stock ($36 × 100 shares) in the Money Out side of the options chart, because the investor spent money to purchase the stock. Next, enter the $400 that the investor paid for the option (4 × 100 shares per option) in the Money Out side of the options chart because the investor purchased the option. Because the Money In side of the chart is empty, the investor's maximum potential gain is unlimited.

(×4) Money Out	Money In
$3,600	
$400	

2. Find the investor's maximum potential loss.

You've already determined the maximum potential gain; therefore, you need to exercise the option to get the maximum potential loss. The investor purchased a put option, so you have to enter the $3,000 (30 strike price × 100 shares per option) in the Money In side of the options chart, because *puts switch* (the premium and the strike price go on opposite sides of the options chart). Total up the two sides, and you see that you have $1,000 more Money Out than Money In, so the investor's maximum potential loss is $1,000 per option. Because this investor has four options and 400 shares, you need to multiply the $1,000 by four to get the maximum loss of $4,000.

(×4) Money Out	Money In
$3,600	
$400	$3,000
$4,000	$3,000

Maximum loss = $1,000 per option × 4 = $4,000

Here's how you find the investor's break-even point: In this case, the investor purchased the stock for $36 per share and purchased the option for $4 per share. Therefore, this investor needs the price of the stock to go to $40 ($36 + $4) in order to break even:

Break-even point (call spread) = 36 + 4 = 40

Dividends and splits, more or less

This section addresses what happens to an option contract when a company declares a dividend or splits its stock (see Chapter 6 for more info on splits and dividends). I begin with the basics and move forward from there.

Stock dividends

When a company declares a stock dividend, here's what'll happen to option contracts:

- The number of option contracts will remain the same.
- The strike price will decrease.
- The number of shares per option contract will increase.

Please peruse the following example to see how this works out. Here, the investor's initial position is

4 ABC Sep 65 call options (100 shares per option)

If ABC declares a 5 percent stock dividend, you can find the investor's position on the *ex-dividend date* (the first day the stock trades without the dividend).

Because ABC is giving a 5 percent stock dividend, there'll be 105 shares per option instead of 100 (5 percent more shares). To find the new strike price, multiply the original 65 call options by 100 shares per option to get 6,500. Next, divide the 6,500 by the 105 shares per option to get a new strike price of 61.90 (rounded to the nearest cent). The new position is

4 ABC Sep 61.90 call options (105 shares per option)

Cash dividends *do not* affect listed options. For example, suppose that an investor owns 1 ABC Oct 40 call option and ABC declared a $0.50 cash dividend. Although the price of the stock would decrease by $0.50, the option would still read 1 ABC Oct 40 call.

Regular forward splits

Dealing with a regular forward split is relatively easy. In this case, you're dealing with a 2-for-1, 3-for-1, 4-for-1, and so on. I cover your approach to tackling uneven splits in the next section. In an anything-for-1 split, here's what happens:

- ✔ The number of option contracts increases.
- ✔ The strike price decreases.
- ✔ The number of shares per option remains the same (normally 100).

Check out the following example, where the investor has an initial position of

> 2 DEF Jul 60 calls (100 shares per option)

If DEF Corporation announces a 3-for-1 split, the investor's position on the ex-dividend date would be

> 6 DEF Jul 20 calls (100 shares per option)

In this case, the investor would have three options for every one that he or she had before, and the strike price would be ⅓ of what it was before:

$$2 \times \frac{3}{1} = \frac{6}{1} = 6 \text{ option contracts}$$

$$60 \times \frac{1}{3} = \frac{60}{3} = 20 \text{ strike price}$$

Notice how you multiply the contracts by ¾ and multiply the strike price by the reciprocal (⅓).

A good way to double check your work for all dividends and splits is to multiply the number of option contracts by the strike price and then by the number of shares per option. Do the same thing after you adjust the numbers for the dividend or split. Compare the answers. You should get the same number. If you don't, you did something wrong.

Uneven and reverse splits

Uneven splits are similar to dividends in the respect that the number of option contracts remains the same but the strike price and the number of shares per option change. Uneven splits are splits that are not for 1 (for example 3-for-2, 4-for-3, 5-for-2, and so on). Look at the following example, where the investor has an initial position of

> 3 GHI Jun 50 calls (100 shares per option)

If GHI announces a 5-for-2 split, the investor's position on the ex-dividend date would be

> 3 GHI Jun 20 calls (250 shares per option)

First, because the investor is going to have 5 shares for every 2 that he or she had before, you have to multiply the shares per option by 5/2:

$$100 \text{ shares} \times \frac{5}{2} = \frac{500 \text{ shares}}{2} = 250 \text{ shares per option}$$

Next, you have to multiply the strike price by ⅖:

$$50 \text{ strike price} \times \frac{2}{5} = \frac{100}{5} = 20 \text{ new strike price}$$

To work out a reverse split (for example, 3-for-5, 2-for-3, and so forth), use the same process. Be aware that for reverse splits, the strike price increases and the shares per option decrease.

Non-Conforming Options

Certain options fit somewhat outside the realm of standard option terms. This section covers two qualifiers that change an option.

Spending time on LEAPS: Long-term options

LEAPS is short for Long-term Equity AnticiPation Securities. The initial expiration for most options is 9 months. LEAPS, however, can have expirations dates of up to three years. Investors can purchase LEAPS on a large variety of stocks, the Dow, the S&P 100, and the S&P 500.

Setting limits with capped options

You can spot a capped index option because it has the word *CAPS* next to it. Capped index options are traded on the S&P 100 and the S&P 500. *Capped options* have a limited maximum gain or loss because the option will be capped at 30 points in-the-money. You can assume that the cap interval for a capped option is 30 points in-the-money unless the question gives you a different cap interval (which it most likely won't). Look at the example, which finds the maximum loss and maximum gain for an investor with the following order ticket:

> Buy 1 OEX CAPS 450 call at 7

Holders of options don't have to exercise them, so the investor can lose no more than the premium. The maximum loss is $700 ($7 \times 100$ shares per option).

The maximum gain is $2,300. If the investor had paid nothing for the option, the maximum this investor could make would've been $3,000 (30 points in-the-money $\times$ 100 shares per option). However, this investor paid $700 for the option, so the most he or she could make is $2,300.

For Further Review

Although this chapter works through the more difficult and more commonly tested areas of the Series 7 relating to options, you also need to have a good handle on the following topics:

- Registered option's principal (ROP)
- Compliance registered option's principal (CROP)
- Senior registered option's principal (SROP)
- Chicago Board Options Exchange (CBOE)

- ✔ Order book official (OBO)
- ✔ Options risk disclosure document (ODD)
- ✔ Order support system (OSS)
- ✔ Options Clearing Corporation (OCC)
- ✔ Foreign currency options
- ✔ Yield-based options
- ✔ Debt options
- ✔ Index options
- ✔ American style versus European style
- ✔ Last trade, last exercise, and expiration of an option
- ✔ Opening and closing rotations
- ✔ Automatic exercise at expiration
- ✔ Bull or bear spreads
- ✔ Tax treatment of options
- ✔ Options of the same type, series, or class
- ✔ Hedging
- ✔ Covered options versus uncovered (naked) options
- ✔ Routing an option order
- ✔ Margin on options
- ✔ Position and exercise limits

Part IV

Playing Nicely: Serving Your Customers and Following the Rules

The 5th Wave — By Rich Tennant

"All right, ready everyone! We've got some clown out here who looks interested."

In this part . . .

For the Series 7 exam (and in your real-life career as a stockbroker), you're required to know the market conditions that affect your customers' portfolios and the rules that regulate your responsibilities when you're opening, closing, transferring, and handling your customers' accounts. Then, for when your customers' portfolios sky-rocket in value (thanks to your expertise and brilliant recommendations, of course), the Series 7 tests you on your understanding of the tax breaks available so your customers can keep more of the money you helped them earn instead of giving it away to Uncle Sam.

In this part, I detail the tools you have at your disposal — not just to scrutinize customers' accounts but also to monitor market conditions that can affect their investments. I also familiarize you with the markets where securities trade. And in addition to giving you an overview of income tax breaks and helping you distinguish long-term from short-term capital gains and losses for income tax purposes, I discuss the effect of retirement plans and contribution limits on your customers' income taxes. Finally, I review the essential rules for care and protection of your customers' accounts, and I talk a bit about the agencies that make sure you play by the rules.

Chapter 13

Doing a Little Market Research: Portfolio and Securities Analysis

· ·

In This Chapter

▶ Analyzing a customer's needs

▶ Comparing fundamental analysis to technical analysis

▶ Looking at the money supply

▶ Reviewing additional topics tested

· ·

1n terms of choosing securities, throwing darts at a list of stocks seems to have fallen out of favor. So has drawing company names out of a hat. But hey, no problem. Your psychic powers may not be the most reliable, but you still have tons of tools that can help you get a good idea of where the market's heading and how certain securities may perform.

One of your main jobs as a registered representative is to figure out the best investments for your customers. To help lead people down the path of riches, you have to analyze customers' portfolios and the market and try to find a good fit.

In this chapter, I cover topics relating to portfolio analysis, securities analysis, and money supply. I've made a majority of this chapter about analyzing a customer's financial conditions and what happens with money supply. Don't worry, though — I don't leave out technical and fundamental analysis; I just focus on the information that can help you get the best score on the Series 7.

Know Your Customer: Portfolio Analysis

Not all investors are able to take the same amount of risk, so what's an excellent recommendation for one customer may be disastrous for another. When opening an account with a new customer, beginning with a portfolio analysis of the client's current holdings and needs is important so you can help more effectively. When you open such an account, you fill out a new account form with your customer's help (for details on the info that appears here, see Chapter 16). One important element on the form is the customer's investment objectives, which tell you how much risk the customer is willing to take. Of course, a customer's investment objectives aren't written in stone — they can change during his or her lifetime, so you also need to keep up with the customer's life changes.

The Series 7 exam takes your ability to evaluate a customer's needs into consideration — so naturally, you get tested on it. The following sections explain investment objectives, what factors impact these goals, and how you can allocate assets and appropriately manage portfolios so your investments are just about right.

Understanding investment objectives

Investments aren't exactly one-size-fits-all, so asking a client about his or her investment objectives can be a real help. As a financial expert, you'll likely have to help clients pin down what their goals should be. I help you find out how in the next section, but for now, here are some possible investment objectives:

- **Preservation of capital:** Investing in safe securities such as U.S. government bonds, municipal bonds, high rated corporate bonds, and so on

- **Current income:** Investing in securities (such as bonds, preferred stock, income funds, and so on) that'll provide interest or cash dividends

- **Capital growth:** Investing in the stock of relatively new companies or ones that have a high growth potential

- **Total return:** Investing in a combination of stocks and bonds, looking for both growth and income

- **Tax advantages:** Investing in securities (such as municipal bonds, direct participation programs, retirement plans, and so on) that give tax breaks

- **Liquidity:** Looking to purchase securities that can be bought and sold easily

- **Diversification:** Investing in securities from several different companies, municipalities, and/or the U.S. government to offset the risk associated with only owning one security

- **Speculation:** Investing in securities with higher risk in an attempt to maximize profits if the securities move in the right direction

- **Trading profits:** Looking to buy and sell securities on a constant basis

- **Long-term or short-term:** Looking to tie up money for either a long time or a short time

When recommending securities to your customers, you need to make recommendations that fit their investment objectives. Some customers may fit into more than one category (for example, looking for diversification and liquidity). All customers should have a diversified portfolio (own several different securities and/or types of securities). If a customer can't afford to diversify, you should be recommending mutual funds (for info on mutual funds and other packaged securities, check out Chapter 10).

The following question tests your ability to answer a question about investment objectives:

Mr. Johnson is a 60-year old investor who is heavily invested in the market. Mr. Johnson is looking to invest in more securities with a high degree of liquidity. Which of the following investments would you LEAST likely recommend?

(A) DPPs

(B) Blue-chip stocks

(C) T-bills

(D) Mutual funds

The answer is A. Because Mr. Johnson is looking for securities with a high degree of liquidity, you'd least likely recommend DPPs (direct participation programs), or limited partnerships, because they're the most difficult investments to get in and out of. Not only do you need to prequalify the investor, but the investor also has to be accepted by the general partner (see Chapter 11 for details). However, blue-chip stocks, T-bills, and mutual funds can all be bought and sold fairly easily.

Looking at factors that influence your customer's investment profile

If an investor is clueless about how much risk he or she should be taking, your job is to help your client figure it out. Think of yourself of the Sherlock Holmes of the investing world and use the information you have available, such as your client's age, whether he or she has a family, how much money he or she has, and so on. Additionally, feel your client out to try to get an idea of how much risk he or she is comfortable taking.

Money, money, money: Checking out financial information

Obviously, financial factors influence future investments. To get an idea of your client's needs, you can start by looking at your customer's financial profile, which includes

- **Your client's net worth:** The investor's current assets, current liabilities, the amount of marketable securities the client owns, and whether he or she is invested in a retirement plan

- **Money available for investing:** The client's current income, current expenses, and the amount of money he or she has available for investments

- **Additional background items:** Whether he or she owns a home, whether he or she has life and/or disability insurance, the client's tax bracket, and his or her credit score

Money isn't everything: Considering nonfinancial influences

In addition to the customer's financial profile (see the preceding section), you need to be aware of nonfinancial considerations so you can choose appropriate investments. These considerations may include whether this customer is responsible for his or her family, the customer's age, the employment of other family members (for example, whether they work for a bank, broker-dealer, or insurance company), educational plans for self or children, and so on. Here's how such factors can affect an investor's objectives:

- **Age:** Older investors usually can't handle as much risk as younger investors.

- **Changes in marital status:** Recently married couples may be looking for securities that provide a certain degree of safety; for instance, they may be looking to buy a house. New divorcees may face more or fewer financial responsibilities in addition to changes in income, affecting their willingness to take risk.

- **Family responsibilities:** Investors who have a family would normally not be as comfortable investing in more speculative securities.

- **Education:** Parents who need to save for kids' college may need to invest in securities that are not only safer but also allow for a smaller investment now for a bigger return in the future, such as zero-coupon bonds or T-STRIPS.

- **Investment experience:** As a customer gets more used to investing, he or she may be willing to take more risk.

Keep updated with your customer's lives. Not only will this effort make it seem like you care (which of course I hope you do), but it'll also help you keep updated on changing investment objectives and help you keep the investments in line with the objectives.

Splitting up with asset allocation

Asset allocation is the process of dividing an investor's portfolio among different asset classes such as bonds, stock, and cash. The main purpose of asset allocation is to reduce risk by diversifying the investor's portfolio. Asset allocation differs from investor to investor depending on the investor's risk tolerance.

Strategic asset allocation

Strategic asset allocation refers to the types of investments that should make up a long-term investment portfolio. Typically, the normal strategic asset allocation model suggests that you subtract the investor's age from 100 to determine the percentage of the portfolio that should be invested in stocks. For example, a 40-year-old investor should have 60 percent invested in stocks and 40 percent invested in bonds and cash or cash equivalents (such as a money market fund). A 70-year-old investor should have 30 percent invested in stocks and 70 percent invested in bonds and cash or cash equivalents.

Strategic asset allocation gives you a good starting point. If you have an aggressive investor, put a higher percentage into stocks than the model suggests; if you have a conservative investor, put a lower percentage into stock.

Tactical asset allocation

Tactical asset allocation refers to rebalancing a customer's portfolio due to market conditions. For example, if the stock market is expected to do well in the short-term, you put a higher percentage into stocks. If the stock market is expected to do poorly over the short-term, you lower the percentage of stocks and purchase more fixed income securities (bonds). Later sections in this chapter can give you more info on how to analyze securities and markets.

Strategizing with portfolio management policies

In addition to all the other investment choices, investors may have a defensive investment strategy, an aggressive investment strategy, or some combination of the two. An investor who adopts a *defensive investment strategy* has safety of principal and interest as a top priority. A defensive investment strategy includes investments such as

- Blue-chip stocks with low volatility (stocks of well-established, financially stable companies — see Chapter 6)
- AAA rated bonds (Chapter 7)
- U.S. government bonds (Chapter 7)

An investor who adopts an *aggressive investment strategy* is attempting to maximize gains by investing in securities with higher risk. An aggressive portfolio strategy includes

- Investing in securities such as highly volatile stocks (Chapter 6)
- Investing in put and/or call options (Chapter 12)
- Buying securities on margin (Chapter 9)

Although defensive and aggressive strategies are clearly defined, most investors have a *balanced portfolio* (aggressive/defensive), which includes securities included in both an aggressive and defensive portfolio.

Know Your Securities and Markets: Securities Analysis

Although many brokerage firms have their own analysts, you do need to know some of the basics of securities analysis to pass the Series 7. In this section, I cover investment risks that your customers face and show you the differences between technical and fundamental analysis.

Regarding risk

Investors face many risks (and hopefully many rewards) when investing in the market. You need to understand the risks because not only can this knowledge make you sound like a genius, but it can also help you score higher on the Series 7:

- ✔ **Market (systematic) risk:** The risk that a security will decline due to negative market conditions; all securities have market risk

- ✔ **Business (non-systematic) risk:** The risk that a corporation doesn't perform to expectations

- ✔ **Credit risk:** The risk that the principal and interest aren't paid on time; Moody's, Standard & Poor's, and Fitch are the main bond-rating companies

- ✔ **Liquidity (marketability) risk:** The risk that the security is not easily traded; long-term bonds and limited partnerships have more liquidity risk

- ✔ **Interest (money rate) risk:** The risk that bond prices will decline with increasing interest rates (use the idea behind the seesaw from Chapter 7: when interest rates increase, outstanding bond prices decrease); all bonds (even zero-coupon bonds) are subject to interest risk

- ✔ **Reinvestment risk:** The risk that interest and dividends received will have to be reinvested at a lower rate of return; zero coupon bonds, T-bills, T-STRIPS, and so on have no reinvestment risk because they don't receive interest payments

- ✔ **Purchasing power (inflation) risk:** The risk that the return on the investment is less than the inflation rate; long-term bonds and fixed annuities have high inflation risk; to avoid inflation risk, investors should buy stocks and variable annuities

- ✔ **Capital risk:** The risk of losing all money invested (for options [Chapter 12] and warrants [Chapter 6]); because options and warrants have expiration dates, purchasers may lose all money invested at expiration; to reduce capital risk, investors should buy investment-grade bonds

- ✔ **Regulatory (legislative) risk:** The risk that law changes will affect the market

For the Series 7 exam, to determine the best investment for a customer, pay close attention to the risk(s) mentioned. If the question isn't specific about the type of risk, use strategic asset allocation to determine the best answer (see the earlier "Splitting up with asset allocation" section for more information).

Deciding what to buy: Fundamental analysis

Although most analysts use some combination of fundamental analysis and technical analysis to make their securities recommendations, for Series 7 exam purposes, you need to be able to differentiate between the two types. This section discusses fundamental analysis; I cover technical analysis later in "Deciding when to buy: Technical analysis."

Fundamental analysts perform an in-depth analysis of companies. They look at the management of a company and its financial condition (balance sheets, income statements, the industry, management, earnings, and so on) and compare it to other companies in the same industry. In addition, fundamental analysts even look at the overall economy and industry conditions to determine whether an investment is good to buy.

In simplest terms, fundamental analysts decide *what to buy*.

A fundamental analyst's goal is to determine the value of a particular security and decide whether it's underpriced or overpriced. If the security is underpriced, a fundamental analyst recommends buying the security; if the security is overpriced, he or she recommends selling or selling short (selling on margin) the security.

The following sections explain some of the fundamental analyst's tools of the trade and how to use them.

Balance sheet components

The *balance sheet* provides an image of a company's financial position at a given period of time. The Series 7 exam tests your ability to understand the components (see Figure 13-1) and how financial moves that the company makes (buying equipment, issuing stock, issuing bonds, paying off bonds, and so on) affect the balance sheet. In general, understanding how a balance sheet works is more important than being able to name all the components.

Assets	**Liabilities**
Current assets	Current liabilities
Fixed assets	Long-term liabilities
Intangible assets	
	Stockholder's equity (net worth)
	Par value (common)
	Par value (preferred)
	Paid-in capital
	Treasury stock
	Retained earnings

Figure 13-1:
Components of a balance sheet.

People call this statement a balance sheet because the assets must always balance out with the liabilities plus the stockholder's equity.

Assets are items that a company owns. They include

- **Current assets:** Owned items that are easily converted into cash within the next 12 months; included in current assets are cash, securities, accounts receivable, inventory, and any prepaid expenses (like rent or advertising)

- **Fixed assets:** Owned items that aren't easily converted into cash; included are property, plant(s), and equipment; because fixed assets wear down over time, they can be depreciated

- **Intangible assets:** Owned items that don't have any physical properties; included are items such as trademarks, patents, formulas, goodwill (a value based on the reputation of a company — for example, the name McDonalds is probably worth more than Fred's Sloppy Burgers), and so on

Liabilities are what a company owes. They may be current or long-term:

- **Current liabilities:** Debt obligations that are due to be paid within the next 12 months; included in current liabilities are *accounts payable* (what a company owes in bills), wages, debt securities due to mature, *notes payable* (the balance due on money borrowed), declared cash dividends, and taxes

- **Long-term liabilities:** Debt obligation due to be paid after 12 months; included in long-term liabilities are mortgages and outstanding corporate bonds

Stockholder's equity (net worth) is the difference between the assets and the liabilities (basically, what the company is worth). This value includes

- **Par value of the common stock:** The arbitrary amount that the company uses for bookkeeping purposes; if a company issues 1,000,000 shares of common stock with a par value of $1, the par value on the stockholder's-equity portion of the balance sheet is $1,000,000

- **Par value of the preferred stock:** The value that the company uses for bookkeeping purposes (usually $100 per share); if the company issues 10,000 shares of preferred stock, the par value on the stockholder's equity portion of the balance sheet is $1,000,000

- **Paid in capital:** The amount over par value that the company receives for issuing stock — for example, if the par value of the common stock is $1 but the company receives $7 per share, the paid in capital is $6 per share; the same theory holds true for the preferred stock

- **Treasury stock:** Stock that was outstanding in the market but was repurchased by the company

- **Retained earnings:** The percentage of net earnings the company holds after paying out dividends (if any) to its shareholders

Balance sheet calculations

If I were to give you all the calculations that fundamental analysts derive from the balance sheet, you'd likely be cursing under your breath (or possibly out loud). The good news is that the likelihood of your having to perform these calculations on the Series 7 is remote. The most important thing for you to know is what happens to components of the balance sheet when the company makes certain transactions (sells stock or bonds, redeems bonds, and so on).

Here are some formulas that you do need to know for the Series 7 exam:

Working capital = current assets – current liabilities

Assets = liabilities + stockholder's equity

Net worth = assets – liabilities

Note: The last two equations say the same thing in two different ways. The reason that I list both of them is for ease of use. Depending on the question you get, one will be easier to use than the other.

If, for instance, ABC Corp. issues 10,000 bonds at par value, you can use these formulas to figure out what'll happen to the net worth and working capital. You may not even have to plug in numbers. As far as the net worth goes, you can see that it remains unchanged. The company brings in $10,000,000 by issuing 10,000 bonds at $1,000 par. However, because ABC has to pay off the $10,000,000 at maturity, the liabilities go up by the same amount:

Net worth = assets ↑ – liabilities ↑

Working capital is the amount of money a company has to work with right now. The company brings in cash by issuing the bonds, which is a current asset, but doesn't have to pay off the bonds for several years, so the current liabilities remain the same. If the current assets increase and the current liabilities remain the same, the working capital increases:

Working capital ↑ = current assets ↑ – current liabilities

When a company issues bonds, assume that it's a long-term liability, not short-term, unless the question specifically states that the company is issuing short-term bonds.

The following question tests your ability to answer a balance-sheet-equation question:

DEF Corp. is in the process of buying a new $50,000 computer system. If it is paying for the computer system with available cash, what is the effect on the balance sheet?

(A) The net worth decreases and the working capital remains the same.

(B) The net worth remains the same and the working capital remains the same.

(C) The net worth decreases and the working capital decreases.

(D) The net worth remains the same and the working capital decreases.

The answer is D. The company is exchanging one asset for another, and the overall liabilities remain the same, so the net worth of the company doesn't change. However, the company is using a current asset (cash) to purchase a fixed asset (the computer system), so the working capital (the amount of money that the company has to work with) decreases:

> Net worth = assets − liabilities
>
> Working capital ↓ = current assets ↓ − current liabilities

Take a look at the following scenarios and see whether you can determine what'll happen to the balance sheet. Here's what happens when a company

- **Declares a cash dividend:** When a company declares a cash dividend, that cost becomes a current liability to the company. Because current liabilities are part of the overall liabilities owed in the net worth equation, both the net worth and the working capital decrease.

- **Pays a cash dividend:** When the company initially declared the cash dividend, the current liabilities increased, but when the company now pays that dividend, the current liabilities fall. However, the current assets also decrease because the company has to use cash to pay the dividend. If the current assets (and overall assets) decrease and the current liabilities (and overall liabilities) decrease by the same amount, the working capital and net worth both remain the same.

- **Issues stock:** When a company issues stock, it receives cash, which is a current asset (and part of the overall assets). The company doesn't owe anything to investors, so the overall liabilities (and current liabilities) remain the same. Therefore, the net worth and working capital both increase.

When you're dealing with balance sheet equations on the Series 7 exam, write down the equations and think about the questions logically. If something is increasing, use an up arrow, and if something is decreasing, use a down arrow. Hopefully, this notation can help you solve a majority of the balance sheet problems.

Income statement components

An income statement tells you how profitable a company is right now. *Income statements* list a corporation's expenses and revenues for a specific period of time (quarterly, year to date, or yearly). When comparing revenues to expenses, you should be able to see the efficiency of the company and how profitable it is. I don't think you need to actually see a detailed balance sheet from a company, but knowing the components of an income statement is important. Take a look at Figure 13-2 to see the way an income statement is laid out. Most of the items should be self-explanatory.

Net sales
− Cost of goods sold
− Operating expenses (including depreciation)
  Operating profit (earnings before interest and taxes) (EBIT)
− Interest expenses
  Taxable income
− Taxes
  Net income (after-tax income)
− Preferred dividends)
  Earnings available to common stockholders
− Common dividends
  Retained earnings

Figure 13-2:
Sample
income
statement.

Income statement calculations

Here are calculations that can be derived from the income statement that you need to know for the Series 7:

$$\text{Earnings per share (EPS)} = \frac{\text{net income} - \text{preferred dividends}}{\text{No. of common shares outstanding}}$$

$$\text{Price/earnings (P/E) ratio} = \frac{\text{market price}}{\text{EPS}}$$

$$\text{Current yield} = \frac{\text{annual dividends per common share}}{\text{market price}}$$

$$\text{Dividend payout ratio} = \frac{\text{annual dividends per common share}}{\text{EPS}}$$

The following question tests your ability to answer a question on earnings per share:

Zazzoo Corp. has 1,000,000 common shares outstanding. If Zazzoo's net income is $14,000,000, what are the earnings per share?

(A) $0.07

(B) $0.70

(C) $14.00

(D) Cannot be determined without knowing the preferred dividends.

The answer is C. *Cannot be determined* is almost never the answer on the Series 7. Remember that a corporation doesn't need to issue preferred stock, only common stock. Because the question doesn't mention anything about Zazzoo's having preferred stock, you can't assume that they do; the preferred dividends are equal to zero. Therefore, this problem is as easy as dividing the net income by the number of common shares outstanding:

$$\text{EPS} = \frac{\text{net income} - \text{preferred dividends}}{\text{No. of common shares outstanding}} = \frac{\$14,000,000 - 0}{1,000,000} = \$14.00$$

You could *possibly* get a bunch of formulas on the Series 7 exam. However, the most you'll *probably* get is two. Understanding how income statements and balance sheets work is more important than remembering a bunch of formulas. For you die-hard math fans, I mention the formulas that you may want to know in the "For Further Review" section at the end of the chapter. If you feel that you have a handle on everything else that you need for the Series 7 exam and want to get the extra four-tenths or eight-tenths of a point by memorizing all the formulas, go for it.

Deciding when to buy: Technical analysis

Technical analysts look at the market to determine whether the market is bullish or bearish. They look at trendlines, trading volume, new highs and lows, the advance-decline ratio, odd lot volume, short interest, put-to-call ratio (options trading), and so on. These analysts believe that history tends to repeat itself and that past performance of securities and the market indicate its future performance.

Fundamental analysts decide *what to buy,* and technical analysts decide *when to buy* (timing).

Not only do technical analysts chart the market, but they also chart individual securities. Technical analysts try to identify market patterns and patterns of particular stocks in an attempt to determine the best time to purchase or sell. Even though a stock's price may vary a lot from one day to another, when plotting out stock prices over a long period of time, the prices tend to head in a particular direction (up, down, or sideways) and create a *trendline*.

Consolidation is occurring when a stock stays within a narrow trading range. When plotted out on a graph, the trendline is moving horizontally (neither up nor down). If a stock stays within a narrow trading range for a long period of time (months or even years), it creates a *support* (bottom of the trading range) and *resistance level* (top of the trading range). For example, say that XYZ common stock has been trading between $40 and $42 per share for several months; the lower number ($40) is the support, and the higher number ($42) is the resistance.

When a stock declines below its support level or increases above its resistance level, a *breakout* is occurring. When a stock has been trading horizontally (sideways) for a long period of time, a breakout is considered significant. Breakouts are usually a sign that the stock is beginning a new downward or upward trend.

If a stock price is gradually moving down over a period of time, the stock's in a *downtrend*. Conversely, if the stock price is gradually moving upward over a period of time, you're looking at an *uptrend*. Here are a couple patterns technical analysts recognize as reversals of such trends:

✔ **Saucer and inverted saucer:** In a saucer pattern, when the stock prices are plotted for a period of time, they make a saucer shape (gradually decreasing and then gradually increasing). A saucer pattern is a bullish sign or, to be more precise, the reversal of a bearish trend. Conversely, an inverted saucer is exactly the opposite; it's a bearish sign because it's the reversal of a bullish trend.

✔ **Head and shoulders and inverted head and shoulders:** A head and shoulders pattern is formed when the price of a stock has been increasing, hits a high, and then starts decreasing. It involves three peaks, with the center peak as the highest. The two bumps in the road (one on the way up and one on the way down) are the shoulders, and the high is the head. A head and shoulders top formation is a bearish sign because it's the reversal of a bullish trend. I also illustrate an inverted head and shoulders, which is a bullish sign because it's the reversal of a bearish trend.

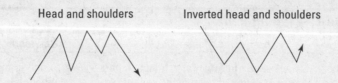

Head and shoulders   Inverted head and shoulders

The key thing to remember about these patterns is that the saucer pattern and inverted head and shoulders patterns are bullish signs and that the head and shoulders and inverted saucer patterns are bearish signs.

The market is said to be *oversold* if a market index such as the DJIA or the S&P 500 is declining but fewer stocks are declining than advancing. If the market is oversold, it's likely a good time to buy. On the other hand, the market's *overbought* if a market index such as the DJIA or the S&P 500 is increasing but fewer stocks are advancing than declining. If the market is overbought, it's likely a good time to sell or sell short (borrow securities to sell on margin).

Follow the Green: Money Supply

The money supply heavily affects the market. If the money supply is higher than average, interest rates go down, people borrow more money, and people spend more money. That all sounds great, but the situation can lead to some negatives, such as higher inflation and the weakening of U.S. currency in relation to foreign currency. The Federal Reserve Board (FRB) has to do a balancing act to help the economy grow at a slow and steady rate. This section deals with how the money supply affects the market and the tools that the Fed uses to control the money supply

Influencing the money supply

Changes in money supply can affect rates of economic growth, inflation, and foreign exchange, so knowing a bit about monetary policy can help you predict how certain securities will fare and how interest rates will change. Take a look at Table 13-1 to see what easing and tightening the money supply can do.

Table 13-1	Effects of Easing and Tightening the Money Supply	
Category	*Easing the Money Supply*	*Tightening the Money Supply*
Economy	It helps the U.S. avoid or get out of a recession. Consumers can borrow money at lower interest rates.	The economy slows down because people aren't spending as much money; the rate of small business failure increases.
Market	As a result of lower interest rates, investors have more money to invest and can purchase more goods. Additionally, businesses don't have to pay as much interest to borrow money, which increases their profits. Both elements can lead to a bullish market.	High interest rates hurt the market because investors don't have extra money to spend. Additionally, corporations have to pay higher interest on loans and therefore report lower earnings. The market becomes bearish.

(continued)

Table 13-1 (continued)

Category	Easing the Money Supply	Tightening the Money Supply
Inflation	Lower interest rates lead to higher inflation. If companies see that customers are spending money freely, they raise their prices.	A tighter money supply helps curb high inflation.
Strength of the U.S. dollar	The U.S. dollar weakens. U.S. exports increase because foreign currency strengthens (people can trade fewer units of foreign currency for more dollars); therefore, buying U.S. products is cheaper for foreign consumers. However, the U.S. dollar loses value when purchasing foreign goods, so foreign imports decrease.	The value of the U.S. dollar rises in relation to foreign currency. The U.S. dollar is subject to supply and demand, so if our money supply is tight, the value of our currency increases. Because the U.S. dollar is strong, importing foreign goods is cheaper for U.S. companies. However, U.S. exports decline because buying U.S. goods becomes more expensive for foreign companies.

When the money supply is eased (easy money), interest rates in general decrease. The Fed can ease the money supply by

- Buying U.S. government securities in the open market
- Lowering the discount rate, reserve requirements, and/or Regulation T (although changing Reg T isn't likely)

Occasionally, the Fed has to tighten the money supply. (Remember, the Fed wants the U.S. economy to grow at a slow, steady pace.) When the money supply is tightened (tight money), interest rates across the board increase. The Fed can tighten the money supply by

- Selling U.S. government securities (pulling money out of the banking system)
- Increasing the discount rate, reserve requirements, and/or Regulation T

The following section tells you more about these tools.

Opening the Federal Reserve Board's toolbox

The Federal Reserve Board, or the Fed, has the authority on behalf of the U.S. government to lend money to banks; it determines the interest rate charged to banks for these loans. You probably remember the chairman of the Fed (formally Alan Greenspan, now Ben Bernanke) coming on TV to announce an increase or decrease in the *discount rate* (the rate the Fed charges banks for loans) and what a big deal it was. The rate the Fed charges impacts the rates banks charge each other and their public customers. Because banks charge customers higher rates than the Fed charges banks, the Fed policy affects consumers as well (through credit card fees, mortgage loans, auto loans, and so on):

Fed \$ →   banks \$ →   customers \$

Taking a look at the Fed setup

Here's a quick lesson in government: Congress established the Federal Reserve System in 1913 to stabilize the country's chaotic financial system. The Fed controls our money supply and, therefore, our economy.

The nation is divided into 12 Federal Reserve Districts, each with its own bank. Each bank prints currency to meet the business needs of its district, and each district is distinguished by a letter printed on the face of the bill.

The Federal Reserve Board in Washington is the parent organization that oversees and controls each of the 12 Federal Reserve District Banks. The seven members of the board are nominated by the President of the United States, subject to confirmation by the Senate. Each board member is appointed for one 14-year term and may not serve a second term. The Chairman of the Board serves a 4-year term that's considered part of his or her 14-year term. The President appoints the chairman, who may serve more than one term in that role.

The Fed has a few tools in its arsenal to help control the money supply (the preceding section explains the effects of tightening and easing the supply). Here's what you need to understand about these tools for the Series 7:

- **Open market operations:** The tool the Fed uses most often, open market operations are the buying or selling of U.S. government bonds or U.S. government agency securities to control the money supply. Open market operations are performed by the Federal Open Market Committee (FOMC). If the Fed sells securities, it pulls money out of the banking system; if the Fed purchases securities in the open market, it puts money into the banking system.

- **The discount rate:** This value is the rate that the 12 Federal Reserve Banks charge member banks for loans. If the discount rate increases, the money supply tightens; by contrast, if the discount rate decreases, the money supply eases.

- **Reserve requirement:** The reserve requirement is the percentage of customers' money that banks are required to keep on deposit in the form of cash. If the Fed increases the reserve requirement, banks have less money to lend to customers, so interest rates increase (supply and demand).

- **Regulation T:** Reg T is the percentage that investors must pay when purchasing securities on margin (see Chapter 9 for details). Regulation T is currently set at 50 percent, and it doesn't change very often. If the Fed raises the rate, investors have less cash, which tightens up the money supply.

Interest rate indicators

The Series 7 designers expect you to recognize some signs that interest rates have increased or decreased. If the following values are high, the money supply will tighten up. The money supply is subject to supply and demand the same way securities are, so if interest rates increase due to the tightening of the money supply, you can assume that interest rates across the board will increase. For example, if the Fed raises the reserve requirements, you can expect interest rates on savings accounts to increase, credit card rates to increase, bond yields to increase, mortgage rates to increase, and so on. Conversely, if interest rates decrease, you can assume that interest rates decrease across the board. Here are some key interest rate indicators:

- **Reserve requirements:** This value is the percentage of bank deposits that may not be loaned to customers (controlled by the Fed).

- **Discount rate:** The discount rate is the interest rate that the Fed charges to member banks for loans. The discount rate is the lowest rate for all loans.

- **Fed Funds rate:** The Fed Funds rate is the interest rate that banks, broker-dealers, and financial institutions charge each other for loans. If one bank doesn't have enough money to meet the reserve requirements, the bank can borrow money from another bank that has excess reserves. In most cases, a Fed Funds loan is a loan between banks, usually overnight. It's the most volatile of all interest rates (it changes the most often).

- **Call loan rate (broker loan rate):** This value is the interest rate that banks charge brokerage firms for customers' margin accounts. When customers borrow money from a broker-dealer to purchase securities on margin, the broker-dealer in turn borrows money from a bank to cover the loan that it made to the customer.

- **Prime rate:** This value is the interest rate that banks charge their best customers (usually corporations) for loans.

Looking at easy money and tight money yield curves

Yield curves are graphic representations of bond yields as compared to the amount of time until maturity. Although you aren't likely to have an exhibit relating to yield curves on the Series 7 exam, visualizing the different yield curves can really help you answer multiple choice questions about yield curves:

- **Normal (easy money) yield curve:** This figure is the type of yield curve that you'd expect; you expect the yields on long-term debt securities to be higher than the yields on short-term debt securities. If you were going to tie your money up for a year, you may be happy with a 6 percent yield, but if you were tying your money up for 30 years, you may want to yield at least 8 percent.

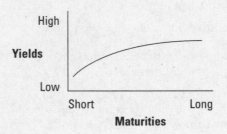

- **Inverted (tight money) yield curve:** This curve is opposite of what you'd expect. In a tight money yield curve, short-term debt securities are actually paying higher yields than long-term debt securities. Not cool.

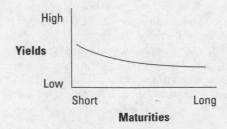

- **Flat yield curve:** When you plot this situation out on a graph, the yields on long-term and short-term debt securities are pretty much the same.

The following question tests your yield curve knowledge:

During a period of tight money, when the yield curve is inverted, which of the following securities is likely to have the highest yield?

(A) T-bills

(B) Commercial paper

(C) T-notes

(D) AA rated corporate bonds

The answer is B. Because you're dealing with an inverted yield curve and tight money, short-term debt securities have higher yields than long-term debt securities. The two short-term debt securities listed are T-bills and commercial paper, so if you pick T-bills, you're on the right track. However, because T-bills are issued by the U.S. government and are considered very safe, they'd have lower yields than commercial paper (corporate debt securities with maturities of 270 days or less).

For Further Review

For you to be as prepared as possible to take the Series 7 exam, you should also have a grasp of the items in this section. Look over these additional analysis-related topics and make sure you know them prior to braving the Series 7:

- Economic indicators
- Sources of information
- U.S. balance of payments
- M1, M2, and M3 money supply
- Business cycle: expansion, peak, contraction, trough
- Terms: gross domestic product (GDP), consumer price index (CPI), inflation, deflation
- Keynesian, supply side, and monetarist economics
- Types of issues: blue-chip, cyclical, countercyclical, defensive, growth company
- Risk related to purchasing growth stock, cyclical stock, speculative stock, defensive stock, utilities, and so on
- Alpha coefficient and beta coefficient
- Capital asset pricing model (CAPM)
- Aggressive versus defensive portfolio management
- Liquidity of a company: current ratio, quick assets, acid test ratio
- A company's risk of bankruptcy: debt-to-equity ratio, bond ratio
- How a company uses its assets: inventory turnover ratio, cash flow
- How profitable a company is: margin-of-profit ratio, net profit ratio
- Earnings per share: fully diluted earnings per share, price-earnings ratio, current yield, dividend payout ratio
- Asset coverage: net asset value per bond, bond interest coverage, book value per share

- ✔ Return on common equity
- ✔ Accelerated versus straight-line depreciation
- ✔ Accumulation/distribution
- ✔ Moving averages
- ✔ Trading channels
- ✔ Stabilization
- ✔ Indexes, averages, and composites

Chapter 14

Going to Market: Orders and Trades

• •

• •

*P*art of your function as a registered rep will be to understand and explain to customers (and potential customers) how the stock market works. I designed this chapter with that in mind (along with the fact that you need to know this stuff for the Series 7, of course).

In this chapter, I cover the basics of exchanges and the over-the-counter market, along with some of the active participants who help the market run smoothly (at least most of the time). Pay particular attention to the "Talking about order types" and the "Factoring in order features" sections because you'll definitely use that information every day after you pass the Series 7 exam. As always, practice questions and a "For Further Review" section await.

Shopping at Primary and Secondary Markets

Depending on whether the securities are new or outstanding, they're trading in either the primary or secondary market. This section deals with the differences between the two.

Buying new in the primary market

The primary market (new issue market) is broken down into two categories, depending on whether the company has ever issued securities before. A security that has never been offered or sold to the public is considered a *new issue*. When securities are sold in the primary market, a bulk of the sales proceeds go to the issuer, and the balance goes to the underwriter (who buys the securities from the issuer and sells them to the public). Here are the two types of offerings on the primary market:

✔ **Initial public offering (IPO):** An IPO is the first time a company ever sells stock to the public to raise money. When a company is in the process of issuing securities for the first time, it's said to be *going public*.

> ✔ **Primary offering:** When a company initially offers securities, it usually holds some back for future use; it later pulls those securities out of storage and sells them in a primary offering. For example, a company may be authorized to sell 2,000,000 shares of common stock, but in its initial public offering, it sells only 800,000. At this point, 1,200,000 new shares have never been offered to the public. One year later, when the company needs to raise additional capital to build a new warehouse, it can sell some of the remaining 1,200,000 shares in a primary offering.

Buying used in the secondary market

When the securities are already trading in the market, the sales proceeds go to another investor instead of to the issuer. The secondary market, also called the *aftermarket*, consists of four categories (see the following section for info on trading on exchanges versus over-the-counter markets):

> ✔ **First market (auction market):** The first market is the trading of listed securities on the exchange floor, such as the New York Stock Exchange (NYSE).
>
> ✔ **Second market (over-the-counter market):** This market is the trading of unlisted securities over-the-counter (by phone or computer).
>
> ✔ **Third market:** The third market is comprised of exchange-listed securities trading over-the-counter (OTC) — traders are calling in their orders or ordering online. All AMEX and NYSE securities and most of the securities listed on other exchanges can be traded OTC.
>
> ✔ **Fourth market:** The fourth market is the trading of securities between institutions without the use of a brokerage firm. Fourth market trades are reported on Institutional Networks, or Instinet, a computerized system for institutional traders.

You're more likely to get a question on the third or fourth market than the first or second.

Making the Trade

After securities are issued publicly, securities may trade on an exchange or on the over-the-counter (OTC) market.

Auctioning securities at securities exchanges

Exchanges are auction markets, where bidders and sellers get together to execute trades. I'm sure you've seen movies or TV shows featuring the New York Stock Exchange. It definitely looks very chaotic (and like it's a good place to have a heart attack or develop an ulcer). However, some sort of order is definitely there: All exchanges have a trading floor where all trades are executed. Each security listed on an exchange has its own *trading post* (location) on the floor where the auction takes place. Brokers looking to purchase shout out and/or make hand signals to indicate the price they're willing to spend to buy a particular security. Sellers, in turn, shout out the price they're willing to sell a security for. If buyers and sellers can come to an agreement, a trade is made.

The main exchange that the Series 7 tests you on is the New York Stock Exchange (NYSE), but you should be aware of others, such as the American Stock Exchange (AMEX), the Philadelphia stock exchange, Chicago Board Options Exchange, and the Pacific stock exchange. *Listed securities* are ones that satisfy minimum requirements and are traded on a regional or national exchange like the NYSE. Listed securities may trade on the exchange or in the OTC market.

Although thousands of people may seem to be on the floor of the exchange, you don't need to be aware of too many titles. Most of the people on the floor of the exchange fall into one of three categories:

- **Floor brokers:** These individuals act as agents in executing buy or sell orders on behalf of their firm's customers. A floor broker may also facilitate buying and selling for his or her firm. Floor brokers receive buy or sell orders from their firms and either transfer the orders to a specialist or trade with another floor broker.

- **Two dollar brokers (independent brokers):** These people assist floor brokers in getting their orders executed on busy days. (By the way, they're called two dollar brokers because many, many years ago, they used to receive $2 per trade. Commissions may have gone up a bit since then.)

- **Specialists:** These market professionals manage the auction market trading for a particular security (or for a few securities, if not actively traded). For more information about a specialist, visit "Taking a Look inside the Specialist's Book," toward the end of this chapter.

Negotiating trades over-the-counter

Unlike exchanges, the OTC market is a negotiated market. Instead of yelling out bid and ask prices, traders buy and sell securities by way of telephone or computer transactions. There's no central location for trading OTC securities. Thousands of securities — both listed and unlisted — are traded this way. In fact, *unlisted securities,* which aren't listed on an exchange, can only trade OTC.

The OTC equities market is divided into NASDAQ issues (issues that meet the NASDAQ listing requirements) and non-NASDAQ issues.

U.S. government and municipal bonds trade only over-the-counter.

The NASD Automated Quotation service (NASDAQ) is an electronic quotation system that displays bid and ask prices of the most actively traded OTC stocks. Additionally, NASDAQ also includes quotes of preferred stock, convertible bonds, and warrants. The NASDAQ market is divided into two components:

- **NASDAQ National Market (NNM or NMS):** This market includes the largest and most actively traded stocks trading OTC. The NASDAQ National Market provides a market for over 3,900 companies, including giants such as Microsoft and Intel. To be listed on the NASDAQ National Market, a company has to have a minimum number of shares outstanding, at least 400 round lot (100 shares) shareholders, and shares with a minimum bid price of at least $5. A majority of NASDAQ stocks are NNM issues, which are *marginable* (can be purchased on margin — see Chapter 9 for info on margin accounts).

- **Capital market stocks:** These securities were formerly called *small cap stocks.* These stocks trade OTC but don't meet the listing requirements of NNM stocks.

To make trades, people need accurate, current info on bid and ask prices. Not everyone can get the same amount of information, though. Here are the *access levels* of NASDAQ (the computer displays with NASDAQ information):

- ✔ **Level I:** The most basic level of NASDAQ, this quotation screen displays up-to-the-minute inside bid and ask prices for several hundred OTC stocks. Level I is the computer screen that you'll most likely have on your desk when you're working as a registered rep.

- ✔ **Level II:** The second level of NASDAQ provides up-to-the-minute bid and ask prices of each market maker (dealers or principals) for a security. Most brokerage firm traders use this level.

- ✔ **Level III:** The most complete level of NASDAQ, this level not only shows the bid and ask prices of all market makers but also allows a market maker to enter and change quotes.

Understanding the Role of a Broker-Dealer

In order for a firm to be considered a broker-dealer, it must buy and sell securities from its own account and act as middlemen (or middlewomen) for securities not in inventory. Here are the differences between the brokers and dealers:

- ✔ **Broker:** A firm is acting as a broker when it doesn't use its own inventory to execute a trade. A broker charges a *commission* (sales charge) for acting as a middleman between a buyer and seller.

  For Series 7 exam purposes, the term *broker* and *agent* may be used interchangeably. A registered representative is sometimes called an agent or stockbroker because he or she acts as an intermediary between buyers and sellers.

- ✔ **Dealer:** A firm is acting as a dealer when it's using its own inventory to execute a trade. When a dealer sells securities to a customer using its own inventory, it charges a *markup* (sales charge). When a dealer buys securities from a customer for its own inventory, it charges a *markdown* (reducing the price a customer receives by charging a sales charge). Firms become dealers in the hopes that the securities it has in its own inventory increase in price so that the dealer can benefit from the appreciation.

  The terms *dealer, principal,* and *market maker* may be used interchangeably on the Series 7 exam.

Capacity refers to whether a firm is acting as a broker or dealer, and it must always be disclosed on the *confirmation* (receipt of trade). If a firm is acting as a broker, the commission always needs to be disclosed on the confirmation. However, if a firm is acting as a dealer, the markup or markdown doesn't always have to be disclosed.

A firm can't act as a broker and a dealer for the same trade. In other words, charging a markup (or markdown) and a commission on the same trade would be a violation. (For info on rules and regulations, see Chapter 16.)

To help you remember the differences between a broker and a dealer, think of a real estate broker. A real estate broker (or agent) acts as an intermediary between sellers and buyers and charges a commission, just like a stockbroker does.

Receiving Orders from Customers

Here's where the rubber meets the road. You can receive several types of orders from customers along with numerous order qualifiers. This section explains the types of orders and how to execute them.

Talking about order types

You can definitely expect a few questions on the Series 7 exam relating to orders. The following sections explore the order types.

Market order

A *market order* is for immediate execution at the best price available. A majority of the orders that you'll receive will be market orders. Here are the varieties they come in:

- **Buy order:** When an investor places a market order to buy, he or she is not price-specific; the investor will be purchasing the security at the lowest ask price (the lowest price at which someone's willing to sell the security). An investor who's purchasing a security wants the price to increase (after the sale, of course) and is establishing a bullish position.

- **Sell order:** When an investor places a market order to sell, he or she is not price-specific and will be selling the security at the highest bid price (the highest price someone's willing to pay for the security).

- **Selling short:** Selling short occurs when an investor sells securities that he or she doesn't own. The investor is actually borrowing securities from a lender to sell. Here's how it works: Say an investor borrowed 100 shares of ABC stock and sold them short at $40 per share, thus receiving $4,000. The borrower doesn't owe the lender $4,000; he or she owes the lender 100 shares of ABC stock. After a month or two, when ABC is trading at $20 per share, the borrower could purchase the 100 shares for $2,000 and return them to the lender, making a nice $2,000 profit (excluding commission costs). A short seller is bearish (wants the price of the security to decrease). If the price increases instead, the short seller has to buy the stock in the market at a higher price, thus losing money.

When you purchase a security, the most you can lose is the amount invested. When you're short a security, your maximum loss potential is unlimited because the price of the stock can keep climbing and you'd have to spend more money to cover your short position. Additionally, because of the additional risk, all short sales must be executed in a margin account. Chapter 9 can tell you more about margin accounts.

Stop order

A stop order is used for protection; it tries to limit how much an investor can lose. Depending on whether an investor has a long or short stock position, he or she may enter a buy stop order or a sell stop order:

- **Buy stop:** These orders protect a short position (when an investor sells borrowed securities). A buy stop tells you to buy a security if the market price touches a particular price or higher. Investors who are short the stock make money when the price of the stock decreases; however, if the price increases, they lose money. For example, an investor who's short ABC stock currently trading at $25 could enter a buy stop order on ABC at $30. If ABC reaches $30 or above, the order is triggered and the order becomes a market order for immediate execution at the next price.

✔ **Sell stop:** These orders protect a long position (when an investor purchases stock); They tell you to sell a security if the market price touches a particular price or lower. Investors who are long stock make money when the price of the stock increases; if the price decreases, they lose money. For example, an investor who is long DEF stock currently trading at $50 could enter a sell stop order on ABC at $45. If DEF reaches $45 or below, the order is triggered and the order becomes a market order for immediate execution at the next price, whether higher or lower than $45.

Limit order

A customer who's specific about the price he or she wants to spend or receive for a security places a limit order; this order says the customer doesn't want to pay more than a certain amount or sell for less. Depending on whether an investor is interested in buying or selling, he or she could enter a buy limit or sell limit order:

✔ **Buy limit:** Investors who want to purchase a security place these orders. A buy limit order is a directive to buy a particular security at the limit price or lower. For example, suppose DEF stock is trading at $35 per share but one of your customers doesn't want to pay more than $30 per share. You could place a buy limit order in at $30. If the price of DEF ever reaches 30 or below, there's a good chance that your customer will end up with the stock.

✔ **Sell limit:** Investors who want to sell a security place sell limit orders. A sell limit order is a directive to sell a particular security at the limit price or higher. For example, suppose one of your customers owns LMN stock, which is currently trading at $62 per share, but he wants to receive at least $70 per shares if he's going to sell it. This customer could place a sell limit on LMN at $70 per share. If LMN touches or goes above $70 per share, there's a good chance that the stock will be sold.

Because stop and limit orders are price-specific, they may or may not be executed. Additionally, even if limit orders do reach or surpass the limit price, the order may not be executed if more orders were placed ahead of the investor's.

Stop limit order

A *stop limit order* is a combination of a stop and limit order (see the preceding sections); it's a buy stop or sell stop order that becomes a limit order after the stop price is reached. For example, an order that reads "sell 1,000 HIJ at 41 stop, 40.75 limit" means that the sell stop order will be triggered as soon as HIJ reaches 41 or below (the stop price). If this were just a stop order, the stock would be sold on the next trade (no matter what the price). Because this is a stop limit order, after the order is triggered, it becomes a limit order to buy at 40.75 or above (the limit price). In other words, this customer is interested in selling his or her stock if it drops to 41 but wants to receive at least 40.75 per share.

Handling limit and stop orders

One of the exhibits that you may see on the Series 7 exam is a ticker tape. You may have to determine the price at which a limit order is executed or a stop order is triggered. Using the *BLiSS* and *SLoBS* acronyms can help you out tremendously when you're trying to keep the prices straight:

✔ **BLiSS (buy limit or sell stop):** The BL stands for *buy limit,* and the SS stands for *sell stop.* All BLiSS orders are entered *at or below* the market price of the security. Another thing to remember about BLiSS orders is that they get reduced on the *ex-dividend date* (the first day a stock trades without a dividend).

The *BL* in BLiSS helps you remember that the orders are placed BeLow the market price.

✔ **SLoBS (sell limit or buy stop):** The SL stands for *sell limit,* and the BS stands for *buy stop.* All SLoBS orders are entered *at or above* the market price of the security. Unlike BLiSS orders, SLoBS orders remain the same on the ex-dividend date.

A good way for you to remember that SLoBS orders remain unchanged on the ex-dividend date is to remember the phrase "once a slob, always a slob."

The following question tests your understanding of trigger and execution prices:

An investor enters an order to sell MNO at 34 stop. The ticker following entry of the order is as follows:

34.75, 34.60, 34.45, 34.20, 34.10, 33.95, 34.25, 34.30, 34, 33.80

At which prices was the order triggered and executed?

(A) Triggered at 33.95 and executed at 33.80

(B) Triggered at 34.10 and executed at 33.95

(C) Triggered at 33.95 and executed at 34.25

(D) Triggered at 34.25 and executed at 33.80

The answer is C. The investor wants to limit losses, so he or she entered an order to sell if the price dips too low. The order was triggered at 33.95 and executed at 34.25. This is a sell stop order, which is a BLiSS order. BLiSS orders are triggered at or below the order price. In this case, the first transaction that was at or below 34 was 33.95, which is the trigger price. Because this is a stop order, it became a market order for immediate execution and was completed on the next trade (34.25).

When you're dealing with stop limit orders, remember that the order is first a stop order; after the stop order is triggered, it becomes a limit order. The following question tests your ability to answer a stop limit question:

Julia Jingleham purchased 1,000 shares of XYZ Corp. at $45 per share. To limit her losses, a couple of weeks later, Julia places an order to sell 1,000 shares of XYZ at 43 stop 42.90 limit. The ticker following entry of the order is as follows:

43.64, 43.27, 43.30, 43.09, 42.95, 42.87, 42.85, 42.90, 42.94, 43

The order was triggered at

(A) 42.95 and executed at 42.87

(B) 42.95 and executed at 42.90

(C) 42.87 and executed at 42.94

(D) 42.87 and executed at 42.85

The answer is B. Julia Jingleham placed this sell stop limit order to sell the stock if it drops to 43 but not sell it at less than 42.90 per share. Take care of the stop portion first, so look for where the sell stop order is triggered. Sell stop orders are BLiSS orders that are triggered at or below the stop price. The first trade that's at or below 43 is 42.95. Now that the order is triggered, it becomes a sell limit order at 42.90. Sell limit orders are SLoBS orders that are executed at or above the market price. When you move ahead from the point where it was triggered, the first trade that's at or above 42.90 is 42.90.

Factoring in order features

Besides knowing the basic types of orders (market, stop, and limit — see "Talking about order types"), you should have a handle on some additional features that may be added to the order to make your customers happy. A lot of them exist, but for the most part, the name of the order feature pretty much explains what it is:

- **Day:** If a day order hasn't been filled by the end of the trading day, it's canceled. All price-specific orders (stop and limit) are assumed to be day orders unless marked to the contrary.

- **Good-till-canceled (GTC):** Good-till-canceled orders are also called *open orders* because the order is kept open until executed or canceled. For example, say that an investor wants to purchase ABC stock at $30. While the price of ABC is at $35, he or she could enter an open buy limit order for ABC at $30. If the price of ABC ever hits $30 or below, the order will likely be executed; however, if the price of ABC never hits $30 or below, the order stays open until canceled. Regardless of when an open order is placed, a specialist clears it out of his or her book at the end of April or October and the order has to be re-entered.

- **Not held (NH):** This order gives the broker discretion about when to execute the trade. Typically, investors use not held orders when the broker believes he or she can get the customer a better price later in the day.

  Not held orders deal only with timing. For registered reps to choose the security, number of shares, and/or whether to buy or sell, the customer needs to open a discretionary account, which requires a written power of attorney. See Chapter 16 for details.

- **Fill or kill (FOK):** This order instructs a floor broker to immediately execute an entire order at the limit price or better or else to cancel it.

- **Immediate or cancel (IOC):** These limit orders are similar to FOK orders except that the order may be partially filled. Any portion of the order that's not completed is canceled.

- **All or none (AON):** These limit orders have to be executed in their entirety or not at all. AON orders don't have to be filled immediately (several attempts to fill the order completely are allowed) and may be day orders or good-till-canceled orders.

  As of 2005, the NYSE does not accept AON or FOK orders.

- **At the open:** These orders are to be executed at the security's opening price. At the open orders can be market or limit orders, but if they aren't executed at the opening price, they're canceled. These orders allow for partial execution.

- **At the close:** This order is to be executed at the closing price (or as near as possible). If this order isn't completed, it's canceled.

✔ **Do not reduce (DNR):** This order says not to reduce the price of a stop or limit order in response to a dividend. For example, say that QRS stock is currently trading at $50 on the day prior to the ex-dividend date. If QRS previously announced a $0.50 dividend, the next day's opening price would be $49.50. If a customer had placed a DNR limit order to buy 1,000 shares of QRS at $45, the order wouldn't be reduced by the $0.50 dividend.

✔ **Alternative:** The alternative order is also known as a *one cancels the other order* or an *either/or order*. This type of order instructs the broker to execute one of two orders and then cancel the other. For example, say Mr. Smith owns stock at $60 per share. He could enter a sell stop order at $55 for protection and a sell limit order at $70 in the event that the stock price increases. If one of the orders is executed, the other order is canceled immediately.

Reading the Ticker Tape

The ticker tape is also known as the *consolidated tape*. For subscribers, the tape delivers real-time (within 90 seconds) reports of securities transactions as they occur on different exchanges. The consolidated tape is broken down into Network A and Network B. Network A reports transactions in New York Stock Exchange (NYSE) listed securities, and Network B reports American Stock Exchange (AMEX) listed securities, as well as securities listed on regional exchanges. Take a look at an example of a quote shown on a typical ticker tape:

$$\text{MSFT}_{2K} = 29.76 \blacktriangle 0.16$$

Here are the five parts of a basic ticker-tape quote and how they fit with the example:

1. **The ticker symbol — MSFT**

   Each symbol represents a particular company.

2. **The number of shares traded — 2K**

   In this case, 2,000 shares were traded. If fewer than 1,000 shares are traded, the full volume is shown. For example, 400 shares would appear as 400, without any letter next to it. The abbreviations (for kilos, millions, and billions) are as follows: K = 1,000, M = 1,000,000, and B = 1,000,000,000.

3. **The price for the last trade — 29.76**

   Here, the last trade took place at $29.76

4. **The change in direction from the previous day's closing price — ▲**

   In this case, the triangle is pointing up, so the price is higher. If the triangle points down, the price of the stock is lower than the previous day's closing price.

5. **The difference in price from the previous days' closing price — 0.16**

   In this case, the stock is trading 16 cents higher than the previous day's closing price.

Alphabet soup: Other ticker symbols and meanings

For your personal knowledge, I've compiled a list of additional symbols that may be placed after the symbol of a security. Although you aren't likely to see these on the Series 7 exam, you'll be dealing with them after you begin your journey as a registered rep:

A = Class A shares

B = Class B shares

C = Continuance (NASDAQ exception)

D = New issue

E = Delinquent with SEC filings

F = Foreign

G = First convertible bond

H = Second convertible bond

I = Third convertible bond

J = Voting share (special)

K = Nonvoting common stock

L = Miscellaneous

M = 4th class preferred stock

N = 3rd class preferred stock

O = 2nd class preferred stock

Q = In bankruptcy

S = Shares of a beneficial interest

T = With warrants or rights

U = Units

V = Pending issue and distribution

Y = American Depositary Receipt

Z = Miscellaneous situation

You can quickly tell whether a security is trading on an exchange such as NYSE or AMEX by the number of letters. If the symbol for the security has three letters or less, it's listed on an exchange. If the security has four letters, the stock is trading on NASDAQ.

Although you're not as likely to see extra letters on the Series 7 exam as the standard three- or four-letter stock symbols, you should be aware of some of them. The ticker symbol will be followed by a period and then an extra letter to provide the following info:

Symbol	Meaning
.X	Mutual funds
.W	Warrants
.R	Rights
.P	Preferred stock

You may run across a bunch of other symbols (like the ones listed in the sidebar), but these four are all you need for the Series 7. After you pass, you can look into the other ones.

Taking a Look inside the Specialist's Book

A *specialist* is a member of a stock exchange who's responsible for maintaining a fair and orderly market on a particular security. A specialist not only maintains an inventory of stock but also posts bid and ask prices and executes trades for other broker-dealers. A specialist acts as both a broker (executing trades for others) and a dealer (buying and selling securities for his or her own inventory) and tries to keep trading as active as possible.

A specialist's main function is to maintain a fair and orderly market for a particular security. A specialist can't compete with a public order; he or she can only narrow the gap between the bid and ask prices if it gets too wide by placing a buy or sell order in between the highest bid and lowest ask prices.

Specialist's books aren't written documents like they used to be; now they've gone electronic, but they're still called *specialist's books, display books,* or just *books.* The book receives and displays orders to specialists and allows them to execute and then publish orders to the consolidated (ticker) tape.

Take a good look at the specialist's book and see how it works, because the Series 7 exam may include it as an exhibit; see Table 14-1.

Table 14-1	Specialist's Book (ABC Stock)	
BID	*39*	*ASK (OFFER)*
8 Golden Sec. GTC	.00	7 Livingston Broker-Dealer STOP
7 Pride Broker-Dealer GTC	.01	
4 Vizzion Klempt 14 Orlando Securities	.02	
	.03	
	.04	
6 Martin Bros. STOP GTC	.05	12 High Profit Securities GTC
	.06	6 Brown and White

When you're looking at the specialist's book, the left-hand side (under BID) indicates bid prices that investors are willing to pay for a security (potential buyer). The right-hand side (under ASK) indicates the prices investors are willing to accept for selling the security (potential seller).

On each side of the chart are names of broker-dealers looking to buy and sell the security. The numbers to the left of the names represent how many *hundreds* of shares the investors are looking to buy or sell. For example, the 8 next to Golden Securities on the bid side represents the fact that Golden Securities is looking to buy 800 shares of ABC stock at $39 good till canceled (GTC).

A specialist's book keeps track of stop and limit orders. Market orders aren't kept in a book because they're for immediate execution at the best price available. Any order with the word STOP next to it is obviously a stop order, and all the rest are limit orders. Stop orders are *not active* when placed in a specialist's book. Stop orders are triggered (activated) at the price placed in the book but then become market orders for immediate execution at the next price, whatever that may be. All orders in the specialist's book are day orders unless marked GTC. See "Receiving Orders from Customers" for more info on order types.

A customer entering a market order would either buy at the best ask price or sell at the best bid price.

As you can imagine, the Series 7 can ask numerous questions about a specialist's book. No matter what the question, you need to ignore the stop orders (pretend that they aren't there) because you can't be sure what price the order will be executed at, if at all. The following points are examples of information that the Series 7 may ask for. For the data, please refer back to the exhibit in Table 14-1:

- ✔ **Inside market:** After ignoring the stop orders, the *inside market* is the highest bid price and the lowest ask price.

  In this case, the highest bid is 39.02 (Vizzion Klempt and Orlando Securities) and the lowest ask is 39.05 (High Profit Securities).

- ✔ **Size of the market:** The size of the market is the number of shares (or round lots) that are available at the best prices (highest bid and lowest ask) after you ignore the stop orders. You represent it as

  Shares at highest bid price × shares at lowest ask price

  Ignoring the Martin Bros. stop, Vizzion Klempt and Orlando Securities offer the highest bid at 39.02. Vizzion Klempt wants 400 shares and Orlando wants 1,400, for a total of 1,800 shares. Ignoring the Livingston Broker-Dealer stop, High Profit Securities offers the lowest ask price at 39.05; High Profit wants to sell 1,200 shares. The size of the market is therefore 1,800 x 1,200, or 18 x 12 (if given in round lots, units of 100 shares).

- ✔ **Spread:** The *spread* is the difference between the highest bid and lowest ask (ignoring the stop orders).

  In this case, the spread is $39.05 – 39.02, or $.03.

  The narrower the spread, the more actively traded the security. Because investors are buying at the lowest ask price and selling at the highest bid, there's a built-in loss, which is the difference between those two numbers (the spread). If you have a $2 spread between the highest bid and lowest ask, the price of the stock would have to increase by $2 in order for investors to break even (excluding commissions). As you can imagine, a security like that wouldn't garner much demand.

- ✔ **Where a specialist can enter a bid for his or her own inventory:** Remember that a specialist can't compete with a public order. A specialist's duty is to keep trading as active as possible, so a specialist can enter a bid (or ask) in between the highest bid and lowest ask.

  Using this exhibit, acceptable bids from a specialist would be 39.03 or 39.04.

For Further Review

Please take a look at the following items one at a time and make sure you have a strong grasp on each of them as well as the related info in this chapter:

- ✔ Uptick and upbid rules
- ✔ Non-NASDAQ issues (pink sheets and OTC Bulletin Board)
- ✔ Yellow sheets
- ✔ Stopping stock
- ✔ Priority, parity, precedence

- Automated order execution system
- Consolidated Quotation Service (CQS)
- SuperDot (Designated Order Turnaround System)
- SuperMontage
- Trades reported out of sequence
- Odd lot trades
- Firm quotes and subject quotes
- Workable indication
- Firm with recall option
- Arbitrage and risk arbitrage
- Trading halts
- Selling short against the box

Chapter 15

Making Sure the IRS Gets Its Share

● ●

In This Chapter

▶ Outlining the breakdown of taxes and income

▶ Seeing how the IRS taxes securities

▶ Checking taxes on gifts and inheritances

▶ Comparing the different types of retirement plans

▶ Reviewing additional topics tested

● ●

Yes, it's true what they say: The only sure things in life are death and taxes. Although taxes are an annoying necessity, investors do get tax breaks if they invest in securities for a long period of time, and you need a good understanding of the tax discounts investors receive. Additionally, the Series 7 exam tests your ability to recognize the different types of retirement plans, the specifics about each one, and the tax advantages.

In this chapter, I cover tax categories and tax rules — topics from distinguishing between types of taxes to calculating capital gains for securities received as gifts. And although enjoying retirement isn't quite as certain as pushing up daisies, I explain Uncle Sam's claim on the cash investors put into IRAs, Keoghs, and other retirement plans. As always, you can also count on some example questions and suggestions for further review.

Everything in Its Place: Checking Out Tax and Income Categories

All the lines on the tax forms should be a clue that the IRS likes to break things down into categories. The following sections explain progressive and regressive taxes, as well as the types of personal income.

Touring the tax categories

The supreme tax collector (the IRS) has broken down taxes into a couple categories according to the percentage individuals pay. Your mission is to understand the different tax categories and how they affect investors:

▸ **Progressive taxes:** These taxes affect high-income individuals more than they affect low-income individuals; the more taxable money individuals have, the higher their income tax bracket. Progressive taxes include taxes on personal income (see the next section), gift taxes, and estate taxes (see "Presenting Gift and Inheritance Tax Rules"). The Series 7 contains more questions on progressive taxes than on regressive taxes.

✔ **Regressive taxes:** These taxes affect individuals earning a lower income more than they affect people earning a higher income; everyone pays the same rate, so individuals who earn a lower income are affected more because it's a higher percentage of their income. Examples of regressive taxes are payroll, sales, property, excise, gasoline, and so on.

Looking at types of income

The three main categories of income are earned, passive, and portfolio. (If you're especially interested in the details of how investments are taxed, you can find more information at www.irs.gov.) You need to distinguish among the different categories because the IRS treats them differently:

✔ **Earned (active) income:** People generate this type of income from activities that they're actively involved in. Earned income includes money received from salary, bonuses, tips, commissions, and so on. Earned income is taxed at the individual's tax bracket.

✔ **Passive income:** This type of income comes from enterprises in which an individual isn't actively involved. Passive income includes income from limited partnerships (see Chapter 11) and rental property. When you see the words *passive income* on the Series 7, immediately start thinking that it comes from a limited partnership (DPP). Passive income is in a category of its own and can only be written off against passive losses.

✔ **Portfolio income:** This type of income includes interest, dividends, and capital gains derived from the sale of securities. The following section can tell you more on taxes on portfolio income. Portfolio income may be taxed at the investor's tax bracket or a lower amount, depending on the holding period.

Note: Gifts and inheritances are not considered income. For more on such sources of money, see "Presenting Gift and Estate Tax Rules."

Noting Taxes on Investments

You need to understand how dividends, interest, capital gains, and capital losses affect investors. To make your life more interesting, the IRS has given tax advantages to people who hold onto investments for a long period of time, so familiarize yourself with the types of taxes that apply to investments and how investors are taxed.

Interest income

Interest income that bondholders receive may or may not be taxable, depending on the type of security or securities held:

✔ **Corporate bond interest:** Interest received from corporate bonds is taxable on all levels (federal, state, and sometimes local).

✔ **Municipal bond interest:** Interest received from municipal bonds is federally tax free; however, investors may be taxed on the state and local level, depending on the issuer of the bonds (see Chapter 8).

✔ **U.S. government securities interest:** Interest received from U.S. government securities such as T-bills, T-notes, T-STRIPS, and T-bonds is taxable on the federal level but is exempt from state and local taxes.

Even though T-bills, T-STRIPS, and any other zero-coupon bonds don't generate interest *payments* (because the securities are issued at a discount and mature at par), the difference between the purchase price and the amount received at maturity is considered interest and is subject to taxation.

Dividends

Dividends may be in the form of cash, stock, or product. However, cash dividends are the only ones that are taxable in the year that they're received. The following sections discuss dividends in cash, in stock, and from mutual funds.

Cash dividends

Since 2003, cash dividends received from stocks are taxed at a maximum rate of 15 percent, provided the customer has held onto the stock for at least 61 days. The 61-day holding period starts 60 days prior to the *ex-dividend date* (the first day the stock trades without dividends). If the investor has held the stock for less than the 61-day holding period, he or she is taxed at his or her regular tax bracket.

Stock dividends

Stock dividends don't change the overall value of investment, so the additional shares received are not taxed (for details, see Chapter 6). However, stock dividends do lower the cost basis per share for tax purposes. The cost basis is used to calculate capital gains or losses.

Dividends from mutual funds

Dividends and interest generated from securities that are held in a mutual fund portfolio are passed through to investors. The type(s) of securities in the portfolio and the length of time the fund held the securities dictate how the investor is taxed. Here's how mutual fund dividends are taxed:

Federally Tax Free	*15 Percent*	*Ordinary Income*
Municipal bond funds	Stock funds	Corporate bond funds
Long-term capital gains	Short-term capital gains	

One of the great things about owning mutual funds is that they're nice enough to let you know what taxes you're going to be subject to. At the end of the year, you get a statement that lets you know how much you received in dividends, in short-term capital gains, and in long-term capital gains.

The mutual fund determines the long-term or short-term gains by its holding period, not the investors'. Also remember that you'd be subject to capital gains tax and taxes on dividends even if the money were reinvested back into the fund.

At the sale: Capital gains and losses

Capital gains are profits made when selling a security, and *capital losses* are losses incurred when selling a security. To determine whether an investor has a capital gain or capital loss, you have to start with the investor's cost basis. The *cost basis* is used for tax purposes and includes the purchase price plus any commission (although on the Series 7 exam, the test designers usually don't throw commission into the equation). The cost basis remains the same unless it's adjusted for accretion or amortization (see "Cost basis adjustments on bonds: Accretion and amortization," later in the chapter).

Incurring taxes with capital gains

An investor realizes *capital gains* when he or she sells a security at a price higher than the investor's cost basis. Capital gains on any security (even municipal and U.S. government bonds) are fully taxed on the federal, state, and local level.

A capital gain isn't realized until a security is *sold*. If the value of an investment increases (appreciates) and the investor doesn't sell, the investor doesn't incur capital gains taxes.

Capital gains are broken down into two categories, depending on the holding period of the securities:

- **Short-term capital gains:** These gains are realized when a security is held for *one year or less*. Short-term capital gains are taxed at the *investor's tax bracket*.

- **Long-term capital gains:** These gains are realized when a security is held for *more than one year*. To encourage investors to buy and hold securities, long-term capital gains are currently taxed at a maximum rate of *15%*.

Offsetting gains with capital losses

An investor realizes a capital loss when selling a security at a value lower than the cost basis. Investors can use capital losses to offset capital gains and reduce the tax burden. As with capital gains, capital losses are also broken down into short-term and long-term:

- **Short-term capital losses:** An investor incurs these losses when he or she has held the security for *one year or less*. Investors can use short-term capital losses to offset short-term capital gains.

- **Long-term capital losses:** An investor incurs these losses when he or she has held the security for *more than one year*. Long-term capital losses can offset long-term capital gains.

When an investor has a net capital loss, the investor can write off $3,000 per year against his or her earned income and carry the balance forward to the next year.

The following question involves capital-loss write-offs:

In a particular year, Mrs. Jones realizes $30,000 in long-term capital gains and $50,000 in long-term capital losses. How much of the capital losses would be carried forward to the following year?

(A) $3,000

(B) $17,000

(C) $20,000

(D) $30,000

The answer is B. Mrs. Jones has a net capital loss of $20,000 ($50,000 loss minus the $30,000 gain). Mrs. Jones writes off $3,000 of that capital loss against her earned income and carries the additional loss of $17,000 forward to write off against any capital gains she may have the following year. In the event that Mrs. Jones doesn't have any capital losses the following year, she can still write off $3,000 of the $17,000 and carry the remaining $14,000 forward to the following year.

The wash sale rule: Adjusting the cost basis when you can't claim a loss

To keep investors from claiming a loss on securities (which investors could use to offset gains on another investment — see the preceding section) while repurchasing substantially (or exactly) the same security, the IRS has come up with the *wash sale rule;* according to this rule, if an investor sells a security at a capital loss, the investor can't repurchase the same security or anything convertible into the same security for 30 days prior to or after the sale and be able to claim the loss. An investor won't end up in handcuffs for violating the wash sale rule; he or she simply can't claim the loss on his or her taxes.

However, the loss doesn't go away if investors buy the security within that window of time — investors get to adjust the cost basis of the security. For instance, if an investor were to sell 100 shares of ABC at a $2-per-share loss and purchase 100 shares of ABC within 30 days for $50 per share, the investor's new cost basis (excluding commissions) would be $52 per share ($50 purchase price plus the $2 loss on the shares sold), thus lowering the amount of capital gains he or she would face on the new purchase.

The following question tests your understanding of the wash sale rule:

If Melissa sells DEF common stock at a loss on June 2, for 30 days she can't buy

   I. DEF common stock

   II. DEF warrants

   III. DEF call options

   IV. DEF preferred stock

(A) I only

(B) I and IV only

(C) I, II, and III only

(D) I, II, III, and IV

The answer is C. You need to remember that Melissa sold DEF at a loss; therefore, she can't buy back the same security (like in Roman numeral I) or anything convertible into the same security (like Roman numerals II and III) within 30 days to avoid the wash sale rule. Warrants give an investor the right to buy stock at a fixed price (see Chapter 6), and call options give investors the right to buy securities at a fixed price (Chapter 12). However, Roman numeral IV is okay because DEF preferred stock is a different security and is not convertible into DEF common stock (unless it's convertible preferred, which it isn't; if it were convertible, the question would've told you so). For Melissa to avoid the wash sale rule, she can't buy DEF common stock, DEF convertible preferred stock, DEF convertible bonds, DEF call options, DEF warrants, or DEF rights for 30 days. However, she can buy DEF preferred stock, DEF bonds, or DEF put options (the right to sell DEF).

Cost basis adjustments on bonds: Accretion and amortization

You use accretion and amortization when figuring out taxes on bonds; you simply adjust the cost of the bond toward par in the time that the bond matures. For more info on amortization and accretion, check out Chapter 7 and read on.

Accretion

When investors purchase bonds at a discount, the discount must be accreted over the life of the bond. *Accretion,* which involves adjusting the cost basis (price paid) of the bond toward par each year that the bond is held, increases both the cost basis of the bond and the reported interest income.

To determine the annual accretion, find the difference between the cost of the bond and par value; divide the result by the original number of years to maturity.

The following question tests your understanding of accretion:

Mr. Dancer purchases a 5 percent corporate bond with 10 years to maturity at 80. What would be Mr. Dancer's annual reported income on this bond?

(A) $20

(B) $30

(C) $50

(D) $70

The answer is D. Mr. Dancer purchased the bond at 80 ($800), and you can assume that it matures at $1,000 (par) in 10 years (you can always assume $1,000 par unless otherwise stated — see Chapter 7). You need to take the $200 difference and divide it by 10 years to get $20. Mr. Dancer's reported income would be $70 ($50 interest plus $20 accretion).

Be prepared to answer questions about the annual accretion and yearly reported income and to calculate the capital gain or loss the investor would incur if selling the bond before maturity.

The following question tests your ability to figure out the capital gain or loss on a bond purchased at a discount:

Ms. Jones purchased a 7 percent DEF corporate bond at 80 with 10 years to maturity. Six years later, Ms. Jones sold the bond at 85. What is the gain or loss?

(A) $50 gain

(B) $70 loss

(C) $150 loss

(D) None of the above

The answer is B. First adjust the cost basis of the bond in the time the bond matures:

$$\$800 \xrightarrow{\text{10 years}} \$1,000$$

The bond was purchased at $800 (80 percent of $1,000 par) and matures at $1,000 par in 10 years. Next, take that $200 difference and divide it by the 10 years to maturity:

$$\text{Annual accretion} = \frac{\$200}{10 \text{ years}} = \$20$$

Then take the $20 per year accretion and multiply it by the *number of years* that the investor held the bond:

$20 per year × 6 years = $120 total accretion

Next, add the total accretion to the purchase price of the bond to determine the investor's adjusted cost basis:

$800 original cost + $120 total accretion = $920 (adjusted cost basis)

After that, compare the adjusted cost basis to the selling price to determine the gain or loss:

$920 adjusted cost basis – $850 selling price = $70 capital loss

Ms. Jones incurred a $70 capital loss on her sale of the DEF bond, which she can use to offset capital gains on other investments (see the earlier section titled "Offsetting gains with capital losses").

All discount bonds, except municipal bonds purchased in the secondary market (outstanding bonds), are accreted. If a municipal bond is purchased as an original issue discount (OID), the accretion is treated as part of the tax-free interest. If an investor purchases a municipal bond in the secondary market at a discount, the bond is not accreted, but the difference between the purchase price and selling price (or redemption price) is treated as a capital gain.

Amortization

When bonds are purchased at a premium, the premium can be amortized over the life of the bond. You *amortize* the bond by adjusting the cost basis of the bond towards par each year that the bond is held; amortization decreases the cost basis of the bond and decreases the reported interest income.

To find the yearly amortization, divide the difference between the purchase price and par value by the original number of years to maturity.

The following question involves annual amortization:

Mrs. Sheppard purchases a 7 percent corporate bond with 20 years to maturity at 110. If Mrs. Sheppard decides to amortize the bond, what is the annual reported income?

(A) $5

(B) $65

(C) $70

(D) $75

The answer is B. Because Mrs. Sheppard purchased the bond at 110 ($1,100) and you can assume that it matures at $1,000 (par) in 20 years, you need to take the $100 difference and divide it by 20 years to get $5. Mrs. Sheppard's reported income would be $65 ($70 interest minus $5 amortization).

Corporate bondholders can elect to amortize their premium bonds or not; however, all municipal bondholders must amortize their premium bonds, whether they were purchased as a new issue or in the secondary market (used).

You can use the same basic formula that you used for accretion to determine the gain or loss on an amortization problem (see the preceding section). Only the first couple steps change. You still take the difference between the purchase price and par value and divide it by the number of years until maturity, which gives you the annual amortization. Then you multiply the annual amortization by the number of years the investor held the bond. At this point, you need to subtract that amount from the purchase price instead of adding it to the purchase price to get the adjusted cost basis. Then, as you do with accretion problems, you compare the adjusted cost basis to the selling price to determine the gain or loss.

Presenting Gift and Estate Tax Rules

Fortunately, you need to know only limited information on gift and estate tax rules for the Series 7. Although some of your clients may receive a gift or inheritance of money, paintings, a car, a little red wagon, or whatever, you only need to be concerned with a gift or inheritance of securities. Both gift taxes and estate taxes are progressive taxes (the higher the tax bracket, the higher the percentage of tax paid). Additionally, the recipient is never responsible for the taxes on the gift or inheritance. The main thing that you need to focus on is the recipient's cost basis for the securities.

Gift taxes

A gift tax is a progressive tax imposed on the transfer of certain goods. In the event that a gift tax is due, it's always paid by the donor, not the recipient. For example, if someone makes a gift to a minor in an UGMA account (see Chapter 16), the donor of the gift, not the minor, is responsible for any taxes due.

The IRS does allow some gift-tax loopholes. Anyone can give a gift of up to *$12,000 per person per year* that's free from the gift tax, and gifts between spouses aren't subject to gift taxes.

To help determine capital gains or losses (see "At the sale: Capital gains and losses"), when a gift of securities is made, the recipient assumes the donor's cost basis (purchase price of the security) as long as the securities have increased in value. If the securities decrease in value after the original purchase, the recipient assumes the cost basis of the securities on the date of the gift.

The following question tests your understanding of how the cost basis carries over with gifts of securities:

Mary Johnson purchased 100 shares of LLL common stock at a price of $60 per share. She gives the securities to her son Zed when the market price is $75 per share. What is Zed's cost basis per share?

(A) $60 per share

(B) $67.50 per share

(C) $75 per share

(D) It depends on the holding period

The answer is A. Because LLL increased in value since the original purchase, Zed would assume his mother's cost basis.

This question concerns the cost basis of a gift when the market price of the stock falls:

John Johnson purchased 1,000 shares of DIM Corp. common stock at $40 per share. DIM subsequently decreased in price to $30 per share, and John gave the securities to his father-in-law Mike. Two years later, Mike sold the stock for $37 per share. What is Mike's tax situation regarding the sale of the DIM stock?

(A) $30,000

(B) $35,000

(C) $37,000

(D) $40,000

The answer is A. Because DIM decreased from the original purchase price, Mike would assume the cost basis of the DIM stock on the date of the gift, which was $30,000 (1,000 shares × $30).

Note: You're more likely to get a Series 7 question about a security's increasing in value before the gift is given.

Estate taxes

Inheriting securities is a little more straightforward than receiving gifts of securities. When an individual receives securities as a result of an inheritance, he or she *always* assumes the cost basis of the securities on the date of the owner's death. Additionally, securities received by inheritance are always taxed as long-term.

When a person dies, estate taxes are normally paid before assets are transferred to beneficiaries. Because the estate pays the taxes on the securities, the tax liabilities aren't passed along to the beneficiaries.

Exploring Retirement Plan Tax Advantages

I place retirement plans in with taxes because retirement plans give investors tax advantages. When you're reviewing this section, zone in on the differences and similarities among the different types of plans. The contribution limits are important but not as important as understanding the plan specifics and who'd be qualified to open which type of plan.

Qualified versus non-qualified plans

The IRS may dub employee retirement plans as qualified or non-qualified. The distinction concerns whether they meet IRS and Employee Retirement Income Security Act (ERISA) standards for favorable tax treatment.

Tax-qualified plans

A *tax-qualified plan* meets IRS standards to receive a favorable tax treatment. When you're investing in a tax-qualified plan, the contributions into the plan are made from pre-tax dollars and are deductible against your taxable income. Not only are contributions into the plan tax deductible, but the account also grows on a tax-deferred basis, so you won't be taxed until you withdraw money from the account at retirement. The two types of tax-qualified retirement plans are defined contribution and defined benefit plans. These include 401(k)s, profit-sharing plans, and money-purchase plans. Most corporate pension plans are tax-qualified plans.

Because investors don't pay tax on the money initially deposited or on the earnings, the entire withdrawal from a tax qualified plan is taxed at the investor's tax bracket, which is normally lower at retirement. Additionally, distributions taken before age 59½ are subject to a 10 percent tax penalty (10 percent added to the investor's tax bracket).

Non-qualified plans

Obviously, a non-qualified plan is the opposite of a qualified plan. *Non-qualified plans,* such as deferred compensation plans and payroll deduction plans, do not meet IRS and ERISA standards for favorable tax treatment. If you're investing in a non-qualified retirement plan, deposits are not tax-deductible (they're made from after-tax dollars); however, because you're dealing with a retirement plan, earnings in the plan do build up on a tax-deferred basis. People may choose to invest in non-qualified plans because either their employer doesn't have a qualified plan set up or the investment guidelines are not as strict (investors may be able to contribute more and in a wider choice of securities).

Because investors have already paid tax on the money initially deposited but not on the earnings, withdrawals from non-qualified plans are only partially taxed at the investor's tax bracket. The investor is taxed only on the amount above the contributions.

IRA types and contribution limits

You'll likely be tested on a few different types of retirement plans and possibly the contribution limits. When you're looking at this section, understand the specifics of the types of plans and view the contribution limits as secondary. The contribution limits change pretty much yearly, and the Series 7 questions may not change that often. If you have a rough idea of the contribution limits, you should be okay.

Traditional IRAs (individual retirement accounts)

IRAs are tax-qualified retirement plans, so deposits made into the account are made from pre-tax dollars (they're tax-deductible). IRAs are completely funded by contributions that the *holder of the account* makes. Regardless of whether individuals are covered by a pension plan, they can still deposit money into an IRA. Here's a list of some of the key points of IRAs:

- The maximum contribution per person is $4,000 per year ($5,000 in 2008), with an additional catch-up payment of $1,000 per person allowed for investors age 50 or older.

- A husband and wife can have separate accounts with a maximum contribution of $4,000 per year each.

- Contributions into the IRA are fully deductible for individuals not covered by employer pension plans.

If investors are covered by an employer pension plan, deposits into an IRA may or may not be tax-deductible. Although I think that the chances of your being tested on the values are slim, if an individual is covered by an employer pension plan and earns up to $50,000 per year ($80,000 jointly), deposits made into an IRA are fully deductible. The deductions are gradually phased out and disappear when an individual earns more than $60,000 per year ($100,000 jointly).

✔ When an investor starts to withdraw funds from an IRA, the investor is taxed on the entire withdrawal (the amount deposited, which was not taxed, and the appreciation in value). The withdrawal is taxed as ordinary income.

✔ Withdrawals can't begin before age 59½, or investors have to pay an early withdrawal penalty of 10 percent added to the investor's tax bracket. An investor isn't subject to the 10 percent tax penalty in cases of death, disability, first-time homebuyers, and higher education. Obviously, dead retirees won't be making withdrawals, but their beneficiaries would be. In this case, the beneficiaries wouldn't be hit with the 10 percent penalty.

✔ Withdrawals must begin by April 15 of the year after the investor reaches age 70½. Investors who don't take their withdrawal amount by that time are subject to a 50 percent tax penalty on the amount they should've withdrawn.

✔ Deposits into IRAs are allowed up to April 15 (tax day) to qualify as a deduction for the previous year's taxes.

Roth IRAs

Anyone who doesn't make too much money can open a Roth IRA. The key difference between a traditional IRA and a Roth IRA is that withdrawals from a Roth IRA are tax free. However, deposits made into the Roth IRA are not tax-deductible (made from after-tax dollars). Provided that the investor has held onto the Roth IRA for over five years and has reached age 59½, he or she can withdraw money from the Roth IRA without incurring any taxable income on the amount deposited or on the appreciation in the account.

The maximum that an individual may contribute to a traditional IRA and Roth IRA is $4,000 per year combined (or $5,000 if over age 50). As of 2008, the contribution limit goes up to $5,000, with a catch-up contribution of $1,000 allowed for individuals age 50 and older.

A limitation placed on Roth IRAs is that investors who earn more than $110,000 per year ($160,000 per year jointly) can't contribute to a Roth IRA.

Simplified employee pensions (SEP-IRAs)

A SEP-IRA is a retirement vehicle designed for small business owners, self-employed individuals, and their employees. SEP-IRAs allow participants to invest money for retirement on a tax-deferred basis. Employers can make tax-deductible contributions directly to their employees' SEP-IRAs. As of 2007, the maximum employer contribution to each employee's SEP-IRA is 25 percent of the employee's compensation (salary, bonuses, and overtime) or $45,000 (subject to cost of living increases in the following years), whichever is less. Employees who are part of the plan may still make annual contributions to a traditional or Roth IRA.

For Further Review

For you to be as prepared as possible to take the Series 7 exam, you should also have a grasp of the items in this section. Look over these additional tax- and retirement-plan-related topics and make sure you know them prior to taking the test:

- Foreign security taxes
- Tax (bond) swap
- LIFO, FIFO, or identified shares
- Taxes on securities owned by a corporation
- Keogh plans
- Coverdell IRA
- Rollovers
- Employee Retirement Income Security Act (ERISA)
- Defined contribution plans
- Defined benefit plans
- Savings incentive match plans for employees (SIMPLEs)
- 401k
- 403b (tax-sheltered annuities)
- Section 529 plans
- Vesting
- Early withdrawal penalties
- Allowable contributions
- Penalties for excess contributions

Chapter 16

No Fooling Around: Rules and Regulations

First off, I'd like to apologize for having to include this chapter. Unfortunately, rules are a part of life and part of the Series 7. When you're reading this, please remember that I didn't make the rules — but I do my best to make them as easy to digest as possible. Rules have become increasingly important on the Series 7 exam, especially since the Patriot Act came into the picture.

In this chapter, I cover topics related to rules and regulations. First, I help you understand who the guardians of the market are and their roles in protecting customers and enforcing rules. I also place considerable emphasis on opening, closing, transferring, and handling customers' accounts. And of course, I proved practice questions and the "For Further Review" section to guide you on your way.

The Market Watchdogs: Securities Regulatory Organizations

To keep the market running smoothly and to make sure investors aren't abused (at least too much), regulatory organizations stay on the lookout. Although you don't need to know all the minute details about each of them, you do have to know the basics. For additional information on the New York Stock Exchange (NYSE) and the National Association of Securities Dealers (NASD), you can visit (or revisit) Chapter 14.

The Securities and Exchange Commission

The Securities and Exchange Commission, or SEC, is the major watchdog of the securities industry. Congress created the SEC to regulate the market and to protect investors from fraudulent and manipulative practices. All broker-dealers who transact business with investors and other broker-dealers must register with the SEC. And that registration means something: All broker-dealers have to comply with SEC rules or face censure (an official reprimand), limits on activity, suspension or suspension of one or more associated persons (such as a registered rep or principal), a fine, and/or having their registration revoked.

SEC investigations may lead to a civil (financial) complaint being filed in a federal court. They may seek disgorgement (taking away of) of ill-gotten gains, civil money penalties, and injunctive relief (cease and desist order from the court). If the matter is criminal in nature, the investigation is conducted by the U.S. Attorney's Office and the grand jury.

Among its other numerous functions, you should be aware that the SEC also enforces the following acts:

- **Securities Act of 1933:** The Act of 1933 requires the full and fair disclosure of all material information about a new issue.

- **Securities Exchange Act of 1934:** The Act of 1934, which established the SEC, was enacted to protect investors by regulating the over-the-counter (OTC) market and exchanges (such as the NYSE). Chapter 14 can tell you more about markets. In addition, the Act of 1934 regulates

  - The extension of credit in margin accounts (see Chapter 9)

  - Transactions by insiders

  - Customer accounts

  - Trading activities

- **The Trust Indenture Act of 1939:** This act prohibits bond issues valued at over $5,000,000 from being offered to investors without an indenture. The trust *indenture* is a written agreement that protects investors by disclosing the particulars of the issue (coupon rate, maturity date, any collateral backing the bond, and so on). As part of the Trust Indenture Act of 1939, all companies must hire a trustee who's responsible for protecting the rights of bondholders.

- **Investment Company Act of 1940:** This act regulates the registration requirements and the activities of investment companies.

- **Investment Advisers Act of 1940:** This act requires the registration of certain investment advisers with the SEC. An *investment adviser* is a person who receives a fee for giving investment advice. Any investment advisers with at least $25 million of assets under management or people who advise an investment company must register with the SEC. All other investment advisers have to register on the state level. The Investment Advisers Act of 1940 regulates

  - Record-keeping responsibilities

  - Advisory contracts

  - Advertising rules

  - Custody of customers' assets and funds

Self-regulatory organizations

As you can imagine, due to the unscrupulous nature of some investors and registered representatives, the SEC's job has to be overwhelming. Fortunately, a few self-regulatory organizations (SROs) are there to take some of the burden off of the SEC's shoulders. Although membership isn't mandatory, most broker-dealers are members of one or more SROs. SRO rules are usually stricter than those of the SEC.

The four types of SROs you need to know for the Series 7 are the NASD, MSRB, NYSE, and CBOE:

- **National Association of Securities Dealers:** The NASD is a self-regulatory organization that's responsible for the operation and regulation of the NASDAQ stock market and the OTC (over-the-counter) market. The NASD is responsible for making sure that members follow not only NASD rules but also the rules set forth by the SEC. Additionally, the NASD handles complaints against member firms and may take disciplinary action if necessary (see "Handling complaints," later in this chapter). The NASD is also responsible for administering securities exams such as the Series 7 (now you know who to blame).

- **Municipal Securities Rulemaking Board:** The MSRB was established to develop rules that banks and securities firms have to follow when underwriting, selling, buying, and recommending municipal securities (check out Chapter 8 for info on municipal bonds). The MSRB is subject to SEC oversight but does not enforce SEC rules.

  The MSRB makes rules for firms (and representatives) who sell municipal bonds but does not enforce them.

- **New York Stock Exchange:** The NYSE is the oldest and largest stock exchange in the United States. The NYSE is responsible for listing securities, setting exchange policies, and supervising the exchange and member firms. As with the NASD, the NYSE has the power to take disciplinary action against member firms.

- **Chicago Board Options Exchange:** The CBOE is an exchange that makes and enforces option exchange rules.

The NASD and NYSE can fine, suspend, censure (reprimand), and expel members; however, the NASD and NYSE can't imprison members who violate the rules and regulations.

Look at Series 7 questions with the words *guarantee* or *approve* in them very carefully. The NASD, SEC, NYSE, and so on do *not* approve or guarantee securities. Any statement that says that they do is false.

Following Protocol when Opening Accounts

The Series 7 examiners seem to be focusing more and more on the handling of customer accounts. You need to know what to do to open accounts, how to take customer orders, the rules for sending out confirmations, and so on.

Filing the facts on the new account form

When you're opening any new account for a customer, the new account form needs some basic information. Getting this information will be your responsibility (or the responsibility of the broker-dealer). Here's a list of the items that need to be on the new account form:

- The name(s) and address(es) of the individual(s) who'll have access to the account

- The customer's date of birth (the customer must be of legal age to open an account)

- The type of account the customer is opening (cash, margin, options, and so on)

- The customer's Social Security number (if the customer is an individual) or tax ID number (if the customer is a business)

- The customer's occupation, employer, and type of business (certain limitations are placed on customers who work for banks, broker-dealers, insurance companies, and so on)

✔ The customer's citizenship

✔ Bank references and the customer's net worth and annual income

✔ Whether the customer is an insider of a company

✔ Investment objectives (see Chapter 13)

✔ The registered representative's and principal's signature

Additionally, only individuals who are legally competent may open accounts.

The following question tests your ability to answer a question about opening a new account:

Which of the following people must sign a new account form?

   I. The customer

   II. The customer's spouse

   III. The registered representative

   IV. A principal

(A) I and II only

(B) III and IV only

(C) I and IV only

(D) I, III, and IV only

The answer is B. When you're opening a new account for a customer, the new account form requires only your signature and a principal's (manager's) signature. Make sure you don't assume extenuating circumstances. You need the customer's signature on a new account form only if the customer is opening a margin account. Additionally, you need the spouse's signature only if you're opening a joint account. Because the question doesn't say that the account is being opened jointly, you can't assume that it is.

Word on the street: Numbered accounts

A *street name* or *numbered account* is an account registered in the name of the broker-dealer with an ID number. Street name accounts give the investor a certain degree of privacy and help facilitate the trading of securities (because the brokerage firm, not the customer, signs the certificates). You need to know a few rules about street name accounts for the Series 7:

✔ You need a written statement from the customer attesting to the ownership of the account.

✔ The street name account may be changed into a regular account at any time.

✔ All margin accounts must be in street name.

The Patriot Act

The Patriot Act was enacted in 2001 to help identify and catch terrorists. As part of the Patriot Act, broker-dealers are required to

✔ Verify the identity of new customers

✔ Keep records of the information used to identify the customer

✔ Verify that a customer doesn't appear on any list of known terrorists or terrorist organizations (the U.S. Treasury keeps this list)

Selecting the appropriate type of account

Investors can open many different types of accounts through a broker-dealer. You need a basic understanding of the types of accounts for the Series 7 exam. Fortunately, most of them are pretty straightforward.

Single and joint accounts

Some investors prefer to share; others like to go it alone. Whatever their preference, adults can open up accounts that fit their needs:

- ✔ **Single accounts:** Naturally, this account is in the name of *one person*. The key thing for you to remember is that individuals may not open accounts in other people's names without written permission (power of attorney).

- ✔ **Joint accounts:** This account is in the name of more than one person. All individuals named on the account have equal trading authority for the account. For Series 7 exam purposes, you need to be familiar with two types of joint accounts:

  - **Joint tenants with rights of survivorship (JTWROS):** With this type of joint account, when a joint tenant named on the account dies, his or her portion of the account passes on to the surviving joint tenant. These accounts are usually set up almost exclusively for husbands and wives.

  - **Joint with tenants in common (JTIC):** With this type of account, when one tenant of the account dies, his or her portion of the account becomes part of his or her estate. JTICs are usually set up for individuals who aren't related.

The following question tests your knowledge of account types:

All of the following people may open a joint account EXCEPT

(A) Two friends

(B) A husband and wife

(C) A parent and minor son

(D) Three strangers

The answer is C. A joint account is an account in the name of more than one adult. Answers A, B, and D are all possible for joint accounts; however, an account opened for a minor must be a custodial account, which I discuss in the next section.

Custodial accounts

A *custodial account* is set up for a child who's too young to have his or her own account. A custodian (adult) makes the investment decisions for the account. Any adult can open a custodial account for a minor, so the people named on the account don't have to be related.

Custodial accounts may be referred to on the Series 7 exam as UGMA or UTMA accounts because they fall under the Uniform Gifts to Minors Act or Uniform Transfer to Minors Act. A *UTMA account* is an extension of the UGMA account that allows gifts in addition to cash and securities to be transferred to the minor. The additional gifts allowed are art, real estate, patents, and royalties.

Additionally, because the minor is too young to make investment decisions for himself or herself, some rules are specific for custodian accounts:

- ✔ There can only be one custodian and one minor per account.

- ✔ The minor is responsible for the taxes (the minor's Social Security number is registered for the account).

- ✔ The account is registered in the name of the custodian for the benefit of the minor (the custodian is responsible for endorsing all certificates).

- ✔ The account can't be held in street name (in the name of the broker-dealer with an ID number — see the earlier section "Word on the street: Numbered accounts").

- ✔ Securities can't be traded on margin or sold short (Chapter 9 covers margin accounts).

- ✔ Anyone may give a gift of cash or securities to the minor. The gift is irrevocable (can't be refused or sent back by the custodian).

- ✔ If an account receives rights, the custodian can't let the rights expire. (See Chapter 6 for info on rights.) Because rights have value, a custodian can exercise or sell the rights.

Custodial accounts are for minors, so as soon as a minor reaches the age of majority, which is determined by state, the custodial account is terminated and the account is transferred to a single account in the name of the (former) minor.

Discretionary accounts

Decision-making can be stressful, and some investors don't want to deal with it. With a *discretionary account,* an investor can give you (the registered rep) the right to make trading decisions for the account. All discretionary accounts need a *written power of attorney* signed by the investor, which gives trading authorization to the registered rep.

If a customer places an order but doesn't specify the security, the number of shares or units, and/or whether the customer wants to buy or sell, you need a written power of attorney. If you don't have a written power of attorney, you can't do anything but decide when to place the order (timing). For example, suppose one of your customers calls you and says that he or she wants to sell 100 shares of ABC common stock and you believe you can get a better price later in the day. The customer can give you verbal permission to place the order at your discretion. This type of order is called a *market not held order* and is usually good only for the day.

Here are some specific rules for discretionary orders that you're likely to see on the Series 7 exam:

- ✔ Each discretionary order must be marked as *discretionary* on the order ticket.

- ✔ As with other orders, principals must sign each order ticket.

- ✔ A principal needs to review discretionary accounts regularly to make sure reps don't trade excessively to generate commissions, which is called *churning.*

A *fiduciary* is anyone who can legally make decisions for another investor. Examples of fiduciaries are custodians (UGMA accounts), a registered rep having power of attorney, an executor of an estate, a trustee, and so on.

Corporate accounts

Only incorporated businesses can open corporate accounts. If you're opening a corporate account, you need to obtain the tax ID number of the corporation, which is similar to an individual's Social Security number. Additionally, you need to obtain a copy of the *corporate resolution,* which lets you know who you should be taking trading instructions from (so you don't get a call like, "Hi, I'm Joe Blow, the janitor for XYZ Corporation, and I'd like to purchase 1,000 shares of ABC for our company").

If a corporation wants to open a margin account (accounts where they're borrowing some money from the broker-dealer to purchase securities — see Chapter 9), you also need a copy of the corporate charter (bylaws). The corporate charter has to allow the corporation to purchase securities on margin.

Partnership accounts

Two or more individual owners of a business that's not set up as a corporation may set up a partnership account. All partnerships must complete a partnership agreement, which the broker-dealer has to keep on file. The *partnership agreement,* like a corporate resolution, states who has trading authorization for the account so you know who you're supposed to be taking orders from.

Trading by the Book When the Account Is Open

After you've opened a new account, you have to follow additional rules and regulations to keep working in the business. You need to know how to receive trade instructions and how to fill out an order ticket, as well as settlement and payment dates for different securities.

Filling out an order ticket

When you're working as a registered rep, completing documents such as order tickets will become second nature because you'll have them in front of you. When you're taking the Series 7, you don't get that luxury, but you still need to know the particulars about what to fill out.

Getting the particulars on paper (or in binary)

When your customer places an order, you have to fill out an order ticket. Order tickets may be on paper or entered electronically. Regardless of how you enter the order, it needs to contain the following information:

- The registered rep's identification number
- The customer's account number
- The description of the security (stocks, bonds, symbol, and so on)
- The number of shares or bonds that are being purchased or sold
- Whether the registered rep has discretionary authority over the account
- Whether the customer is buying, selling long (selling securities that are owned), or selling short (selling borrowed securities — see Chapter 9)
- For option tickets, whether the customer is buying or writing (selling), is covered or uncovered, and is opening or closing (see Chapter 12 for info on options)
- Whether it's a market order, good-till-cancelled (GTC) order, day order, and so on
- Whether the trade is executed in a cash or margin account
- The time of the order
- The execution price

Figure 16-1 shows you what standard paper order tickets may look like.

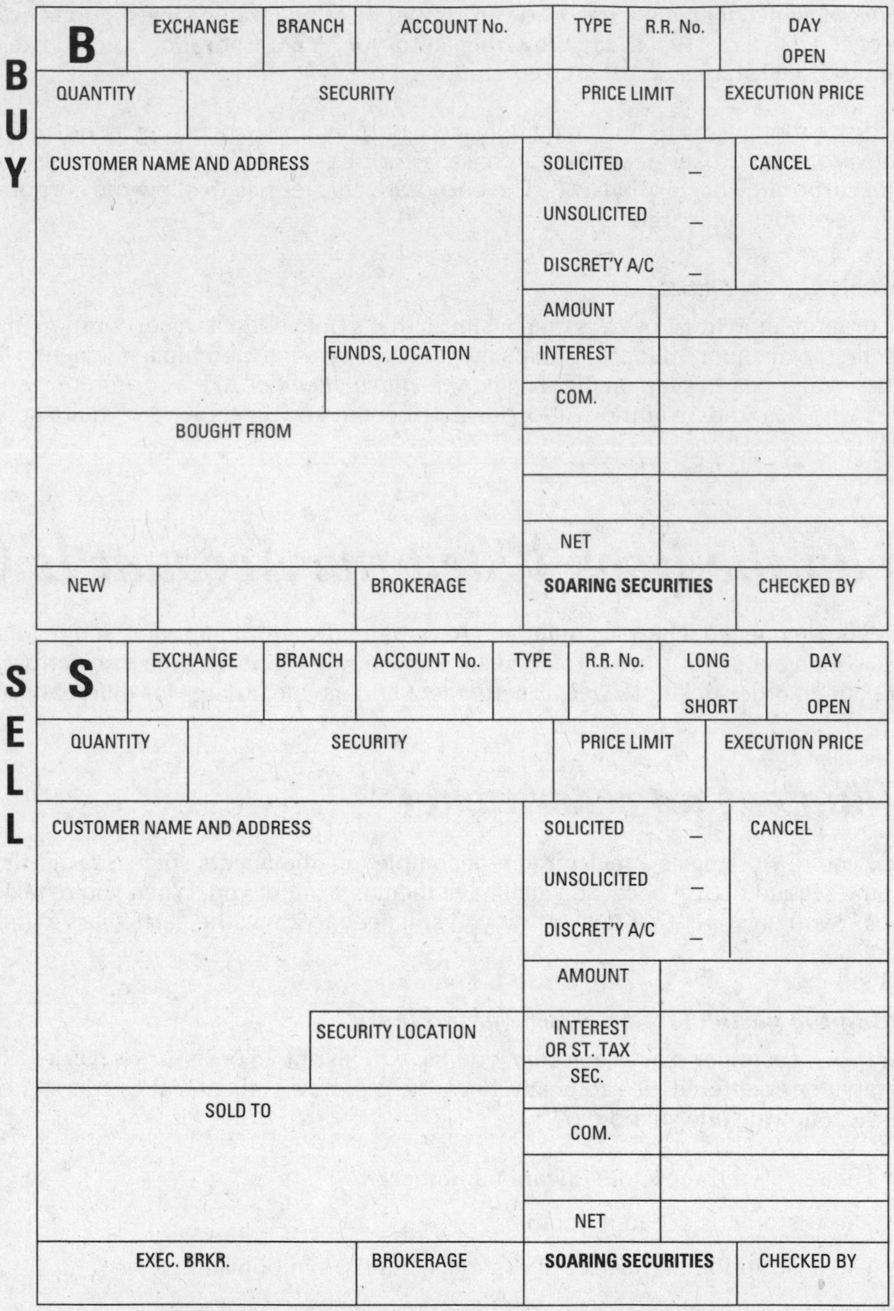

B	EXCHANGE	BRANCH	ACCOUNT No.	TYPE	R.R. No.	DAY OPEN

BUY

QUANTITY	SECURITY	PRICE LIMIT	EXECUTION PRICE

CUSTOMER NAME AND ADDRESS

SOLICITED _   CANCEL

UNSOLICITED _

DISCRET'Y A/C _

AMOUNT

FUNDS, LOCATION   INTEREST

COM.

BOUGHT FROM

NET

NEW		BROKERAGE	**SOARING SECURITIES**	CHECKED BY

S	EXCHANGE	BRANCH	ACCOUNT No.	TYPE	R.R. No.	LONG SHORT	DAY OPEN

SELL

QUANTITY	SECURITY	PRICE LIMIT	EXECUTION PRICE

CUSTOMER NAME AND ADDRESS

SOLICITED _   CANCEL

UNSOLICITED _

DISCRET'Y A/C _

AMOUNT

SECURITY LOCATION   INTEREST OR ST. TAX

SEC.

SOLD TO   COM.

NET

EXEC. BRKR.	BROKERAGE	**SOARING SECURITIES**	CHECKED BY

Figure 16-1:
Buy and sell
order tickets
have
spaces for
the info you
need to
make a
trade.

Designating unsolicited trades

Normally, you'll be recommending securities in line with a customer's investment objectives. If, however, the customer requests a trade that you think is unsuitable, it's your duty to inform him or her about it. You don't have to reject the order (it *is* the customer's money, and you're in the business to generate commission). If the customer still wants to execute the trade, simply mark the order as *unsolicited,* which takes the responsibility off of your shoulders.

A trip to the principal's office: Securing a signature

Principals are managers of a firm. All brokerage firms, no matter how small, must have at least one principal. When you open or trade an account, you have to bring the new account form or order ticket to a principal to sign. Principals need to approve all new accounts, all trades in accounts, and all advertisements and sales literature; they also handle all complaints (lucky break for you!). A principal doesn't have to approve a prospectus or your recommendations to your customers.

Although you'll generally bring an order ticket to a principal right after taking an order, the principal can sign the order ticket later in the day. On the Series 7 exam, you'd answer that the principal needs to approve the trade on the same day, not before or immediately after the trade.

Checking your calendar: Payment and settlement dates

Securities that investors purchase have different payment and settlement dates. Here's what you need to know:

- ✔ **Trade date:** The day the trade is executed; an investor who buys a security owns the security as soon as the trade is executed, whether or not he or she has paid for the trade

- ✔ **Settlement date:** The day the issuer updates its records and the certificates are delivered to the buyer's brokerage firm

- ✔ **Payment date:** The day the buyer of the securities must pay for the trade

Unless the question specifically asks you to follow NASD or NYSE rules (which I doubt it will), assume the Fed payment dates in Table 16-1. The NASD and NYSE rules both require payment for securities to be made no later than the settlement date, but the Federal Reserve Board states that the payment date for corporate securities is five business days after the trade date.

Table 16-1	Regular Way Settlement and Payment Dates	
Type of Security	**Settlement Date (in Business Days after the Trade Date)**	**Payment Date (in Business Days after the Trade Date)**
Stocks and corporate bonds	3	5
Municipal bonds	3	3
U.S. government bonds	1	1
Options	1	5

Cash trades (same-day settlement) require payment for the securities and delivery of the securities on the same day as the trade date.

The *when, as, and if issued (when-issued transaction)* method of delivery is used for a securities issue that's been authorized and sold to investors before the certificates are ready for delivery. This method is typically used for stock splits, new issues of municipal bonds, and Treasury securities (U.S. government securities). The settlement date for when-issued securities can be any of the following:

- A date to be assigned
- Three business days after the securities are ready for delivery
- On the date determined by the NASD

Confirming a trade

A *trade confirmation* (receipt of trade) is the document you send to a customer after a trade has taken place. You have to send out trade confirmations after each trade, at or before the completion of the transaction (the settlement date). Here's a list of information included in the confirmation:

- The customer's account number
- The registered rep's ID number
- The trade date
- Whether the customer bought (BOT) or sold (SLD)
- The number of shares of stock or the par value of bonds purchased or sold
- The yield (if bonds)
- Committee on Uniform Security Identification Procedures (CUSIP) number, a security ID number
- The price of the security
- The total amount paid or received, not including commission
- The commission, which is added on purchases and subtracted on sales; if the broker-dealer purchased for or sold from its own inventory, the markdown or markup doesn't have to be disclosed
- The *net amount,* or the amount the customer paid or received after adding or subtracting the commission; if the investor purchased or sold bonds, the accrued interest is added or subtracted during this calculation.

Meeting the requirements for good delivery

In the securities industry, good delivery doesn't mean "in 30 minutes or it's free" (even the pizza delivery places don't promise that anymore). To constitute good delivery of certificates, the securities have to be in a certain form. The transfer agent is responsible for good delivery. Here are the general requirements:

- It must be in good physical condition.
- It must be endorsed.
- The exact number of shares or bonds must be delivered.
- The correct denomination of the certificates must be delivered.

And here are the requirements for good delivery of specific securities:

- ✔ **Bearer (coupon) bonds:** These unregistered bonds must be in $1,000 or $5,000 denominations only.

  For a bearer bond to be in good delivery form, it must be delivered with all unpaid coupons (representing interest payments) attached. See Chapter 7 for more info on bonds.

- ✔ **Registered bonds:** These bonds must be in multiples of $1,000 par value with a maximum par value of $100,000.

- ✔ **Stock:** Because the most easily traded unit of stock is 100 shares (a round lot), stock certificates must be in denominations of one of the following:

  - Multiples of 100 shares — 100, 200, 300, 400, and so on

  - Divisors of 100 shares — 1, 2, 4, 5, 10, 20, 25, 50, or 100

  - Units that add up to 100 shares — 40 shares + 60 shares, 91 + 9, 80 + 15 + 5, and so on

Odd lot trades (less than 100 shares) or odd lot portions of orders are exempt from the good delivery rule.

The following question tests your ability to answer a good delivery question:

All of the following are considered good delivery for a 560-share order EXCEPT

(A) two 200-share certificates, one 100-share certificate, and one 60-share certificate

(B) fifty-six 10-share certificates

(C) six 60-share certificates, five 30-share certificates, and five 10-share certificates

(D) one 400-share certificate and two 80-share certificates

The answer is D. Answer A is good because the 200-share certificates and 100-share certificates are multiples of 100 shares, and the 60-share trade (odd lot portion) is exempt. Answer B is good because 10 is a divisor of 100 (it goes into 100 evenly). Answer C is good because 60 + 30 + 10 adds up to 100, and the extra 60-share certificate is exempt because it's an odd-lot portion. However, answer D is bad delivery because even though the 400-share certificate is okay, the two 80 share certificates aren't good because they don't add up to 100.

Always look at the shares first to determine whether you have good delivery. I see a lot of students look at the number of certificates before they check the number of shares per certificate. The Series 7 designers want to know more about your understanding of concepts than your multiplication and addition skills, so you probably won't have to figure out the total number of shares in each answer choice — they should all add up to the number of shares in the order (in the preceding example, 560).

Following up with account statements

An *account statement* gives the customer information about his or her holdings in the account along with the market value at the time the statement was issued. Customers are supposed to receive account statements on a regular basis. This should be pretty easy for you to remember. Here's how often you have to send out statements, from most to least often (remember the acronym *AIM*):

- **Active accounts:** If any trading was executed within the month, the customer must receive an account statement for that month.

- **Inactive accounts:** If the customer is not actively trading his or her account and is just holding a position, an account statement must be sent out at least quarterly (every three months).

- **Mutual funds:** No matter how much (or little) trading was done, a customer needs to receive an account statement semiannually (every six months).

Keeping your dividend dates straight

When customers are purchasing securities of a company that's in the process of declaring a dividend or paying a dividend, you need to be able to tell those customers whether they're entitled to receive the dividend. Because stock transactions settle in three business days, the customers are entitled to the dividend if they purchased the securities at least three days prior to the *record date*. Here's a list of the four need-to-know dates for the Series 7 exam:

- **Declaration date:** The day that the corporation officially announces that a dividend will be paid to shareholders.

- **Ex-dividend date:** The first day that the stock trades without dividends; an investor purchasing the stock on the ex-dividend date isn't entitled to receive the dividend; because stock transactions take three business days to settle, the ex-dividend date is automatically two business days before the record date.

  The ex-dividend date is the day that the price of the stock is reduced by the dividend amount. (Chapter 6 can tell you more about dividends and related calculations.)

- **Record date:** The day the corporation inspects its records to see who gets the dividend; to receive the dividend, the investor must be listed as a stockholder in company records.

- **Payment (payable) date:** The day that the corporation pays the dividend.

As you can see from the diagram, the buyer receives the dividend if he or she purchases the stock before the ex-dividend date. If the stock is purchased after the ex-dividend date, the seller receives the dividend.

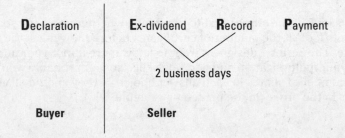

To help you remember the sequence of dates, use the phrase *Don't Eat Rubber Pickles*. I know it sounds ridiculous, but the more ridiculous, the easier it is to remember.

The board of directors must announce three dates: the declaration date, the record date, and the payment date. The ex-dividend date doesn't need to be announced because it's automatically two business days before the record date. However, mutual funds have to announce all four dates because they may set their ex-dividend date at any time (even on the record date).

The following question tests your ability to answer a dividend question:

Wedgie Corp. has just announced a $0.50 cash dividend. If the record date is Wednesday, March 10, when is the last day an investor can purchase the stock and receive the dividend?

(A) March 4

(B) March 5

(C) March 7

(D) March 8

The answer is B. In order for an investor to purchase the stock and receive a previously declared dividend, he or she must purchase the stock at least one business day before the ex-dividend date. This question is a little more difficult because you have a weekend to take into consideration.

The ex-dividend date is March 8, which is two business days prior to the record date. This investor had to buy the stock before the ex-dividend date in order to receive the dividend, so he or she had to buy it March 5 or before (because the 6th and 7th were Saturday and Sunday). The last day an investor can purchase the stock and receive the dividend is March 5.

If a stock is sold short (if the investor is selling a borrowed security), the lender of the stock sold short is entitled to receive the dividend. (See Chapter 9 for details on margin accounts.) Also, the trades in the example problems are regular way settlement (three business days after the trade date); remember that cash transactions settle on the same day as the trade date. In case of dividends, if an investor purchases stock for cash, he or she would receive the dividend if he or she purchased the stock anywhere up to and including the record date.

Handling complaints

It's bound to happen sooner or later, no matter how awesome you are as a registered rep: One of your customers is going to complain about something (like unauthorized trades, guarantees, and so on). Complaints aren't considered official unless they're in writing. The NASD wants you to follow the proper procedure for handling complaints. The following sections cover formal and informal proceedings.

Code of procedure

The *code of procedure* is the NASD's formal procedure for handling securities-related complaints between public customers and members of the securities industry (broker-dealers, registered reps, clearing corporations, and so on). The public customer has the choice of taking the complaint to the formal code of procedure or the informal code of arbitration (see the next section).

In the code of procedure, the District Business Conduct Committee (DBCC) has the first jurisdiction over complaints. If the customer or member isn't satisfied with the results, he or she can appeal the decision to the NASD Board of Governors. Decisions are appealable all the way to the Supreme Court.

Code of arbitration

The *code of arbitration* is an informal hearing (heard by two to three arbiters) that's primarily conducted for disputes between members of the NASD. Members include not only broker-dealers but also individuals working for member firms.

For example, if you (a registered rep) have a dispute with the broker-dealer that you're working for, you can take the broker-dealer to arbitration. If a customer has a complaint against a broker-dealer or registered rep, the customer has the choice of going through code of procedure (see the preceding section) or code of arbitration, unless the customer has given prior written consent (usually by way of the new account form) that he or she will settle disputes only through arbitration.

The decisions in arbitration are binding and nonappealable, so they're less costly than court action.

Transferring accounts

If a customer wants to transfer an account from one broker-dealer to another, the customer has to fill out an account transfer form with the new broker-dealer listing the securities held at the old broker-dealer. Transfer instructions are then sent from the new broker-dealer to the old one.

The old broker-dealer has *three business days* to either validate or take exception (for an invalid account number, wrong Social Security number, and so on) to the transfer instructions sent from the new broker-dealer. After the old broker-dealer validates the account, that dealer has *three business days* to transfer the account to the new broker-dealer.

Committing Other Important Rules to Memory

Brokers and investors must follow numerous rules in order to keep themselves from facing fines or worse. In this section, I list a few of the more important rules.

Obeying the Telephone Act of 1991

To make sure that certain standards are used when calling potential customers (such as not calling them at midnight) the Telephone Act of 1991 was created. When you're dealing with potential customers on the phone, you need to know these rules:

- ✔ You can't make calls before 8:00 a.m. or after 9:00 p.m. local time of the potential customer.

- ✔ You have to give your name, company name, company address, and phone number.

- ✔ If you get a potential customer who's tired of being called, you should place that person on a *do not call list*.

- ✔ You may not send unsolicited ads by fax machine.

The Telephone Act of 1991 applies to potential customers. If you have an existing customer, you may call before 8:00 a.m. or after 9:00 p.m., if requested. This act applies to all sales calls (except those from nonprofit organizations).

Sticking to the NASD 5% markup policy

The NASD 5% policy is more of a guideline than a rule. The policy was enacted to make sure that investors receive fair treatment and aren't charged excessively for broker-dealer services in the over-the-counter (OTC) market. The guideline says that brokerage firms shouldn't charge commissions, markups, or markdowns of more than 5 percent for standard trades.

The following trades are subject to the NASD 5% markup policy:

- **Principal (dealer) transactions:** A firm buys securities for or sells securities from its own inventory and charges a markdown or markup.

- **Agency (broker) transactions:** A firm acts as a middleman (broker) and charges a commission.

- **Riskless (simultaneous) transactions:** A firm buys a security for its own inventory for immediate resale to the customer (riskless to the firm).

- **Proceeds transactions:** A firm sells a security and uses the money to immediately buy another security. You must treat this transaction as one trade (you can't charge on the way out and on the way in).

The NASD 5% markup policy covers *over-the-counter trades of outstanding, non-exempt securities with public customers.* If securities are exempt from SEC registration, they're exempt from the NASD 5% policy. Additionally, if a dealer paid $20 per share to have a security in inventory (dealer cost) and the market price is $8 per share, the dealer can't charge customers $20 per share so that they don't take a loss.

Under extenuating circumstances, the brokerage firm may charge more. Justifiable reasons for charging more (or less) than 5 percent include

- Difficulty buying or selling the security because the market price is too low or too high

- Having a small trade — for example, if a customer placed an order for $100 worth of securities, you'd lose your shirt if you were to charge only 5% ($5); in this case, you wouldn't be out of line if you were to charge 100 percent (by the same token, if a customer purchases $1,000,000 worth of securities, 5 percent [$50,000] would be considered excessive)

- Availability of the security

- Expenses involved in executing the trade

- Dealing with odd lot trades (for details, see "Meeting the requirements for good delivery," earlier in this chapter)

- Trading non-liquid securities

- Executing transactions on foreign markets

Avoiding violations

You should be aware of some violations not only for the Series 7 exam but also so you stay out of trouble. Some of the violations are more connected with broker-dealers and some with registered reps:

- **Commingling of funds:** Combining a customer's fully paid and margined securities or combining a firm's securities with customer securities

- **Interpositioning:** Having two securities dealers act as agents for the same exact trade so that two commissions are earned on one trade

- **Gifts:** Giving or receiving a gift of more than $100 per customer per year; business expenses (lunch, dinner, hotel rooms, and so on) are exempt from this MSRB rule (see "Self-Regulatory Organizations," earlier in this chapter)

- **Freeriding:** A customer's buying securities and selling them without paying for the purchase

- **Backing away:** A failure of a securities dealer to honor a firm quote

- **Churning:** When a registered rep excessively trades a customer's account for the sole purpose of generating commission

- **Matching orders:** The illegal manipulation of the price of a security (trading back and forth to artificially raise or lower the price of a security); people could match orders by executing a buy and a sell order of the same security at the same time with two different brokerage firms — for example, buying 1,000 shares of DEF from firm A while selling 1,000 shares of DEF through brokerage firm B

- **Painting the tape:** Creating the illusion of trading activity due to misleading reports on the consolidated tape — for example, reporting a trade of 10,000 shares of stock as two separate trades for 5,000 shares each

- **Frontrunning:** A violation in which a registered rep executes a trade for him- or herself, his or her firm, or a discretionary account based on knowledge of a block trade (10,000 shares or more) before the trade is reported on the ticker tape

- **Prearranged trades:** An illegal agreement between a registered rep and a customer to buy back a security at a fixed price

- **Marking the close/marking the open:** Executing a series of trades within minutes of the open or close of the market to manipulate the price of a security

- **Paying the media:** A violation in which brokerage firms or affiliated persons pay an employee of the media to affect the price of a security; for example, paying a TV stock expert to recommend a security that the firm has in its inventory

- **Freeriding and withholding:** A violation in which an underwriter holds back a hot issue (a new issue in high demand) and sells them later at a higher price; in addition, hot issues can't be sold to other brokerage firms, employees of firms (and their immediate family), or employees of financial institutions (and their immediate family)

Following the money: Anti money-laundering rules

The Bank Secrecy Act establishes the U.S. Treasury Department as the regulator for anti-money laundering programs. All broker-dealers are required to develop programs to detect possible money-laundering abuses. The program is designed to help prevent dirty money that has been *cleaned* (made to look like it came from a legitimate source) from being used to fund terrorist activities, illegal arms sales, drug trafficking, and so on. Here are three stages of money laundering that you must be aware of for the Series 7 exam (please, don't try this at home):

1. **Placement**

   In this initial stage of money laundering, the funds, derived from criminal activity, are transferred into the financial system (typically banks and broker-dealers).

2. **Layering**

   Layering is the money launderers' attempt to disguise the source of the funds, usually by moving the funds from one place to another through a series of transactions.

3. **Integration**

   Integration is the final stage of money laundering, when illegal funds are mixed *(commingled)* with legitimate funds. Launderers usually accomplish this step through businesses that operate using cash, importing and exporting companies, and so on.

Broker-dealers and other financial institutions must report any *cash or cash equivalent* deposits, withdrawals, or transfers of *$10,000 or more* through a Currency Transaction Report (CRT) to FinCEN (the U.S. Treasury Financial Crimes Network). An institution must report suspicious activity of *$5,000 or more* of *any type of transaction* to FinCEN by filing an Suspicious Activity Report (SAR).

Here are some indications of money laundering at the opening of the account:

- Concern with U.S. government reporting requirements
- Reluctance to reveal information about business activities
- Suspect ID such as a license or passport that looks like it was made in someone's basement
- Irrational transactions that are inconsistent with objectives
- Fiduciary (the person who can legally make decisions for another investor) reluctant to provide information about the customer
- The individual lacks general knowledge of his or her industry

And here are some shady signals for after the account is open:

- Depositing large amounts of cash or money orders
- *Structuring* — making cash or cash-equivalent deposits (such as money orders) of just under $10,000 to avoid having them be reported to the U.S. government
- Wire transfers to non-cooperative countries
- Sudden and unexplained wire activity
- Making a deposit and transferring to another party without any business purpose
- Buying a long-term investment and liquidating in the short-term
- Transfers between multiple accounts for no apparent reason
- Depositing bearer bonds and requesting the money immediately
- Total lack of concern about risks and commissions

The signs of money laundering tend to make sense, so when answering a Series 7 exam question about money laundering, think to yourself, "If it looks like a duck and quacks like a duck, it's probably a duck" — or in financial terms, "If it looks and seems like money laundering, it probably is money laundering."

The Investor's Bankruptcy Shield: SIPC

The Securities Investor Protection Corporation (SIPC) protects the customer against broker-dealer bankruptcy (failure). The government created this private, nonprofit organization (not a government agency) in 1970. SIPC protects each separate customer's assets (securities and cash) up to $500,000 total, of which no more than $100,000 is cash.

The following question concerns SIPC coverage:

John Fredericks has a cash account with $200,000 in securities and $300,000 cash and a margin account with $150,000 in equity. Additionally, John has a joint cash account with his wife Mary with $400,000 in securities and $200,000 cash. If John's broker-dealer goes bankrupt, what is his coverage under SIPC?

(A) 450,000

(B) $500,000

(C) $850,000

(D) $950,000

The answer is D. If one of your customers has a cash and margin account titled under one name, as John does, it's treated as though it belongs to one customer. Therefore, John's cash and margin account would be covered up to $500,000, of which no more than $100,000 can be cash. He'd be covered for the $350,000 in securities ($200,000 in securities plus the $150,000 equity) and $100,000 of the $300,000 cash for a total of $450,000. Next, the joint account with his wife would be treated as though from a separate customer. Therefore, that account would be covered for the $400,000 in securities and $100,000 in cash. Add the two together, and you see that John is covered for a total of $950,000 ($450,000 plus $500,000).

If an investor is not fully covered under SIPC, the investor is still owed money by the bankrupt broker-dealer; therefore, the investor becomes a *general creditor* of the firm for the balance owed.

For Further Review

Although I cover the main topics relating to rules and regulations, you need to know plenty more to be properly prepared to take the Series 7. You should have a good grasp on the following:

- Regulation S-P
- Rule 405 — know your customer
- Opening accounts for the employees of other brokerage firms
- Multiple accounts
- Back office procedure (wire room, purchasing and sales, margin, and cashier)
- Prudent man rule and the legal list
- Limited power of attorney and full power of attorney
- Death of an account holder
- Simplified arbitration and simplified industry arbitration

- Penny stock rules
- Trust account
- Seller's option
- Delivery versus payment (DVP)
- Payment and delivery instructions
- Extension of payment dates
- Stock or bond power, power of substitution
- Frozen accounts
- Erroneous reports
- Rejection and reclamation
- Transfer on death
- Ominibus account
- NASD Rule 2790
- Rules for brokers: moonlighting, private securities transactions, and bankruptcy
- Rules for insiders
- Rules for penny stocks
- Rules of fair practice and the uniform practice code
- Office of Supervisory Jurisdiction (OSJ)
- Corporate bankruptcy
- Fidelity bonds
- Rule of financial disclosure
- Nine bond rule
- Proxies
- Advertisements and sales literature
- Record keeping
- Holding customers' mail
- Exam requirements for registered reps
- Don't know (DK) notice

Part V
Putting Your Knowledge to Good Use: A Practice Exam

The 5th Wave   By Rich Tennant

Near The End of a Series 7 Exam...

SERIES 7 EXAM   SERIES 7 EXAM

" Not a problem! Not a problem! I just tripped over the power cord and disconnected his computer as he was about to check his score. I'm sure the computer's okay."

In this part . . .

Okay. This is your time to shine. Grab your sharp-
ened pencils, your stopwatch, and some paper.
Here's where the rubber meets the road and you find out
whether you're an old Model T or a Maserati. If you've followed my advice, completed your Series 7 prep course to
get a handle on the subject matter, and used this book as a
substantive review, you should do well on this exam. After
finishing, make sure you check out the answer explanations
that follow. You should be ready for the real deal if you
score 80 or better the first time you take the practice test.
Your goal of becoming a stockbroker awaits you at the
finish line, and you're almost there! Get ready, get set, go!

Chapter 17

Bring It On: Practice Exam Part I

*H*ere is where you get your chance to shine like a star.

This part of the practice exam has 125 questions in random order, just as they are in the actual Series 7 exam. Please read carefully — many test-takers make careless mistakes because they miss key words or read too quickly. Focus on the information you do need to know and ignore the information that you don't need. Read the last sentence twice to make sure you know what the question is asking.

Mark your answers on the answer key provided or on a separate piece of paper. You may use a basic calculator and scrap paper for notes and figuring. As you're done taking the exam, be sure to circle the questions you find difficult. This step can help you determine what you really need to review.

To simulate the real exam, try to finish part I in 3 hours or less. Please resist the urge to look at the answers and explanations as you work through the exam; save the grading for later. After you finish part I, you can either check your answers (see the answer key at the end of this chapter, or find the answers and detailed explanations in Chapter 18) or take a break and then proceed directly to part II in Chapter 19, where you find the final 125 questions (the break during the actual test is 30–60 minutes long, so you can probably squeeze a snack in there).

Good luck!

Practice Exam Part 1 Answer Sheet

1 Ⓐ Ⓑ Ⓒ Ⓓ	33 Ⓐ Ⓑ Ⓒ Ⓓ	65 Ⓐ Ⓑ Ⓒ Ⓓ	97 Ⓐ Ⓑ Ⓒ Ⓓ
2 Ⓐ Ⓑ Ⓒ Ⓓ	34 Ⓐ Ⓑ Ⓒ Ⓓ	66 Ⓐ Ⓑ Ⓒ Ⓓ	98 Ⓐ Ⓑ Ⓒ Ⓓ
3 Ⓐ Ⓑ Ⓒ Ⓓ	35 Ⓐ Ⓑ Ⓒ Ⓓ	67 Ⓐ Ⓑ Ⓒ Ⓓ	99 Ⓐ Ⓑ Ⓒ Ⓓ
4 Ⓐ Ⓑ Ⓒ Ⓓ	36 Ⓐ Ⓑ Ⓒ Ⓓ	68 Ⓐ Ⓑ Ⓒ Ⓓ	100 Ⓐ Ⓑ Ⓒ Ⓓ
5 Ⓐ Ⓑ Ⓒ Ⓓ	37 Ⓐ Ⓑ Ⓒ Ⓓ	69 Ⓐ Ⓑ Ⓒ Ⓓ	101 Ⓐ Ⓑ Ⓒ Ⓓ
6 Ⓐ Ⓑ Ⓒ Ⓓ	38 Ⓐ Ⓑ Ⓒ Ⓓ	70 Ⓐ Ⓑ Ⓒ Ⓓ	102 Ⓐ Ⓑ Ⓒ Ⓓ
7 Ⓐ Ⓑ Ⓒ Ⓓ	39 Ⓐ Ⓑ Ⓒ Ⓓ	71 Ⓐ Ⓑ Ⓒ Ⓓ	103 Ⓐ Ⓑ Ⓒ Ⓓ
8 Ⓐ Ⓑ Ⓒ Ⓓ	40 Ⓐ Ⓑ Ⓒ Ⓓ	72 Ⓐ Ⓑ Ⓒ Ⓓ	104 Ⓐ Ⓑ Ⓒ Ⓓ
9 Ⓐ Ⓑ Ⓒ Ⓓ	41 Ⓐ Ⓑ Ⓒ Ⓓ	73 Ⓐ Ⓑ Ⓒ Ⓓ	105 Ⓐ Ⓑ Ⓒ Ⓓ
10 Ⓐ Ⓑ Ⓒ Ⓓ	42 Ⓐ Ⓑ Ⓒ Ⓓ	74 Ⓐ Ⓑ Ⓒ Ⓓ	106 Ⓐ Ⓑ Ⓒ Ⓓ
11 Ⓐ Ⓑ Ⓒ Ⓓ	43 Ⓐ Ⓑ Ⓒ Ⓓ	75 Ⓐ Ⓑ Ⓒ Ⓓ	107 Ⓐ Ⓑ Ⓒ Ⓓ
12 Ⓐ Ⓑ Ⓒ Ⓓ	44 Ⓐ Ⓑ Ⓒ Ⓓ	76 Ⓐ Ⓑ Ⓒ Ⓓ	108 Ⓐ Ⓑ Ⓒ Ⓓ
13 Ⓐ Ⓑ Ⓒ Ⓓ	45 Ⓐ Ⓑ Ⓒ Ⓓ	77 Ⓐ Ⓑ Ⓒ Ⓓ	109 Ⓐ Ⓑ Ⓒ Ⓓ
14 Ⓐ Ⓑ Ⓒ Ⓓ	46 Ⓐ Ⓑ Ⓒ Ⓓ	78 Ⓐ Ⓑ Ⓒ Ⓓ	110 Ⓐ Ⓑ Ⓒ Ⓓ
15 Ⓐ Ⓑ Ⓒ Ⓓ	47 Ⓐ Ⓑ Ⓒ Ⓓ	79 Ⓐ Ⓑ Ⓒ Ⓓ	111 Ⓐ Ⓑ Ⓒ Ⓓ
16 Ⓐ Ⓑ Ⓒ Ⓓ	48 Ⓐ Ⓑ Ⓒ Ⓓ	80 Ⓐ Ⓑ Ⓒ Ⓓ	112 Ⓐ Ⓑ Ⓒ Ⓓ
17 Ⓐ Ⓑ Ⓒ Ⓓ	49 Ⓐ Ⓑ Ⓒ Ⓓ	81 Ⓐ Ⓑ Ⓒ Ⓓ	113 Ⓐ Ⓑ Ⓒ Ⓓ
18 Ⓐ Ⓑ Ⓒ Ⓓ	50 Ⓐ Ⓑ Ⓒ Ⓓ	82 Ⓐ Ⓑ Ⓒ Ⓓ	114 Ⓐ Ⓑ Ⓒ Ⓓ
19 Ⓐ Ⓑ Ⓒ Ⓓ	51 Ⓐ Ⓑ Ⓒ Ⓓ	83 Ⓐ Ⓑ Ⓒ Ⓓ	115 Ⓐ Ⓑ Ⓒ Ⓓ
20 Ⓐ Ⓑ Ⓒ Ⓓ	52 Ⓐ Ⓑ Ⓒ Ⓓ	84 Ⓐ Ⓑ Ⓒ Ⓓ	116 Ⓐ Ⓑ Ⓒ Ⓓ
21 Ⓐ Ⓑ Ⓒ Ⓓ	53 Ⓐ Ⓑ Ⓒ Ⓓ	85 Ⓐ Ⓑ Ⓒ Ⓓ	117 Ⓐ Ⓑ Ⓒ Ⓓ
22 Ⓐ Ⓑ Ⓒ Ⓓ	54 Ⓐ Ⓑ Ⓒ Ⓓ	86 Ⓐ Ⓑ Ⓒ Ⓓ	118 Ⓐ Ⓑ Ⓒ Ⓓ
23 Ⓐ Ⓑ Ⓒ Ⓓ	55 Ⓐ Ⓑ Ⓒ Ⓓ	87 Ⓐ Ⓑ Ⓒ Ⓓ	119 Ⓐ Ⓑ Ⓒ Ⓓ
24 Ⓐ Ⓑ Ⓒ Ⓓ	56 Ⓐ Ⓑ Ⓒ Ⓓ	88 Ⓐ Ⓑ Ⓒ Ⓓ	120 Ⓐ Ⓑ Ⓒ Ⓓ
25 Ⓐ Ⓑ Ⓒ Ⓓ	57 Ⓐ Ⓑ Ⓒ Ⓓ	89 Ⓐ Ⓑ Ⓒ Ⓓ	121 Ⓐ Ⓑ Ⓒ Ⓓ
26 Ⓐ Ⓑ Ⓒ Ⓓ	58 Ⓐ Ⓑ Ⓒ Ⓓ	90 Ⓐ Ⓑ Ⓒ Ⓓ	122 Ⓐ Ⓑ Ⓒ Ⓓ
27 Ⓐ Ⓑ Ⓒ Ⓓ	59 Ⓐ Ⓑ Ⓒ Ⓓ	91 Ⓐ Ⓑ Ⓒ Ⓓ	123 Ⓐ Ⓑ Ⓒ Ⓓ
28 Ⓐ Ⓑ Ⓒ Ⓓ	60 Ⓐ Ⓑ Ⓒ Ⓓ	92 Ⓐ Ⓑ Ⓒ Ⓓ	124 Ⓐ Ⓑ Ⓒ Ⓓ
29 Ⓐ Ⓑ Ⓒ Ⓓ	61 Ⓐ Ⓑ Ⓒ Ⓓ	93 Ⓐ Ⓑ Ⓒ Ⓓ	125 Ⓐ Ⓑ Ⓒ Ⓓ
30 Ⓐ Ⓑ Ⓒ Ⓓ	62 Ⓐ Ⓑ Ⓒ Ⓓ	94 Ⓐ Ⓑ Ⓒ Ⓓ	
31 Ⓐ Ⓑ Ⓒ Ⓓ	63 Ⓐ Ⓑ Ⓒ Ⓓ	95 Ⓐ Ⓑ Ⓒ Ⓓ	
32 Ⓐ Ⓑ Ⓒ Ⓓ	64 Ⓐ Ⓑ Ⓒ Ⓓ	96 Ⓐ Ⓑ Ⓒ Ⓓ	

1. Which of the following is TRUE about the par value of common stock?

   (A) It represents an arbitrary value on a corporation's books.

   (B) It is directly linked to the market value of the security.

   (C) It represents the amount of money investors receive for redeeming their shares.

   (D) It represents the amount of money shareholders will receive if the corporation goes into bankruptcy and its assets are liquidated.

2. At a shareholder's meeting, three positions are up for election on the board of directors. If the voting is done on a cumulative basis and an owner has 1,000 shares, which of the following are acceptable ways to vote?

   I.   1,000 votes for one candidate

   II. 3,000 votes for one candidate

   III. 1,000 votes for each of three candidates

   IV. 3,000 votes for each of three candidates

   (A) I, III, and IV only

   (B) II, III, and IV only

   (C) I, II, and III only

   (D) I, II, III, and IV

3. Lee Digsworth III purchases 10 ABC convertible bonds at 120 that are convertible at $25. The bonds are due to mature in 27 years at par value, and they pay a coupon rate of 9 percent. What is the current yield of the bonds?

   (A) 6.8 percent

   (B) 7.5 percent

   (C) 9 percent

   (D) (Annual interest – annual amortization) ÷ market price

4. Mike Sparticus would like to purchase $30,000 of TOGA Aggressive Growth mutual fund. How many shares can Mike purchase if the NAV is $12.00, the POP is $13.11, and the sales charge percent is as follows?

Breakpoint	Sales Charge %
$0–$9,999	8½%
$10,000–$19,999	7½%
$20,000–$29,999	6½%
$30,000–$49,999	5½%
$50,000 and up	4½%

   (A) 2,288

   (B) 2,304

   (C) 2,362

   (D) 2,370

5. Which TWO of the following option investors will receive the dividend if the option is exercised prior to the ex-dividend date?

   I.   The holder of a call option

   II. The holder of a put option

   III. The writer of a call option

   IV. The writer of a put option

   (A) I and II

   (B) III and IV

   (C) I and IV

   (D) II and III

6. Which of the following securities are exempt from SEC registration?

   I.   Private placements

   II. Intrastate offerings

   III. Interstate offerings

   IV. Variable annuities

   (A) I and II only

   (B) I and III only

   (C) I, II, and IV only

   (D) I, III, and IV only

7. When is the last time an investor may trade a listed option?

   (A) 11:59 p.m. EST on the Saturday after the third Friday of the expiration month

   (B) 10:59 p.m. EST on the Saturday after the third Friday of the expiration month

   (C) 5:30 p.m. EST on the third Friday of the expiration month

   (D) 4:00 p.m. EST on the third Friday of the expiration month

8. While studying a particular stock, a technical analyst notices that it is in a "head and shoulders top formation." Which of the following best describes a head and shoulders top formation?

   (A) Reversal of a bearish trend

   (B) Reversal of a bullish trend

   (C) Bearish

   (D) Bullish

9. Which of the following MUST be a closed-end fund?

   (A) NAV — 9.20, POP — 10.00

   (B) NAV — 4.45, POP — 4.65

   (C) NAV — 22.00, POP — 23.00

   (D) NAV — 11.40, POP — 13.00

10. The Fed announces an increase in the discount rate from 5 percent to 5½ percent. Which TWO of the following will MOST likely occur after the increase?

    I. Outstanding debenture prices will rise.

    II. Outstanding debenture prices will fall.

    III. U.S. imports of foreign goods will be more competitive.

    IV. U.S. exports will be more competitive.

    (A) I and III

    (B) I and IV

    (C) II and III

    (D) II and IV

11. Which of the following BEST illustrates the calculation of a net revenue pledge as it relates to municipal bonds?

    (A) Net revenues ÷ (operation + maintenance)

    (B) (Gross revenues – [operation + maintenance]) ÷ debt service

    (C) (Net revenues + operation + maintenance) ÷ (principal + interest)

    (D) (Gross revenues – debt service) ÷ (principal + interest)

12. An investor purchases an ABC corporate debenture with a 7 percent coupon and a basis of 7 percent. If the bond is to be called in five years with a yield to call of 7¼ percent, how much did the investor pay for the bond?

    (A) Below $1,000

    (B) $1,000

    (C) Above $1,000

    (D) 7^4

13. Which of the following BEST describes dollar cost averaging as it pertains to mutual fund investing?

    (A) Maintaining a fixed dollar amount invested in mutual funds

    (B) Investing a fixed dollar amount periodically into the same investment

    (C) Purchasing a fixed number of shares periodically

    (D) None of the above

14. Which of the following are TRUE of ADRs?

    I. The investor does not receive the actual certificate.

    II. The investor cannot receive dividends in cash.

    III. The actual shares are held in a custodian bank.

    IV. They represent receipts for U.S. securities that trade in foreign countries.

    (A) I and III only

    (B) I, II, and IV only

    (C) I, III, and IV only

    (D) I, II, III, and IV

15. All of the following are money market instruments EXCEPT

    (A) ADRs

    (B) CDs

    (C) T-bills

    (D) Repos

16. An investor purchases a callable convertible bond that is currently trading in the market at 96. The bond is convertible at $25. If the basis is 7.5 percent and the nominal yield is 7 percent, what is the current yield?

    (A) 7 percent

    (B) 7.29 percent

    (C) 7.34 percent

    (D) 7.5 percent

17. Which of the following is/are TRUE regarding variable annuities?

    I.   The payouts depend upon the performance of the securities in the separate account.

    II. Investors may claim deductions for the current year as long as they have deposited money into the annuity prior to April 15 of the following year.

    III. "Life with period certain" provides the highest payouts.

    IV. The assumed interest rate is the annual rate of return necessary to beat the S&P 500.

    (A) I only

    (B) I, II, and III only

    (C) II, III, and IV only

    (D) II and III only

18. An investor purchases 1,000 shares of DIM at $20 per share in a margin account. If this is the initial transaction and Reg T is 55 percent, what is the loan value?

    (A) $2,000

    (B) $9,000

    (C) $10,000

    (D) $11,000

19. An investor is long 1 DIP Jul 80 put for 9 and is short 1 DIP Jul 70 put for 3. In which TWO ways could the investor profit from this position?

    I.   The difference in the premiums widens.

    II. The difference in the premiums narrows.

    III. The options expire unexercised.

    IV. The options are exercised.

    (A) I and III

    (B) I and IV

    (C) II and III

    (D) II and IV

20. You would like to show potential customers some of your option picks and how you might be able to make them money. Advertisements pertaining to past option recommendations must include which of the following?

    (A) Whether your firm acted as a selling group member within the last three years

    (B) A listing of all of the securities recommendations made by your firm during the past year

    (C) All option recommendations made by your firm in the last year

    (D) All straddle positions presently held by your firm

Use the following information to answer questions 21–22.

Specialist's Book: ABC Common Stock

BID	Price	ASK
12 Salomon	**24.**	
6 Merrill (GTC) 4 Morgan	.10	
27 Goldman	.20	5 Reynolds (stop)
	.30	
	.40	
9 Bear (stop)	.50	8 Salomon 6 Paine
	.60	12 Merrill
	.70	5 Goldman

21. What is the inside market?

    (A) 24.00–24.70

    (B) 24.10–24.50

    (C) 24.20–24.50

    (D) 24.20–24.70

22. Where can the specialist enter a quote for his own inventory?

    (A) Less than 24

    (B) Greater than 24.70

    (C) 24.20

    (D) 24.30

23. Mary was a registered representative for 16 years and left the business for a while due to a nasty divorce. Mary would like to get back into the business and rebuild her book. She is required to take her exams all over again if she has been unaffiliated with a broker/dealer for more than

    (A) One year

    (B) Two years

    (C) Five years

    (D) Ten years because of her length of employment as a registered representative

24. If a corporation issues 10,000 shares of 8 percent preferred stock ($100 par), which of the following will increase?

    I. Current assets

    II. Quick assets

    III. Net worth

    IV. Total liabilities

    (A) I and III only

    (B) I and II only

    (C) I, II, and III only

    (D) I, II, III, and IV

25. All of the following are considered leading indicators EXCEPT

    (A) M1

    (B) unemployment figures

    (C) building permits

    (D) industrial production

26. All of the following are exempt from the Trust Indenture Act of 1939 EXCEPT

    (A) debentures

    (B) T-bonds

    (C) GO bonds

    (D) revenue bonds

27. John Bearishnikoff has a numbered account with his broker-dealer. John's holdings are as follows:

    $150,000 in corporate debentures

    $100,000 in common stock

    $50,000 in preferred stock

    $50,000 in warrants

    $150,000 in cash

    If John's broker-dealer declares bankruptcy, how much is John covered for?

    (A) $350,000

    (B) $400,000

    (C) $450,000

    (D) $500,000

28. Which of the following are TRUE of open-end investment companies but NOT closed-end investment companies?

    I. Investors may redeem their shares.

    II. Only common stock may be issued.

    III. Investors purchase at the NAV plus a commission.

    IV. New shares are constantly being issued.

    (A) I and II only

    (B) I and III only

    (C) I, II, and IV only

    (D) II, III, and IV only

29. According to Rule G-39, which of the following is TRUE of cold-calling?

    I. Calls must be made after 8:00 a.m. or before 9:00 p.m. local time of the customer.

    II. Calls must be made after 8:00 a.m. or before 9:00 p.m. local time of the caller.

    III. The caller must disclose his name and the firm's name.

    IV. The caller must disclose the firm's telephone number and/or address.

    (A) I and III only

    (B) I, III, and IV only

    (C) II and III only

    (D) II, III, and IV only

30. Which of the following will cause an increase in the deficit of the U.S. balance of payments?

    I. U.S. investors' buying ADRs

    II. A drop in the discount rate

    III. The tightening of the U.S. dollar

    IV. Foreign investors' buying U.S. companies

    (A) I and III only

    (B) II and IV only

    (C) II, III, and IV only

    (D) II and III only

31. All of the following are possible reasons for investors to write covered calls EXCEPT

    (A) to hedge a long stock position

    (B) to increase the yield on the investor's portfolio

    (C) to generate a profit when the market price of the underlying security drops significantly

    (D) both A and B

32. An investor has the following option positions:

    Short 1 ABC Oct 50 call at 3

    Write 1 ABC Oct 45 put at 4

    The investor has created a

    (A) debit spread

    (B) credit spread

    (C) short combination

    (D) short straddle

33. ABC common stock is trading at $44. Which TWO of the following options are "in-the-money"?

    I. ABC Oct 40 calls

    II. ABC Oct 40 puts

    III. ABC Oct 50 calls

    IV. ABC Oct 50 puts

    (A) I and II

    (B) III and IV

    (C) II and III

    (D) I and IV

34. An investor purchases ten DUD convertible bonds at 90. The bonds are convertible at $25. One month after the purchase, the customer converts the bonds into common stock when the stock is trading at $23. If the customer sells the stock in the market at this point, what is the tax consequence as a result of these transactions?

    (A) No gain or loss
    (B) $20 capital gain
    (C) $20 capital loss
    (D) $200 capital gain

35. The holders of which of the following securities are considered owners of the corporation?

    I.   Mortgage bondholders
    II. Convertible debenture holders
    III. Preferred stockholders
    IV. Warrant holders

    (A) I and II only
    (B) I, II, and IV only
    (C) III only
    (D) III and IV only

36. Unless otherwise stated, a CMO has a Standard and Poor's rating of

    (A) AAA
    (B) AA
    (C) A
    (D) BBB

37. Mrs. Bullishinski enters an order to buy 100 shares of DIM at 40 stop limit. The ticker following entry of the order is as follows:

    39.75, 40, 40.25, SLD 40, 39.88, 40

    The order was triggered at

    (A) 39.75 and executed at 40
    (B) 40 and executed at 39.88
    (C) 40.25 and executed at 40
    (D) 40 and not executed

38. Readham & Wheepe Broker-Dealer Corporation purchases 10,000 shares of DROP common stock for their own inventory at a price of $27 per share. Several weeks later, DROP is quoted in the market at 25–25.25. If the brokerage firm wishes to sell 1,000 shares to one of its customers, which of the following prices must the brokerage firm use as a basis for their markup?

    (A) 25
    (B) 25.12
    (C) 25.25
    (D) 27

39. Regarding the NASD 5% policy, which of the following is/are TRUE?

    I.   The type of security is not a consideration.
    II. Riskless transactions are not covered by the 5% policy.
    III. Securities sold through a prospectus are exempt from the 5% policy.
    IV. The 5% policy is used as a guideline for open-end investment company sales.

    (A) III only
    (B) I, II, and III only
    (C) II and IV only
    (D) I, III, and IV only

40. Which of the following types of bonds has a mandatory sinking fund?

    (A) Term bonds
    (B) Series bonds
    (C) Balloon bonds
    (D) Serial bonds

41. An investor purchases an XYZ 8 percent callable bond at 80. The bond matures in ten years. If the investor sells the bond at 87 in six years, what is the gain or loss?

    (A) $70 gain
    (B) $130 loss
    (C) $50 loss
    (D) $10 gain

42. An investor purchases an XYZ 8 percent callable bond at 80. If the bond matures in ten years, how much does the investor have to claim on his or her taxes each year?

    (A) $8

    (B) $80

    (C) $90

    (D) $100

43. A customer purchases a new issue of GO bonds. The confirmation sent to the customer must include all of the following EXCEPT

    (A) the settlement date

    (B) the nominal yield and maturity date

    (C) the current yield calculated at the time of sale

    (D) the customer's name

44. The Federal Reserve Board controls the money supply by

    I. changing the discount rate

    II. changing the prime rate

    III. engaging in open-market operations

    IV. changing the reserve requirements

    (A) I and II only

    (B) I, III, and IV only

    (C) II, III, and IV only

    (D) I, II, III, and IV

45. Which of the following does NOT occur during the cooling-off period?

    (A) Due diligence meeting

    (B) The issuance of the preliminary prospectus (red herring)

    (C) Stabilizing the issue

    (D) Blue-skying the issue

46. Which of the following is responsible for approving an over-the-counter stock for purchase on margin?

    (A) The FRB

    (B) The NASD

    (C) Any exchange

    (D) The state securities commissioner

47. Interest received from which of the following investments is free from state income tax in all states?

    I. Revenue bonds issued to build toll booths

    II. Treasury bonds

    III. Bonds issued by the Commonwealth of Puerto Rico

    IV. GNMAs

    (A) I, II, and III only

    (B) II and III only

    (C) II, III, and IV only

    (D) I, II, and IV only

48. A registered representative is opening a new account for a customer. According to the "know your customer" rule, the rep should determine which of the following?

    I. The customer's date of birth

    II. The customer's investment objectives

    III. The customer's risk tolerance

    (A) I and II only

    (B) I and III only

    (C) II and III only

    (D) I, II, and III

49. Who is the issuer and guarantor of all listed options?

    (A) The OCC

    (B) The OAA

    (C) The ODD

    (D) The CBOE

50. DORK Corp., a U.S. company that supplies rubber products, shipped a supply to France. If DORK is to receive payment in French Francs in 30 days, which of the following is the BEST strategy for DORK Corp. to hedge its currency exposure?

    (A) Buy euro calls

    (B) Buy euro puts

    (C) Buy U.S. dollar calls

    (D) Buy U.S. dollar puts

51. Which of the following does NOT change the strike price of a listed option?

    (A) A $0.60 dividend

    (B) A 2-for-1 stock split

    (C) A 10 percent stock dividend

    (D) A 3-for-2 stock split

52. DEF common stock has a market price of $60 per share and earnings per common share of $6. If DEF Corp. announces a 2-for-1 stock split, which TWO of the following are TRUE after the split?

    I.   The PE ratio is 10.

    II. The PE ratio is 5.

    III. The EPS remains at $6.

    IV. The EPS reduces to $3.

    (A) I and III

    (B) I and IV

    (C) II and III

    (D) II and IV

53. All of the following are considered allowable tax deductions for an oil and gas limited partnership EXCEPT

    (A) principal expenses on a loan

    (B) interest expenses on a loan

    (C) depletion

    (D) depreciation

54. All of the following may trade in the secondary market EXCEPT

    I.   Fed funds

    II. repurchase agreements

    III. American Depositary Receipts

    IV. bankers' acceptances

    (A) I and III only

    (B) II and IV only

    (C) I and II only

    (D) III and IV only

55. An investor buys 4 ABC Oct 60 puts for 3 each and purchases 400 shares of ABC for $65 per share. Six months later, ABC is trading in the market at $67 per share. At what market price does this investor break even, excluding commissions?

    (A) 57

    (B) 62

    (C) 63

    (D) 68

56. The Fed is about to announce the largest sale of T-bills in recent history. An investor who wishes to profit from this anticipated sale should do which TWO of the following?

    I.   Buy T-bond yield calls

    II. Buy T-bond yield puts

    III. Buy T-bond calls

    IV. Buy T-bond puts

    (A) I and III

    (B) I and IV

    (C) II and III

    (D) II and IV

57. Which of the following includes a zero-minus tick?

    (A) 40, 40.25, 40.25, 40.38, 40.25, 40

    (B) 27.13, 27.38, 27.38, 27.25, 27.25

    (C) 9.63, 9.88, 10, 10, 9.88, 10

    (D) 63.75, 63.50, 63.38, 63.25, 63.38

58. Lee Dimwitty is in the process of purchasing a municipal GO bond in the secondary market for 92. The nominal yield of the bond is 6 percent and the basis is 6.6 percent. If Mr. Dimwitty is in the 28 percent tax bracket, what is the taxable equivalent yield for this bond?

    (A) 6 percent

    (B) 6.6 percent

    (C) 8.3 percent

    (D) 9.16 percent

59. Individuals giving specific investment advice for a fee are required to have passed which exams?

    (A) The Series 7 and Series 66

    (B) The Series 7, Series 63, and Series 65

    (C) The Series 65 and Series 63

    (D) A, B, or C

60. Melvin has a portfolio of securities with a lot of liquidity. Melvin has an additional $20,000 to invest and would like to keep the liquidity due to a business opportunity that may be coming his way. Which of the following investments would you LEAST likely recommend?

    (A) A long-term bond fund

    (B) An oil and gas limited partnership

    (C) Blue-chip stocks

    (D) Zero-coupon bonds

61. Which of the following are NOT TRUE regarding the Uniform Gifts to Minors Act?

    I. The donor may not be the custodian for the account.

    II. Purchases in the account may be made only in a margin account.

    III. If a stock in the account receives rights, the rights must be exercised.

    IV. The custodian is responsible for all taxes due from the account.

    (A) I and III only

    (B) I, III, and IV only

    (C) II and III only

    (D) I, II, III, and IV

62. A technical analyst notices that the market is generally consolidating. What does this mean?

    (A) The trendline is moving upward.

    (B) The trendline is moving downward.

    (C) The trendline is moving sideways.

    (D) All securities are trading within 10 percent of their trading range for the previous week.

63. What is the MOST likely reason for an investor to write covered call options?

    (A) To increase the yield on the investor's portfolio

    (B) To provide maximum protection in the event of a bear market

    (C) To be able to purchase shares at a discount if the stock price increases dramatically

    (D) To help the investor lock in profits on the long securities

64. A customer opens a long margin account by purchasing $30,000 in securities. The customer signs a loan consent agreement, a credit agreement, and a hypothecation agreement. All of the following are TRUE EXCEPT

    (A) The customer's securities will be held in street name.

    (B) The customer will have to pay interest on the debit balance.

    (C) A portion of the securities may be pledged as collateral for a loan.

    (D) A change in the market value of the securities would affect the debit balance.

65. A variable annuity has an assumed interest rate of 4½ percent, but the separate accounts annualized return is only 4 percent. Which TWO of the following are TRUE?

    I. The value of the accumulation unit will rise.

    II. The value of the accumulation unit will fall.

    III. The value of the annuity unit will rise.

    IV. The value of the annuity unit will fall.

    (A) I and III

    (B) I and IV

    (C) II and III

    (D) II and IV

66. Zowee Securities holds a joint account for Mr. and Mrs. Zazzo. Mr. Zazzo calls his registered representative at Zowee and tells him to "sell 100 shares of ZZZ common stock out of the account and send me a check to my name only." As the registered rep, you are required to tell Mr. Zazzo that

    (A) you need to talk to his wife before executing the transaction because it is a joint account

    (B) you will execute the trade right away and make sure that the check is made out to his name

    (C) you will execute the trade right away but the check will have to be in his and his wife's name

    (D) you need to clear it with your principal prior to taking his order

67. One of your customers believes that interest rates are going to decrease over the next ten years. Your customer is looking for investment advice. Which of the following bonds are appropriate investments for this investor?

    I. Adjustable rate bonds with ten-year maturities

    II. Ten year bonds that are non-callable

    III. 15 year bonds callable at par in ten years

    IV. 15 year put bonds that can be put back to the issuer starting in five years

    (A) I and III only

    (B) II and IV only

    (C) I, III, and IV only

    (D) II, III, and IV only

68. One of your customers has never invested in a DPP. Which of the following are considerations for her prior to investing?

    I. The goals of the partnership

    II. The general manager's experience

    III. The projected time frame for the partnership to become profitable

    IV. Whether she has enough liquidity in other investments

    (A) I and II only

    (B) I, II, and IV only

    (C) I, III, and IV only

    (D) I, II, III, and IV

69. Which of the following is NOT TRUE regarding warrants?

    (A) Warrants can trade separately from the common stock of the same company.

    (B) Warrants are longer-term than rights.

    (C) Warrants provide the holder with a perpetual interest in the issuer's common stock.

    (D) Warrants are sometimes called "sweeteners" because they are issued to make a new bond or stock offering more attractive to investors.

70. Which of the following are considered "immediate family" under NASD Rule 2790?

    I. Mother-in-law

    II. Uncle

    III. Grandfather

    IV. Sister

    (A) I and III only

    (B) II and IV only

    (C) I and IV only

    (D) II, III, and IV only

71. Joanne Smithy would like to invest in mutual funds, but she is not sure what she should be looking for. You should inform her that the most important thing to consider when selecting mutual funds is the fund's

    (A) sales charge

    (B) investment objectives

    (C) management fees

    (D) redemption fees

72. Which of the following transactions is considered structured?

    I. Mr. and Mrs. Johnson each transfer $9,900 to the same brokerage account on the same day.

    II. Mr. Jones wires $9,000 to the same account on three separate occasions during the same week.

    III. Two customers with no relation wire $9,000 to each of their own accounts one time.

    (A) I and II only

    (B) I and III only

    (C) II and III only

    (D) I, II, and III

73. Which of the following statements are TRUE regarding municipal bond GO issues?

    I. GO bonds are issued by the federal government and therefore are exempt from federal taxes.

    II. Municipal GO bonds are exempt from SEC registration.

    III. GO bonds are issued to fund revenue producing facilities.

    IV. The largest backing for GO bonds is property taxes.

    (A) II and IV only

    (B) I, II, and III only

    (C) I, II, and IV only

    (D) I, II, III, and IV

74. On the same day, a customer purchases one XYZ Oct 60 call at 6 and sells one XYZ Oct 70 call at 2. What is this investor's maximum potential gain?

    (A) $200

    (B) $400

    (C) $600

    (D) $1,000

75. A customer is long 100 shares of QHI at $45 and sells 1 QHI Jul 60 call at 2. Six months later, QHI is trading at $50 per share. If the customer sells the stock at the current market price and closes the option at 4, what is the gain or loss?

    (A) $300

    (B) $500

    (C) $700

    (D) $1,100

76. A doctor earns $140,000 per year and has no retirement plans except a traditional IRA. If this doctor contributes the maximum $4,000 per year to the IRA, what are the tax consequences?

    (A) The IRA contributions are fully tax-deductible.

    (B) The IRA contributions are only partially tax-deductible.

    (C) The IRA contributions are not tax-deductible.

    (D) The IRA contributions are not allowed because of the doctor's income level.

77. John Dough is the chairman of BIGI Corporation. BIGI will be announcing a major acquisition of SMLL Corporation in the coming weeks. John is so excited that he shares this information with his friend Fred. Immediately after hearing the news, Fred calls his broker and purchases call options on SMLL Corp. Which of the following is TRUE regarding insider trading rules?

    (A) They were violated by John.

    (B) They were violated by Fred.

    (C) Neither A nor B

    (D) Both A and B

78. Melvin Markowitz would like to open a cash account at your firm and give trading authorization to his sister Marlene. Which of the following documents is required for you to open the account?

    I.   A new account form

    II. A hypothecation agreement

    III. A limited power of attorney

    IV. A joint account agreement

    (A) I and III only

    (B) I, II, and IV only

    (C) I, III, and IV only

    (D) I, II, III, and IV

79. Which of the following is NOT TRUE regarding the U.S. balance of payments?

    (A) The more goods that the U.S. imports, the more money leaves the country.

    (B) The more goods that the U.S. exports, the more money comes into the country.

    (C) When U.S. investors purchase foreign securities, the U.S. balance of payments increases.

    (D) When U.S. investors purchase foreign securities, the U.S. balance of payments decreases.

80. A customer places a market order to sell 200 shares of ZYX Corp. The initial execution reports shows that the trade occurred at 26.25 per share. However, upon further scrutiny, the firm discovers that the trade was actually made at 26.00 per share. Which of the following is TRUE regarding this transaction?

    (A) The customer will receive $5,200 less any commissions.

    (B) The customer will receive $5,250 less any commissions.

    (C) The customer will receive $5,200 initially and may take the brokerage firm to court for the additional $50.

    (D) The customer will receive $5,200 from the transaction initially and the registered rep will be required to make up the $50 difference within ten business days.

81. An investor has a margin account with a market value of $30,000 and a debit balance of $12,000. What is the buying power?

    (A) $0

    (B) $3,000

    (C) $6,000

    (D) $18,000

82. A customer has placed an order to sell 200 shares of ABC common stock at market. The customer delivers two 100-share certificates to the broker-dealer to complete the trade. Upon examination of the certificates, it is noticed that the customer signed only one and left the other one blank. What is the correct procedure regarding the certificates?

    (A) Return both certificates to the customer by certified mail for proper endorsement and let him know that they must be returned within three business days.

    (B) Return the unsigned certificate to the customer by certified mail for proper endorsement and let him know that it must be returned within three business days.

    (C) Hold onto the certificates and send the customer a stock power along with instructions that must be signed and returned by the customer.

    (D) Deliver all certificates to the transfer agent as is.

83. You are setting up a strategic asset allocation plan for one of your 60-year old customers. Which of the following is MOST correct?

    (A) Having your customer invest 40 percent of his/her portfolio in stocks and 60 percent in bonds and cash

    (B) Having your customer invest 60 percent of his/her portfolio in stocks and 40 percent in bonds and cash

    (C) Having your customer invest 30 percent of his/her portfolio in bonds, 30 percent in stock, and 40 percent in cash and cash equivalents

    (D) Having your customer invest 60 percent of his/her portfolio in bonds, 20 percent in stocks, and 20 percent in commodities

84. Vic Vantage has held onto his ZIMB restricted stock for 1½ years. There are 2.5 million shares of ZIMB outstanding. Vic filed Form 144 on Tuesday, July 10. The ZIMB weekly trading volume for the previous 5 weeks is as follows:

Week Ending	Trading Volume
July 6	26,000
June 29	24,000
June 22	28,000
June 15	27,000
June 8	22,000

What is the maximum number of shares that Vic can sell under Rule 144?

(A) 25,000

(B) 25,250

(C) 25,400

(D) 26,250

85. Maxine Moolah is a 65-year-old investor. If you help her determine that she should have a "defensive investment" strategy, which of the following types of investments are suitable for Maxine?

I. Blue chip stocks

II. AAA rated bonds

III. High-yield bonds

IV. Call options

(A) I and II only

(B) I and III only

(C) II, III, and IV only

(D) I, II, and IV only

86. Mr. Bearclaw has a margin account with a current market value of $27,000 and a debit balance of $15,000. Which of the following are TRUE?

I. The account is currently restricted.

II. The account has an SMA of $1,500.

III. Mr. Bearclaw will receive a margin call for $1,500.

IV. Mr. Bearclaw will receive a mainte-nance call if the market value drops below $20,000.

(A) I and III only

(B) I, III, and IV only

(C) I and IV only

(D) II and IV only

87. The resistance level is

(A) the upper portion of the trading range of a security

(B) the lower portion of the trading range of a security

(C) the average trading range of a security

(D) none of the above

88. Juanita Jingleham would like to purchase municipal bonds through your firm. If you sell her the bonds out of your firm's inven-tory, which of the following is TRUE?

(A) The sale is subject to the NASD 5% policy.

(B) You are required to disclose the rating of the bonds on your customer's confirmation.

(C) You should take into consideration the total amount of the sale when deter-mining the markup charged.

(D) You are required to disclose the amount of commission on the confir-mation to the customer.

89. Mary Moneymountain purchased 1 HHH Jul 40 call at 6 and 1 HHH Jul 35 put at 3. HHH increased to 37 at expiration. If Mary has not previously exercised either option, what is her gain or loss?

    (A) $700 loss

    (B) $900 loss

    (C) $300 gain

    (D) $900 gain

90. Which of the following orders are considered discretionary and require a written power of attorney to complete the order?

    I. An order that specifies only the number of shares to be purchased and the particular security to buy and leaves the price and/or time to purchase up to the registered rep

    II. A market order that specifies only which security to sell

    III. A limit order that specifies the price and the security that is to be purchased

    (A) I and II only

    (B) II and III only

    (C) I and III only

    (D) I, II, and III

91. The S&P 500 has been increasing on a constant basis, but the number of stocks that are advancing as compared to the number declining is starting to level off. A technical analyst might say that the market is

    (A) oversold

    (B) overbought

    (C) volatile

    (D) stable

92. JAMB common stock is being sold to a syndicate during an underwriting for $8.50 per share. The public offering price is $9.50 per share and the manager's fee is $0.15 per share. If the concession is $0.50 per share, what is the additional takedown?

    (A) $1.00

    (B) $0.85

    (C) $0.50

    (D) $0.35

93. Jeemco broker-dealer is part of a syndicate that is offering new shares of DIP Corp. common stock to the public. There are 2,000,000 shares being offered to the public, and Jeemco is allocated 300,000 shares. After selling its allotment, 500,000 shares remain unsold by other members. How much of the remaining shares is Jeemco responsible for?

    I.   75,000 shares if the offering was on an Eastern account basis

    II. 75,000 shares if the offering was on a Western account basis

    III. 0 shares if the offering was on an Eastern account basis

    IV. 0 shares if the offering was on a Western account basis

    (A) I and II only

    (B) II and III only

    (C) I and IV only

    (D) III and IV only

94. Zack Zellig purchased 100 shares of FRM common stock at $40 per share. Zack additionally paid a commission of $2 per share. If ABC pays a 10 percent stock dividend, what is the tax status of Zack's investment?

    (A) He has 100 shares at a cost basis of $40.00 per share.

    (B) He has 100 shares at a cost basis of $42.00 per share.

    (C) He has 110 shares at a cost basis of $40.00 per share.

    (D) He has 110 shares at a cost basis of $38.18 per share.

95. Which of the following statements are TRUE regarding callable municipal revenue bonds?

I. Callable bonds usually have a higher yield than non-callable bonds.

II. When interest rates increase, callable bonds increase in price more than non-callable bonds.

III. The issuer normally calls the bonds when interest rates are decreasing.

IV. In the event that the bonds are called, call premiums are set to make up the lost interest payments that the investors would have received if the bond hadn't been called.

(A) I and III only

(B) I, II, and III only

(C) I, II, and IV only

(D) I, II, III, and IV

96. Michelle opens a custodial account for her 9-year-old niece Patricia. Which of the following statements are TRUE?

I. The account cannot be opened because Michelle is not Patricia's parent.

II. Michelle cannot share the custodian job with Patricia's father.

III. All trades in the custodial account must be on margin.

IV. When Patricia reaches the age of majority, the account will be switched to her name.

(A) I and III only

(B) II and IV only

(C) I, III, and IV only

(D) II, III, and IV only

97. Which of the following are short-term municipal notes?

I. PNs

II. BANs

III. AONs

IV. RANs

(A) I, II, and III only

(B) I, II, and IV only

(C) II, III, and IV only

(D) II and IV only

98. Kowabunga Ironing Board Corp. has announced in a recent tombstone advertisement that it is issuing $4,000,000 worth of convertible mortgage bonds with a coupon rate of 6½ percent. The bonds are convertible into common stock at $20. The maturity date is Oct 2026. Which TWO of the following are TRUE?

I. The bonds are backed by the full faith and credit of Kowabunga.

II. The bonds are backed by a lien on property owned by Kowabunga.

III. The conversion ratio is 20.

IV. The conversion ratio is 50.

(A) I and III

(B) I and IV

(C) II and III

(D) II and IV

99. One of your customers is interested in purchasing equity securities. If her main focus is to receive dividends, which of the following investments would you LEAST likely recommend?

(A) ABC common stock

(B) DEF preferred stock

(C) GHI warrants

(D) JKL convertible preferred stock

100. Over the years, one of your customers purchased 10,000 shares of DUD stock in 500-share increments whenever he had extra money. The stock has been extremely volatile since your customer started purchasing DUD, and your customer would like to sell off 3,000 shares of DUD but would like to limit his tax liability. What accounting method would you recommend to your customer to limit the amount of capital gains taxes he will have to pay?

    (A) FIFO

    (B) LIFO

    (C) Identified shares

    (D) Average cost

101. All of the following statements are TRUE regarding discretionary accounts EXCEPT

    I. All order tickets must be marked "discretionary."

    II. A hypothecation agreement is required for all discretionary accounts

    III. All discretionary accounts must be approved by a principal

    IV. A written power of attorney is required for all discretionary accounts

    (A) I and III only

    (B) II only

    (C) I, III, and IV only

    (D) I, II, III, and IV

102. DPPs that invest in raw land are considered

    (A) speculative investments

    (B) conservative investments

    (C) income-producing investments

    (D) none of the above

103. All of the following are acceptable stabilizing bids for a new issue with a public offering price of $20 per share EXCEPT

    (A) $19.50

    (B) $19.75

    (C) $20.00

    (D) $20.25

104. Investors face an unlimited loss potential in which of the following situations?

    (A) They bought a call option and are short the stock.

    (B) They sold a put option and are short the stock.

    (C) They sold a call option and are long the stock.

    (D) They sold a put option and are long the stock.

105. Account statements must be sent out to customers at least

    (A) daily

    (B) weekly

    (C) monthly

    (D) quarterly

106. Which TWO of the following are TRUE about Treasury STRIPS?

    I. The security's principal and interest is paid at maturity.

    II. The security's interest is paid semi-annually and the principal is paid at maturity.

    III. Investors must pay tax on interest earned annually.

    IV. Investors do not pay tax on interest earned until maturity.

    (A) I and III

    (B) I and IV

    (C) II and III

    (D) II and IV

107. Mary has a short margin account with a credit balance of $5,600 and an SMV of $4,000. How much excess equity does Mary have in her margin account?

    (A) None

    (B) $400

    (C) $800

    (D) $1,600

108. The purchase of a put option as compared to selling a stock short has all of the following advantages EXCEPT

   (A) the investor is not required to make up dividend payments on the borrowed stock

   (B) there is no loss on the time value as the put option is held

   (C) the investor can hold interest in the same amount of securities with less expense

   (D) the investor does not face an unlimited maximum loss potential

109. Which of the following statements are TRUE regarding Roth IRAs?

   I. Earnings in the Roth accumulate tax-free.

   II. Withdrawals from a Roth IRA are not taxable, provided that the investor has satisfied the holding period.

   III. Contributions are made from pre-tax dollars.

   IV. Contributions are made from after-tax dollars.

   (A) I and III only

   (B) I and IV only

   (C) I, II, and III only

   (D) I, II, and IV only

110. Chicago, IL, is issuing $10,000,000 worth of callable bonds in the coming months. Which of the following is NOT TRUE about the call feature of these municipal bonds?

   (A) If the issue has a serial maturity, longer term bonds will be called first.

   (B) The call feature allows issuers to eliminate those bonds with unfavorable indenture provisions.

   (C) An announcement of a call must be made prior to the call date.

   (D) Most municipalities like to add a call feature in the indenture to make the issue more marketable.

111. Kathy Knox has an unrestricted long margin account at BD Securities. If the value of Kathy's securities in the account increases by $2000, her SMA will

   (A) increase by $1,000

   (B) increase by $2,000

   (C) decrease by $4,000

   (D) decrease by $1,000

112. Michael Mintek would like to move his account from Varnish Brokerage to Waxman Securities. Which of the following must take place for this to happen?

   I. Michael must complete and sign an account transfer form from Waxman Securities.

   II. Varnish Brokerage must validate the account transfer form filled out by Michael.

   III. Varnish Brokerage must cancel any of Michael's open orders.

   IV. Varnish Brokerage has ten business days in which to complete the transfer.

   (A) I and II only

   (B) I and III only

   (C) I, II, and III only

   (D) I, II, III, and IV

113. A double-barreled municipal bond is

   (A) automatically exempt from federal and state taxes

   (B) backed by the full faith and credit of the municipality if revenues from the backing project are insufficient

   (C) automatically exempt from state and local taxes only

   (D) a municipal bond that is indirectly backed by the U.S. government

114. Approval of shareholders is required if a corporation would like to

    I.   split its stock

    II. reverse split its stock

    III. give investors a cash dividend

    IV. give investors a stock dividend

    (A) I and II only

    (B) III and IV only

    (C) I, II, III, and IV

    (D) None of the above

115. All of the following are possible ways of investing in variable annuities EXCEPT

    (A) single payment immediate annuity

    (B) single payment deferred annuity

    (C) periodic payment deferred annuity

    (D) periodic payment immediate annuity

116. A local municipality decides to issue bonds to build a public park. Which of the following characteristics of the issuer should be considered when analyzing this municipal GO bond issue?

    I.   Insurance covenants

    II. Ad valorem tax rate

    III. Flow of funds

    IV. Budgetary practices

    (A) I and III only

    (B) II and IV only

    (C) I, II, and III only

    (D) I, II, III, and IV

117. Which of the following investment strategies is a long combination?

    (A) Sell 1 XZX Jun 40 call; sell 1 XZX Jun 40 put

    (B) Buy 1 XZX Jun 40 call; buy 1 XZX Jun 40 put

    (C) Buy 1 XZX Jun 40 call; buy 1 XZX Jun 30 put

    (D) Buy 1 XZX Jun 40 call; sell 1 XZX Jun 30 put

118. Which of the following are TRUE regarding industrial development revenue bonds?

    I.   The money raised is used to construct a facility for a private corporation.

    II. The bonds are issued by municipalities.

    III. The bonds are backed by the full faith and credit of the municipality.

    IV. The bonds are backed by lease payments made by the private corporation.

    (A) I and III only

    (B) I and IV only

    (C) II and III only

    (D) I, II, and IV only

119. Which of the following are violations of the "wash sale rule"?

    I.   20 days after selling ABC stock at a loss, the customer buys an ABC convertible bond.

    II. 35 days prior to selling ABC stock at a loss, the customer buys ABC warrants.

    III. 15 days after selling ABC stock at a loss, the customer buys an ABC put option.

    IV. 30 days after selling ABC stock at a loss, the customer buys an ABC call option.

    (A) I and IV only

    (B) I, II, and IV only

    (C) I and III only

    (D) I, III, and IV only

120. Which of the following technical theories assumes that the small investor is usually wrong?

    (A) Odd lot theory

    (B) Short interest theory

    (C) Dow theory

    (D) Volume theory

121. Which of the following trades is/are subject to the NASD 5% policy?

    I. Riskless transactions

    II. Markdowns on stocks that were bought from a customer for the dealer's inventory

    III. Markups on stocks that were sold to a customer from the dealer's inventory

    IV. Commissions charged to a customer on securities bought on an agency basis

    (A) I only

    (B) III and IV only

    (C) II, III, and IV only

    (D) I, II, III, and IV

122. If the Fed raises the reserve requirements, which TWO of the following are MOST likely to happen?

    I. Interest rates will increase.

    II. Interest rates will decrease.

    III. Outstanding bond prices will decrease.

    IV. Outstanding bond prices will increase.

    (A) I and III

    (B) I and IV

    (C) II and III

    (D) II and IV

123. It is required that all of the following are reviewed by a principal EXCEPT

    (A) customers' written complaints

    (B) interoffice memos

    (C) letters recommending securities to clients of an agent

    (D) form letters that are to be sent to all customers

124. Under the Investment Advisers Act of 1940, which of the following is considered an investment adviser?

    (A) A newspaper column that gives general investing advice

    (B) A radio program that gives general investing advice to certain age groups

    (C) An investment letter available by paid subscription that gives specific advice based on a customer's specific situation

    (D) A broker who gives free advice prior to the customer's making a trade

125. An official notice of sale is published to indicate that a municipal offering is going to be made

    (A) on a negotiated basis

    (B) on a competitive basis

    (C) privately

    (D) any of the above

Answer Key for Part 1 of the Practice Exam

1. A	26. A	51. A	76. A	101. B
2. C	27. C	52. B	77. D	102. A
3. B	28. C	53. A	78. A	103. D
4. C	29. B	54. C	79. C	104. B
5. C	30. A	55. D	80. A	105. D
6. A	31. C	56. B	81. C	106. A
7. D	32. C	57. B	82. C	107. A
8. B	33. D	58. D	83. A	108. B
9. D	34. D	59. D	84. D	109. D
10. A	35. C	60. B	85. A	110. D
11. B	36. A	61. D	86. C	111. A
12. B	37. B	62. C	87. A	112. C
13. B	38. C	63. A	88. C	113. B
14. A	39. A	64. D	89. B	114. A
15. A	40. A	65. B	90. B	115. D
16. B	41. C	66. C	91. B	116. B
17. A	42. D	67. B	92. D	117. C
18. B	43. C	68. D	93. C	118. D
19. B	44. B	69. C	94. D	119. A
20. C	45. C	70. C	95. A	120. A
21. C	46. A	71. B	96. B	121. D
22. D	47. B	72. A	97. B	122. A
23. B	48. D	73. A	98. D	123. B
24. C	49. A	74. C	99. C	124. C
25. D	50. B	75. A	100. C	125. B

Making the Grade

Here's how the Series 7 exam is scored:

- ✔ You get one point for each correct answer.
- ✔ You get zero points for each incorrect answer.

A passing score is 70 percent. To calculate your grade for this half of the exam, multiply the number of correct answers by 0.8 or divide it by 125. Whatever grade you get, make sure you round down, not up. For example, a grade of 69.6 is a 69 percent, not a 70. If you got 88 or more questions right, you're getting a passing score so far.

Of course, you simply need 175 correct answers on the whole test. So you could get only 50 questions correct here and still pass if you get a perfect score on the next part (I wouldn't recommend this strategy, though).

The actual test contains ten additional experimental questions (five in each part) that don't go toward your actual score. You can't tell these questions apart from the questions that do count, so you may have to answer a few more questions right to get your 70 percent. Don't sweat it. Simply come prepared, stay focused, and do your best.

Chapter 18

Answers and Explanations to Practice Exam Part I

*C*ongratulations — if you've reached this point, you've completed part I of the practice exam in Chapter 17. (If you haven't, flip back and take the test. You don't want to spoil all the surprises, do you?) You can either stop here and review your answers, or if you're really, really brave, you can go to part II of the practice test in Chapter 19. If you're going to part II, take a 30–60 minute break before proceeding (like in the real exam).

Review, review, review. And if I haven't mentioned this yet, reviewing would definitely be a good idea. Look at the questions you had problems with, retake all the questions you got wrong, and make sure you get them right the second (or third) time around.

Wait at least a week or two before taking the same test again. Retaking the test won't help your cause if you're just memorizing the answers.

1. **A.** The par value of stock is a bookkeeping value, and it has no effect on the market value of the security. Shares of stock are sold to other investors and aren't redeemed the way bonds and mutual fund shares are.

2. **C.** The key to this question is that shareholders are voting on a *cumulative* voting basis. Cumulative voting helps smaller shareholders gain representation on the board of directors. Because this investor has 1,000 shares and three positions are open on the board of directors, he has 3,000 votes (1,000 shares × 3 open positions) that he can use any way he chooses. In other words, he can use all his votes for one candidate, split his votes three ways, or use any combination of votes he likes. Answers I, II, and III are all possible. Answer IV would require this investor to have 9,000 total votes (3,000 votes × 3 candidates). If the question were to involve statutory or regular voting, the investor could vote only 1,000 shares each for each of the three candidates.

3. **B.** This problem is one of those questions that add meaningless information. The last sentence asks, "What is the current yield of the bonds?" Therefore, you need only the annual interest and the market price. The fact that Lee has 10 bonds, that the bonds are convertible, and that they mature in 27 years means nothing. To determine that the current yield is 7.5 percent, use the following formula:

$$\text{Current yield} = \frac{\text{annual interest}}{\text{market price}}, \text{ so } \frac{\$90 \ (9\% \times \$1{,}000 \text{ par})}{\$1{,}200 \ (120\% \times \$1{,}000 \text{ par})} = 7.5\%$$

4. **C.** Because Mike is purchasing $30,000 worth of TOGA Aggressive Growth Fund, he won't be paying the current public offering price (POP) of $13.11 because he'll receive a breakpoint (discounted price) for a large dollar purchase. Looking at the chart directly below the question, you can see that Mike will pay a sales charge of only 5½ percent. To determine that Mike will pay $12.70 per share, you have to recalculate the POP for investors depositing between $30,000 and $49,999. The POP is determined by dividing the net asset value (NAV) by the difference between 100 percent and the sales charge percent:

$$POP = \frac{NAV}{100\% - \text{sales charge \%}}, \text{ so } \frac{\$12.00}{100\% - 5\frac{1}{2}\%} = \frac{\$12.00}{94\frac{1}{2}\%} = \$12.70$$

Because Mike is investing $30,000, divide that amount by the cost per share ($12.70); you find out that he can purchase 2,362 shares:

$$\frac{\$30,000}{\$12.70} = 2,362 \text{ shares}$$

5. **C.** What you need to identify in this question is which investor would be buying the stock if an option were exercised. The holder (owner) of a call option has the right to buy the stock, and the writer (seller) of a put option has the obligation to buy the stock if the option's exercised. The answer is C.

6. **A.** Roman numeral I is part of all the answer choices; therefore, you know that part of the answers is correct. Private placements are exempt from SEC registration under Regulation D. *Intra*state offerings (offerings of securities in one state) are exempt from SEC registration but do need to be registered on the state level. *Inter*state offerings (offerings of securities in several states) and *variable* annuities must be registered. Therefore, A is the correct answer.

7. **D.** The last time a customer can trade (close) an option is 4:00 p.m. EST (or thereabout) on the third Friday of the expiration month. The last time a customer can exercise an option is 5:30 p.m. EST on the third Friday of the expiration month; options expire 11:59 p.m. EST on the Saturday after the third Friday of the expiration month.

Examiners may give you Central Standard Time (CST) rather than Eastern Standard Time (EST) in option questions because most options trade on the Chicago Board Options Exchange (CBOE). If they give you CST, subtract one hour from the Eastern times.

8. **B.** A head and shoulders top formation is a bearish sign, but the answer choice that best describes it is a *reversal* of a bullish trend. A technical analyst would look at the formation and say that the stock has reached a high and is starting to reverse and go down.

9. **D.** Any of the choices could be a closed-end fund, but answer D *must* be a closed-end fund. To be an open-end fund, the public offering price (POP) can't be below the net asset value (NAV) and the sales charge can't be more than 8½ percent of the amount invested. The sales charge for answer D exceeds 8½ percent, so it has to be a closed-end fund. Use the following formula to determine the sales charge:

$$\text{Sales charge \%} = \frac{POP - NAV}{POP}, \text{ so } \frac{\$13.00 - \$11.40}{\$13.00} = \frac{\$1.60}{\$13.00} = 12\%$$

10. **A.** This question is challenging because you have to answer two separate questions in one. If the Federal Reserve Board (FRB, or Fed) increases interest rates, you can assume that interest rates in general will increase. If interest rates increase, outstanding bond prices (in this case, debentures) will fall.

If the interest rates increase, the U.S. money supply will tighten up, making the dollar stronger. If the U.S. dollar is stronger, the U.S. will import more goods and export less. In II and III, you can replace the phrase *more competitive* with the word *cheaper*.

11. **B.** Municipal revenue bonds are backed by money that a revenue-producing facility (such as toll booths, municipal hospitals, and so on) brings in. Normally, a net revenue pledge backs revenue bonds. In a *net revenue pledge,* operation and maintenance are the first expenses the local government pays out of the gross revenues it receives. After operation and maintenance are paid, the municipality pays the debt service (principal and interest on the bonds).

12. **B.** If you use the seesaw (see Chapter 7) to answer this question, you see that the bond was purchased at $1,000 par. Because the coupon rate (nominally yield or NY) is 7 percent and the basis or yield to maturity is 7 percent, the seesaw is level, as the following figure shows. The fact that the bond has a call premium and that the investor would end up receiving 7¼ percent after five years has no bearing on the answer.

	7%		7%	
Bond price	**NY**	**CY**	**YTM**	**YTC**

13. **B.** Dollar cost averaging allows investors to purchase shares at an average cost per share that's less than the average price per share. *Dollar cost averaging* is investing the same dollar amount into the same investment periodically (for example, investing $1,000 per month into ABC Growth Fund). The average cost per share is lower when the price is fluctuating because the investor can purchase more shares when the price is low and fewer shares when the price is high.

14. **A.** American Depositary Receipts (ADRs) are receipts for foreign securities trading in the U.S., not U.S. securities trading in foreign countries as IV suggests. If you eliminate the answers that include IV, the only answer that works is choice A.

15. **A.** Money market instruments are short-term debt securities that usually mature in one year or less. ADRs (American Depositary Receipts or American Depositary Shares), which are receipts for foreign securities traded in the U.S., are not debt securities, they're equity securities. The correct answer is A. All the other answer choices are types of money market instruments.

16. **B.** This question adds meaningless information to try to trip you up. When determining the current yield of a bond, you divide the annual interest of $70 (7% nominal yield × $1,000 par) by the market price of $960 (96 × $1,000 par), as shown here:

$$\text{Current yield} = \frac{\text{annual interest}}{\text{market price}}, \text{ so } \frac{\$70}{\$960} = 7.29\%$$

17. **A.** *Variable annuities* are retirement plans that insurance companies issue. The payout depends on the performance of the securities in a separate investment account that insurance companies hold. The better the securities in the separate account perform, the higher the payouts. You know Roman numeral I is true, so you can eliminate answers C and D. All variable annuities have an assumed interest rate (AIR) that is independent of the S&P 500. Investors may deposit money into an IRA (not a variable annuity) up until April 15 and be able to claim it on the previous year's taxes. Straight life annuities provide the highest payout because after the investor dies, nobody receives payments. The answer is A.

18. **B.** The *loan value* is the amount that the broker-dealer can lend to the customer in a margin account. The loan value is the difference between Regulation T and 100 percent. Because Regulation T is 55 percent in this case, the loan value is 45 percent. The total purchase is $20,000 (1,000 shares × $20 per share), so the loan value is $9,000 (45% × $20,000).

19. **B.** This investor has a debit spread because she paid more money for the option she purchased than she received for the option she sold. This investor already has a loss, and she needs the option(s) to be exercised in order to make a profit (statement IV). This investor also needs the difference in the premiums to widen (to have her option go in-the-money) to be able to make a profit (statement I). The correct answer is B.

20. **C.** When showing a customer (or potential customer) some of your previous picks, you have to include all similar picks for the past year. Because you'd like to show this customer your option picks, you need to include all option picks for the past year, not just the ones that made money.

21. **C.** When looking at a specialist's book, ignore the stop orders. Looking at the remaining orders, choose the highest bid price and the lowest ask price to get the inside market. The highest bid (highest price) is Goldman at 24.20, and the lowest ask (lowest price) is Salomon and Paine at 24.50. C is the correct answer.

22. **D.** A specialist can't compete with public orders and can enter quotes only in between the highest bid price and lowest ask price. Ignoring the stop orders, the highest bid and lowest ask is 24.20–24.50 respectively. The only answer choice that's in between those numbers is 24.30.

23. **B.** The fact that Mary went through a nasty divorce is irrelevant (except for telling you why she'd leave the wonderful world of stockbroking); however, Mary's having been out of the business for more than two years would be a problem. Any registered representative who has been unaffiliated with a broker/dealer for more than two years has to take the licensing exams (such as a Series 7 or Series 63) again in order to work as a stockbroker.

24. **C.** When a corporation issues stocks or bonds, it's bringing cash into the company. Cash is a current asset and a quick asset (an asset convertible into cash in a 3–5 month period), which means that I and II are true. The *net worth* of the corporation equals assets minus liabilities. When a corporation issues stock, it doesn't owe money to investors, so the liabilities don't increase. Therefore, answer IV is false. If the assets increase and the liabilities remain the same, the net worth of the corporation increases. Therefore, statement III is correct. Your answer is C.

25. **D.** *Leading indicators* give you an idea of how the economy may perform in the near future. Included in the leading indicators are the M1 money supply, unemployment figures, and the number of new building permits. Industrial production is considered a coincidental indicator; it gives you an idea of how the economy is performing right now.

26. **A.** The Trust Indenture Act of 1939 is an act that covers issues of corporate bonds. Therefore, T-bonds (U.S. government bonds), GO bonds (municipal bonds), and revenue bonds (municipal bonds) are exempt from the act. *Debentures* are corporate bonds that are backed by the full faith and credit of the issuer.

27. **C.** The maximum Securities Investor Protection Corporation (SIPC) coverage for an investor in the event of the broker-dealer's bankruptcy is $500,000, of which no more than $100,000 can be cash. In this case, the investor is covered for only $100,000 of the $150,000 in cash and is covered in full for all the securities. Because he has $350,000 in securities and is covered for $100,000 cash, his coverage is $450,000. If the broker-dealer goes bankrupt, John becomes a general creditor of the firm for the remaining $50,000 cash.

28. **C.** Open-end investment companies (mutual funds) continuously offer new shares at the public offering price (POP), which includes a sales charge, not at the NAV plus commission. Open-end investment companies may only issue common stock. Closed-end investment companies can issue common stock, preferred stock, and bonds. One difference between open- and closed-end shares is that investors have to redeem open-end shares with the issuer; those particular shares can't be sold to another investor. Therefore, answers I, II, and IV are all true; answer III is true of closed-end shares, not open-end. The answer is C.

29. **B.** Rule G-39 is a Municipal Securities Rulemaking Board (MSRB) rule. The rule has to do with cold-calling potential customers; it doesn't cover existing customers or communications with other brokers or dealers. As a registered representative, you have to make all cold calls between 8:00 a.m. and 9:00 p.m. local time of the potential customer. The registered representative needs to disclose his or her name, the firm's name, the firm's phone number and/or address, and that the call is a sales call.

30. **A.** To answer questions that deal with the U.S. balance of payments, follow the money. If more money comes into the U.S., the balance of payments increases; if more money goes out of the U.S., the deficit of the U.S. balance of payments increases.

    Take each answer and look at which way the money would go. If U.S. investors are buying American Depositary Receipts (ADRs), which are receipts for foreign securities trading in the U.S., money would go out of the U.S. Thus, answer I is correct. If you look at choices A through D, only choice A includes the Roman numeral I, so that's your answer. Answer II (a drop in the discount rate) would ease U.S. money supply, and the country would be exporting more, thus bringing more money into the U.S. However, you're looking for an answer that increases the deficit. Answer III (the tightening of the U.S. dollar) is the other correct answer. A tightening of the U.S. dollar would have the U.S. importing more; the dollar would be strong, sending more money out of the U.S. Answer IV (foreign investors' buying U.S. companies) would bring more money into the United States, so you can eliminate that choice. The answer is A.

31. **C.** Writing covered call options (selling call options on the stock that an investor owns) helps increase the yield on a stock because the seller of the option receives the premium. This move is also a partial hedge (protection) because if the price of the stock held drops by the premium amount, the investor still wouldn't have a loss. For example, if an investor buys 100 shares of ABC common stock for $40 per share and then sells 1 ABC Oct 40 call for a premium of 6, the price of the stock can go all the way down to $34 per share ($40 per share – $6 premium per share received) without any loss to the investor. However, if the price drops significantly (answer C) the investor would have a loss, not a gain.

32. **C.** You can cross off answers A and B right away because to have a spread, the investor has to have one buy and one sell. This investor has sold two options and therefore has either a short combination or short straddle. To tell which one she has, look at the expiration months and the strike prices. If they're all the same, you have a straddle. If either is different, as in this case (50 and 45 are different strike prices), the investor has a combination.

33. **D.** Call options go in-the-money when the price of the stock is above the strike price. Because the stock is trading at $44, the ABC 40 call option (answer I) is in-the-money. Put options go in-the-money when the price of the stock is below the strike price. This means that the ABC 50 put option (answer IV) is in-the-money because the stock price is below 50. The answer is D.

34. **D.** For this question, you have to determine the conversion ratio (the number of shares the bonds are convertible into). The bonds are convertible at $25, so $25 is the conversion price. Use the following formula:

$$\text{Conversion ratio} = \frac{\text{par}}{\text{conversion price}}, \text{ so } \frac{\$1,000}{\$25} = 40 \text{ shares}$$

The stock is trading at $23, so multiply the conversion ratio by the selling price:

40 shares × $23 per share = $920

The investor bought the bonds for $900 each (90 percent of $1,000 par) and converted each bond into 40 shares of stock that were worth $920 all together. Because the investor originally bought ten bonds and profited $20 per bond, he sees a total gain of $200.

35. **C.** Bondholders (answers I and II) are creditors of a company. For this question, you want the owners of a company — the common and preferred stockholders. Because *common stockholders* isn't an answer choice, the correct answer is C. Warrants give the owner the right to buy stock at a fixed price, but warrant holders don't become owners until they use their warrants to purchase stock.

36. **A.** Collateralized Mortgage Obligations (CMOs) normally have a Standard & Poor's rating of AAA because they're made up of GNMA, FNMA, and FHLMC securities. GNMAs are directly backed by the U.S. government, and FNMAs and FHLMCs are U.S. government agency securities that are considered very safe.

37. **B.** You have to break this order into two parts. The first part of the order is a "buy stop at 40." A buy stop is a SLoBS (sell limit, buy stop) order, which would be triggered at or above 40. Looking at the ticker, the first order at or above 40 is 40. After the order is triggered, it becomes a buy limit order. A buy limit is a BLiSS (buy limit, sell stop) order, which would be executed at or below 40. Looking at the ticker, the next trade at or below 40 is the SLD 40. However, *SLD* means that the trade was reported out of sequence and you have to jump to the next trade at or below 40. The next trade at or below 40 is 39.88, and that's where the order would be executed.

38. **C.** The dealer needs to consider all factors except dealer cost (the price that the dealer paid to have the security in his or her inventory). The dealer must charge the current market price. Investors buy at the ask price of $25.25 plus a markup.

39. **A.** The NASD 5% policy is a guideline, not a rule. Over-the-counter (OTC) broker-dealers shouldn't charge more than 5 percent on normal-size trades with customers. Answer I is false because the type of security is significant: This policy is for non-exempt OTC securities. Answer II is false because the policy does cover riskless transactions (purchases of securities for the broker-dealers inventory for immediate resale to a customer). Answer III is correct because securities sold through a prospectus (new securities) are exempt from the 5% policy. Answer IV is false because open-end investment companies (mutual funds) may charge up to 8½ percent of the amount invested. The correct answer is A.

40. **A.** A *sinking fund* is an account where issuers deposit money to pay off bonds at maturity. Because the entire principal amount is due all at one time, issuers of term bonds are usually required to have a sinking fund.

41. **C.** To answer this question, you have to accrete the bond. First, take the difference between the purchase price of $800 (80 percent of $1,000 par) and $1,000 par; then divide that value by the number of years until maturity:

$$\text{Annual accretion} = \frac{\text{par value} - \text{market price}}{\text{years until maturity}} = \frac{\$1,000 - \$800}{10 \text{ years}} = \$20$$

Next, multiply the $20-per-year accretion by the number of years the investor held the bond and add that to the purchase price to get the new cost basis:

20×6 years = $120

$120 + $800 = $920 cost basis

The investor's cost basis is $920, and he sold the bond at $870 (87 percent of $1,000 par); therefore, the investor lost $50.

42. **D.** This investor has to claim the $80-per-year interest (8% interest rate × $1,000 par) plus the annual accretion of $20. His tax liability is based on $100 per bond per year.

43. **C.** The confirmation the customer receives has to include the settlement date, the coupon rate (nominal yield), and the customer's name, not the current yield of the bond.

44. **B.** The *prime rate* is the rate that banks charge their best customers for loans. This rate is controlled by banks, not the Federal Reserve Board (FRB, or the Fed). You can eliminate Roman numeral II; the only answer left is B. The FRB does control the discount rate (the rate that the FRB charges banks for loans), open-market operations (buying and selling U.S. government securities), and the reserve requirements (the percentage of deposits that banks need to have on hand each night).

45. **C.** The cooling-off period takes place when a security is in the process of registration and hasn't been sold to any investors yet. A stabilizing bid occurs when the dealers purchase the new shares in the market when the price starts to drop too quickly. For a stabilizing bid to occur, the security has to be sold, and it can't be sold in the process of registration. The correct answer is C.

46. **A.** The Federal Reserve Board (yes, the Fed once again) determines which securities investors can purchase on margin.

47. **B.** Revenue bonds are state-tax-free only to investors within the issuers' home state. The interest on Treasury bonds is state-tax-free in all states. Puerto Rico bonds are triple tax-free bonds, and the interest is exempt from federal, state, and local taxes. Ginnie Maes (GNMAs) are subject to interest tax on all levels. II and III are true, so the answer is B.

48. **D.** According to the *know your customer rule* (Rule 405), you're required to know the customer's name, date of birth, address, and Social Security number. You should also know the customer's investment objectives and risk tolerance, although it's not a strict requirement if you can obtain this information from other sources.

49. **A.** The Options Clearing Corporation (OCC) is the issuer and guarantor of all listed options. The OCC determines which securities will have options and guarantees that the holder of an option can exercise that option.

50. **B.** First, cross off answers C and D, because options on U.S. currency don't exist. Because DORK Corp. is getting paid in euros, the company is concerned about the decline of the euro. Buying euro puts which give the company the right to sell euros at a fixed price, protects DORK Corp. if the value of the euro declines.

51. **A.** Cash dividends don't affect listed options. For example, if you own 1 DEF Oct 40 call and DEF declares a $0.60 dividend, you still own 1 DEF Oct 40 call even though the price of the stock was reduced. Stock splits and stock dividends do affect the number of option contracts, the strike price, and/or the number of shares per option contract.

52. **B.** Following a 2-for-1 split, the corporation has twice as many shares outstanding, cutting the earnings per share (EPS) in half. Because the EPS was $6, it would now be $3, so IV is correct.

    After a 2-for-1 split, each investor owns two shares for every one that she owned before and the price per share is cut in half ($30). The price/earnings (PE) ratio becomes 10, which means I is correct and your answer is B:

    $$PE\ ratio = \frac{market\ price}{EPS},\ so\ \frac{\$30}{\$3} = 10$$

53. **A.** Interest expenses, depletion, and depreciation are all acceptable deductions for an oil and gas limited partnership. However, principal expenses (repayment of the money borrowed) aren't deductible.

54. **C.** *Fed funds* are usually overnight loans from one bank to another to help meet reserve requirements. These funds pass between two parties and don't trade in the secondary market. *Repurchase agreements* (Repos) are usually overnight loans using U.S. government securities as collateral that likewise don't trade in the secondary market. I and II are therefore correct. Both American Depositary Receipts (ADRs) and bankers' acceptances can trade to other investors in the secondary market. The correct answer is C.

55. **D.** The easiest way to calculate the break-even point for stock and option problems is to look at the purchase and/or sale price for each transaction. This investor has 4 options representing 400 shares (100 shares per option) and owns 400 shares of the same stock.

For break-even point questions, as long as the number of shares is equal on both sides (which they're supposed to be on the Series 7 exam), the number of shares doesn't come into play.

This investor bought the stock at $65 per share and spent $3 per share for the options. Because this investor spent $68 per share, he needs the stock to reach $68 per share in order to break even.

56. **B.** The selling of U.S. government securities such as T-bills pulls money out of the banking system and deposits it with the Federal Reserve Board (the Fed). Pulling a large amount of money out of the banking system tightens money and makes interest rates increase. If interest rates are going to increase, a wise investor should buy T-bond yield calls and T-bond puts. There's an inverse relationship between outstanding bond prices and interest rates (yields): When rates go up, prices go down. B is the right answer.

57. **B.** When the trading price of a security goes down and stays down at the same price for the next trade, you have a zero-minus tick. Choice D has no back-to-back repeats, so that answer's out. A, B, and C all contain zero-plus ticks, in which the price goes up and stays up at the same price for the next trade. Only B includes a zero-minus tick (in bold):

27.13, 27.38 (+), 27.38 (0+), 27.25 (–), **27.25 (0–)**

58. **D.** This question is one in which you have to wade through some useless information. To determine the taxable equivalent yield (TEY), you need the yield to maturity (or nominal yield if you don't know the yield to maturity) of the municipal bond and the investor's tax bracket. Check out the following formula for finding the TEY:

$$\text{TEY (taxable equivalant yield)} = \frac{\text{municipal yield}}{100\% - \text{tax bracket}}, \text{ so } \frac{6.6\%}{72\%} = 9.16\%$$

59. **D.** The question describes someone who's working as an investment adviser. *Investment advisers* give specific advice in return for a flat fee or a percentage of the customer's managed assets. The investment adviser must hold either the Series 66 or Series 65 license. The Series 66 is a combination of the Series 63 (state license exam) and the Series 65 (investment adviser), and it's good only for individuals who have passed (or are going to pass) the Series 7.

60. **B.** Melvin is looking for liquidity because he may need the money soon. Answers A, C, and D allow Melvin a certain amount of liquidity because he can sell the stocks or bonds in the market and can redeem the shares of the bond fund whenever he wants. A limited partnership would be the last thing that you'd recommend to Melvin because of the suitability requirements associated with partnerships and the difficulty of getting in and out of them.

61. **D.** All the choices listed are false. The donor or anyone else may be the custodian for the account. All trades have to be paid for in full and can't be purchased on margin. If the account receives rights, the custodian can exercise or sell them but can't let them expire. The minor, not the custodian, is responsible for the taxes in the account.

62. **C.** A *trendline* is the line on a price chart for a security that indicates its direction (up, down, or sideways). A trendline that's consolidating is moving sideways (staying within a certain trading range).

63. **A.** An investor who writes covered call options (who writes an option on stock she owns) is trying to increase the yield on her portfolio. Although this position would limit the upside on the stock that the investor owns, the strategy is ideal for when the stock isn't moving. The investor can write covered call options, receive the premium, and limit the risk because she has the stock to deliver if the option is exercised.

64. **D.** When opening a long margin account, the customer has to sign a credit agreement (because the customer is borrowing money from the broker-dealer) and a hypothecation agreement. The hypothecation agreement allows the broker-dealer to pledge a percentage of the margin account to use as collateral to borrow money from a lending institution. The loan-consent agreement is optional but is required by most broker-dealers, and it allows the brokerage firm to lend the margined securities to other brokers. The false answer is D, because the debit balance is the amount that the customer borrowed from the broker-dealer; it doesn't change unless the customer borrows more money, sells securities, or puts money into the account or unless it's charged interest in the account.

65. **B.** The *assumed interest rate* (AIR) of a variable annuity is the percentage needed on the investments in the separate account of a variable annuity in order to receive the expected payouts upon retirement. The value of an accumulation unit rises during the pay-in phase because the value of the securities in the separate account rises by 4 percent per year. The value of the annuity unit during the pay-out phase falls because it doesn't reach the expected 4½ percent per year on the investments in the separate account.

66. **C.** A *joint account* is an account in the name of more than one person. Mr. or Mrs. Zazzo can request the sale of securities in the account and have a check sent out, but the check has to include the names of all the people on the account. You can't have the check made out to Mr. Zazzo's name alone.

67. **B.** When interest rates decrease, the price of the outstanding bonds increases. If you look at the answers one at a time, you can see which investments make sense. Answer I doesn't work because the adjustable-rate bond's interest rate decreases if interest rates drop. Answer II is good because an investor can lock in a rate that's high right now; if interest rates drop, the investor profits by selling his bond at a premium. Answer III doesn't make sense because the bonds are callable; if interest rates drop, the issuer will call the bonds back from this investor and he won't be able to sell at a premium. Answer IV makes sense because the bonds are put bonds. This investor would be able to control the bond and put it back to the issuer if interest rates increase, or he could hold onto (or sell) the bond if interest rates drop.

68. **D.** All the answers make sense. Certainly, the goals of the partnership (for example, building an office building) are probably the most important. Because Roman numeral I is in all the answers, you don't even really have to look at that one. The general manager's (general partner's) experience is important — you need to find out whether she has had other successful endeavors. The time frame for the partnership to become profitable (the crossover point) is significant because the investor usually needs a few years to earn a profit. Additionally, all investors of partnerships need liquidity in other investments in case the partnership needs a loan.

69. **C.** *Warrants* give the investor the right to purchase stock of a particular company at a specified price. Warrants are long-term and are sometimes — but not always — perpetual (everlasting). Answer C states that warrants provide the holder perpetual interest in the issuer's common stock. Because that statement is definite, it's wrong.

70. **C.** *Immediate family* includes you, your spouse, your children, you and your spouse's parents, and you and your spouse's siblings in addition to anyone you fully support, not including pets. Cousins, nieces, nephews, grandchildren, grandparents, uncles, and aunts aren't considered part of the immediate family (no matter how often they come over to raid your refrigerator).

71. **B.** All the choices listed are important, but the investment objectives (whether it's a growth fund, income fund, municipal bond fund, and so on) are most important. After the investor has determined (or after you've helped her determine) which investment objective is appropriate, she can start comparing funds within the same category for sales charges, management fees, redemption fees, and so on.

72. **A.** A structured transaction is an indication of money laundering. Transactions of $10,000 or more in cash, money orders, wires, and so on in one day have to be reported to the IRS as possible money laundering. In addition, broker-dealers have to file a suspicious activity report (SAR) on behavior that seems illogical or serves no apparent purpose. Roman numerals I and II have more than one transaction of just under $10,000 going into the same account by wire or transfer. This activity looks suspicious and is considered structuring.

73. **A.** *General obligation (GO) bonds* are municipal bonds issued by local governments, and the largest backing is property taxes. The interest received on GO bonds is exempt from federal taxes. If you know that municipal bonds are issued by local governments, not the U.S. government, you can eliminate Roman numeral I and, therefore, answer choices B, C, and D.

74. **C.** The easiest way to calculate the maximum potential gain for this question is to put the numbers in an options chart. Check out the following figure:

Money Out	Money In
$600	$200
$6,000	$7,000
$6,600	$7,200

First, put the two premiums in the chart. The investor is buying the XYZ Oct 60 call at 6, so you put $600 (6 × 100 shares per option) in the Money Out portion of the chart. Next, the investor sold the XYZ Oct 70 call at 2, so you put $200 ($2 × 100 shares per option) in the Money In portion of the chart. Because you have $400 more Money Out than Money In, this value is the investor's maximum potential loss.

To determine the maximum potential gain, you need to exercise both options. When exercising the XYZ Oct 60 call, you exercise at the strike price of 60 and you put the $6,000 (60 strike price × 100 shares per option) in the chart under the premium of $600. Call option exercises go on the same side of the chart as its premium. After you've completed that step, you need to exercise the other option. You come up with $7,000 (70 strike price × 100 shares per option). Put the $7,000 under its premium of $200. Total up both sides, and you see that you have $600 more in than out. The $600 difference is this customer's maximum potential gain.

75. **A.** Here's a question where an options chart can make your life easier. Follow these steps:

Money Out	Money In
$4,500	$200
$400	$5,000
$4,900	$5,200

The first step is to put the stock transaction and the option transaction in the chart. This investor bought 100 shares of QHI stock at $45. Take the $4,500 (45 × 100 shares) and put it in the Money Out portion of the chart, because that's money out of the investor's pocket.

Next, take the premium from the option sold at $200 (2 × 100 shares per option) and put that in the Money In portion of the chart, because that money goes into the investor's pocket. After that, the problem says that the investor sold the stock at $50 per share. Put the $5,000 in the Money In portion of the chart, because that money went into the investor's pocket. Now you have to complete the last transaction of closing the option at 4. Take the $400 and put it in the Money Out portion of the chart; the investor originally sold the option and to close, so the investor has to buy. When buying, money goes out of the investor's pocket. Total up both sides, and you see that the investor has a gain of $300.

76. **A.** All individuals may contribute up to $4,000 per year or 100 percent of earned income, whichever is less, to an IRA. Individuals over the age of 50 can make a $1,000 catch-up contribution, which doesn't come into play in this question. Because this investor doesn't have any other retirement plan, the amount deposited into the IRA is fully deductible.

77. **D.** If insider trading rules are violated, as they clearly are in this case, both the giver and receiver are guilty.

78. **A.** Notice that Roman numeral I is in every answer choice. You don't even need to look at that answer. All new accounts need a new account form, no matter what type of account it is. Because Melvin would like to give trading authorization to his sister, you need a signed power of attorney from Melvin stating that Marlene has trading authority over the account. You do not need a hypothecation agreement because you're dealing with a cash account, not a margin account. You don't need a joint account agreement because this account is a single account, not a joint account.

79. **C.** The balance of payments has to do with money coming in or going out of the U.S. Focus in on C and D right away, because they give you opposing answers. Most of the time when you have opposing answers, one of them is correct. Because you're looking for a false answer here, the correct answer is C. When U.S. investors purchase foreign securities, that action sends money out of the country and the U.S. balance of payments decreases instead of increasing.

80. **A.** When a customer places a market order, the customer pays or receives the best price available at the time of the order. The reported value of the trade is a "whoops" (the brokerage firm made a mistake), but the customer receives only the amount that the trade was executed for, less any commission.

81. **C.** The buying power is the dollar amount of securities that the investor can buy on margin with the excess equity (SMA) in the account.

The investor has a long market value (LMV) of $30,000 and a debit balance (DR) of $12,000, which means that the customer's equity (EQ) is $18,000:

LMV − DR = EQ, so $30,000 − $12,000 = $18,000

Regulation T says that when you buy on margin, you can borrow no more than 50 percent of the price of the security. Therefore, multiply Regulation T by the LMV to get the amount of equity necessary to be at the Regulation T (50 percent) requirement. With the LMV at $30,000 and the Regulation T at 50 percent (you can assume 50 percent), the equity should be at $15,000:

Reg T × LMV = Regulation T requirement, so 50% × $30,000 = $15,000

Because the investor has $18,000 in equity, she has an additional $3,000 that she can use to buy more securities on margin (18,000 − 15,000 = 3,000).

So, the buying power is the dollar amount of securities that you can purchase on margin using your excess equity (SMA — special memorandum account). With Regulation T at 50 percent, this investor can buy an additional $6,000 worth of securities on margin using her $3,000 SMA.

82. **C.** The correct thing to do is to hold onto the certificates so you don't have to worry about getting them back. Your firm should send the customer a stock power to sign and return, which is equivalent to the customer's signing the actual certificates.

83. **A.** As investors grow older, they shouldn't take as much risk. You should occasionally rebalance your customer's portfolios by shifting them out of stocks and into more bonds (fixed income securities) and cash or cash equivalents (for example, money market instruments). As a rule of thumb, subtract the customer's age from 100 to formulate the percentage that the customer should have in stocks. Because this customer is 60 years old, he or she should have 40 percent (100 – 60) invested in stocks and have the balance in bonds and cash.

84. **D.** According to Rule 144, the maximum amount of restricted stock that can be sold after the one-year holding period is 1 percent of the outstanding shares or the average weekly trading volume for the previous four weeks, whichever is greater. Here's your calculation:

$$1\% \times 2{,}500{,}000 \text{ shares} = 25{,}000$$

Your answer of 25,000 is one possibility. However, you also have to check to see whether the average trading volume for the previous four weeks is greater than that. The question gives you the previous five weeks, but you need only the previous four. In this case, the first four are the most recent:

$$
\begin{array}{r}
26{,}000 \\
24{,}000 \\
28{,}000 \\
+\ 27{,}000 \\
\hline
105{,}000
\end{array}
$$

Next, divide the 105,000 shares by 4 to get the average:

$$\frac{105{,}000}{4} = 26{,}250$$

Because 26,250 is greater than 25,000, 26,250 is your answer. Choose D.

85. **A.** A defensive strategy is for someone who doesn't like to take a lot of risk. Out of the listed choices, blue chip stocks from well-established companies and AAA rated bonds would work for Maxine. High-yield bonds (junk bonds) and call options are much riskier and wouldn't fit into Maxine's investment strategy.

86. **C.** To determine the status of Mr. Bearclaw's margin account, take the customer's current market value or, in this case, long market value (LMV), and subtract the debit balance (DR) to get the customer's equity (EQ):

$$LMV - DR = EQ, \text{ so } \$27{,}000 - \$15{,}000 = \$12{,}000$$

Next, multiply Regulation T (50 percent) by the LMV to get the amount of equity that the customer should have in the account to be at the Regulation T requirement:

$$\text{Reg T} \times LMV = \text{Regulation T requirement, so } 50\% \times \$27{,}000 = \$13{,}500$$

This value is greater than the customer's actual equity, so the account has no excess equity, or SMA; because II is false, you can rule out answer D. This customer needs to have $13,500 in equity to be at 50 percent. Because this investor has only $12,000 in equity, the account is restricted by $1,500. The account can be left restricted as long as it doesn't fall below minimum maintenance. To determine how low the market value can drop before Mr. Bearclaw receives a maintenance call, use the following formula:

$$\frac{4 \times DR}{3} = \frac{4 \times \$15{,}000}{3} = \frac{\$60{,}000}{3} = \$20{,}000$$

If the market value of the securities held in Mr. Bearclaw's account falls below $20,000, he'll receive a maintenance call.

87. **A.** The *resistance level* is the upper portion of a stock's trading range. If a stock has a trading range of 40 to 45, the 45 is the resistance level and the 40 is the support level. You assume that if a stock breaks out of the support or resistance level, a new trading range will be established. The answer is A.

88. **C.** The sale of municipal bonds isn't subject to the NASD 5% policy because the security is exempt, so you know A is wrong. You're not required to disclose the rating to the customer because the customer can look it up herself and the rating can change; eliminate B. When the broker-dealer sells bonds from inventory, he or she charges customers a markup, not a commission. Thus, you know D is wrong and C is correct — you should consider the total amount of the sale when calculating the markup.

89. **B.** You don't even need to work this one out on a chart. You can automatically assume that there are 100 shares per option contract. Mary purchased the HHH 40 call for a premium of $600 (6 × 100 shares per option) and purchased the HHH 35 put for a premium of $300 (3 × 100 shares per option). For the call option to be in-the-money at expiration, the price of the stock has to be above 40. For the put option to be in-the-money at expiration, the price of the stock has to be below 35. Because neither option is in-the-money, Mary loses the entire $900 that she invested.

90. **B.** A registered representative needs a written power of attorney to execute an order for a customer if the customer doesn't specify whether he's buying or selling, doesn't specify the particular security, and/or doesn't specify how many shares or what dollar amount to purchase. The registered representative can determine the timing or price to execute the order without a written power of attorney. Answer I doesn't require a written power of attorney, so therefore, the only answer that works is B.

91. **B.** If the market has been increasing on a steady basis but is starting to slow down, the market may be overbought. (If a technical analyst believes that the market is overbought, she'll likely advise investors to sell.)

92. **D.** The *spread* is the difference between the public offering price and the amount the issuer receives. In this case, the spread is $1.00 ($9.50 – $8.50). You can break down the spread into the syndicate manager's fee ($0.15) and the takedown of $0.85 ($1.00 spread – $0.15 manager's fee). If the syndicate members sell shares to the public themselves, they receive the takedown. The concession is the amount selling groups earn when they sell shares to the public. The additional takedown is the profit syndicate members make on shares that the selling group sells. Because the syndicate members have to pay $0.50 out of their $0.85, the additional takedown is $0.35.

93. **C.** If a syndicate is set up on a Western account (divided account) basis, syndicate members are finished when they sell all their shares. You can think of the wild, wild West, because each man is out for himself. If the underwriting is established on an Eastern (undivided) account basis, syndicate members are responsible for a portion of the shares left unsold by other members for the same percentage as the original offering. In this question, the syndicate member is initially responsible for 15 percent of the offering (300,000 ÷ 2,000,000), so the syndicate member is responsible for 15 percent of the unsold shares. Fifteen percent of 500,000 shares is 75,000 shares, so the answer is C.

94. **D.** Zack has a total of 110 shares including the 10 percent stock dividend. Zack initially paid a total of $4,200, including the $2-per-share commission. If you divide the $4,200 by 110 shares, you come up with a cost basis of $38.18 per share.

95. **A.** You don't have to look at Roman numeral I because it's included in all the answers. Roman numeral II is false because when interest rates increase, bond prices fall. Because Roman numeral II is in answers B, C, and D, the only correct answer is A. Roman numeral III is true because an issuer would be likely to call the bonds when interest rates decrease because the issuer could issue new bonds with lower coupon rates and save money. Roman numeral IV is false because call premiums (the penalty an issuer has to pay for calling bonds early) are not tied to lost interest (coupon) payments.

96. **B.** This custodial account is a Uniform Gifts to Minors Act (UGMA) account. Any adult can be a custodian for the account; however, you can have only one minor and one custodian per UGMA account. This situation makes Roman numeral I false and II true. Because only answers B and D are still possible, look at the differences in the choices. Both have IV in common, so you know that it's correct. You only have to look at Roman numeral III. III is incorrect because UGMA accounts must be cash accounts and securities can't be purchased on margin. The answer is B.

97. **B.** Project notes (PNs), bond anticipation notes (BANs), and revenue anticipation notes (RANs) are all short-term municipal notes. All or none (AON) is an order qualifier or a type of underwriting. The examiners may give you this question to trick you because AON looks like it may belong because it has three letters and ends in N and PN looks like it doesn't fit because it has only two letters.

98. **D.** Kowabunga is issuing mortgage bonds, which are backed by a lien on the property that Kowabunga owns. In the event of default, the property will be sold in order to pay off the bondholders. You can determine the conversion ratio (the number of shares the bond is convertible into) by using the following formula:

$$\text{Conversion ratio} = \frac{\text{par}}{\text{conversion price}}, \text{ so } \frac{\$1{,}000}{\$20} = 50 \text{ shares}$$

99. **C.** You wouldn't recommend warrants to an investor who wants dividends. Warrants give the holder the right to purchase stock at a fixed price. Because warrants aren't stock, holders don't receive dividends.

100. **C.** Normally, if the customer doesn't specify a different order, the first securities purchased are the first ones sold (FIFO). This customer would like to limit tax liability. The way to do that is to identify the shares that he wants to sell. If the customer sells the shares that he purchased when the price was high, he can reduce his capital gains tax.

101. **B.** *Discretionary accounts* give the registered representative the right to enter transactions for a customer at the registered representative's judgment. A hypothecation agreement is required for margin accounts but not discretionary accounts, so II is the false answer you're looking for. All the other possible answer choices are correct. The answer is B.

102. **A.** Direct participation programs (DPPs) are organized as limited partnerships. Raw land is a speculative (risky) investment because the land purchased may or may not become valuable in the future. Raw land doesn't provide income but does create a tax liability.

103. **D.** A syndicate puts in a stabilizing bid if the price of a new security starts dropping too quickly in the market. Stabilizing bids must be at or slightly below the public offering price of the security. Because $20.25 is above the public offering price, it's unacceptable. The answer is D.

104. **B.** Sellers of options always face more risk than buyers. The situation in answer B is the riskiest because this investor faces an unlimited maximum loss potential on the stock that he sold short. The investor will eventually have to cover the short position by purchasing the stock in the market. Because there's no limit as to how high the price of the stock can go, his potential loss is unlimited.

105. **D.** Customers need to receive account statements at least quarterly (every three months). If the account is active (the customer made any trades within the month), you have to send out a monthly account statement. Account statements for mutual funds have to be sent out at least once every six months.

106. **A.** Treasury STRIPS (Treasury receipts) are T-bonds and T-notes that are stripped of their coupons and principal. They're direct obligations of the U.S. government. Treasury STRIPS are issued at a discount and mature at par value; therefore, the interest accrues but isn't paid until maturity. Therefore, I is true and II is false. Treasury STRIPS should be accreted and the investor should pay taxes on the yearly accretion. Like the other two statements, III and IV are mutually exclusive. III is correct, so your answer is A.

107. **A.** Mary doesn't have any excess equity in her margin account because the account is restricted. First you have to set up the account correctly. Because this account is short rather than long, you use the SMV + EQ = CR formula. Mary has a credit balance (CR) of $5,600 and a short market value (SMV) of $4,000, which means that Mary's equity is $1,600:

    SMV + EQ = CR, so $4,000 + EQ = $5,600; EQ = $1,600

    To determine whether the account has excess equity (SMA) or is restricted, multiply the 50 percent Regulation T requirement by the short market value of $4,000:

    Reg T × SMV = Regulation T requirement, so 50% × $4,000 = $2,000

    Mary should have at least $2,000 in equity to be at the Regulation T requirement. Because Mary has only $1,600 in equity, the account is restricted by $400.

108. **B.** The false answer here is B. There's no time value when selling a stock short, but the premium of an option is made up of intrinsic value (how much the option is in-the-money) and time value (how long the investor has to use the option). The longer an investor holds an option, the lower the time value.

109. **D.** Roman numeral I is in all of the answer choices, so you don't even have to look at that one. Contributions to Roth IRA are made from after-tax dollars because the investor can't write off and deduct the contributions from his or her taxes. However, the investor can withdraw the entire contribution amount plus the amount that the account has gone up in value without paying any tax.

110. **D.** The false answer is definitely D. Call features make a bond offering less marketable because the bond is riskier for investors (they don't know how long they'll be able to hold the bonds). In fact, issuers pay a higher coupon rate on callable bonds so investors will purchase them.

111. **A.** In an unrestricted long margin account with Regulation T at 50 percent (which you have to assume for the Series 7 exam), the SMA (excess equity) will go up exactly one-half the amount that the account goes up in value. A is correct.

112. **C.** To transfer his account, Michael has to fill out an account transfer form with the new brokerage firm. As soon as the new brokerage firm contacts the old one, the old brokerage firm has to cancel all of Michael's open orders and freeze his account. The old firm has three business days to validate the transfer form that Michael filled out, plus an additional four business days to transfer Michael's account.

113. **B.** A double-barreled municipal bond is a combination of a revenue and general obligation (GO) bond. If revenues from the revenue producing facility that are backing the bond are insufficient, the bond is backed by the full faith and credit (taxing power) of the municipality.

114. **A.** Shareholder approval is necessary if a corporation wants to split its stock. Only the board of directors decides dividends; shareholders can't vote on dividends.

115. **D.** A deferred annuity is when an investor makes a lump sum payment into an annuity and starts receiving payouts sometime in the future. An immediate annuity is when the investor deposits a lump sum payment into an annuity and starts receiving payments immediately. However, under no circumstances will an insurance company start paying on an annuity prior to the investor's paying into it. Therefore, choices A, B, and C are all possible payment plans, but D isn't.

116. **B.** This problem is a nice easy one if you remember that covenants (promises stated on the indenture) are used for revenue bonds, not general obligation (GO) bonds. Roman numeral I is in all the answers except for B. When analyzing municipal GO bonds, ad valorem taxes (property taxes) are important, as are budgetary practices. However, the flow of funds (the way a municipality spends the money received from its revenue producing facility) is important to revenue bonds, not GO bonds.

117. **C.** Because *long* means *to buy,* an investor of a long combination would have two buys and no sells. A *long combination* is buying a call and buying a put on the same stock with different expiration months and/or different strike prices. Answer C fits the bill because the strike prices are different. Answer B is a long straddle because the expiration months and the strike prices are the same.

118. **D.** *Industrial development revenue bonds* (IDRs or IDBs) are municipal bonds in which the proceeds are used to construct or purchase a facility for the benefit of a private user (corporation). Because these bonds are backed by lease payments that the corporation makes rather than by the municipality, IDRs are considered the riskiest municipal bonds.

119. **A.** The *wash sale rule* states that when a customer sells a security at a loss, the customer can't buy the same security or anything convertible into the same security within 30 days before or after the sale and claim the loss. Roman numeral I is a violation because the customer is buying a bond that's convertible into the ABC stock that he sold at a loss within the past 30 days. Roman numeral II is out because the transaction doesn't occur within 30 days of selling the security at a loss. Answer III isn't a violation because put options give the investor the right to sell the stock, not buy the stock. IV is the other answer that violates the rule because the investor bought call options (the right to buy the stock) within 30 days of selling the security at a loss.

120. **A.** The *odd lot theory* states that the small investor is usually wrong. Smaller investors buy odd lots (fewer than 100 shares). Someone who believes in the odd lot theory watches odd lot transactions and goes the opposite direction (for example, if the smaller investors are buying, he would be selling). Many theorists believe that smaller investors don't receive or react to new information fast enough and by the time they get in on the action, it's too late.

121. **D.** All the choices given are subject to the *NASD 5% policy.* The 5% policy is a guideline, not a strict rule. Basically, broker-dealers shouldn't charge more than 5 percent for normal-sized trades when dealing with a public customer. Chapter 16 explains which trades are subject to the policy.

122. **A.** If the Fed raises the reserve requirements (the percentage of deposits that the bank has to have on hand each night), the banks won't be able to lend as much money, tightening the money supply. If the money supply is tight, interest rates increase. There's an inverse relationship between outstanding bond prices and interest rates. If interest rates increase, outstanding bond prices fall.

123. **B.** A principal of a firm doesn't need to review interoffice memos. Principals have to review both documents that are sent to public customers and customers' written complaints.

124. **C.** An investment adviser is someone who gives specific investment advice to investors for a fee. Answer C is an investment adviser because of the subscription fee and the specific advice.

125. **B.** A municipality publishes a notice of sale to let dealers know that it's accepting bids on a new municipal issue. If the municipality is accepting bids, the offering is considered competitive. By contrast, if the municipality chooses the underwriter(s) directly, you're looking at a negotiated offering. The answer is B.

Chapter 19

Nothing but Net: Practice Exam Part II

● ●

*1*f you've just finished part I and are continuing to part II, please make sure that you give your brain a rest for at least half an hour before starting this half. Just like part I, this part of the practice exam has 125 questions. For those of you who couldn't wait to take part II and bypassed part I, I review the test basics here.

As in the real Series 7 exam, the questions in part I and part II are in random order. Please read carefully. You can limit your careless mistakes by focusing in on the key words. Zone in on the information you do need to know to answer the question and ignore the information that doesn't help you. I suggest reading the last sentence twice to make sure you know what the question's asking. You may use scrap paper and a basic calculator for figuring.

Mark your answers on a separate piece of paper or on the upcoming answer sheet. As you're taking the exam, circle or highlight the questions that are giving you problems. After taking and grading the exam, look over the questions that you got wrong and the questions that you circled or highlighted. Review the test, retake all the questions that you circled or answered wrong, and make sure that you get them right this time. To simulate the real exam, try to finish this part in 3 hours or less. Please resist the urge to look at the answers and explanations until you've finished the exam. You can check answers at the end of this chapter or get detailed explanations in Chapter 20. Good luck!

Practice Exam Part II Answer Sheet

1 Ⓐ Ⓑ Ⓒ Ⓓ	33 Ⓐ Ⓑ Ⓒ Ⓓ	65 Ⓐ Ⓑ Ⓒ Ⓓ	97 Ⓐ Ⓑ Ⓒ Ⓓ
2 Ⓐ Ⓑ Ⓒ Ⓓ	34 Ⓐ Ⓑ Ⓒ Ⓓ	66 Ⓐ Ⓑ Ⓒ Ⓓ	98 Ⓐ Ⓑ Ⓒ Ⓓ
3 Ⓐ Ⓑ Ⓒ Ⓓ	35 Ⓐ Ⓑ Ⓒ Ⓓ	67 Ⓐ Ⓑ Ⓒ Ⓓ	99 Ⓐ Ⓑ Ⓒ Ⓓ
4 Ⓐ Ⓑ Ⓒ Ⓓ	36 Ⓐ Ⓑ Ⓒ Ⓓ	68 Ⓐ Ⓑ Ⓒ Ⓓ	100 Ⓐ Ⓑ Ⓒ Ⓓ
5 Ⓐ Ⓑ Ⓒ Ⓓ	37 Ⓐ Ⓑ Ⓒ Ⓓ	69 Ⓐ Ⓑ Ⓒ Ⓓ	101 Ⓐ Ⓑ Ⓒ Ⓓ
6 Ⓐ Ⓑ Ⓒ Ⓓ	38 Ⓐ Ⓑ Ⓒ Ⓓ	70 Ⓐ Ⓑ Ⓒ Ⓓ	102 Ⓐ Ⓑ Ⓒ Ⓓ
7 Ⓐ Ⓑ Ⓒ Ⓓ	39 Ⓐ Ⓑ Ⓒ Ⓓ	71 Ⓐ Ⓑ Ⓒ Ⓓ	103 Ⓐ Ⓑ Ⓒ Ⓓ
8 Ⓐ Ⓑ Ⓒ Ⓓ	40 Ⓐ Ⓑ Ⓒ Ⓓ	72 Ⓐ Ⓑ Ⓒ Ⓓ	104 Ⓐ Ⓑ Ⓒ Ⓓ
9 Ⓐ Ⓑ Ⓒ Ⓓ	41 Ⓐ Ⓑ Ⓒ Ⓓ	73 Ⓐ Ⓑ Ⓒ Ⓓ	105 Ⓐ Ⓑ Ⓒ Ⓓ
10 Ⓐ Ⓑ Ⓒ Ⓓ	42 Ⓐ Ⓑ Ⓒ Ⓓ	74 Ⓐ Ⓑ Ⓒ Ⓓ	106 Ⓐ Ⓑ Ⓒ Ⓓ
11 Ⓐ Ⓑ Ⓒ Ⓓ	43 Ⓐ Ⓑ Ⓒ Ⓓ	75 Ⓐ Ⓑ Ⓒ Ⓓ	107 Ⓐ Ⓑ Ⓒ Ⓓ
12 Ⓐ Ⓑ Ⓒ Ⓓ	44 Ⓐ Ⓑ Ⓒ Ⓓ	76 Ⓐ Ⓑ Ⓒ Ⓓ	108 Ⓐ Ⓑ Ⓒ Ⓓ
13 Ⓐ Ⓑ Ⓒ Ⓓ	45 Ⓐ Ⓑ Ⓒ Ⓓ	77 Ⓐ Ⓑ Ⓒ Ⓓ	109 Ⓐ Ⓑ Ⓒ Ⓓ
14 Ⓐ Ⓑ Ⓒ Ⓓ	46 Ⓐ Ⓑ Ⓒ Ⓓ	78 Ⓐ Ⓑ Ⓒ Ⓓ	110 Ⓐ Ⓑ Ⓒ Ⓓ
15 Ⓐ Ⓑ Ⓒ Ⓓ	47 Ⓐ Ⓑ Ⓒ Ⓓ	79 Ⓐ Ⓑ Ⓒ Ⓓ	111 Ⓐ Ⓑ Ⓒ Ⓓ
16 Ⓐ Ⓑ Ⓒ Ⓓ	48 Ⓐ Ⓑ Ⓒ Ⓓ	80 Ⓐ Ⓑ Ⓒ Ⓓ	112 Ⓐ Ⓑ Ⓒ Ⓓ
17 Ⓐ Ⓑ Ⓒ Ⓓ	49 Ⓐ Ⓑ Ⓒ Ⓓ	81 Ⓐ Ⓑ Ⓒ Ⓓ	113 Ⓐ Ⓑ Ⓒ Ⓓ
18 Ⓐ Ⓑ Ⓒ Ⓓ	50 Ⓐ Ⓑ Ⓒ Ⓓ	82 Ⓐ Ⓑ Ⓒ Ⓓ	114 Ⓐ Ⓑ Ⓒ Ⓓ
19 Ⓐ Ⓑ Ⓒ Ⓓ	51 Ⓐ Ⓑ Ⓒ Ⓓ	83 Ⓐ Ⓑ Ⓒ Ⓓ	115 Ⓐ Ⓑ Ⓒ Ⓓ
20 Ⓐ Ⓑ Ⓒ Ⓓ	52 Ⓐ Ⓑ Ⓒ Ⓓ	84 Ⓐ Ⓑ Ⓒ Ⓓ	116 Ⓐ Ⓑ Ⓒ Ⓓ
21 Ⓐ Ⓑ Ⓒ Ⓓ	53 Ⓐ Ⓑ Ⓒ Ⓓ	85 Ⓐ Ⓑ Ⓒ Ⓓ	117 Ⓐ Ⓑ Ⓒ Ⓓ
22 Ⓐ Ⓑ Ⓒ Ⓓ	54 Ⓐ Ⓑ Ⓒ Ⓓ	86 Ⓐ Ⓑ Ⓒ Ⓓ	118 Ⓐ Ⓑ Ⓒ Ⓓ
23 Ⓐ Ⓑ Ⓒ Ⓓ	55 Ⓐ Ⓑ Ⓒ Ⓓ	87 Ⓐ Ⓑ Ⓒ Ⓓ	119 Ⓐ Ⓑ Ⓒ Ⓓ
24 Ⓐ Ⓑ Ⓒ Ⓓ	56 Ⓐ Ⓑ Ⓒ Ⓓ	88 Ⓐ Ⓑ Ⓒ Ⓓ	120 Ⓐ Ⓑ Ⓒ Ⓓ
25 Ⓐ Ⓑ Ⓒ Ⓓ	57 Ⓐ Ⓑ Ⓒ Ⓓ	89 Ⓐ Ⓑ Ⓒ Ⓓ	121 Ⓐ Ⓑ Ⓒ Ⓓ
26 Ⓐ Ⓑ Ⓒ Ⓓ	58 Ⓐ Ⓑ Ⓒ Ⓓ	90 Ⓐ Ⓑ Ⓒ Ⓓ	122 Ⓐ Ⓑ Ⓒ Ⓓ
27 Ⓐ Ⓑ Ⓒ Ⓓ	59 Ⓐ Ⓑ Ⓒ Ⓓ	91 Ⓐ Ⓑ Ⓒ Ⓓ	123 Ⓐ Ⓑ Ⓒ Ⓓ
28 Ⓐ Ⓑ Ⓒ Ⓓ	60 Ⓐ Ⓑ Ⓒ Ⓓ	92 Ⓐ Ⓑ Ⓒ Ⓓ	124 Ⓐ Ⓑ Ⓒ Ⓓ
29 Ⓐ Ⓑ Ⓒ Ⓓ	61 Ⓐ Ⓑ Ⓒ Ⓓ	93 Ⓐ Ⓑ Ⓒ Ⓓ	125 Ⓐ Ⓑ Ⓒ Ⓓ
30 Ⓐ Ⓑ Ⓒ Ⓓ	62 Ⓐ Ⓑ Ⓒ Ⓓ	94 Ⓐ Ⓑ Ⓒ Ⓓ	
31 Ⓐ Ⓑ Ⓒ Ⓓ	63 Ⓐ Ⓑ Ⓒ Ⓓ	95 Ⓐ Ⓑ Ⓒ Ⓓ	
32 Ⓐ Ⓑ Ⓒ Ⓓ	64 Ⓐ Ⓑ Ⓒ Ⓓ	96 Ⓐ Ⓑ Ⓒ Ⓓ	

1. Skunkneel Balanced is an open-end investment company. When Skunkneel advertises with a prospectus, it MUST

   I.   include a disclaimer with wording that states "past performance might not be indicative of future performance"

   II. only make statements that are true

   III. omit certain facts that investors might find confusing

   IV. state that the fund is not monitored by any governmental body

   (A) I, II, and III only

   (B) II and IV only

   (C) I, II, and IV only

   (D) I, II, III, and IV

2. An investor would like to put away money for her 3-year-old child's higher education. Which of the following investments would be MOST suitable to meet this investor's needs?

   (A) Blue chip stocks

   (B) Zero-coupon bonds

   (C) Growth company stocks

   (D) CDs

3. All of the following describe treasury stock EXCEPT

   (A) It is issued stock that has been repurchased by the company.

   (B) It is stock that was previously authorized but is still unissued.

   (C) Investors receive no dividends.

   (D) It has no voting rights.

4. A customer buys a 10 percent New York municipal bond with a sinking fund provision in the secondary market at 120. If the bond matures in eight years, what is the approximate amount of amortization after holding the bond for five years?

   (A) $95

   (B) $125

   (C) $200

   (D) Municipal bonds cannot be amortized.

5. Bull and Bull Brokerage sent Steve a confirmation of his latest trade of Dimco common stock. Which of the following items should be on the confirmation?

   I.   The trade date and the settlement date

   II. Whether Bull and Bull acted as an agent or principal

   III. The name of the security and how many shares were traded

   IV. The amount of commission paid if Bull and Bull acted as an agent

   (A) I and III only

   (B) I, II, and III only

   (C) I, III, and IV only

   (D) I, II, III, and IV

6. ABDE Corp., a new company, has held back some of its shares for later use. According to shelf distribution rules, ABDE can sell the shares over the course of the next _____ without having to reregister the shares.

   (A) 90 days

   (B) 180 days

   (C) 270 days

   (D) 2 years

7. All of the following are TRUE of a broker's broker EXCEPT

   (A) They maintain the anonymity of their clients.

   (B) They maintain no inventory of municipal bonds.

   (C) They deal only with institutional customers and municipal brokers.

   (D) They deal only with public customers.

8. All of the following are good delivery for a trade of 880 shares EXCEPT

   (A) one certificate for 800 shares, 40 for 2 shares each

   (B) two certificates for 400 shares each, 20 for 4 shares each

   (C) three certificates for 200 shares each, 4 for 70 shares each

   (D) four certificates for 200 shares each, 8 for 10 shares each

9. The formula for cash flow is

   (A) cash flow = net income − depreciation

   (B) cash flow = gross income + depreciation + depletion

   (C) cash flow = net income + depreciation + depletion

   (D) cash flow = gross income − depletion + depreciation

10. Which of the following is TRUE of special tax bonds?

    (A) They are backed by excise taxes.

    (B) They are backed by charges on the property that benefits.

    (C) They are general obligation bonds.

    (D) They are issued by, and backed by, the full faith and credit of the federal government.

11. Which of the following entities is responsible for preparing the legal opinion for an issue of municipal bonds?

    (A) The syndicate manager

    (B) The municipal issuer

    (C) A bond counsel

    (D) The trustee

12. Rod Bullhorn is a resident of Ohio. Mr. Bullhorn purchased an Ohio municipal bond. What is the tax treatment of the interest that Rod earns on his Ohio bond?

    (A) It is exempt from local taxes only.

    (B) It is exempt from state taxes only.

    (C) It is exempt from federal taxes only.

    (D) It is exempt from federal, state, and local taxes.

13. IMP stock tends to move in the opposite direction of the economy. IMP would be termed

    (A) cyclical

    (B) countercyclical

    (C) blue-chip

    (D) defensive

14. ABCD Corp. has filed a registration statement with the SEC and is currently in the cooling-off period. Biff Spanky Corp. is the lead underwriter for ABCD and is in the process of taking indications of interest. Which TWO of the following are TRUE regarding indications of interest?

    I. They are binding on Biff Spanky Corp.

    II. They are binding on the customers.

    III. They are not binding on Biff Spanky Corp.

    IV. They are not binding on the customers.

    (A) I and II

    (B) III and IV

    (C) I and IV

    (D) II and III

15. A trade of securities between a bank and an insurance company without using the services of a broker-dealer would take place on the

    (A) first market

    (B) second market

    (C) third market

    (D) fourth market

16. While building his/her book, a newly registered representative would like to work weekends as a DJ at a local nightclub to earn a little extra income. He/she would be required to tell his/her

    (A) broker-dealer only

    (B) broker-dealer and the NASD

    (C) broker-dealer and the NYSE

    (D) none of the above

Use the following exhibit to answer question 17. **Note:** *P* stands for *put,* and *a* stands for *not traded.*

HLP	Strike	May	Aug	Nov
60.50	50	12	14.50	16
60.50	50p	a	0.50	1.25
60.50	60	2	3.25	5
60.50	60p	1.50	2.75	4

17. If an investor buys an HLP Nov 60 put and writes an RST Nov 50 put, what is the maximum gain?

    (A) $275

    (B) $325

    (C) $675

    (D) $725

18. An official notice of sale does NOT contain which of the following?

    (A) The name of the bond counsel

    (B) The rating of the bond

    (C) Interest and payment dates

    (D) Method and place of settlement

19. An investor owns 10 MMM May 50 calls. RST increases to $60, and the investor exercises the calls. The investor tells her registered rep to sell the stock immediately after purchase. If all of these trades are executed in a margin account, how much must the investor deposit?

    (A) $3,000

    (B) $30,000

    (C) $35,000

    (D) No deposit is required.

20. Mr. and Mrs. Smith opened a joint account several years ago as a JTWROS. Mr. Smith was involved in a severe car accident and didn't survive. Upon receiving confirmation of Mr. Smith's passing, what must be done with the account?

    (A) The entire account is transferred to Mrs. Smith.

    (B) Mr. Smith's portion of the account is transferred to his estate.

    (C) The account is divided up depending on percentage invested.

    (D) None of the above.

21. As a wise registered representative, you should keep track of not only the market and different securities but also each investor's investment objectives. Which of the following changes might affect a customer's investment objectives?

    I.   Growing older

    II. Getting married

    III. Having a child who will soon be going to college

    IV. Obtaining greater investment experience

    (A) I and III only

    (B) II and III only

    (C) I, II, and III only

    (D) I, II, III, and IV

22. According to SEA Rule 145, full disclosure must be made to shareholders in the event of all of the following EXCEPT

    (A) stock splits

    (B) reclassifications

    (C) mergers or consolidations

    (D) transfer of assets

23. What is the main function of a market maker?

    (A) Holding securities in its own account to help facilitate trading

    (B) Selling NASDAQ securities on an agency basis

    (C) Selling NYSE securities on an agency basis

    (D) Selling securities out of its own inventory while charging a commission

24. Which of the following would be deemed control securities?

    I. Securities owned by an officer of the issuer

    II. Securities owned by a director of the issuer

    III. Securities owned by an investor who owns 10 percent or more of any class of a corporation's outstanding securities

    IV. Securities owned by an investor who owns 5 percent or more of a corporation's voting stock

    (A) I and III only

    (B) I, II, and III only

    (C) III and IV only

    (D) I, II, III, and IV

25. Inflation for the past year is at an all-time high. Which of the following is the best indicator of inflation?

    (A) CPI

    (B) GDP

    (C) M1

    (D) Currency exchange rate

26. An investor would like to strengthen his portfolio by adding some defensive stocks. Which of the following stocks would be considered defensive?

    I. Appliance company

    II. Tobacco

    III. Alcohol

    IV. Automotive

    (A) I and IV only

    (B) II and III only

    (C) I, III, and IV only

    (D) II, III, and IV only

27. Francine Franzwitz purchased 400 shares of DIM preferred stock paying a yearly dividend of $8 per share. Francine originally purchased the stock on February 21, 2007. Exactly one year later on February 21, 2008, Francine sold the stock for a profit of $1,200. Which TWO of the following are TRUE relating to the tax treatment of Francine's transactions?

    I. The dividends will be taxed as passive income.

    II. The dividends will be taxed as ordinary income.

    III. The sale will be taxed as a long-term capital gain.

    IV. The sale will be taxed as a short-term capital gain.

    (A) I and III

    (B) I and IV

    (C) II and III

    (D) II and IV

28. Which of the following tranches is considered the safest?

    (A) PAC

    (B) TAC

    (C) Companion

    (D) Z

29. Tom Smith is interested in purchasing an Atlanta municipal general obligation bond. The bonds were originally issued with a serial maturity. If Tom believes that interest rates are going to drop over the next 20 to 30 years, which maturity would you advise him to buy?

    (A) The longest term

    (B) The shortest term

    (C) A combination of all of the different maturities

    (D) There is no way to tell

30. The market took a beating last week and one of your customer's margin accounts is restricted. Which of the following is TRUE?

I. Your customer cannot borrow any additional money from your firm.

II. Your customer must deposit funds to take the account out of restricted status.

III. All additional securities purchases by this customer must be in cash.

IV. The equity in your customer's account has fallen below 50 percent of the long market value.

(A) I, III, and IV only

(B) I, II, and III only

(C) I and II only

(D) IV only

31. If there is a discrepancy in the details of a trade between two firms, what will be sent out to the contra-broker?

(A) A notice of sale

(B) A DK notice

(C) A rehypothecation form

(D) Form 144

32. Joanie Johnson is pursuing an aggressive stock buying strategy. Which of the following investments would BEST suit Joanie's needs?

(A) ABC stock with a beta coefficient of 0.80

(B) LMN stock with a beta coefficient of 1.0

(C) XYZ stock with a beta coefficient of 1.20

(D) Blue-chip stock

33. Your firm was involved in the underwriting of GO municipal bonds for Suffolk, NY. The syndicate manager notifies your firm that the underwriting was oversubscribed. How does the syndicate manager determine which orders are filled first?

(A) As stated in the bond indenture

(B) As stated in the agreement among underwriters

(C) First ordered, first served

(D) In a way that the syndicate manager determines to be fair and equitable

34. Mr. Bulleshi purchases a COW Aug 40 put at 3 and also writes a COW Aug 50 put at 9. Mr. Bulleshi will be able to make a profit if

I. The premium difference narrows to less than 6.

II. The premium difference widens to more than 6.

III. Both options expire unexercised.

IV. Both options are exercised.

(A) I or III

(B) I or IV

(C) II or III

(D) II or IV

35. The market price of a security is the same as the exercise price. If it stays that way, which TWO of the following investors would have a profit?

I. The writer of an at-the-money straddle

II. The writer of an at-the-money call

III. The purchaser of an at-the-money put

IV. The purchaser of an at-the-money call

(A) I and II

(B) III and IV

(C) I and III

(D) II and IV

36. DIM Corp. has 8 percent participating preferred stock. The 8 percent represents the

(A) minimum dividend payment

(B) maximum dividend payment

(C) actual dividend payment

(D) percentage ownership of the company

37. Which of the following sources would provide an investor with the BEST information about municipal bonds in the primary market?

(A) *The Bond Buyer*

(B) *The Blue List*

(C) *Munifacts*

(D) *Yellow Sheets*

38. Which TWO of the following orders are NOT held in a specialist's book?

I. Not-held orders

II. Stop orders

III. Limit orders

IV. Market orders

(A) I and II

(B) II and III

(C) III and IV

(D) I and IV

39. All of the following money market instruments trade without accrued interest EXCEPT

(A) T-bills

(B) bankers' acceptances

(C) certificates of deposit

(D) commercial paper

40. All of the following are TRUE about a bond selling at a discount EXCEPT

(A) The market price is lower than the par value.

(B) The current yield is greater than the coupon rate.

(C) Interest rates most likely declined after the bonds were issued.

(D) The yield-to-maturity is greater than the nominal yield.

41. The indenture of a corporate bond would include all of the following EXCEPT the

(A) nominal yield

(B) rating

(C) collateral backing the bond (if any)

(D) maturity date

42. A buy-in would occur when which of the following happens?

(A) The buyer of a security fails to pay for the trade by the payment date.

(B) The seller of a security fails to deliver the securities that were sold.

(C) Both A and B.

(D) Neither A nor B.

43. TUV Corp. has issued 7 percent participating preferred stock. The 7 percent represents the

(A) minimum dividend payment

(B) maximum dividend payment

(C) dividend payment

(D) average dividend payment

44. XYZ convertible bonds are trading in the market for 88. XYZ is convertible into common stock at $20. If the common stock is 10 percent below parity, what is the price of the common stock?

(A) 15.84

(B) 16.38

(C) 17.25

(D) 17.68

45. Straight-line amortization of a municipal bond purchased at a premium will cause which TWO of the following?

I. Reduction of the bond's cost basis by equal amounts each year

II. Increase of the bond's cost basis by equal amounts each year

III. Increase of the amount of potential capital gain each year

IV. Reduction of the amount of potential capital gain each year

(A) I and III

(B) I and IV

(C) II and III

(D) II and IV

46. Fawn Frammer is out of the country and would like to sell the stock that she keeps at home in her safe. Because she doesn't have access to the securities, you let her know that she can sell her stock short to lock in the price. If Fawn takes your advice, what would be her position?

(A) A straddle

(B) Short against the box

(C) A combination

(D) Longing against the short

47. One of your customers purchases a new municipal bond at a discount. Which TWO of the following are TRUE?

   I. The discount on the bond must be accreted.

   II. The discount on the bond would not be accreted.

   III. The customer would be subject to a capital gain if he/she holds the bond to maturity.

   IV. The customer would not be subject to a capital gain if he/she holds the bond to maturity.

   (A) I and III

   (B) I and IV

   (C) II and III

   (D) II and IV

48. Anne would like to create a "short combination" using her existing option. Anne is short 1 XYZ Aug 80 call. Which of the following option positions should Anne purchase or sell?

   (A) Long 1 XYZ Aug 90 put

   (B) Long 1 XYZ Aug 80 put

   (C) Short 1 XYZ Aug 70 put

   (D) Short 1 XYZ Aug 80 put

49. An investor holds a portfolio of securities that includes a significant amount of preferred stocks. Which of the following is the best option strategy to protect against a decline in the value of the preferred stock?

   (A) Buy interest rate calls

   (B) Buy interest rate puts

   (C) Buy index option puts

   (D) Buy index option calls

Use the following exhibit to answer question 50.

Income Statement for DIM Corp.	
Net sales	$10,000,000
Operating expenses	− $6,000,000
EBIT	$4,000,000
Bond interest	− $500,000
Taxable income	$3,500,000
50% tax	− $1,750,000
Net income	$1,750,000
Preferred dividends	− $500,000
	$1,250,000
Common dividends	− $300,000
Retained earnings	$950,000

Market price of the common stock: $13

Common shares outstanding: 1,000,000

Annual common dividend: $0.60

Depreciation: $200,000

50. What is the EPS of DIM Corp.?

   (A) $0.30

   (B) $0.60

   (C) $1.25

   (D) $2.40

51. The settlement date for a WI security is

   (A) a date to be assigned

   (B) one business day

   (C) three business days

   (D) seven calendar days

52. All of the following information is required on a red herring EXCEPT

   (A) the final offering price

   (B) the purpose for which the issuer is raising the funds

   (C) a statement in red lettering stating that items on the preliminary prospectus are subject to change before the final prospectus is issued

   (D) the issuer's history and financial status

53. A tombstone advertisement would include which of the following?

    I.   A listing of syndicate members

    II. An offering price

    III. A listing of the selling group members

    IV. Where investors can obtain a prospectus

    (A) I and IV only

    (B) I, III, and IV only

    (C) I, II, and IV only

    (D) I, II, and III only

54. A municipal bond trader may do any of the following EXCEPT

    (A) request bids

    (B) enter offers on behalf of a broker-dealer

    (C) rate a municipal bond's credit worthiness

    (D) position a broker-dealer's inventory

55. An investor buys a municipal bond in the secondary market for 105. The bond has ten years until maturity. Six years later, the investor sells the bond for 102. What is the investor's gain or loss?

    (A) $30 capital loss

    (B) $20 capital gain

    (C) $20 capital loss

    (D) No gain or loss

56. ABC Corp. issued 20-year convertible bonds with an "antidilution" covenant. If ABC declares a stock dividend, which TWO of the following are TRUE?

    I.   The conversion ratio would increase.

    II. The conversion ratio would decrease.

    III. The conversion price would increase.

    IV. The conversion price would decrease.

    (A) I and III

    (B) I and IV

    (C) II and III

    (D) II and IV

57. Which of the following situations requires a broker-dealer to file a currency transaction report?

    (A) A customer purchases $40,000 worth of stock with a personal check.

    (B) A customer opens an account with $12,000 cash.

    (C) A customer opens an account with a wire transfer from his checking account for $32,000.

    (D) A customer deposits bearer bonds with a par value of $50,000.

58. Spanky Corp. (SPNK) is issuing new shares to existing shareholders through a rights offering. The current market price of SPNK is $30 per share, and the stock is being offered to current shareholders at $22 and 10 rights. What is the theoretical value of a cum-right?

    (A) $0.73

    (B) $0.80

    (C) $2.00

    (D) $2.20

59. Which of the following best describes systematic risk?

    (A) The risk that a security can decline due to negative market conditions

    (B) The likelihood of default by a particular issuer

    (C) The risk that a security cannot keep pace with the inflation rate

    (D) The risk that the issuer does not perform to expectations

60. Which of the following is considered the MOST secure municipal revenue bond?

    (A) IDRs

    (B) Moral obligations

    (C) PHAs

    (D) Special assessment bonds

61. Zeb Zbridger purchased 1,000 shares of ZZZ common stock three years ago at a cost of $40 per share. Zeb gives the stock to his son Zack when the market value is $50 per share. Which TWO of the following are TRUE of this transaction?

    I.   Zeb may be subject to a gift tax.

    II. Zack may be subject to a gift tax.

    III. Zack's cost basis is $40 per share.

    IV. Zack's cost basis is $50 per share.

    (A) I and III

    (B) I and IV

    (C) II and III

    (D) II and IV

62. Harry Bullbed has recently invested in an oil and gas DPP as a limited partner. You can tell Harry that he can do all of the following EXCEPT

    (A) help manage the DPP

    (B) inspect all of the DPP's books

    (C) invest in other competing oil and gas DPPs

    (D) sue the general partner of the DPP

63. You are about to take your first order for options. Place the following option transactions in sequential order starting from the first.

    I.   The ROP approves the account.

    II. The customer is sent an ODD.

    III. The customer sends in an OAA.

    IV. The transaction is executed.

    (A) I, II, III, IV

    (B) II, I, III, IV

    (C) II, I, IV, III

    (D) III, I, IV, II

64. Jon is an investor with quite a lot of money. Jon is in the highest income tax bracket. He is looking for an investment for his situation that would give him an advantage over other investors in lower tax brackets. Which of the following securities would you MOST likely recommend?

    (A) Municipal bonds

    (B) T-bonds

    (C) High-yielding bonds

    (D) Stocks from different growth companies

65. Which of the following is NOT a factor that would affect the marketability of a municipal bond?

    (A) The rating

    (B) The dated date

    (C) The maturity

    (D) The issuer's name

66. All of the following are ways of diversifying a municipal bond portfolio EXCEPT

    (A) buying bonds with different maturities

    (B) buying bonds of different quality

    (C) buying bonds from different geographical regions

    (D) buying a larger or smaller quantity of bonds

67. Bernice Bearishnikoff is a registered representative who works for Bullwork and Bearsleep Securities. Bernice has just learned of the death of one of her customers. Which of the following actions should Bernice take regarding her deceased customer's account?

    (A) Mark her customer's account as deceased.

    (B) Cancel all open orders.

    (C) Wait for the proper legal papers.

    (D) All of the above.

68. Which of the following does NOT reduce the debit balance in a long margin account?

    (A) Cash dividends

    (B) Liquidation of long stock

    (C) Stock dividends

    (D) Cash deposits

69. DURF Corp. common stock is currently trading in the market for $16 per share. DURF Corp. pays an annual dividend of $0.80 per share and has an earnings per share of $4. What is the PE ratio?

    (A) 4

    (B) 5

    (C) 20

    (D) Cannot be determined

70. All of the following are considered quick assets EXCEPT

    (A) cash

    (B) accounts receivable

    (C) inventory

    (D) marketable securities

71. Mervin Mazon purchased 100 U.S. government T-bonds. Which of the following is TRUE?

    (A) The purchase of the bonds will settle in one business day, and payment is due one business day after the trade date.

    (B) The purchase of the bonds will settle in one business day, and payment is due five business days after the trade date.

    (C) The purchase of the bonds will settle in three business days, and payment is due three business days after the trade date.

    (D) The purchase of the bonds will settle in three business days, and payment is due five business days after the trade date.

72. A customer enters an order to buy 100 shares of JKL at 50 stop limit when the market price is 49.75. The ticker tape after the order shows the following transactions:

JKL	MNO
49.80, 49.75, 50, 50.13, 50.25, 50.13, 49.88	61.14, 60.25

    The order was elected (triggered) at

    (A) 49.75

    (B) 50

    (C) 50.13

    (D) 50.25

73. Referring to the preceding example, the first trade where the order could have been executed is

    (A) 50

    (B) 50.13

    (C) 49.88

    (D) The order could not have been executed.

74. T-bonds issued by the U.S. government have been issued in which form since the mid-1980s?

    (A) Bearer

    (B) Book entry

    (C) Fully registered

    (D) Partially registered

75. All of the following securities earn interest EXCEPT

    I.   Treasury STRIPS

    II. Treasury bonds

    III. treasury stock

    IV. Treasury bills

    (A) I and IV only

    (B) II and III only

    (C) III only

    (D) IV only

76. A customer receives dividends on securities held in a margin account at Needum Securities. If this customer chooses to leave the dividend in the account, which TWO of the following will occur?

    I.   The equity will increase.

    II. The equity will decrease.

    III. The debit balance will increase.

    IV. The debit balance will decrease.

    (A) I and III

    (B) I and IV

    (C) II and III

    (D) II and IV

77. All of the following are TRUE regarding special assessment bonds EXCEPT

    (A) The bonds are backed with ad valorem taxes.

    (B) They are considered revenue bonds.

    (C) The property owners who benefit from the improvements pay increased taxes to back the bonds.

    (D) They are considered a type of GO bond.

78. Mrs. Ballyhoo writes ten naked puts on WIG stock. What is the maximum loss that Mrs. Ballyhoo can incur?

    (A) (Strike price − the premium) × 100 shares × 10 options

    (B) (Strike price + the premium) × 100 shares × 10 options

    (C) The entire premium received

    (D) Unlimited

79. An investor purchases 200 shares of DIM Corp. at $65 per share and purchases 2 RST Oct 60 puts at 7. What is the customer's break-even point?

    (A) 53

    (B) 58

    (C) 67

    (D) 72

80. DIM Lighting, Inc., bonds are convertible at $40. If DIM's common stock is trading in the market for $38 and the bonds are trading for 80, which of the following statements are TRUE?

    I.   The bonds are trading below parity.

    II. The stock is trading below parity.

    III. This is an excellent arbitrage situation for an astute investor.

    IV. The bonds are convertible into 20 shares of common stock.

    (A) I and III only

    (B) I and IV only

    (C) II and III only

    (D) II, III, and IV only

81. An investor has a margin account with $40,000 market value and $14,000 debit balance. If the investor wants to purchase an additional $20,000 of stock in this account, what amount must the investor deposit?

    (A) $10,000

    (B) $4,000

    (C) $2,000

    (D) $0

82. A customer calls up to get the current bid and ask prices on JABB common stock. You have a Level I machine. Which of the following quotes given to the customer would NOT be acceptable?

    (A) "It is trading at 45.25 to 45.40 subject."

    (B) "It is currently trading at 45.25 to 45.40."

    (C) "It is 45.25 to 45.40."

    (D) "Last time I looked, it was 45.25 to 45.40."

83. M2 money supply includes all of the following EXCEPT

    (A) jumbo CDs

    (B) time deposits

    (C) money in circulation

    (D) checking accounts

84. A syndicate is offering 15,000,000 new shares to the public on an Eastern account basis. A member of the syndicate is responsible for selling 4,500,000 shares. After selling its entire allotment, 3,000,000 shares are left unsold by other members. How many additional shares is the firm responsible for selling to the public?

    (A) 0

    (B) 200,000

    (C) 400,000

    (D) 900,000

85. A fundamental analyst is examining the balance sheets of a few different companies to try to make a stock pick. The fundamental analyst can view (or determine) all of the following information from the balance sheet EXCEPT

    (A) inventory

    (B) stockholder's equity

    (C) current liabilities

    (D) earnings per share

86. An investor is long 1 ACE Aug 65 call for 5 and 1 WXYZ Aug 65 put for 8. WXYZ drops to 50 just prior to expiration. The investor buys the stock in the market and exercises the put. After the call expires, what is the gain or loss?

    (A) $200 gain

    (B) $200 loss

    (C) $1,000 gain

    (D) $1,000 loss

Use the following information to answer question 87.

	BID	OFFER
WOW Aug 50 call	4	4.25
WOW Aug 50 put	3	3.25
WOW Aug 60 call	1	1.25
WOW Aug 60 put	8	8.25

87. How much would an investor creating a debit call spread have to pay (disregarding commissions)?

    (A) $200

    (B) $225

    (C) $300

    (D) $325

88. An IDR is backed by

    (A) the local municipality if the corporate guarantor cannot meet its debt obligation

    (B) the corporate guarantor only

    (C) the state in which the facility is located

    (D) none of the above

89. When a municipality issues a revenue bond under a net revenue pledge, which expense will be paid first from the revenues received?

    (A) Bond principal and interest

    (B) Operation and maintenance

    (C) Debt service reserve

    (D) Renewal and replacement

90. An investor is long 100 shares of YYY stock originally purchased at $70 per share. This investor subsequently wrote a YYY Jul 75 call at 3 when YYY was trading at $68 per share. What is this investor's maximum potential loss?

    (A) $300

    (B) $6,500

    (C) $6,700

    (D) $7,800

91. An investor purchases 10 XYZ Oct 40 calls for a premium of 6 each. These options will expire

    (A) on the third Saturday in October

    (B) on the third Friday in October

    (C) on the Saturday following the third Friday in October

    (D) on a date to be assigned by the seller of the option

92. A municipality decides to call its bonds due to mature in 2015 and to finance the call by issuing bonds with a maturity date of 2035. This is known as

    (A) redeeming

    (B) advance refunding

    (C) pre-refunding

    (D) refunding

93. JMM stock is trading at 30.75. JMM Jul 25 calls are trading at a premium of 7. What is the time value of the JMM Jul 25 calls?

    (A) $0

    (B) $125

    (C) $575

    (D) $700

94. Which of the following orders guarantee a specific price or better?

    (A) Buy limits and sell stops

    (B) Sell limits and buy stops

    (C) Buy stops and sell stops

    (D) Buy limits and sell limits

95. Black Hole is an oil DPP. One of the limited partners of the DPP is Lena Johnson. Lena signed a recourse loan on behalf of Black Hole. If Black Hole defaults on the loan, which of the following is TRUE?

    (A) Creditors could pursue Lena's personal assets to help repay the loan.

    (B) Creditors could pursue the personal assets of Black Hole's general manager.

    (C) Creditors would be last in line to collect any assets that Black Hole has left over after paying other creditors.

    (D) Cannot be determined.

96. The public offering price (POP) of a mutual fund share is

    (A) net asset value – sales charge

    (B) net asset value + sales charge

    (C) net asset value × sales charge

    (D) net asset value + (8½% × NAV)

97. An investor sells short 1,000 shares of GHI at $60. If GHI goes up to $64, how much is the account restricted?

    (A) $0

    (B) $2,000

    (C) $4,000

    (D) $6,000

98. A syndicate has just won a bid on a new issue of municipal bonds. The syndicate is expected to start receiving orders for this issue. The normal order for filling orders from highest priority to lowest priority is

    I. designated

    II. syndicate

    III. member

    IV. presale

    (A) II, III, I, IV

    (B) IV, II, III, I

    (C) IV, II, I, III

    (D) I, IV, II, III

99. All of the following are types of state registration of new issues EXCEPT

    (A) filing

    (B) coordination

    (C) qualification

    (D) communication

100. The Securities Act of 1933 is the act that

    (A) created the Securities and Exchange Commission

    (B) regulates margin and the short sale of securities

    (C) covers the registration of new issues on the state level

    (D) requires full and fair disclosure of material information regarding new issues

101. *The Bond Buyer's* 11-bond index is made up of which of the following grades of bonds?

    I. AAA

    II. AA

    III. A

    IV. BBB

    (A) I and II only

    (B) I, II, and III only

    (C) II, III, and IV only

    (D) III only

102. Inflation has been running rampant over the last couple of years. It is expected that the Fed will increase interest rates to try to curb the inflation. Knowing this information, a municipality would most likely issue

    (A) long-term bonds

    (B) short-term bonds

    (C) intermediate-term bonds

    (D) any of the above

103. All of the following are potential benefits of a long-term equipment leasing program EXCEPT

    (A) capital appreciation potential

    (B) a steady stream of income

    (C) depreciation deductions to offset income

    (D) operating expenses to help offset revenues

104. Michael Moneysworth III has held shares of ABC stock for 11 months. Which of the following transactions by Michael would affect his holding period on the ABC stock?

    I. Selling ABC stock "short against the box"

    II. Buying ABC call options

    III. Buying ABC put options

    IV. Selling ABC put options

    (A) I and III only

    (B) II and III only

    (C) I, II, and IV only

    (D) None of the above

105. Which of the following is the BEST indication of demand for new municipal issues?

    (A) The visible supply

    (B) The placement ratio

    (C) *The Bond Buyer's* index

    (D) The revenue bond index

106. Which of the following entities could claim depletion deductions?

    (A) Real estate DPPs

    (B) Oil and Gas DPPs

    (C) Transportation companies

    (D) Pharmaceutical companies

107. One of your customers decides to take it upon herself to do a little securities analysis. She feels pretty confident about one of her picks but would like to know what "a beta of 1" means. You can inform her that a stock with a beta of 1 should be

    (A) less volatile than the market

    (B) equally as volatile as the market

    (C) more volatile than the market

    (D) countercyclical

108. An oil and gas limited partnership is going to write off its equipment on an accelerated basis. Modified accelerated depreciation, when compared to straight line depreciation,

    (A) provides for greater write-offs in the early years

    (B) provides for greater write-offs in the later years

    (C) provides for an adjustable write-off schedule after the first three years

    (D) provides for salvage value at the end of the depreciation period

109. Vision-Skunk has a no-load growth fund. Which of the following is FALSE regarding the no-load fund?

    (A) No fees are charged to shareholders.

    (B) Investors are not charged a sales charge.

    (C) It is sold directly to investors without using the services of a broker-dealer.

    (D) Investors can redeem their shares at any time.

110. Which of the following is true regarding Pink Sheets?

    I. They provide information on exchange-listed securities.

    II. They provide information on OTC securities.

    III. They list the names of the market makers for particular stocks.

    IV. They provide firm quotes for securities listed on NASDAQ.

    (A) I, II, and III only

    (B) II, III, and IV only

    (C) II and III only

    (D) I, II, and IV only

111. Which of the following is/are TRUE regarding advertisements of investment companies used by your firm?

    I. They must be approved by a principal of the firm in writing prior to the first use.

    II. They must be approved by the NASD prior to the first use.

    III. They must be filed with the NASD prior to the first use.

    IV. They must be filed with the NASD within ten days of the first use.

    (A) I only

    (B) I and II only

    (C) II and III only

    (D) I and IV only

112. Which of the following is TRUE of Regulation A offerings?

    (A) They are also called private placements.

    (B) They can only raise up to $10,000,000 in any 12-month period.

    (C) They use an offering circular instead of a prospectus.

    (D) They are limited to 35 unaccredited investors per year.

113. A municipality decides to issue new revenue bonds to fund the construction of a new highway. Toll booths will be placed on the highway to pay off the revenue bond debt. Which of the following are important factors in assessing the safety of this revenue bond?

    I.   Engineering report

    II. Flow of funds

    III. Debt per capita

    IV. Assessed property values

    (A) I and II only

    (B) III and IV only

    (C) I, III, and IV only

    (D) II, III, and IV only

114. You get a job working for JJJ Corp., an investment banking firm. JJJ can do all of the following EXCEPT

    (A) underwrite new issues

    (B) advise an issuer on how to raise money

    (C) become a syndicate manager

    (D) sell securities on an agency basis

115. One of your customers believes that interest rates are going to rise. If your customer is correct, which TWO of the following option strategies would be profitable?

    I.   Buy T-bond calls

    II. Buy T-bond puts

    III. Sell T-bond calls

    IV. Sell T-bond puts

    (A) I and II

    (B) I and IV

    (C) II and III

    (D) II and IV

116. DORF Corp. has 10,000,000 shares of authorized stock. It has issued 8,500,000 shares and has since repurchased 300,000 shares. The number of outstanding shares is

    (A) 10,000,000

    (B) 8,500,000

    (C) 8,800,000

    (D) 8,200,000

117. An investor buys an OEX CAPS 350 call for 7. At what price would OEX have to pass before automatic exercise?

    (A) 357

    (B) 320

    (C) 380

    (D) 387

118. The sale of securities with an agreement to buy them back at a higher price on an agreed upon future date is called

    (A) a Repo

    (B) a reverse Repo

    (C) tax-exempt commercial paper

    (D) a revenue anticipation note

119. A specialist on the CBOE is called an

    (A) OCC

    (B) OAA

    (C) ODD

    (D) OBO

120. All of the following are examined by a fundamental analyst EXCEPT

    (A) EPS

    (B) balance sheets

    (C) the industry

    (D) market timing

121. Which of the following ratios could indicate a high risk of bankruptcy for a corporation?

    (A) High inventory turnover ratio

    (B) Low PE ratio

    (C) High debt-to-equity ratio

    (D) High current ratio

122. A municipality would like to issue new bonds through a competitive offering. The official notice of sale published by this municipality should include which of the following information?

    I. The allotment for each syndicate member

    II. Whether the bidders must include a NIC or TIC bid

    III. The reoffering yield

    IV. The amount of the good-faith deposit

    (A) I and II only

    (B) II and IV only

    (C) I and III only

    (D) I, II, and IV only

123. Dippy Doodads Corp. (DPY) issued cumulative preferred stock. DPY missed its last two dividend payments to their 7.2 percent cumulative preferred stockholders. The par value of the cumulative preferred stock is $100. DPY has had strong sales in its gizmo division and would like to pay a $1.50 dividend to its common shareholders next quarter. If there are 2,000,000 common shareholders and 1,000,000 cumulative preferred shares outstanding, how much would DPY have to pay in dividends next quarter?

    (A) $1,500,000

    (B) $3,000,000

    (C) $4,800,000

    (D) $8,400,000

124. Which of the following is the BEST after-tax investment for an individual investor in the 28 percent tax bracket?

    (A) 5 percent T-bond

    (B) 4¾ percent AAA rated corporate bond

    (C) 4½ percent preferred stock

    (D) 4½ percent GO bond

125. An investor purchases a British pound 130 put for a premium of 3. If the contract size is 30,150, what is the cost of this option?

    (A) $90.450.00

    (B) $9,045.00

    (C) $904.50

    (D) $90.45

Answer Key for Part II of the Practice Exam

1. C	26. B	51. A	76. A	101. A
2. B	27. D	52. A	77. B	102. A
3. B	28. A	53. C	78. A	103. A
4. B	29. A	54. C	79. D	104. A
5. D	30. D	55. D	80. A	105. B
6. D	31. B	56. B	81. B	106. B
7. D	32. C	57. B	82. C	107. B
8. C	33. B	58. A	83. A	108. A
9. C	34. A	59. A	84. D	109. A
10. A	35. A	60. C	85. D	110. C
11. C	36. A	61. A	86. A	111. D
12. D	37. A	62. A	87. D	112. C
13. B	38. D	63. C	88. B	113. A
14. B	39. C	64. A	89. B	114. D
15. D	40. C	65. B	90. C	115. C
16. A	41. B	66. D	91. C	116. D
17. D	42. B	67. D	92. D	117. C
18. B	43. A	68. C	93. B	118. A
19. D	44. A	69. A	94. D	119. D
20. A	45. A	70. C	95. A	120. D
21. D	46. B	71. A	96. B	121. C
22. A	47. B	72. B	97. D	122. B
23. A	48. C	73. C	98. C	123. D
24. B	49. A	74. B	99. D	124. D
25. A	50. C	75. C	100. D	125. C

Knowing the Score

Here's how the Series 7 exam is scored:

- ✔ You get one point for each correct answer.
- ✔ You get zero points for each incorrect answer.

A passing grade is 70 percent. In other words, you need at least 175 correct answers on the whole test to get one step closer to your Nobel Prize in stockbrokerage (okay, economics). That's an average of about 88 correct answers per part.

To calculate your score for this part only, multiply the number of correct answers by 0.8 or divide it by 125. If you're one of the brave ones who took both parts I and II in one sitting, you can multiply your correct answers by 0.4 or divide them by 250. Whatever grade you get, make sure you round down, not up. For example, a grade of 69.6 is a 69 percent, not a 70.

Chapter 20

Answers and Explanations to Practice Exam Part II

• •

Congratulations! You've just completed part II of the practice exam (unless you're just randomly flipping through the book). After grading both parts I and II, you should have a good idea of where you stand regarding the Series 7 exam. Kudos if you did really well on both parts I and II.

As with the first part, review all the questions that you got wrong and the ones you struggled with. Test yourself again by answering all the questions you highlighted and the questions you answered incorrectly, and make sure you get them right this time! Please give yourself a week or two before taking the same test again. Memorizing answers can give you a false sense of security, and you won't get an accurate forecast of how well you'll do on the Series 7 exam (you certainly don't want your score to be as unpredictable as the weather). You can take an additional test on the CD that comes with this book. I encourage you to take as many Series 7 practice exams as possible.

1. **C.** All prospectuses must include a disclaimer stating that *past performance may not be indicative of future performance.* I'm sure you've heard statements similar to that when listening to radio or TV advertisements. Certainly, Roman numeral II makes sense because anti-fraud rules always apply and mutual fund issuers can't lie about their products. Notice that II is in all the answer choices. Roman numeral III states that the prospectus can omit facts about the fund. Logically, you can assume that the prospectus has to include all material facts about the fund, confusing or not. Additionally, the prospectus must include a statement that says that *the fund is not monitored by a governmental body.* This goes along with the idea that the SEC, NASD, and so on don't guarantee or approve of securities. If a fund were monitored by a government body, the government body would be held responsible if investors were to lose money. I and II are correct and III is not, so the only answer that works is C.

2. **B.** This question gives a perfect example of when an investor should purchase a zero-coupon bond. This investor is planning for a future event (her child's college fund). Investors purchase zero-coupon bonds at a deep discount from par (for example, $400 per bond), and the bonds mature at $1,000 par and don't pay interest along the way. This type of bond allows the investor to invest a smaller amount of money now in return for a larger amount of money at maturity.

3. **B.** Answers A and B are saying two opposing things, and you're looking for the false statement. Therefore, A or B is most likely the correct answer. *Treasury stock* is issued stock that the issuing corporation has repurchased, so your answer is B. Treasury stock doesn't have any voting rights and doesn't receive dividends; therefore, C and D are incorrect.

4. **B.** Amortization reduces the cost basis of bonds (those purchased at a price greater than $1,000 par) over several years. Check out the following equation:

$$\text{Annual amortization} = \frac{\text{market price} - \text{par value}}{\text{years until maturity}}, \text{ so } \frac{\$1,200 - \$1,000}{8 \text{ years}} = \$25$$

This investor purchased the bond for a price of $1,200 (120 percent of $1,000 par), and it matures in eight years at $1,000 par. Divide the $200 difference ($1,200 purchase price minus $1,000 par) by eight years until maturity. You get an answer of $25 per year amortization. This investor is losing $25 per year on the value of her bond (at least as far as the IRS is concerned) — she'll lose $125 ($25 × 5 years) over the course of five years. The answer is B.

5. **D.** When a customer receives a confirmation (receipt of trade), the confirmation has to include the trade and settlement date (regardless of whether the trade was completed on a principal or agency basis), the name of the security, how many shares were traded, and the amount of commission if traded on an agency basis. The answer is D, all four Roman numerals.

6. **D.** *Shelf registration* is an SEC provision that allows an issuer to register a new issue without having to sell all the securities at once. Shelf registration allows the issuer to hold back securities for up to two years without having to reregister them.

7. **D.** This problem is another one of those questions whose answer choices make it a little easier. Answers C and D say opposite things, so one of them has to be the exception you're looking for.

A broker's broker basically acts as a broker for brokers. People in this field maintain the anonymity of their clients, and because they're brokers and not dealers, they don't keep an inventory of securities. Broker's brokers deal only with institutional customers and municipal brokers; they don't deal with public customers at all, so the answer is D.

8. **C.** To determine good delivery, always look at the shares. The certificates must be in multiples of 100 shares (for example, 100, 200, 300, and so on), divisors of 100 shares (1, 2, 4, 5, 10, 20, 25, and 50), or shares that add up to 100 (for example, 80 + 20, 75 + 15, 60 + 30 + 10, and so on). Answer A is okay because 800 is a multiple of 100 and 2 is a divisor of 100. Answer B is fine because 400 is a multiple of 100 and 4 is a divisor of 100. Answer D works because 200 is a multiple of 100 and 10 is a divisor of 100. Answer C is the bad one because even though 200 is a multiple of 100, 70 doesn't divide into 100 evenly, and nothing matches up with the 70 shares to make the total add up to 100.

9. **C.** *Cash flow* measures the financial health of a company. Cash flow is determined by taking the net income (after-tax income) and adding back in the depreciation and depletion deductions. Depreciation and depletion are added back in because they're write-offs for a company but are not out-of-pocket expenses.

Cash flow = net income + depreciation + depletion

Please note that only companies that deal with natural resources (for example, oil, minerals, lumber, and so on) may claim depletion deductions.

10. **A.** *Special tax bonds* are a type of municipal bond that's funded (backed) by taxes on certain items (excise taxes). *Excise taxes* are taxes on nonessential goods such as gasoline, alcohol, and tobacco.

11. **C.** A *legal opinion* is a statement by a bond attorney (counsel) affirming that the interest received from a particular municipal bond meets the requirements to be exempt from federal taxation. All municipal bonds must be accompanied by a legal opinion unless the issue is marked as *ex-legal* (a municipal bond that trades without a legal opinion).

12. **D.** When purchasing a municipal bond issued within your home state, the interest received is triple tax-free and is exempt from federal, state, and local taxes. Additionally, if you purchase a bond issued by a U.S. territory (such as Puerto Rico, U.S. Virgin Islands, Guam, Samoa, and Washington, D.C.), the interest is also triple-tax free. If you purchase a bond issued by another state, the interest is exempt from federal taxes only.

13. **B.** A *cyclical* stock moves in the same direction as the economy. Therefore, a *countercyclical* stock moves in the opposite direction of the economy. Investors buy countercyclical stocks to balance out their portfolios and to protect themselves in the event of economic decline. Gold stocks tend to be countercyclical because they usually do well when the market is doing poorly and vice versa. *Defensive* stocks tend to do well no matter what. Some examples of defensive stocks are food companies, alcohol, tobacco, pharmaceuticals, and so on. *Blue-chip* stocks are from well-established companies with a history of good earnings.

14. **B.** Indications of interest for a new offering are binding neither on the customer nor on the broker-dealer. For example, a customer may tell you that he wants to buy 1,000 shares of this new issue when it's available and then change his mind later. By the same token, the broker-dealer isn't obligated to have 1,000 shares available to sell to the customer when the issue is available.

15. **D.** A trade between institutions without using the services of a broker-dealer takes place on the fourth market. Fourth market trades usually take place using electronic communications networks (ECNs).

16. **A.** When a registered representative takes a job outside of his or her firm, he or she is moonlighting. Moonlighting rules for registered representatives require the individual to disclose this information to the employer only.

17. **D.** Before you begin, you have to locate the premiums on the exhibit. The premium for the HLP Nov 60 put that the investor is buying is 4. If you look at the second column, you see the strike prices. Look for the 60 put, which is located at the bottom of that column. Follow that row over to the column that says Nov, and you see the premium of 4. Follow the same procedure to locate the premium for the Nov 50 put. The premium for the Nov 50 put is 1.25 and is positioned two numbers above the premium for the 60 put. Now that you've established the premiums, you can place them in an options chart:

Money Out	Money In
$400	$125

The investor bought the HLP Nov 60 put for $400 (4 × 100 shares per option). Enter the $400 in the Money Out portion of the options chart because the investor paid money to purchase the option. Next, take the $125 (1.25 × 100 shares per option) the investor received for the HLP Nov 50 put that he sold and enter it in the Money In portion of the options chart because the investor received money for selling that option. Stop at this point to see whether that answers the question. You have $275 more money out than money in, which is the investor's maximum loss. The question, however, asks for the maximum gain; therefore, you have to exercise both options.

Money Out	Money In
$400	$125
$5,000	$6,000
$5,400	$6,125

First, to exercise the 60 put, multiply the 60 strike price by 100 shares to get $6,000. Enter $6,000 on the side of the options chart opposite from its premium because *puts switch* (go opposite their premium). Next, exercise the 50 put by multiplying it by 100 shares to get $5,000. Enter $5,000 on the opposite side of the options chart from its premium because puts switch. Add each side up, and you have $725 more money in than money out ($6,125 – $5,400). This investor's maximum gain is $725, and your answer is D.

18. **B.** The *official notice of sale* is an invitation for broker-dealers to bid on a new issue of municipal bonds. The official notice of sale includes the date, time and place of sale, maturities, interest payment dates, call provisions, the amount of good faith deposit, a description of the issue, and so on. The rating of the bond issue comes from ratings companies such as Moody's and Standard & Poor's after the bond is issued.

19. **D.** This particular investor owns the calls that she's exercising. The investor is exercising at a profit of $10 per share (less the premium) and is selling the stock immediately, so no deposit's required. It wouldn't make much sense to have this investor pay $50 per share when exercising the options and then have the brokerage firm send her a check for $60 per share. The key here is that the investor exercised the option and sold the stock on the same day.

20. **A.** This account was set up as joint tenants with rights of survivorship (JTWROS). When an investor with a JTWROS account dies, his or her portion of the account is transferred to the remaining survivors of the account (in this case, Mrs. Smith). Most married couples set up their joint accounts this way to avoid probate issues.

21. **D.** All the choices listed can change a customer's investment objectives. Looking at the situation logically, as a customer grows older, he or she would normally need to be a little more conservative and start switching to fixed-income securities. When a customer gets married, he or she may want to buy a house or start a family and therefore may not be able to take as much risk. If an investor has a child who will be going to college (kids grow up so fast!), the investor has to put money aside for that event. As customers obtain more investment experience, they may want to diversify their portfolios more or take different directions with their accounts.

22. **A.** Rule 145 is an SEC rule that covers major changes within a company. Investors have a right to decide whether to accept a new or different security in exchange for the existing security when a company reclassifies, experiences a merger, consolidates, or transfers assets from another corporation. Stock splits aren't considered a major change and therefore aren't covered under Rule 145.

23. **A.** Market makers (dealers) sell securities out of their own inventory to make trading easier. Market makers charge a markup or markdown, not a commission, so D is wrong. You can eliminate B and C, because all trades from market makers are on a principal basis, not on an agency basis. A is the correct answer.

24. **B.** *Control securities* are securities that officers, directors, or another affiliate of the issuer owns. Any investor who owns 10 percent or more of the outstanding shares of a company has controlling interest. The answer is B. The sale of control securities is subject to the quantity limitations as stated under Rule 144.

25. **A.** The Consumer Price Index (CPI) is the best measure of inflation or deflation. The *CPI* measures price changes in consumer goods and services. The *gross domestic product* (GDP) is the sum of all goods and services produced by a country in one year, and it measures how much the economy is growing. *M1* is a measure of the money supply that includes currency in circulation, checking accounts, and NOW accounts (interest bearing checking accounts). The *currency exchange rate* is the rate at which one currency can be converted into another.

26. **B.** *Defensive* stocks perform consistently no matter how poorly the economy's doing. Companies that sell goods such as alcohol, tobacco, pharmaceutical supplies, food, and so on issue defensive stocks. Appliance-company and automotive stocks aren't defensive because when the economy is doing poorly, investors wait a little longer to buy these items.

27. **D.** Dividends received from stock and interest received from bonds are always taxed as ordinary income. *Passive income* is income that someone receives from limited partnerships only. Long-term capital gains are for securities held for longer than one year. Because this investor held the stock for exactly one year, it's taxed as a short-term capital gain.

28. **A.** The planned amortization class (PAC) tranche is considered the safest because a large portion of the prepayment risk and extension risk associated with collateralized mortgage obligations (CMOs) is absorbed by a companion tranche. The targeted amortization class (TAC) tranche is considered the second safest tranche because it's more subject to prepayment and extension risk than the PAC tranche. A companion tranche absorbs the prepayment and extension risk associated with PAC and TAC tranches and is considered risky because the average life varies greatly with interest rate changes. A Z tranche is the most volatile of the CMO tranches because it receives no payments until all of the CMO tranches are retired.

29. **A.** If an investor believes that interest rates are going to drop over the next 20 to 30 years like Tom does, he should lock in at a high interest rate right now. Buying the longest-term bond makes sense for Tom because he believes that the rates are high right now, and if interest rates drop like he expects them to, he'd be locking in a high rate for a long period of time. Additionally, if interest rates drop, the price of his bond will increase, because there's an inverse relationship between interest rates and bond prices.

30. **D.** If a customer's margin account is restricted (which happens all the time) the equity (EQ) has fallen below the 50 percent Regulation T requirement, so IV is true. You know Roman numeral I is false because the customer can still purchase more securities on margin by coming up with the Regulation T amount of the purchase. At this point, you can answer the question — A, B, and C contain Roman numeral I, so you can select D. The customer doesn't have to take the account out of restricted status unless the account falls below minimum maintenance (25 percent of the current market value). Also, the customer can purchase more securities on margin by depositing fully paid securities into the margin account to meet the margin call of the new securities purchased.

31. **B.** In the event that a discrepancy occurs in a trade between two firms, one of the firms sends out a don't know (DK) notice to the contra-broker (the other firm involved in the trade). Firms use a DK notice for unmatched or uncompared trades. For example, firm A may think it bought 1,000 shares of DEF stock from firm B, but firm B may think firm A bought 1,000 shares of GHI stock. Rehypothecation takes place in a margin account when a broker-dealer pledges a customer's securities as collateral for a loan; Form 144 must be filed with the SEC when restricted stock (stock held by insiders or stock issued through private placement) is sold.

32. **C.** Securities with a beta coefficient of 1.0 are equally as volatile as the market (if the market goes up 5 percent over a given period of time, you'd expect the price of the stock to go up 5 percent). Someone like Joanie, who's pursuing an aggressive stock-buying strategy, would be looking for stocks with a beta greater than 1.0 because they're more volatile than the market. Therefore, the security that would best meet her needs is the XYZ stock, with a beta coefficient of 1.20. This stock would be expected to move more than the market (if the market goes up 10 percent over a given period of time, you'd expect the price of the stock to go up 12 percent). This all sounds great, but if the market goes down 5 percent over a given period of time, you'd expect the price of the stock to fall 6 percent. Stocks with a beta coefficient of less than 1.0 are more defensive securities that don't move as much as the market. Blue chip stocks are securities issued by well-established, stable companies and would not be part of an aggressive stock portfolio.

33. **B.** The agreement among underwriters (the syndicate agreement) states the priority in which orders are to be filled. The normal priority is presale, syndicate (group net), designated, and then member orders. All the presale orders are filled before any syndicate orders, all the syndicate orders are filled before any designated orders, and so on.

34. **A.** In order to answer this question, you need to determine whether you're dealing with a credit or debit spread. Start out by placing the premiums in an options chart:

Money Out	Money In
$300	$900

This investor bought the COW Aug 40 put for a premium of $300 (3 × 100 shares per option). Because the investor bought for $300, place this amount in the Money Out portion of the options chart. Next, the investor sold the COW Aug 50 put for a premium of $900 (9 × 100 shares per option). In this case, put that premium in the Money In portion of the options chart, because the investor received money for selling that option. This investor has a credit spread, because he has more money in than money out. When an investor has a credit spread, he wants the premium difference to narrow (premiums narrow as the options get closer to expiration or move further away from being in-the-money) and he wants the options to expire so he can keep the profit.

35. **A.** In this case, the options aren't in-the-money; they're at-the-money (the market price is the same as the strike price). As long as the options aren't in-the-money, the writers (sellers) of the options will earn a profit. The purchasers earn a profit when the options are in-the-money by more than the premium. The answer is A.

36. **A.** The stated dividend for a participating preferred stock is the minimum dividend that an investor can receive. Participating preferred stock receives its own dividend and a portion of the dividend received by the common stockholders. In this case, the minimum the investor can receive is 8 percent if no common dividend was paid. If a common dividend was paid, the investor would receive greater than 8 percent.

37. **A.** *The Bond Buyer* has the best information on new municipal bonds (primary market). *The Blue List* has the best information about outstanding municipal bonds. *Munifacts* is a newswire service that provides information about new and outstanding municipal bonds. *Yellow Sheets* is a bulletin that gives updated bid and ask prices for over-the-counter (OTC) corporate bonds.

38. **D.** A specialist's book keeps track of stop and limit orders. Market orders are for immediate execution at the best price available and are not placed in the specialist's book. Not-held orders are held by the floor broker who has discretion concerning the time and the price that the order will take place.

39. **C.** This problem is one of those double-negative questions. The phrase "trading without accrued interest EXCEPT" means "Which one trades *with* accrued interest?" The only money market instrument (short-term debt security) that trades with accrued interest is certificates of deposit (CDs). All the other money market instruments are issued at a discount and mature at par value. Holders of CDs receive interest payments; therefore, investors purchasing CDs are required to pay the seller any accrued interest due. That makes the answer C.

40. **C.** You're looking for the false answer. You can prove answers A, B, and D true by setting up a seesaw (see Chapter 7 for details). Answer C is false because when interest rates decrease, outstanding bond prices increase. If interest rates were to decrease after this bond was issued, it'd have to be selling at a premium, not a discount.

41. **B.** The *indenture* (trust indenture) of a bond is a legal contract between the issuer and the trustee representing the investors. The indenture includes the coupon rate (interest rate), the maturity date, collateral backing the bond, and so on. The indenture does not include the rating of the bond. Rating agencies such as Moody's and Standard & Poor's determine the rating.

42. **B.** A buy-in occurs when the seller of a security fails to deliver the securities sold. In this case, the brokerage firm would have to purchase the securities from another investor to deliver to the purchaser. If a customer fails to deliver securities that she has sold, her account is frozen for 90 days, during which time the customer must pay for trades in advance and deliver securities before they can be sold.

43. **A.** Because this question involves participating stock that has been issued by TUV Corp., the minimum payment is 7 percent. Participating preferred stock receives not only the stated dividend (7 percent) but also a portion of the dividend paid to common shareholders, if any. Therefore, the minimum an investor of TUV Corp. participating preferred stock would receive is 7 percent per year; there is no maximum.

44. **A.** When dealing with questions relating to conversion or parity price, you must always first determine the conversion ratio (the number of shares the bond is convertible into). Check out the following equation:

$$\text{Conversion ratio} = \frac{\text{par}}{\text{conversion price}}, \text{ so } \frac{\$1{,}000}{\$20} = 50 \text{ shares}$$

Next determine the parity price of the common stock with the following equation:

$$\text{Parity price of the stock} = \frac{\text{market price of the bond}}{\text{conversion ratio}}, \text{ so } \frac{\$880}{50 \text{ shares}} = \$17.60$$

After that, you still have to reduce the parity price of the stock by 10 percent ($1.76) to make the amount 10 percent below the parity price of the bond:

$17.60 - $1.76 = $15.84

45. **A.** Straight-line amortization of a bond's premium reduces the cost basis of the bond by an equal amount each year. The cost basis of the bond is decreasing each year; therefore, the chance of the holder's selling the bond at a capital gain (above the cost basis) increases each year.

46. **B.** *Shorting against the box* is selling short securities that you already own. Because Fawn doesn't have access to her securities, this strategy would be appropriate for her to lock in the sales price. As soon as she goes short against the box, what happens to the price of the stock doesn't matter, because she'll either make money on the stock she owns and lose money on the stock she shorted or make money on the stock she shorted and lose money on the stock she owns.

47. **B.** All new municipal bonds purchased at a discount must be accreted. The accretion is part of the investor's tax-free interest. If an investor holds a bond to maturity, it won't be taxed as a capital gain or loss. In order to have a capital gain or loss, the investor must sell the security at a price that differs from the cost basis.

48. **C.** A *short combination* is buying a call and buying a put on the same stock with different expiration months and/or strike prices. You can cross off answers A and B right away because you need to have two sells (shorts) to make a short combination. The difference between a straddle and a combination is in the expiration months and the strike prices. If the expiration months are the same and the strike prices are the same, you have a straddle. If the expiration months and/or the strike prices are different, you're looking at a combination.

49. **A.** Preferred stock is similar to bonds in that they're both subject to price decreases if interest rates rise. Preferred stock pays a fixed dividend, and if interest rates increase, the preferred stock decreases in value. An investor can protect himself by buying interest rate calls. If interest rates increase, the value of the preferred stock decreases but the value of the calls increases to offset the loss.

50. **C.** This problem is one of those exhibit questions that looks a little more difficult than it really is. The main issue is remembering the following formula:

$$\text{Earnings per share (EPS)} = \frac{\text{net income} - \text{preferred dividends}}{\text{No. of common shares outstanding}}$$

Look at the exhibit and notice that the preferred dividends were deducted just before the common dividends. If you plug in the numbers, you get your answer:

$$\text{EPS} = \frac{\$1,250,000}{1,000,000 \text{ common shares}} = \$1.25$$

51. **A.** The settlement date for a when issued (WI) security is a date to be assigned. A *when issued security* is one that's been authorized and sold to investors before the certificates are ready for delivery. A WI is also known as a *when, as, and if issued security*.

52. **A.** A red herring is a preliminary prospectus. It includes all the information about the issue except the final offering price. A preliminary prospectus is used during the cooling off period and may be subject to change by the time the final prospectus is sent out.

53. **C.** A tombstone advertisement is printed in a newspaper to solicit indications of interest in a new securities offering. Included in the tombstone advertisement are the names of the syndicate members (underwriters), the name of the issuer, the type of security, and where prospective buyers can obtain a prospectus. The selling group members are not normally included on the tombstone advertisement.

54. **C.** Traders work on positioning a firm's inventory. They can request bids and enter offers for different securities. The rating of a bond's creditworthiness is judged by companies such as Moody's and Standard & Poors, not municipal bond traders; C is the exception you're looking for.

55. **D.** You use amortization for premium bonds (bonds purchased at a price greater than $1,000 par) to reduce the cost basis over several years. Check out the following equation:

$$\text{Annual amortization} = \frac{\text{market price} - \text{par value}}{\text{years until maturity}}, \text{ so } \frac{\$1,050 - \$1,000}{10 \text{ years}} = \$5$$

This investor purchased the bond for a price of $1,050 (105 percent of $1,000 par) and it matures in ten years at $1,000 par. Take the $50 difference ($1,050 purchase price minus $1,000 par) and divide it by the ten years until maturity. You get an answer of $5 per year amortization. If this investor is losing $5 per year on the value of his bond (at least as far as the IRS is concerned), he'll lose $30 ($5 × 6 years) over the course of six years. Next, subtract the $30 from the purchase price of the bond to determine the investor's cost basis after six years:

$1,050 – $30 = $1,020 new cost basis

This investor's cost basis is $1,020, and he sold the bond at $1,020 (102 percent of $1,000 par); therefore, he saw no gain or loss.

56. **B.** An antidilution covenant protects convertible bondholders in the event of stock splits or stock dividends. Because convertible bonds are tied to the price of the underlying stock, the number of shares (the conversion ratio) a bond is convertible into will be adjusted for stock splits or stock dividends. When a company declares a stock dividend, the price of the stock decreases on the ex-dividend date. Each investor will have more shares with a lower market price per share. Just as the market price decreases, the conversion price decreases, so IV is true. If the conversion price decreases, the conversion ratio increases, so Roman numeral I is also true. The answer is B.

57. **B.** When determining whether a broker-dealer has to file a currency transaction report (CTR), look at the size of the trade first. If the transaction is over $10,000 (as they all are in this case) you may have to file one. The next thing to look at is whether the customer is depositing cash or a cash equivalent (for example, a money order) — that's another sign that you may have to file a CTR. Choice B is the only one that involves cash. Some other things that you have to be aware of are whether a customer is wiring money to or from an offshore account.

58. **A.** Rights offerings give current investors the first right to receive stock of a corporation at a discount when the corporation offers new shares. An investor receives one right for every share she owns. To determine the value of a cum-right (stock trading with rights), use the following formula where M = the market price of the stock, S = the subscription price (discounted price) for purchasing shares in the rights offering, and N = the number of rights needed to purchase one share:

$$\frac{M-S}{N+1} = \frac{\$30 - \$22}{10+1} = \frac{8}{11} = \$0.73$$

59. **A.** Systematic risk is the same as market risk. All securities are subject to systematic risk, which is the risk that securities can decline due to negative market conditions. The risk that a security cannot keep pace with the inflation rate (answer choice C) is called *purchasing power risk* or *inflation risk*.

60. **C.** A public housing authority (PHA) bond is considered the safest municipal bond. It's issued by a local public housing authority but backed by the U.S. government. All of the choices listed are types of municipal bonds, but backing by the U.S. government makes PHAs the safest.

61. **A.** Each person may give an individual a gift of up to $12,000 per year that's exempt from gift tax. This gift is for $50,000 worth of securities; therefore, Zeb (the doner) is subject to paying a gift tax. When receiving a gift of securities, the recipient assumes the donor's original cost basis (in this case, $40). The answer is A.

62. **A.** Limited partners can inspect all the partnership's books, invest in other competing partnerships, and sue the general partner, but they can't manage the partnership. That's the job of the general partner.

63. **C.** Investors of options face a considerable risk. Because of that risk, all customers must receive an options risk disclosure document (ODD) prior to opening the account. After the customer receives the ODD, the registered option's principal (ROP) has to approve the account. Next, the transaction is executed. Fifteen days after the ROP approves the account, the customer must sign and send in an options account agreement (OAA), wherein she agrees to abide by the rules of the options exchanges.

64. **A.** The interest received on municipal bonds is federally tax-free. Because Jon is in the highest income tax bracket, he can save more tax money by investing in municipal bonds than other investors in lower tax brackets will. Although the interest received on T-bonds is state tax free, larger savings would be had on municipal bonds because federal taxes are more than state taxes.

65. **B.** The *dated date* is the first day that a bond starts accruing interest and is not a factor in the marketability of a bond. However, the credit rating, the maturity date, and the issuer's name are all important to investors.

66. **D.** Investors can diversify a municipal bond portfolio by buying bonds of different maturities, different qualities, and different geographical regions. You can't diversify a portfolio by buying more or less of the same type of bonds.

67. **D.** When learning of the death of a customer, a registered representative should mark the account as deceased, freeze the account (not do any trading), cancel all open orders (good-till-canceled orders), cancel all written powers of attorney, and await the proper legal papers for guidance about what to do with the account.

68. **C.** To reduce the debit balance (DR) in a long margin account, someone has to deposit money into the account. The debit balance is the amount borrowed from the broker-dealer. You can pay down the debit balance by selling securities in the account, adding fully paid securities, or receiving cash dividends. Stock dividends don't bring cash into the account and therefore can't be used to pay down the debit balance.

69. **A.** You can quickly cross off answer D, because *cannot be determined* is almost never a correct answer on the Series 7 exam. To determine the price/earnings (PE) ratio, use the following formula:

$$PE\ ratio = \frac{market\ price\ of\ the\ stock}{earnings\ per\ share\ (EPS)},\ so\ \frac{\$16}{\$4} = 4$$

The answer is 4, choice A.

70. **C.** *Quick assets* are assets that someone can convert into cash within a 3- to 5-month period. Cash, accounts receivable, and marketable securities that the company owns are all quick assets. Inventory is a current asset but not a quick asset because you can assume that a company will take up to a year to sell its entire inventory.

71. **A.** U.S. government bonds settle in one business day, and payment is due one business day after the trade date.

72. **B.** The first part of the order is a *buy stop at 50*. A buy stop is a SLoBS (sell limit, buy stop) order, which is triggered at or above 50. Looking at the ticker, the first JKL order at or above 50 is 50.

73. **C.** After being triggered at 50, the order becomes a buy limit order at 50. A buy limit is a BLiSS (buy limit, sell stop) order, and you'd execute this order at or below 50. Looking at the ticker, the next trade at or below 50 is 49.88 — your answer is C.

74. **B.** The U.S. government has issued securities in book entry form since the mid 1980s. Book entry securities are sold without delivering a certificate. A central agency keeps the ownership records.

75. **C.** Treasury STRIPS, Treasury bonds, and Treasury bills all earn interest, even though owners of Treasury STRIPS and Treasury bills don't receive interest payments. Treasury STRIPS and Treasury bills are issued at a discount, and they mature at par value; the difference between the purchase price and par value is considered interest. However, *treasury stock* is stock that the issuing corporation repurchases; it doesn't earn interest, so your answer is C.

76. **A.** When a customer receives dividends in a margin account, the action is the same as depositing cash into the account. The debit balance (DR) is reduced by the full amount of the dividend, and the equity (EQ) increases by the full amount of the dividend.

77. **B.** *Special assessment bonds* are a type of general obligation (GO) bond that's backed by taxes assessed on the property that benefits. For example, a municipality may raise funds to put new streetlights in a particular area. In this case, only the people who live in that area will pay additional taxes to back the bond issue. GO bonds receive the largest backing by *ad valorem* (property) taxes, while revenue bonds are issued to fund a revenue producing facility (toll booths, municipal hospitals, and so on) and are backed only by revenues brought in by the facility.

78. **A.** When selling a naked (uncovered) put option, the most the seller could lose is the strike price minus the premium times 100 shares times ten options. Put options go in-the-money when the price of the stock goes down. Because the stock can only go down to zero, the seller can lose money from the strike price down to zero less the premium received. However, because options are for 100 shares, you have to multiply that answer by 100 shares and then by the ten options the customer sold.

79. **D.** The easiest way to calculate the break-even point for stock/option problems is to take a look at what's happening. This investor purchased the stock for $65 per share and then purchased the options for $7 per share. This investor paid $72 ($65 + $7) per share out of pocket and would need the stock to be at $72 per share in order to break even.

80. **A.** In a situation like the one in this problem, you need to calculate the conversion ratio before you can determine any of the answers. Check out the following equation:

$$\text{Conversion ratio} = \frac{\text{par}}{\text{conversion price}}, \text{ so } \frac{\$1{,}000}{\$40} = 25 \text{ shares}$$

You can always assume that par value for a bond is $1,000 unless otherwise stated. Now that you've determined that the bond is convertible into 25 shares, you can use the following equation to figure out the parity price:

Parity price of the bond = market price of the stock × conversion ratio

Parity price of the bond = $38 × 25 shares = $950

Investors of DIM Lighting convertible bonds can convert their bonds trading at $800 (80 percent of 1,000 par) into common stock trading at $950. Therefore, the bonds are trading below parity, and the investor has an excellent arbitrage situation because she can make a quick profit.

81. **B.** Normally an investor purchasing $20,000 worth of stock on margin would have to deposit $10,000 to meet the margin call (you can assume Regulation T is 50 percent of the purchase). First, you have to find out whether this investor has any excess equity in his margin account to help offset the $10,000 payment. Use the following equation: LMV – DR = EQ.

After setting up the equation, enter the market value of the securities under the long market value (LMV). Next, enter the $14,000 under the debit record (DR), also known as the debit balance. When you subtract the DR from the LMV, you come up with an equity (EQ) of $26,000. Multiply Regulation T (50 percent) by the LMV to get the amount of equity the customer should have in the account to be at 50 percent. This investor needs only $20,000 in equity to reach 50 percent, and this investor has $26,000, $6,000 more than necessary:

LMV	–	DR	=	EQ
$40,000	–	$14,000	=	$26,000
	Regulation T × LMV =			$20,000
				$ 6,000 excess equity

The $6,000 is excess equity (SMA — special memorandum account), which she can use to help offset the margin call for the $20,000 worth of stock she wants to buy:

$10,000 margin call – $6,000 excess equity = $4,000 to deposit

82. **C.** The quote in answer C is unacceptable because you're stating a definite price that the customer could purchase or sell at. You have to be careful that you don't give firm quotes (definite quotes) unless your firm is a market maker in the security and you can guarantee that price. All the other answers are acceptable because the customer would know that the price is subject to change.

83. **A.** The M2 money supply includes all of M1 (currency, checking accounts, and NOW accounts) plus savings deposits, time deposits, and money market funds. Jumbo CDs are part of the M3 money supply.

84. **D.** When a syndicate is formed on an Eastern (undivided) account basis, each syndicate member is responsible not only for his or her own allotment but also for a percentage of the shares left unsold by other syndicate members. This syndicate member was responsible for selling 4,500,000 shares of a 15,000,000 share offering, which is 30 percent. After selling its entire allotment, this firm is responsible for selling 30 percent of the shares left unsold:

    $30\% \times 3,000,000$ shares = 900,000 shares

85. **D.** To determine the earnings per share (EPS) of a company, a fundamental analyst has to look at the income statement, not the balance sheet.

86. **A.** You can best work out this question in an options chart. Look at the following setup:

Money Out	Money In
$500	
$800	
$5,000	$6,500
$6,300	$6,500

    This investor bought the WXYZ Aug 65 call for 5, so you enter $500 (5 × 100 shares per option) on the Money Out side of the options chart. The investor also bought the WXYZ Aug 65 put for 8, so enter $800 (8 × 100 shares per option), again on the Money Out side. Next, the investor bought the stock in the market at the market price of $50 per share for a total of $5,000 ($50 per share × 100 shares to cover the put option). The investor spent $5,000 for the stock; therefore, that amount also goes on the Money Out side of the options chart. After that, you exercise the put. You have to exercise the put at its strike price of 65. Calculating 65 × 100 shares per option gives you a price of $6,500, which you enter on the Money In side of the chart because puts switch (go on the opposite side of the option's chart from its premium). Add up each side, and you see that this investor had a gain of $200 ($6,500 in, $6,300 out).

87. **D.** I hope you crossed out the WOW Aug 50 put and the WOW Aug 60 put right away, because you can't create a call spread with puts. To create a debit call spread, the investor has to pay more for the option purchased than he receives for the one he sold. Investors always buy at the offer (ask) price and sell at the bid price. Having this knowledge, the only thing that makes sense is the investor's buying the WOW Aug 50 call for 4.25 and selling the WOW Aug 60 call for 1. Place these values in the options chart to get your answer:

Money Out	Money In
$425	$100

The investor bought the WOW Aug 50 call for $425 (4.25 premium × 100 shares per option), so that goes on the Money Out side of the options chart. Next, enter the $100 (1 premium × 100 shares per option) on the Money In side of the options chart, because the investor received $100 for selling that option. The investor paid $325 more for the option purchased than he received for the option sold.

88. **B.** An industrial development revenue bond (IDR) is a municipal bond that's backed by a private company. The municipality uses the lease payments that the private company makes to pay principal and interest on the bonds. IDRs are considered the riskiest municipal bonds.

89. **B.** *Municipal revenue bonds* are issued to fund something, and they're backed by a revenue-producing facility (such as tollbooths). Municipal revenue bonds are usually structured under a *net revenue pledge*, whereby the issuer pays operation and maintenance before principal and interest on the bonds.

90. **C.** To determine this investor's maximum potential loss, set up the equation in an options chart:

Money Out	Money In
$7,000	$300

This investor purchased 100 shares for $70 per share, totaling $7,000. Because the investor paid $7,000, enter $7,000 in the Money Out portion of the options chart. Next, enter the $300 ($3 premium × 100 shares per option) that the investor received for selling the YYY July 75 call in the Money In side of the options chart. Stop at this point to see whether the chart lets you answer the question yet. Because you're looking for the maximum potential loss and you have more Money Out than Money In, you have your answer. The totals are on opposite sides of the chart, so subtract the two numbers:

$7,000 – $300 = $6,700 maximum potential loss

91. **C.** Listed options expire at 11:59 p.m. EST (10:59 p.m. CST) on the Saturday following the third Friday of the expiration month.

92. **D.** When an issuer pays off old bonds with the proceeds of a new bond issue, it's *refunding* the issue.

93. **B.** The *premium* of an option is made up of intrinsic value (how much the option is in-the-money) and time value (the amount of time an investor has to use the option). Use the following formula:

Premium = intrinsic value + time value

7 = 5.75 + time value

Time value = 1.25

Call options go in-the-money when the price of the stock rises above the strike price. The intrinsic value here is 5.75, because the stock is 5.75 above the strike price (30.75 stock price – 25 strike price). This result means that the time value has to equal 1.25 (that is, $7 premium – 5.75 intrinsic value). Because options are for 100 shares, the answer is $125 (1.25 × 100 shares).

94. **D.** Limit orders are orders that have to take place at a specific price or better. If an investor places a buy limit order on ABC stock at $40, this investor won't pay more than $40 per share if the price ever drops that low. If an investor places a sell limit order on ABC stock at $60, the investor won't accept less than $60 per share if the price ever gets that high. Because the orders are price specific, limit orders may or may not be executed.

95. **A.** Lena signed a recourse loan; therefore, the creditors can pursue her personal assets if Black Hole defaults on the loan. The answer is A.

96. **B.** The public offering price (POP) of a mutual fund is the net asset value (NAV) plus the sales charge, so the answer is B. If you're dealing with a no-load fund, the net asset value and the public offering price are the same.

97. **D.** Whenever an investor sells securities short, the sale has to be executed in a margin account. Short sellers are bearish and want the price of their securities to decrease. This investor will end up with a restricted account because the value of the securities increased. To determine how much the account is restricted, use the following equation: SMV + EQ = CR.

After setting up the equation, enter the market value of the securities ($60,000) under the SMV (short market value). Next, enter the Regulation T amount (50 percent of the SMV) under the EQ (equity), because that's how much the investor has to deposit into the account. Add the SMV and the EQ together to get the CR (credit balance). After you've done that, change the SMV to $64,000 to adjust for the change in the market price; you now have to calculate the new equity. Bring the CR down because that number doesn't change as the SMV goes up or down. Now that the SMV is $64,000 and the CR is $90,000, the EQ has to be $26,000 ($90,000 – $64,000). I've drawn a line through the top numbers because you don't need them from this point on. Multiply Regulation T (you can assume 50 percent) by the new SMV to find the amount of equity (EQ) the investor should have in order to be at 50 percent:

$$
\begin{array}{ccccc}
\text{SMV} & + & \text{EQ} & = & \text{CR} \\
\cancel{\$60,000} & + & \cancel{\$30,000} & = & \cancel{\$90,000} \\
\$64,000 & + & \$26,000 & = & \$90,000 \\
\text{Reg T} \times \text{SMV} & = & \underline{\$32,000} & & \\
& & -\$6,000 \text{ (restricted)} & &
\end{array}
$$

This investor needs $32,000 to be at 50 percent of the SMV. She has only $26,000; therefore, the account is restricted by $6,000.

98. **C.** The normal priority for filling orders received by a syndicate is laid out in the syndicate agreement. Here's the typical order from first- to last-filled: presale, syndicate (group-net), designated, and member.

99. **D.** Issuers can register securities on the state level by filing (notification), through coordination, or through qualification. The Series 63 and Series 66 exams explore this topic in much more detail. *Communication* was just thrown in there as a bogus answer choice because it looks something like the other words.

100. **D.** The Securities Act of 1933 (Full Disclosure Act) covers the *federal* registration of new issues. Companies need to disclose all material information about the issuance of its new securities. *Blue sky laws* cover the registration of issues on the state level. The Securities and Exchange Act of 1934 created the Securities and Exchange Commission (SEC) and established rules for margin accounts and short sales.

101. **A.** *The Bond Buyer's* 11-bond index is a weekly index of 11 of the bonds listed in the 20-bond index (a weekly index of 20 GO bonds with 20 years to maturity rated AAA or AA).

102. **A.** If interest rates are expected to increase, a municipality would most likely issue long-term bonds to lock in a lower interest rate for a long period of time. If the municipality were to issue short-term bonds, it may have to issue new bonds in a few years at a higher interest rate, which would cost more money in interest payments.

103. **A.** Equipment-leasing programs make money by — of course — leasing out equipment. When the equipment gets older, more worn out, or outdated, its value decreases. Therefore, capital appreciation potential (an increasing equipment value) doesn't make sense. Choice A is the answer you're looking for.

104. **A.** When an investor *sells short against the box* (sells a security that he owns short) or buys put options on stock that he owns, the action freezes the holding period, so choices I and III are true. Michael has held the stock for 11 months, so he has a short-term gain or loss because he held the stock 12 months or less. By shorting against the box or buying put options on the same stock, the holding period would remain short-term even if Michael were to hold it for another several months. This concept is important: The IRS doesn't want investors to hold these positions to convert short-term gains to long-term gains because long-term gains are taxed at a lower rate. If the investor has already held the stock for more than 12 months, shorting against the box or buying put options won't affect the tax status; the investment would still be long-term. Buying call options or selling put options wouldn't affect the holding period because the investor is not locking in a gain or loss the way that he or she is when selling short against the box or buying put options on stock he or she owns. The answer is A.

105. **B.** *The Bond Buyer's* placement ratio indicates the number of new municipal issues that have sold within the last week. The *visible supply* is the total dollar volume of municipal offerings expected to reach the market in the next 30 days. *The Bond Buyer's Index* (20-bond index) is a weekly index of 20 GO bonds with 20 years to maturity rated AAA or AA. The *Revenue Bond Index* (Revdex) is a weekly index of 25 revenue bonds with 30 years to maturity, rated A or better.

106. **B.** Only businesses that deal with natural resources (oil, gas, coal, gold, and so on) can claim depletion deductions. *Depletion* is a tax deduction that compensates these businesses for their ever-decreasing supply of the natural resources that provides it with income.

107. **B.** A *beta coefficient* is a way of measuring the volatility of a security or portfolio of securities in relation to the overall market. A beta of 1 indicates that the security's price will move with the market. A beta that's greater than 1 indicates that the security's price is more volatile than the market. A beta lower than 1 indicates that the security's price is less volatile than the market.

108. **A.** Most companies write off depreciation on an accelerated basis instead of a straight-line basis. When writing off on a straight-line basis, the company is writing off an equal amount each year. For example, if a company purchases a tractor-trailer for $100,000 and wants to write it off on a straight line basis over the course of ten years, it would write off $10,000 per year. On an accelerated basis, that same company may write off $25,000 the first year, $18,000 the second year, and so on. By the time the company gets to the ninth and tenth years, the company may be writing off only $2,000 per year.

This situation makes sense if you relate it to a car purchase. When you buy a new car, you lose value pretty much as soon as you drive it off the lot. Additionally, you find a big difference in the price of a car that's 1 year old compared to one that's 2 years old, but you don't see much of a price difference between a 9-year-old car and a 10-year-old car.

109. **A.** No-load funds are mutual funds that don't charge a sales charge; however, they do charge a management fee, so statement A has to be false.

110. **C.** The *Pink Sheets* are a daily publication that contains interdealer wholesale quotes for over-the-counter (OTC) stocks that are too small or too thinly traded to be listed on NASDAQ. Roman numeral II is true (though it's part of all the answer choices, so you can't narrow anything down yet) and IV is false, so you can cross off B and D. The Pink Sheets contain the names of the market makers for the particular stocks, so III is true as well. Pink Sheets don't provide information on exchange-listed securities, so the correct answer is C.

111. **D.** A principal of the brokerage firm has to approve all advertising and sales literature. The NASD doesn't approve advertisements, so answers with Roman numeral II are false (you can cross out B and C). Advertisements relating to investment companies need to be filed with the NASD within ten days after first use, so IV is true and you can eliminate A. The answer is D.

112. **C.** A *Regulation A offering* is an offering of securities valued at $5,000,000 or less within a 12-month period. Regulation A offerings are exempt from the full registration requirements of the Securities Act of 1933. Companies issuing securities through Regulation A offerings make an *offering circular* (an abbreviated prospectus) available to all potential purchasers.

113. **A.** Engineering reports (feasibility studies) and the flow of funds are important to the purchaser of a revenue bond, so the answer is A. Debt per capita (debt per person) and assessed property values are important to investors of general obligation (GO) bonds, which are backed by taxes.

114. **D.** An *investment banking firm* is an institution that's in the business of helping issuers raise capital. Investment bankers may underwrite new issues and advise issuers about how to raise money, and they may become syndicate managers. However, investment bankers aren't allowed to sell securities on an agency basis, because that's the job of a broker.

115. **C.** You find an inverse relationship between interest rates and outstanding bond prices. If a customer believes that interest rates will increase, she believes that outstanding bond prices will decrease. Therefore, this customer is bearish on prices and would employ bearish option strategies like buying puts and selling calls. The correct answer is C.

116. **D.** Outstanding shares equals the number of shares issued minus the number repurchased by the company (treasury stock).

    Outstanding shares = issued shares – treasury stock

    Outstanding shares = 8,500,000 – 300,000 = 8,200,000

117. **C.** *Capped index options* are automatically exercised as soon as the option is 30 points in-the-money. Because call options go in-the-money when the price of the stock goes above the strike price, this option would be automatically exercised at 380 (350 strike price + 30 points in-the-money).

118. **A.** Repurchase agreements, or *Repos,* are money market instruments (short-term debt securities). Repos involve the sale of securities with an agreement to purchase them back at a specified date at a higher price. The difference between the sale price and purchase price represents interest.

119. **D.** The order book official (OBO) is a specialist on the Chicago Board Options Exchange (CBOE).

120. **D.** A fundamental analyst decides *what* to buy, and a technical analyst decides *when* to buy. A fundamental analyst examines answer choices A, B, and C, but market timing falls in the realm of the technical analyst.

121. **C.** A company with a high debt-to-equity ratio owes out a lot of money to bondholders as compared to stockholders' equity. An investor or analyst seeing a company in this position would be concerned about the risk of bankruptcy. A high inventory ratio is a good thing for a corporation. If a corporation is turning over its inventory at a rapid rate, it's obviously getting a lot of sales. A company that has a low price/earnings (P/E) ratio may be a good buy because the market price is low for the earnings made by the company. The current ratio is calculated by dividing the current assets by the current liabilities. A company with a high current ratio would be in a good financial position.

122. **B.** This problem is one of those easy questions if you remember that the syndicate manager and members decide allotment for each syndicate member. The allotment for each member is stated in the syndicate agreement (agreement among underwriters). After you cross off Roman numeral I, the only answer that works is B. The official notice of sale contains bidding details for new municipal issues.

123. **D.** The key to this question is that it involves cumulative preferred stock, which requires the issuer to catch up on the preferred dividends before paying common dividends. Because DPY missed its last two dividend payments, it has to make them up plus the current dividend due before paying a dividend to common stockholders. Perform the following calculation:

7.2% cumulative preferred stock × $100 par value = $7.20 in dividends/year

DPY should be paying $7.20 in dividends to their preferred stockholders per year. However, dividends are paid quarterly, so you have to divide the dividend by 4:

$$\frac{\$7.20}{4} = \$1.80 \text{ quarterly dividend}$$

This answer means that DPY must pay each cumulative stockholder $5.40 ($1.80 × 3 dividend payments) per share before paying the common stockholders. Here's how much that will cost:

$5.40 × 1,000,000 cumulative preferred shares = $5,400,000

Additionally, DPY needs to pay $3,000,000 to the common stockholders ($1.50 × 2,000,000 common shares). DPY owes a total of $8,400,000:

$5,400,000 + $3,000,000 = $8,400,000

124. **D.** To determine the best after-tax investment for an individual investor, look for municipal bonds, because the interest received on municipal bonds is exempt from federal taxation. Then apply the following formula:

$$\text{Taxable equivalent yield (TEY)} = \frac{\text{municipal yield}}{100\% - \text{investor's tax bracket}} = \frac{4.5\%}{100\% - 28\%} = \frac{4.5\%}{72\%} = 6.25\%$$

A *general obligation (GO) bond* is a municipal bond in which the interest received is exempt from taxation. To compare all the listed bonds equally, you need to determine the GO bond's taxable equivalent yield. For this investor, the taxable equivalent yield is 6¼ percent, which is higher than all the other bonds listed. The 6¼ percent represents the coupon rate needed on a taxable bond to be equal to the 4½ percent that he'd be receiving on the tax-free bond.

$$\text{TEY} = \frac{4\frac{1}{2}\%}{100\% - 28\%} = \frac{4\frac{1}{2}\%}{72\%} = 6.25\%$$

125. **C.** The only thing that you have to remember to answer this question is the pricing unit of a penny ($0.01). To get your answer, multiply the premium (which is given) by the contract size (which is also given) and by the pricing unit:

3 × 30,150 × 0.01 = $904.50

Part VI
The Part of Tens

In this part . . .

This part is standard in all *For Dummies* books (and top ten lists are kind of an American institution), so here are two sets of ten tips for your reading pleasure. First, before you go to take the Series 7 exam, check out the ten exam traps to avoid. Next, you've tortured yourself for the past four to six weeks to prepare for the Series 7, so let me help you hit the ground running with ten ways to start your career as a stockbroker off right.

Chapter 21

Ten Series 7 Exam Traps to Avoid

In This Chapter

▶ Identifying the most common mistakes that Series 7 exam-takers make

▶ Uncovering the secrets for avoiding Series 7 exam traps

After all the time, effort, and sacrifice you put into studying, elevating the importance of the Series 7 exam to an unrealistically high level is easy. Step back for a moment. Keep it in perspective. This situation is not life or death. If you don't pass the first time, the worst thing that happens is that you have to retake it.

On the other hand, getting tripped up by some trivial exam traps after you've come this far would be a shame. This chapter lists some common mistakes and gives you some last-minute advice to help you over the last hurdles that stand between you and your first million dollars as a stockbroker.

Easing Up on the Studying

Perhaps you stop studying because you're getting good scores on practice exams and your confidence is high. If you're scoring 80s on exams that you're seeing for the first time, shoot for 85s. If you're getting 85s, shoot for 90s. The point is that you should continue to take exams until the day before your scheduled exam day. I firmly believe that every day away from studying ultimately costs you points on your exam that you can't afford to lose.

By the same token, make sure you don't wait too long before taking the exam. If you have to wait several weeks before you can take the exam, you lose your sense of urgency, and it's almost impossible to keep up the intense level of preparation needed for many months at a time. If you're taking a prep course before you schedule your Series 7, follow your instructor's advice as to when you should take the exam. Even if you're directing your own course of study, after you're passing practice exams consistently with 80s or better, take the test as soon as possible. The longer you wait to take the exam, the more likely you are to forget the key points and complex formulas. If your test date is too far in advance, you also risk falling into the I'll-study-later trap, where you think you can double your efforts later to make up for any wasted time. Overall, losing your sense of urgency leads to complacency and a lack of motivation, which probably aren't skills broker-dealers are looking for in their employees.

Assuming the Question's Intent

You glance at the question quickly and incorrectly anticipate what the exam question is really asking you. You pick the wrong answer because you were in such a rush, you didn't see the word *except* at the end of the question. What a shame.

You don't want to fail the exam when you really knew the material. Read each question carefully, and look for the trick words like *except, not,* and *unless.* Then read all the answer choices before making your selection. (For more info on test-taking strategies that apply to certain question types, see Chapter 3.)

Reading into the Question

You're thinking *but what if* before you even look at the answer choices. When reviewing questions with students, I constantly get questions like "Yeah, but what if he's an insider?" or "What if he's of retirement age?" The bottom line is that you shouldn't add anything to the question that isn't there. Don't be afraid to read the question at face value and select the right answer even if it occasionally seems too easy. Eliminate answer choices that are too much of a stretch, and remember that when two answer choices are opposites, one of them is most likely correct.

Becoming Distracted When Others Finish

You haven't even started looking over the questions you marked for review when the woman next to you leaps from her seat, picks up her results (with a little victory dance), and makes a break for the door.

Don't let people who are taking the exam with you psych you out. If others finish ahead of you, perhaps they're members of Mensa or maybe this is the fifth time they took the exam and practice makes perfect. They may even be taking a totally different exam. Besides the Series 7, the testing centers also offer other securities exams with fewer questions (a 65-question Series 63 exam, a 100-question Series 66 exam, 130-question Series 65 exam, and so on). Keep focused and centered on taking your own exam. The only time you need to be concerned with is your own — whether you're on track. Preserve your sanity by memorizing the time-tracking section from the Cheat Sheet. That way, you'll know you're on schedule and you won't have to worry about how long anyone else is taking to complete the Series 7.

Not Dressing for Comfort

You're trying to calculate the taxable equivalent yield on Mr. Dimwitty's GO bond, but the pencil keeps slipping out of your sweaty hands. You swear the test center has the heat cranked up to 80 degrees. Hmm. Maybe wearing your warmest wool sweater wasn't the best idea.

Dress comfortably. Don't wear a tie that's so tight it cuts off the circulation to your brain. You're under enough stress just taking the exam. Dress in layers. A t-shirt, a sweatshirt, and a jacket are great insulation against the cold. Another advantage is that you can shed layers of clothing (without ending up sitting in your underwear) if the exam room is too warm.

Forgetting to Breathe

You walk into the test center brimming with confidence. All of a sudden the exam begins and some of the words look like they're in a foreign language. Your heart starts pounding, and you feel like you're going to pass out.

If stress becomes overwhelming, your breathing can become shallow and ineffective, which only adds to your stress level. Focus yourself before the exam by closing your eyes and taking a few deep breaths. This same process of closing your eyes and deep breathing is a great way to calm yourself down if you become stressed and anxious at any time during the exam.

Trying to Work Out Equations in Your Head Instead of Writing Them Down

While taking the exam, your memory starts to cloud and, somehow, the fact that two plus two equals five begins to make sense to you and the only formula you can remember is that there are twelve inches in a foot.

Memorize your equations while you're studying for your Series 7 exam so you know them cold before you arrive at the test site. If your nerves are getting the best of you and clouding up your memory, jotting down the more difficult equations that you want to remember as soon as you receive permission to start the exam may be helpful (this process is known as a *brain dump)*. When working out complicated math problems, you have six pieces of scrap paper to work with (and a basic calculator). Use them. For example, some formulas, such as those for determining the debt service coverage ratio or the value of a right (cum rights), require you to find sums and differences before you can divide. Even simple calculations, such as finding averages, can use quite a few numbers. In problems with multiple parts, it's easy for you to accidentally skip steps, plug in the wrong numbers from the question, or forget values that you calculated along the way. Writing things out helps you keep things in place without cluttering your short-term memory.

Spending Too Much Time on One Question

To calculate the number of days of accrued interest on a T-bond, you decide to draw pictures of the calendar for the last four months. As you finish penciling the dates in those tiny boxes, you look at the clock and realize ten minutes have passed. Oops!

All questions have the same point value. If you spend too much time on one question, you may lose points for many questions you didn't have time to even look at because you wasted so much time on the one that gave you trouble. If you find yourself taking too long to answer a question, take your best guess, mark it for review, and return to it later.

Changing Your Answers for the Wrong Reasons

You change an answer just because you already selected that same letter for the preceding three or four questions in a row. Just a touch of paranoia, right?

You've probably been told from the time you first started primary school not to change your answers. Trust your instincts and go with your original reaction. You have only two good reasons to change your answer:

- ✔ You find that you initially forgot or didn't see the words *not* or *except* and you initially chose the wrong answer because you didn't see the tricky word.

- ✔ You find that the answer choice you originally selected is not the best answer after all.

Calculating Your Final Score Prematurely

You waste valuable time concentrating on the number of questions you think you got wrong instead of focusing on the Series 7 exam questions you still have to answer.

All you should do is read each question carefully, scrutinize the answer choices, and select the best answer. You'll find out whether you passed right after you complete the exam; it's not like you need to figure out your possible grade in advance to avoid sleepless nights until you receive your score. If you have additional time, use it to check your answers to the questions you marked for review.

Chapter 22

Ten Ways to Start Your Career Off Right

In This Chapter

▶ Understanding how to survive and prosper as a stockbroker

▶ Socking away (or investing) money

Passing the Series 7 exam can be one of the high points in your life. You've dedicated yourself to attaining your goal, put your life (and partying) on hold while you studied, and fulfilled your commitment to long hours of studying and hard work. You're now ready to reap the rewards. As you begin your new profession, you'll encounter many new hurdles. I give you this chapter to help prepare you for what to expect, and hopefully, to maximize your chances of a long, successful career.

Win at the Numbers Game

As with any other sales job, selling securities to investors is a numbers game. Some people actually track the number of calls it takes to open a new account, but I'm not among them. There are no specific economic benchmarks; however, you may have to make 500 cold calls to get to talk to 150 people. Out of these 150 people, you may generate ten leads. Out of every ten leads, you may open up one account.

The point is that you have to pick up that phone day in and day out and make the calls. If you're making 200 to 300 phone calls per day, you're likely to open an account every few days. However, if you're making 50 phone calls a day, you'll probably open up an account every couple weeks, and unless you hook a whale (a huge investor who likes to trade), you'll have trouble paying for gas in your new car. Remember that you're participating in a numbers game and that every *no* brings you one call closer to a *yes*.

Be an Apprentice

There's no better way to hit the ground running than having a top producer as a role model. Find the person in your firm with sales techniques that are most comfortable for you and invest as much time as possible watching how this mentor conducts himself or herself on a daily basis. Top producers earn the most income because they've found a way to stand out in a competitive market.

Maybe this person can take you under his or her wing and show you the ropes in return for leads you develop while under his or her supervision. You can even have a contract between you and your mentor that sets forth the agreed terms for each of you for a fixed period of time.

Do Your Homework

Take time to find out as much as possible about the securities you're trying to sell. When you know what you're talking about and how to talk, you inspire confidence from potential new customers. Spend some of your free time watching investing programs and reading the *Wall Street Journal* or any other trade magazines or newspapers you can get your hands on. The more you learn, the more comfortable you'll be on the phone, and the more sales you'll make.

Treat the Minnow Like a Whale

More often than not, new customers don't disclose all their financial background to you. However, whether a customer has $10,000 to invest or $10,000,000 to invest, the money is important to him or her. Treat every customer as though he or she is the most valuable person in the world. Who knows? You may be speaking to someone with a lot of money to invest now or someone who will have a lot of money to invest in the future, or he or she may be a friend of someone with substantial resources.

Smile When You Dial

Be positive. You're going to have good days and bad days. You have to accept that as part of the business, but don't let it get you down. If you need to, take a five-minute break to gather your thoughts. If you aren't in a positive state of mind, you'll reflect that in the way you talk to existing or potential customers.

When a Security Falls, Don't Be a Stranger

You can't guarantee success, and that's okay. Savvy investors know that not every investment can end up a winner, no matter how good the situation looks in the beginning. If you recommended a security and it gets beaten down, call your customer. The customer is just waiting to hear from you. This call may be right up there with the most uncomfortable tasks you'll ever have to perform. Remember, however, that a savvy customer is most likely aware of what's going on, and your news won't be a surprise. Customers just want to be comforted and reassured that you'll be there with them — in good times and bad. Hopefully, the other seven or eight securities that you recommended are doing well.

Put In the Hours

Of course, you have to educate yourself about selling your products and cold-calling. In the beginning, be prepared to put in approximately ten hours each day. As you grow more experienced, you'll receive more leads and open more accounts in a shorter period of time, but in the beginning, you have to follow the numbers game in order to earn money while you develop a more confident sales pitch.

Broaden Your Horizons

Consider obtaining other licenses to increase your skills and your ability to compete in the securities and financial industry. For example, the Series 65 or 66 (investment advisor) allows you to receive a fee for giving investment advice; Series 24 (principals license) allows you to manage other registered reps; and a Life, Accident, and Health Insurance license allows you to sell insurance policies to customers. If you take prep courses to obtain these licenses, you may also be exposed to a network of professionals who can be a source of future referrals.

Pay Yourself First

The stock market (and you with it) will have many peaks and valleys, but your financial security doesn't have to be quite so uneven. In the peak times, put away half your earnings when you receive your big paychecks. Tell yourself that you aren't going to make a big purchase until you have a certain amount socked away (see the upcoming section on setting goals). I've seen too many new brokers go out and buy a new car, or a new boat, or whatever with their first big paycheck, expecting to make that much every month. The first time they have a bad month, they're wondering how they're going to make the payments (and possibly pay the rent). Remember, stockbrokers are supposed to be *good* with money. Burying yourself in debt looks kind of bad.

Keep hunger in your efforts, not your stomach

When I first began my career as a stockbroker, the sales manager at the securities firm where I worked began the staff meetings by introducing himself and stating that he'd earned $100,000 his first year in the business and spent $150,000 of it — and he considered that to be a good thing! Somehow that just doesn't make sense either mathematically or logically (no matter how much your spending stimulates the economy). Some of the other trainees at the meeting were very impressed with the sales manager's suggestion, especially when he told us that he stayed hungry by spending so much more than he earned.

I remember looking at the sales manager and the other trainees who were attending this meeting and thinking, "What an idiot!" You'll get a lot of foolish suggestions along the way. If you want to stay hungry, work hard, sock away (or invest) half your earnings, and pretend it isn't there. Otherwise, there may be another reason you're hungry — you can't afford to buy food!

Set Some Goals: The Brass Ring

Focus on your goals. Successful people have realistic short-term and long-term goals and a plan to achieve them. Whether your short term goals are putting $5,000 away per month or opening ten new accounts, identifying what you want to do is the first step in creating a plan for your future.

What's the first thing every broker wants to do with the first big paycheck? You guessed it — buy a new car. Although that glistening Porsche can be an awesome incentive, set yourself smaller milestones to reach prior to making the big purchase. You can break down long-term goals, such as paying for a wedding, buying a new car, or purchasing your first house, into monthly income goals after you've figured out the costs involved. Take a picture of your dream car or house and put it in a frame on your desk to remind you of the reward that awaits you.

Whatever your plan is, setting your mind on what you want, defining the steps you have to take to get there, and focusing your efforts on accomplishing each goal are the essential elements of a lucrative and rewarding career. Remember, you control your destiny.

Appendix

About the CD

Series 7 Exam For Dummies comes complete with a CD-ROM that includes an additional full-length practice exam. This handy appendix helps you use that disc.

System Requirements

Make sure your computer meets the minimum system requirements shown in the following list. If your computer doesn't match up to most of these requirements, you may have problems using the software and files on the CD. You can also find this information in the ReadMe file located in the root directory of the CD-ROM.

- ✔ A PC with a Pentium or faster processor; or a Mac OSX computer with a G3 or faster processor
- ✔ Microsoft Windows 2000 or later; or Mac OSX system software 10.1 or later
- ✔ A CD-ROM drive

If you need more information on the basics, check out these books published by Wiley Publishing, Inc.: *PCs For Dummies,* by Dan Gookin; *Macs For Dummies,* by David Pogue; *Windows XP For Dummies* and *Windows 2000 Professional For Dummies,* both by Andy Rathbone.

Using the CD

To use the CD, follow these steps:

1. **Insert the CD into your computer's CD-ROM drive. The license agreement appears.**

   Note to Windows users: The interface won't launch if you have AutoRun disabled. In that case, go to Start⇨Run. In the dialog box that appears, type D:\start.exe. (Replace D with the proper letter if your CD-ROM drive uses a different letter. If you don't know the letter, see how your CD-ROM drive is listed under My Computer.) Click OK.

   Note for Mac users: The CD icon appears on your desktop; double-click the icon to open the CD and double-click the Start icon.

2. **Read through the license agreement and then click the Accept button if you want to use the CD.**

3. **The CD interface appears. You can choose to either begin taking the practice test from the CD-ROM or install it to your hard drive with just a click of a button (or two).**

   To take the test from the CD, you need to keep the disc inside your CD-ROM drive.

   To install the test on your hard drive, click the Install Tests button and follow the prompts.

4. **Choose one of the tests and begin.**

   To take the test from the CD, click the Take a Test button. Then click the Test 1 or Test 2 button.

   To run the test off your hard drive, access the test from the Start menu. Go to Start⇨Programs⇨Series 7 Exam For Dummies⇨PracticeTest1 or PracticeTest2.

What You'll Find on the CD

As a former Registered Representative and also as an owner and instructor for my securities training school, I know the sacrifice and commitment that you need to prepare for the Series 7 exam, and believe me, I feel your pain! Back when I was preparing for the exam, I would've given almost anything for access to the sophisticated, up-to-date study material and simulated CD exam that's available for Series 7 applicants today.

If you're ready to focus your efforts and invest your time in the exam preparations, your efforts can be well rewarded when you press the life-changing Series 7 exam results button and receive your passing grade. So with you and your success in mind, I created a simulated exam that transports you to test day — not only do you have a sample test in the book, but you also have one on this CD, which is similar to how you'll take the official test.

On this CD are 250 questions on every subject you may see on the exam, all presented to you in random order (which, as you may have figured out by now, means you can take it more than once!). As you take the exam, I strongly recommend that you note which questions you don't answer correctly. Record at least the subject, ideally the whole question, and at the end of the test, you'll have a pretty good idea about what areas you need to brush up on before you go for the Big One.

Try to keep in mind that you should average about 1 minute and 22 seconds per question; that way, you'll be able to assess your ability to efficiently read through the questions and dissect them, as I discuss in Chapter 4.

Although I provide a full-length sample exam in this book, the exam on the CD-ROM is especially helpful because it helps you get used to using a computer for this type of test. Use this sample test as a learning experience so you can clearly identify your strengths and weaknesses and study those areas the most.

When taking the sample exam on the CD, keep the following points in mind in order to put your best click forward:

✔ Read the entire question and all the answer choices before choosing your answer.

✔ Remember your formulas and equations, and apply them to the questions when necessary.

✔ Use scrap paper and a basic calculator if you'd like.

- ✔ Eliminate the absolutely wrong answers first.

- ✔ Choose the correct answer considering *only* the information you need to answer the question while eliminating the surplus facts — you're working in the textbook world, not the real world.

Troubleshooting

I tried my best to compile a CD-ROM that works on most computers with the minimum system requirements. Alas, your computer may differ and the disc may not work properly for some reason.

The two likeliest problems are that you don't have enough memory (RAM) for the programs you want to use or you have other programs running that are affecting installation or running of a program. If you get an error message, such as `Not enough memory` or `Setup cannot continue`, try one or more of the following suggestions and then try using the software again:

- ✔ **Turn off any antivirus software running on your computer.** Installation programs sometimes mimic virus activity and may make your computer incorrectly believe that it's being infected by a virus.

- ✔ **Close all running programs.** The more programs you have running, the less memory is available to other programs. Installation programs typically update files and programs, so if you keep other programs running, installation may not work properly.

- ✔ **Have your local computer store add more RAM to your computer.** This is, admittedly, a drastic and somewhat expensive step. However, adding more memory can really help the speed of your computer and allow more programs to run at the same time.

If you have trouble with the CD-ROM, please call the Wiley Product Technical Support phone number at 800-762-2974. Outside the United States, call 317-572-3994. You can also contact Wiley Product Technical Support at `http://support.wiley.com`. John Wiley & Sons will provide technical support only for installation and other general quality control items. For technical support on the applications themselves, consult the program's vendor.

To place additional orders or to request information about other Wiley products, please call 877-762-2974.

Index

Notes

Notes

Notes

Notes

Wiley Publishing, Inc. End-User License Agreement

READ THIS. You should carefully read these terms and conditions before opening the software packet(s) included with this book ("Book"). This is a license agreement ("Agreement") between you and Wiley Publishing, Inc. ("WPI"). By opening the accompanying software packet(s), you acknowledge that you have read and accept the following terms and conditions. If you do not agree and do not want to be bound by such terms and conditions, promptly return the Book and the unopened software packet(s) to the place you obtained them for a full refund.

1. **License Grant.** WPI grants to you (either an individual or entity) a nonexclusive license to use one copy of the enclosed software program(s) (collectively, the "Software") solely for your own personal or business purposes on a single computer (whether a standard computer or a workstation component of a multi-user network). The Software is in use on a computer when it is loaded into temporary memory (RAM) or installed into permanent memory (hard disk, CD-ROM, or other storage device). WPI reserves all rights not expressly granted herein.

2. **Ownership.** WPI is the owner of all right, title, and interest, including copyright, in and to the compilation of the Software recorded on the physical packet included with this Book ("Software Media"). Copyright to the individual programs recorded on the Software Media is owned by the author or other authorized copyright owner of each program. Ownership of the Software and all proprietary rights relating thereto remain with WPI and its licensers.

3. **Restrictions on Use and Transfer.**

   (a) You may only (i) make one copy of the Software for backup or archival purposes or (ii) transfer the Software to a single hard disk, provided that you keep the original for backup or archival purposes. You may not (i) rent or lease the Software, (ii) copy or reproduce the Software through a LAN or other network system or through any computer subscriber system or bulletin-board system, or (iii) modify, adapt, or create derivative works based on the Software.

   (b) You may not reverse engineer, decompile, or disassemble the Software. You may transfer the Software and user documentation on a permanent basis, provided that the transferee agrees to accept the terms and conditions of this Agreement and you retain no copies. If the Software is an update or has been updated, any transfer must include the most recent update and all prior versions.

4. **Restrictions on Use of Individual Programs.** You must follow the individual requirements and restrictions detailed for each individual program in the "About the CD" appendix of this Book or on the Software Media. These limitations are also contained in the individual license agreements recorded on the Software Media. These limitations may include a requirement that after using the program for a specified period of time, the user must pay a registration fee or discontinue use. By opening the Software packet(s), you agree to abide by the licenses and restrictions for these individual programs that are detailed in the "About the CD" appendix and/or on the Software Media. None of the material on this Software Media or listed in this Book may ever be redistributed, in original or modified form, for commercial purposes.

5. **Limited Warranty.**

   (a) WPI warrants that the Software and Software Media are free from defects in materials and workmanship under normal use for a period of sixty (60) days from the date of purchase of this Book. If WPI receives notification within the warranty period of defects in materials or workmanship, WPI will replace the defective Software Media.

BUSINESS, CAREERS & PERSONAL FINANCE

0-7645-9847-3

0-7645-2431-3

Also available:

- Business Plans Kit For Dummies
  0-7645-9794-9
- Economics For Dummies
  0-7645-5726-2
- Grant Writing For Dummies
  0-7645-8416-2
- Home Buying For Dummies
  0-7645-5331-3
- Managing For Dummies
  0-7645-1771-6
- Marketing For Dummies
  0-7645-5600-2

- Personal Finance For Dummies
  0-7645-2590-5*
- Resumes For Dummies
  0-7645-5471-9
- Selling For Dummies
  0-7645-5363-1
- Six Sigma For Dummies
  0-7645-6798-5
- Small Business Kit For Dummies
  0-7645-5984-2
- Starting an eBay Business For Dummies
  0-7645-6924-4
- Your Dream Career For Dummies
  0-7645-9795-7

HOME & BUSINESS COMPUTER BASICS

0-470-05432-8

0-471-75421-8

Also available:

- Cleaning Windows Vista For Dummies
  0-471-78293-9
- Excel 2007 For Dummies
  0-470-03737-7
- Mac OS X Tiger For Dummies
  0-7645-7675-5
- MacBook For Dummies
  0-470-04859-X
- Macs For Dummies
  0-470-04849-2
- Office 2007 For Dummies
  0-470-00923-3

- Outlook 2007 For Dummies
  0-470-03830-6
- PCs For Dummies
  0-7645-8958-X
- Salesforce.com For Dummies
  0-470-04893-X
- Upgrading & Fixing Laptops For Dummies
  0-7645-8959-8
- Word 2007 For Dummies
  0-470-03658-3
- Quicken 2007 For Dummies
  0-470-04600-7

FOOD, HOME, GARDEN, HOBBIES, MUSIC & PETS

0-7645-8404-9

0-7645-9904-6

Also available:

- Candy Making For Dummies
  0-7645-9734-5
- Card Games For Dummies
  0-7645-9910-0
- Crocheting For Dummies
  0-7645-4151-X
- Dog Training For Dummies
  0-7645-8418-9
- Healthy Carb Cookbook For Dummies
  0-7645-8476-6
- Home Maintenance For Dummies
  0-7645-5215-5

- Horses For Dummies
  0-7645-9797-3
- Jewelry Making & Beading For Dummies
  0-7645-2571-9
- Orchids For Dummies
  0-7645-6759-4
- Puppies For Dummies
  0-7645-5255-4
- Rock Guitar For Dummies
  0-7645-5356-9
- Sewing For Dummies
  0-7645-6847-7
- Singing For Dummies
  0-7645-2475-5

INTERNET & DIGITAL MEDIA

0-470-04529-9

0-470-04894-8

Also available:

- Blogging For Dummies
  0-471-77084-1
- Digital Photography For Dummies
  0-7645-9802-3
- Digital Photography All-in-One Desk Reference For Dummies
  0-470-03743-1
- Digital SLR Cameras and Photography For Dummies
  0-7645-9803-1
- eBay Business All-in-One Desk Reference For Dummies
  0-7645-8438-3
- HDTV For Dummies
  0-470-09673-X

- Home Entertainment PCs For Dummies
  0-470-05523-5
- MySpace For Dummies
  0-470-09529-6
- Search Engine Optimization For Dummies
  0-471-97998-8
- Skype For Dummies
  0-470-04891-3
- The Internet For Dummies
  0-7645-8996-2
- Wiring Your Digital Home For Dummies
  0-471-91830-X

* Separate Canadian edition also available
† Separate U.K. edition also available

Available wherever books are sold. For more information or to order direct: U.S. customers visit www.dummies.com or call 1-877-762-2974.
U.K. customers visit www.wileyeurope.com or call 0800 243407. Canadian customers visit www.wiley.ca or call 1-800-567-4797.

SPORTS, FITNESS, PARENTING, RELIGION & SPIRITUALITY

0-471-76871-5

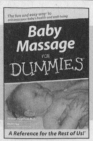

0-7645-7841-3

Also available:

- Catholicism For Dummies
  0-7645-5391-7
- Exercise Balls For Dummies
  0-7645-5623-1
- Fitness For Dummies
  0-7645-7851-0
- Football For Dummies
  0-7645-3936-1
- Judaism For Dummies
  0-7645-5299-6
- Potty Training For Dummies
  0-7645-5417-4
- Buddhism For Dummies
  0-7645-5359-3

- Pregnancy For Dummies
  0-7645-4483-7 †
- Ten Minute Tone-Ups For Dummies
  0-7645-7207-5
- NASCAR For Dummies
  0-7645-7681-X
- Religion For Dummies
  0-7645-5264-3
- Soccer For Dummies
  0-7645-5229-5
- Women in the Bible For Dummies
  0-7645-8475-8

TRAVEL

0-7645-7749-2

0-7645-6945-7

Also available:

- Alaska For Dummies
  0-7645-7746-8
- Cruise Vacations For Dummies
  0-7645-6941-4
- England For Dummies
  0-7645-4276-1
- Europe For Dummies
  0-7645-7529-5
- Germany For Dummies
  0-7645-7823-5
- Hawaii For Dummies
  0-7645-7402-7

- Italy For Dummies
  0-7645-7386-1
- Las Vegas For Dummies
  0-7645-7382-9
- London For Dummies
  0-7645-4277-X
- Paris For Dummies
  0-7645-7630-5
- RV Vacations For Dummies
  0-7645-4442-X
- Walt Disney World & Orlando
  For Dummies
  0-7645-9660-8

GRAPHICS, DESIGN & WEB DEVELOPMENT

0-7645-8815-X

0-7645-9571-7

Also available:

- 3D Game Animation For Dummies
  0-7645-8789-7
- AutoCAD 2006 For Dummies
  0-7645-8925-3
- Building a Web Site For Dummies
  0-7645-7144-3
- Creating Web Pages For Dummies
  0-470-08030-2
- Creating Web Pages All-in-One Desk
  Reference For Dummies
  0-7645-4345-8
- Dreamweaver 8 For Dummies
  0-7645-9649-7

- InDesign CS2 For Dummies
  0-7645-9572-5
- Macromedia Flash 8 For Dummies
  0-7645-9691-8
- Photoshop CS2 and Digital
  Photography For Dummies
  0-7645-9580-6
- Photoshop Elements 4 For Dummies
  0-471-77483-9
- Syndicating Web Sites with RSS Feeds
  For Dummies
  0-7645-8848-6
- Yahoo! SiteBuilder For Dummies
  0-7645-9800-7

NETWORKING, SECURITY, PROGRAMMING & DATABASES

0-7645-7728-X

0-471-74940-0

Also available:

- Access 2007 For Dummies
  0-470-04612-0
- ASP.NET 2 For Dummies
  0-7645-7907-X
- C# 2005 For Dummies
  0-7645-9704-3
- Hacking For Dummies
  0-470-05235-X
- Hacking Wireless Networks
  For Dummies
  0-7645-9730-2
- Java For Dummies
  0-470-08716-1

- Microsoft SQL Server 2005 For Dummies
  0-7645-7755-7
- Networking All-in-One Desk Reference
  For Dummies
  0-7645-9939-9
- Preventing Identity Theft For Dummies
  0-7645-7336-5
- Telecom For Dummies
  0-471-77085-X
- Visual Studio 2005 All-in-One Desk
  Reference For Dummies
  0-7645-9775-2
- XML For Dummies
  0-7645-8845-1

HEALTH & SELF-HELP

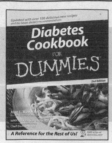

0-7645-8450-2

0-7645-4149-8

Also available:

- Bipolar Disorder For Dummies
  0-7645-8451-0
- Chemotherapy and Radiation
  For Dummies
  0-7645-7832-4
- Controlling Cholesterol For Dummies
  0-7645-5440-9
- Diabetes For Dummies
  0-7645-6820-5* †
- Divorce For Dummies
  0-7645-8417-0 †

- Fibromyalgia For Dummies
  0-7645-5441-7
- Low-Calorie Dieting For Dummies
  0-7645-9905-4
- Meditation For Dummies
  0-471-77774-9
- Osteoporosis For Dummies
  0-7645-7621-6
- Overcoming Anxiety For Dummies
  0-7645-5447-6
- Reiki For Dummies
  0-7645-9907-0
- Stress Management For Dummies
  0-7645-5144-2

EDUCATION, HISTORY, REFERENCE & TEST PREPARATION

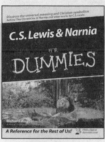

0-7645-8381-6

0-7645-9554-7

Also available:

- The ACT For Dummies
  0-7645-9652-7
- Algebra For Dummies
  0-7645-5325-9
- Algebra Workbook For Dummies
  0-7645-8467-7
- Astronomy For Dummies
  0-7645-8465-0
- Calculus For Dummies
  0-7645-2498-4
- Chemistry For Dummies
  0-7645-5430-1
- Forensics For Dummies
  0-7645-5580-4

- Freemasons For Dummies
  0-7645-9796-5
- French For Dummies
  0-7645-5193-0
- Geometry For Dummies
  0-7645-5324-0
- Organic Chemistry I For Dummies
  0-7645-6902-3
- The SAT I For Dummies
  0-7645-7193-1
- Spanish For Dummies
  0-7645-5194-9
- Statistics For Dummies
  0-7645-5423-9

Get smart @ dummies.com®

- **Find a full list of Dummies titles**
- **Look into loads of FREE on-site articles**
- **Sign up for FREE eTips e-mailed to you weekly**
- **See what other products carry the Dummies name**
- **Shop directly from the Dummies bookstore**
- **Enter to win new prizes every month!**